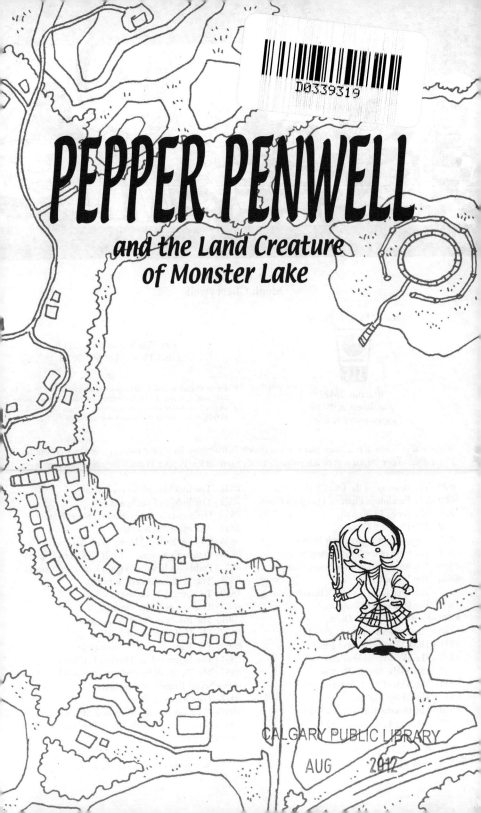

PEPPER PENWELL

and the Land Creature
of Monster Lake

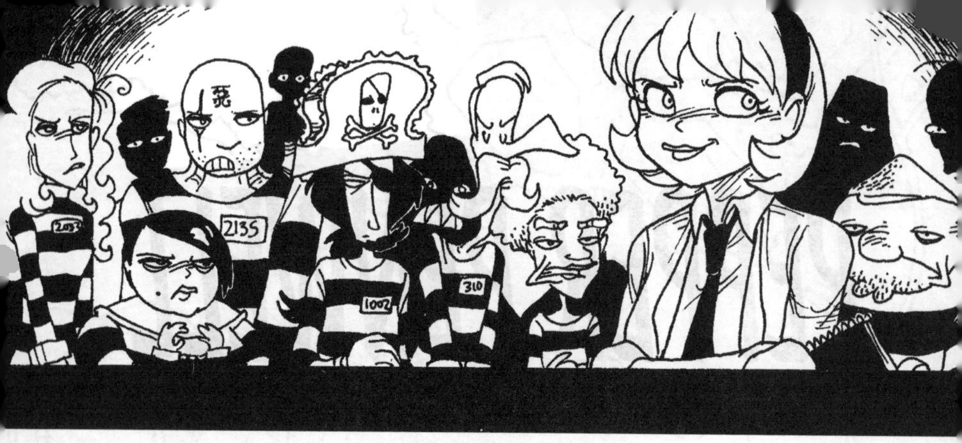
2135
1002
310

written and drawn by
Steph Cherrywell

Published by SLG Publishing

P.O. Box 26427
San Jose, CA 95159
www.slgcomic.com

First Printing: January 2011
ISBN-13: 978-1-59362-205-3

When you've finished this story, please immediately contact your local bookmonger's and politely but firmly request the entire assortment of this month's publications in the Pepper Penwell Investigations series:

#829 - The Revenge of the Old Clock
#830 - The Pendulous Pirate of Dangler's Cove
#831 - Murder by Chocolate
#832 - The Dreadful Drapes
#833 - A Mystery at Arglefumph Manor
#834 - The Case of the Two Creatures
#835 - The Riddle of the Clockwork Chinamen
#836 - The Violin Case
#837 - The Clue in the Corpse's Bloodstream
#838 - The Pantagruel Conspiracy
#839 - Secret of the Little Death
#840 - The Embrace of the Marble Viper
#841 - The Chimney Sweep's Fallacy
#842 - The Woodwind Warning
#843 - Clue in the Badger-Burrow
#844 - The Sign of the Jolly Strumpet
#845 - The Maths Murder
#846 - The Horror of Hadrian's Wall
#847 - Fox, Chicken, Grain, and Death
#848 - The Prancer Incident
#849 - By Light of Turnip-Lantern's Leer
#850 - Beheaded by Poison
#851 - The Indelible Bloaters of Angus
#852 - The Riddle of the Spanx
#853 - Defenestration at Fenchurch Street Station
#854 - The Insoluble Solution
#855 - Case of the Dead Bloke With Knives In
#856 - Puthbert's Key, or What It Unlocked (part 1)
#857 - Puthbert's Key, or What It Unlocked (part 2)
#858 - The Well-Fed Cat of Sumatra
#859 - To Catch A Yorkshireman
#860 - The Voices in the Vicarage
#861 - The Rutabega Salad Conundrum
#862 - The Carbon-Neutral Arsonist
#863 - The Vamp and the Ventriloquist
#864 - The Legend of the Hidden Temple
#865 - The Pirates of Smugglers' Cove and Vice Versa
#866 - Secret Passage at Stonehenge
#867 - The Grapes of Sloth
#868 - The Ghosts of the Werewolf Mummy
#869 - Pepper Penwell's Big Rainy Day Fun Book
#870 - By Bangers Slain

Kindly do collect them all, if you please.

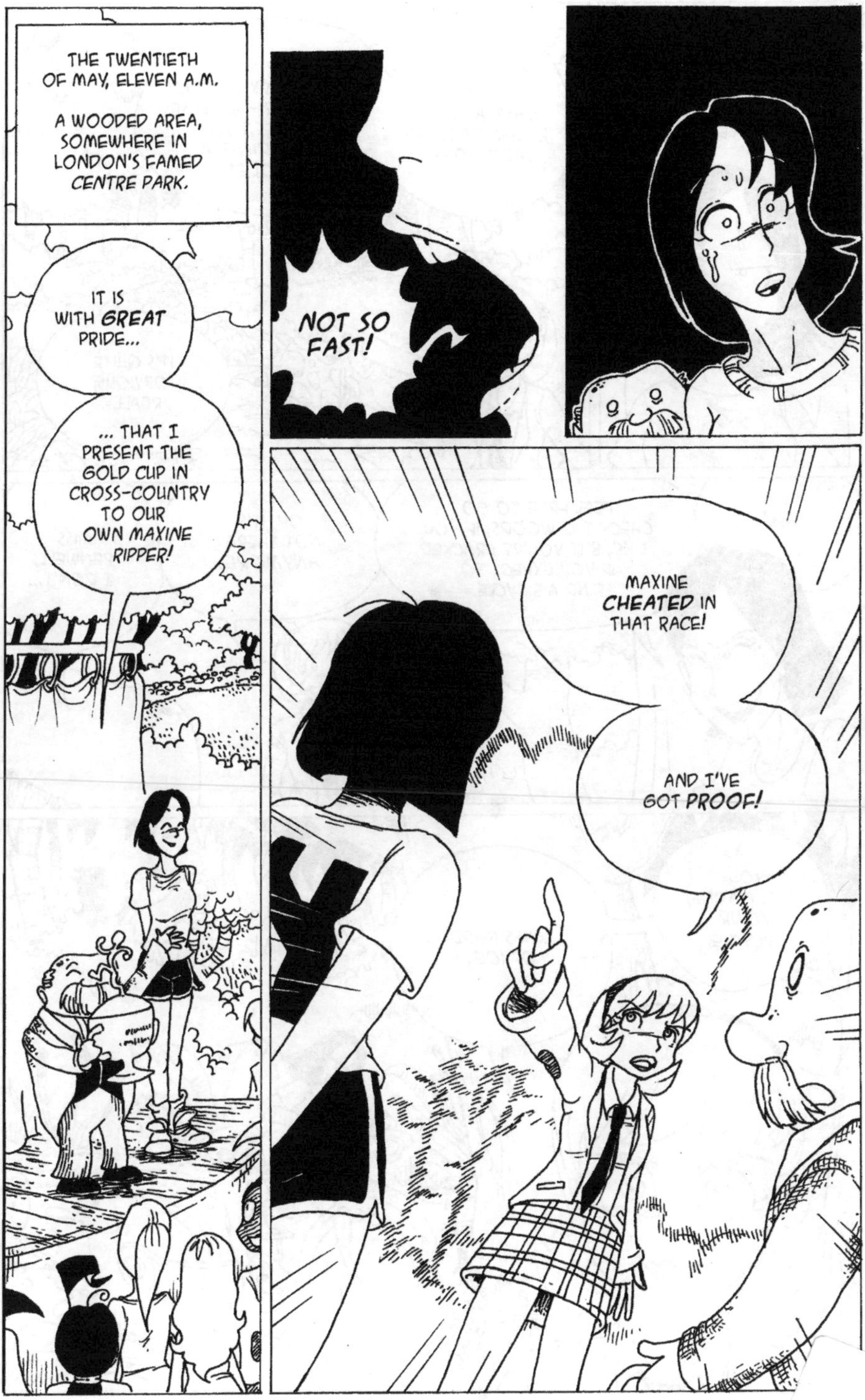
THE TWENTIETH OF MAY, ELEVEN A.M.
A WOODED AREA, SOMEWHERE IN LONDON'S FAMED CENTRE PARK.
IT IS WITH GREAT PRIDE...
... THAT I PRESENT THE GOLD CUP IN CROSS-COUNTRY TO OUR OWN MAXINE RIPPER!
NOT SO FAST!
MAXINE CHEATED IN THAT RACE!
AND I'VE GOT PROOF!

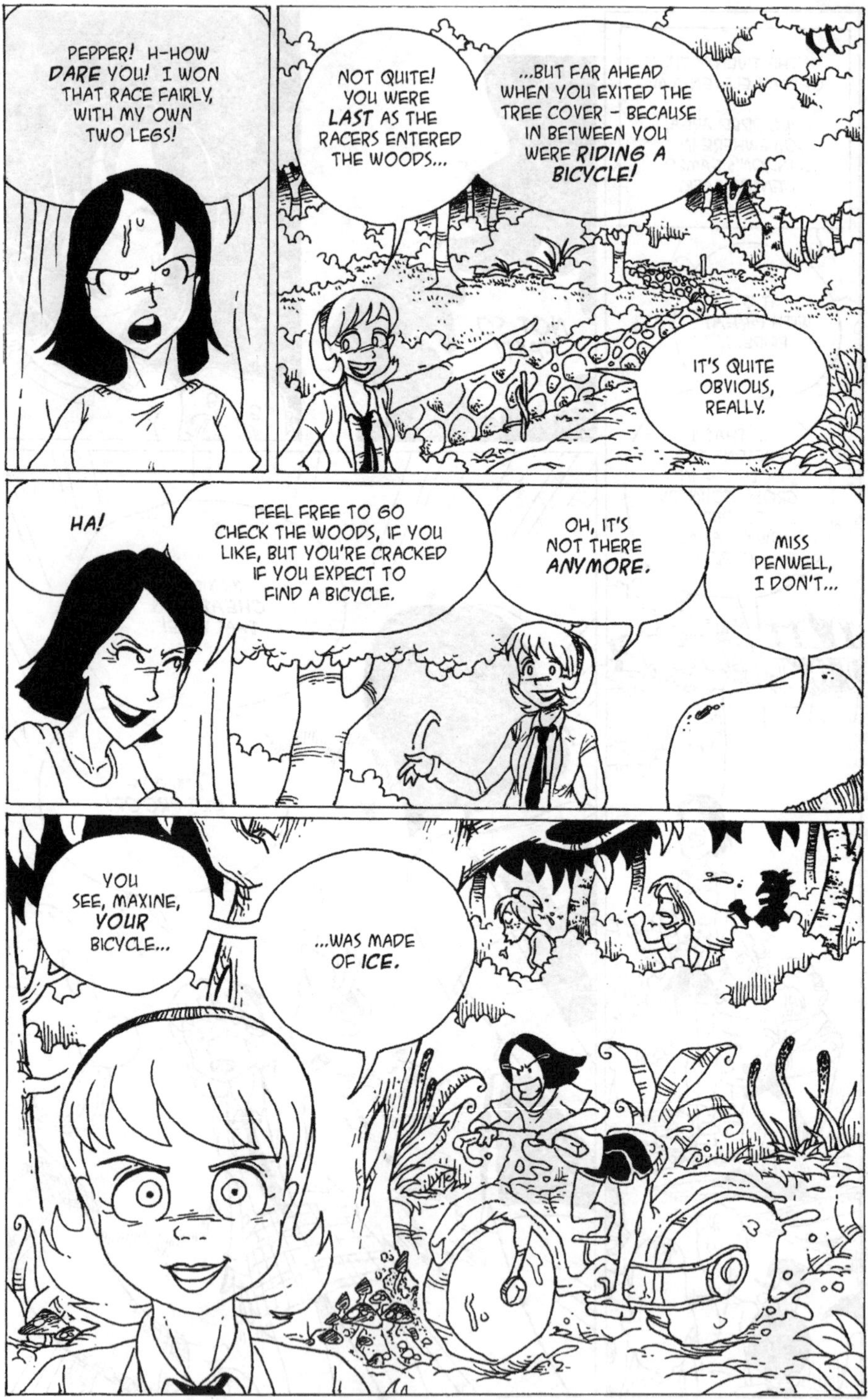
PEPPER! H-HOW DARE YOU! I WON THAT RACE FAIRLY, WITH MY OWN TWO LEGS!
NOT QUITE! YOU WERE LAST AS THE RACERS ENTERED THE WOODS...
...BUT FAR AHEAD WHEN YOU EXITED THE TREE COVER - BECAUSE IN BETWEEN YOU WERE RIDING A BICYCLE!
IT'S QUITE OBVIOUS, REALLY.
HA!
FEEL FREE TO GO CHECK THE WOODS, IF YOU LIKE, BUT YOU'RE CRACKED IF YOU EXPECT TO FIND A BICYCLE.
OH, IT'S NOT THERE ANYMORE.
MISS PENWELL, I DON'T...
YOU SEE, MAXINE, YOUR BICYCLE...
...WAS MADE OF ICE.

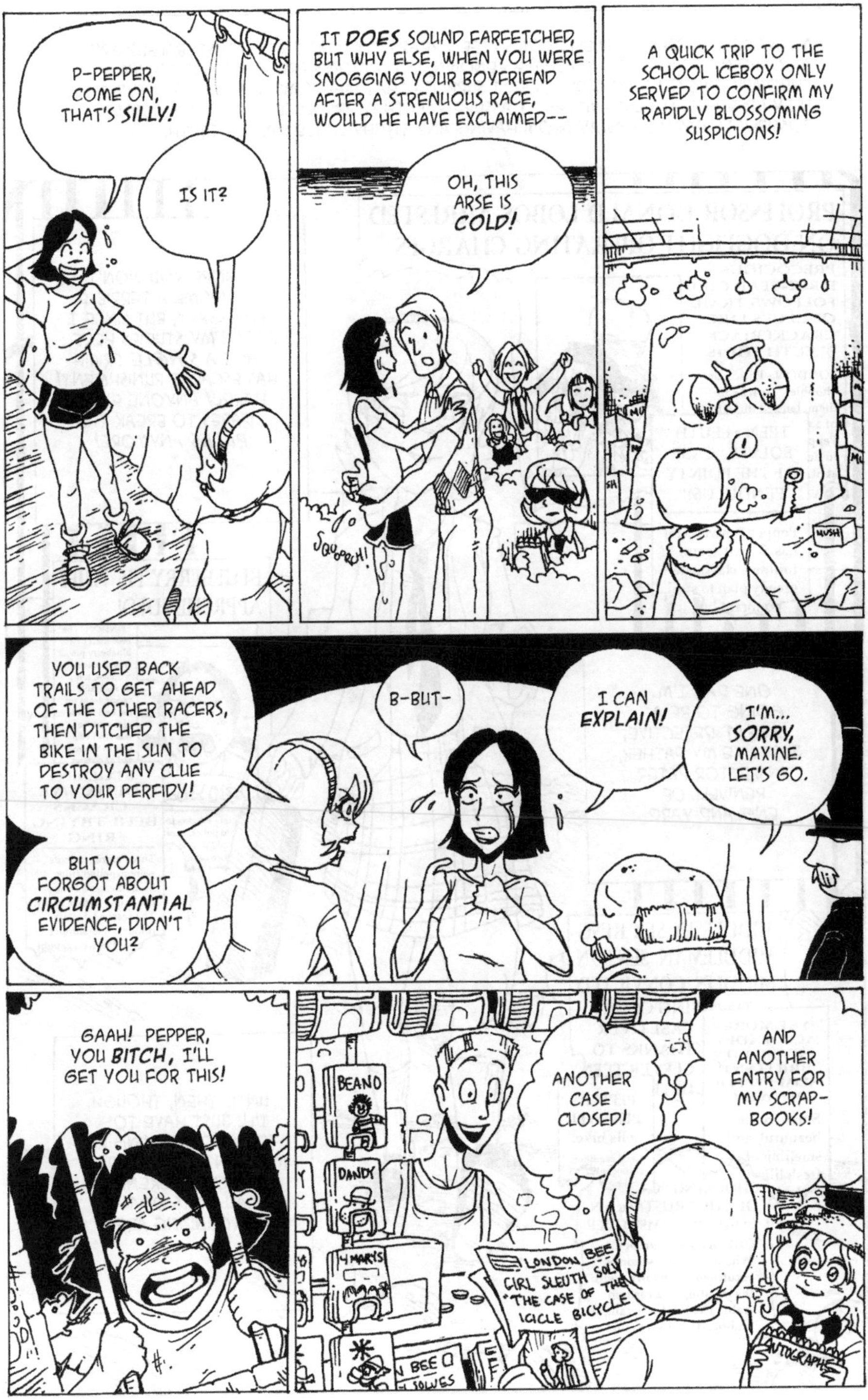
P-PEPPER, COME ON, THAT'S SILLY!
IS IT?
IT DOES SOUND FARFETCHED, BUT WHY ELSE, WHEN YOU WERE SNOGGING YOUR BOYFRIEND AFTER A STRENUOUS RACE, WOULD HE HAVE EXCLAIMED--
OH, THIS ARSE IS COLD!
SQUOOPCH!
A QUICK TRIP TO THE SCHOOL ICEBOX ONLY SERVED TO CONFIRM MY RAPIDLY BLOSSOMING SUSPICIONS!
MUSH
YOU USED BACK TRAILS TO GET AHEAD OF THE OTHER RACERS, THEN DITCHED THE BIKE IN THE SUN TO DESTROY ANY CLUE TO YOUR PERFIDY!
BUT YOU FORGOT ABOUT CIRCUMSTANTIAL EVIDENCE, DIDN'T YOU?
B-BUT-
I CAN EXPLAIN!
I'M... SORRY, MAXINE. LET'S GO.
GAAH! PEPPER, YOU BITCH, I'LL GET YOU FOR THIS!
BEANO
DANDY
4 MARYS
ANOTHER CASE CLOSED!
AND ANOTHER ENTRY FOR MY SCRAP-BOOKS!
LONDON BEE
GIRL SLEUTH SOLV
"THE CASE OF THE ICICLE BICYCLE
AUTOGRAPHS

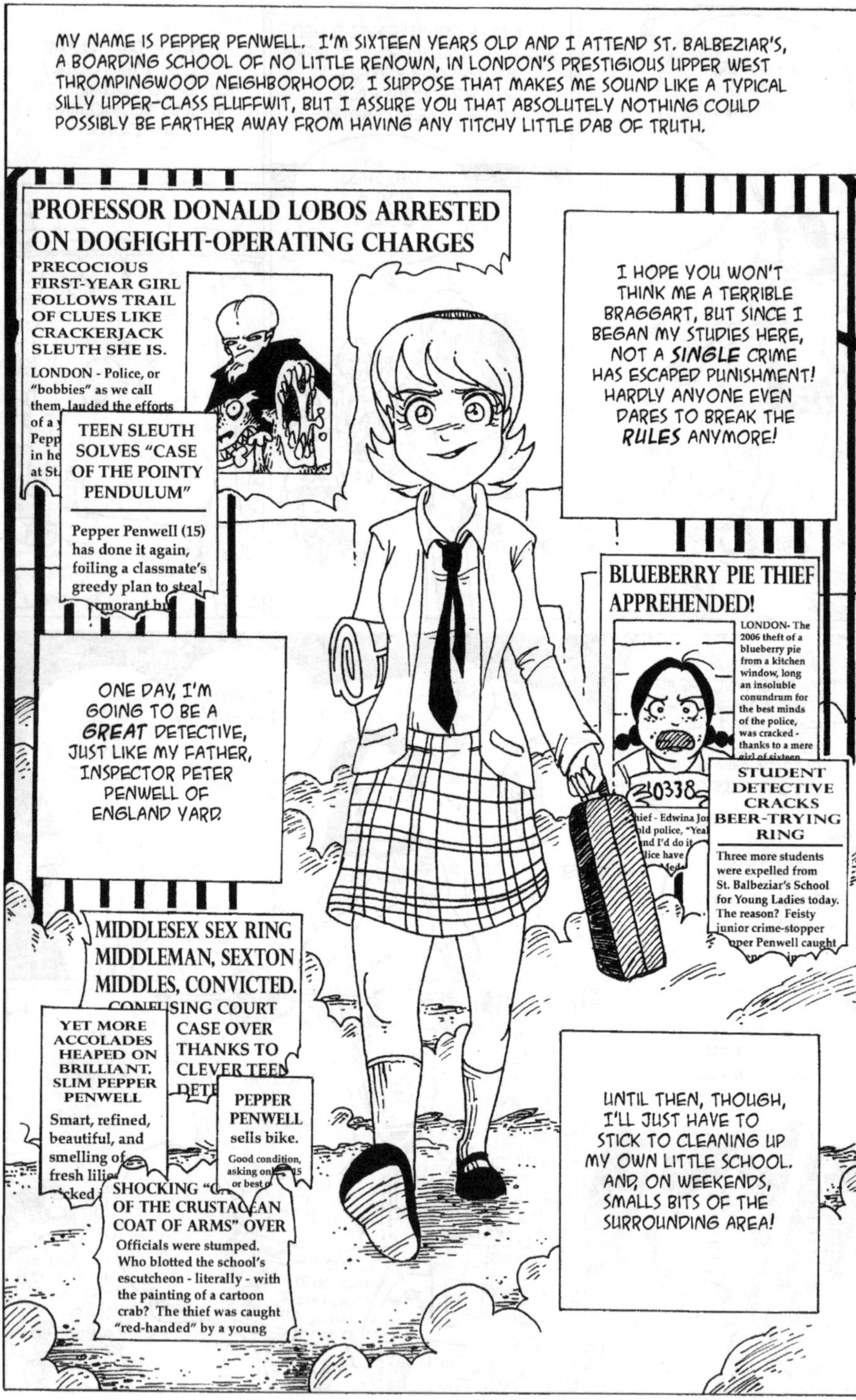
MY NAME IS PEPPER PENWELL. I'M SIXTEEN YEARS OLD AND I ATTEND ST. BALBEZIAR'S, A BOARDING SCHOOL OF NO LITTLE RENOWN, IN LONDON'S PRESTIGIOUS UPPER WEST THROMPINGWOOD NEIGHBORHOOD. I SUPPOSE THAT MAKES ME SOUND LIKE A TYPICAL SILLY UPPER-CLASS FLUFFWIT, BUT I ASSURE YOU THAT ABSOLUTELY NOTHING COULD POSSIBLY BE FARTHER AWAY FROM HAVING ANY TITCHY LITTLE DAB OF TRUTH.
PROFESSOR DONALD LOBOS ARRESTED ON DOGFIGHT-OPERATING CHARGES
PRECOCIOUS FIRST-YEAR GIRL FOLLOWS TRAIL OF CLUES LIKE CRACKERJACK SLEUTH SHE IS.
LONDON - Police, or "bobbies" as we call them, lauded the efforts
TEEN SLEUTH SOLVES "CASE OF THE POINTY PENDULUM"
Pepper Penwell (15) has done it again, foiling a classmate's greedy plan to steal
I HOPE YOU WON'T THINK ME A TERRIBLE BRAGGART, BUT SINCE I BEGAN MY STUDIES HERE, NOT A SINGLE CRIME HAS ESCAPED PUNISHMENT! HARDLY ANYONE EVEN DARES TO BREAK THE RULES ANYMORE!
BLUEBERRY PIE THIEF APPREHENDED!
LONDON- The 2006 theft of a blueberry pie from a kitchen window, long an insoluble conundrum for the best minds of the police, was cracked - thanks to a mere
10338
ONE DAY, I'M GOING TO BE A GREAT DETECTIVE, JUST LIKE MY FATHER, INSPECTOR PETER PENWELL OF ENGLAND YARD.
STUDENT DETECTIVE CRACKS BEER-TRYING RING
Three more students were expelled from St. Balbeziar's School for Young Ladies today. The reason? Feisty junior crime-stopper
MIDDLESEX SEX RING MIDDLEMAN, SEXTON MIDDLES, CONVICTED.
CASE OVER THANKS TO CLEVER
YET MORE ACCOLADES HEAPED ON BRILLIANT, SLIM PEPPER PENWELL
Smart, refined, beautiful, and
PEPPER PENWELL sells bike.
Good condition,
SHOCKING
OF THE CRUSTACEAN COAT OF ARMS" OVER
Officials were stumped. Who blotted the school's escutcheon - literally - with the painting of a cartoon crab? The thief was caught "red-handed" by a young
UNTIL THEN, THOUGH, I'LL JUST HAVE TO STICK TO CLEANING UP MY OWN LITTLE SCHOOL. AND, ON WEEKENDS, SMALLS BITS OF THE SURROUNDING AREA!

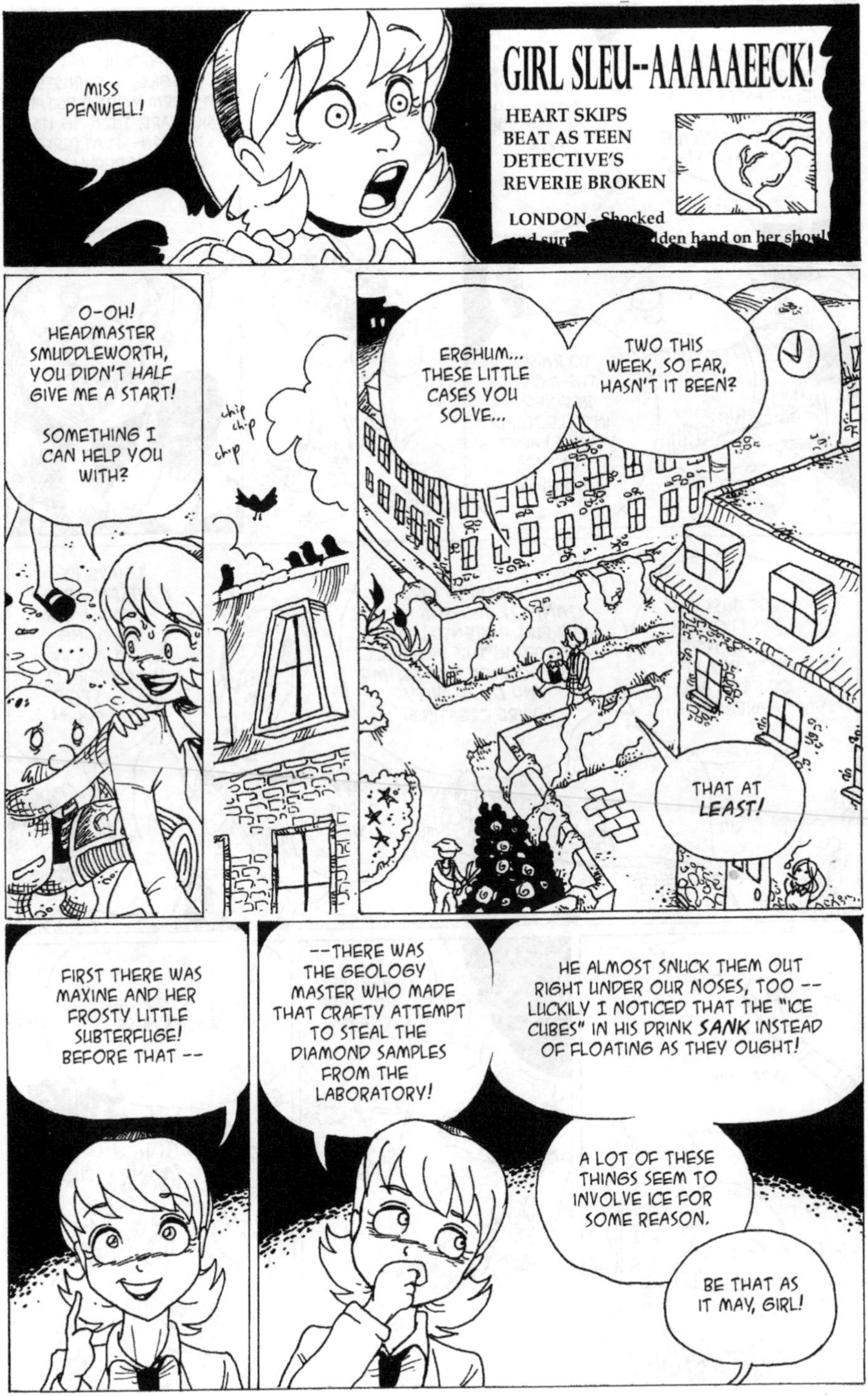
MISS PENWELL!
GIRL SLEU--AAAAAEECK!
HEART SKIPS BEAT AS TEEN DETECTIVE'S REVERIE BROKEN
LONDON - Shocked
O-OH! HEADMASTER SMUDDLEWORTH, YOU DIDN'T HALF GIVE ME A START!
SOMETHING I CAN HELP YOU WITH?
...
chip chip chip
ERGHUM... THESE LITTLE CASES YOU SOLVE...
TWO THIS WEEK, SO FAR, HASN'T IT BEEN?
THAT AT LEAST!
FIRST THERE WAS MAXINE AND HER FROSTY LITTLE SUBTERFUGE! BEFORE THAT --
--THERE WAS THE GEOLOGY MASTER WHO MADE THAT CRAFTY ATTEMPT TO STEAL THE DIAMOND SAMPLES FROM THE LABORATORY!
HE ALMOST SNUCK THEM OUT RIGHT UNDER OUR NOSES, TOO -- LUCKILY I NOTICED THAT THE "ICE CUBES" IN HIS DRINK SANK INSTEAD OF FLOATING AS THEY OUGHT!
A LOT OF THESE THINGS SEEM TO INVOLVE ICE FOR SOME REASON.
BE THAT AS IT MAY, GIRL!

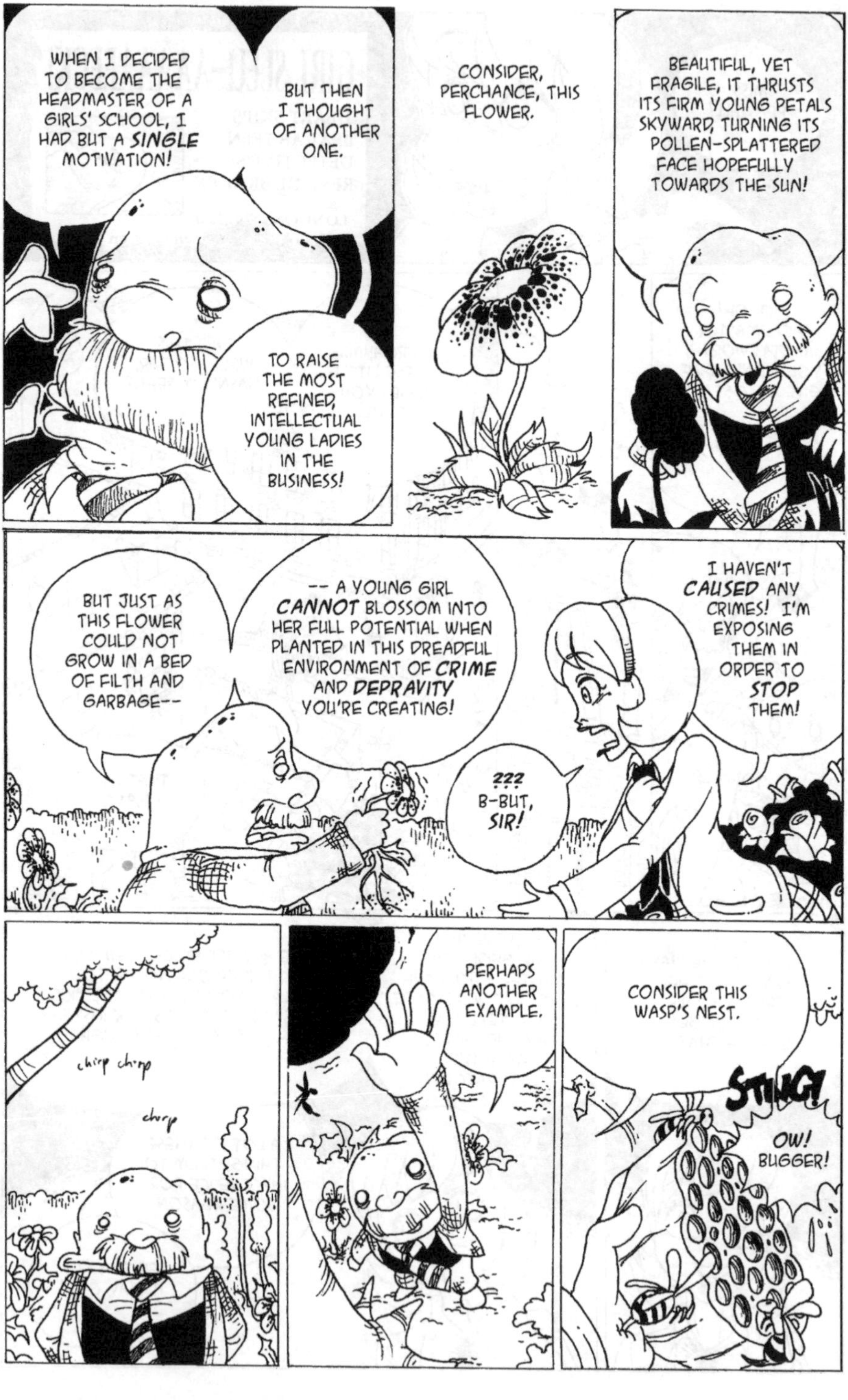
WHEN I DECIDED TO BECOME THE HEADMASTER OF A GIRLS' SCHOOL, I HAD BUT A SINGLE MOTIVATION!
BUT THEN I THOUGHT OF ANOTHER ONE.
TO RAISE THE MOST REFINED, INTELLECTUAL YOUNG LADIES IN THE BUSINESS!
CONSIDER, PERCHANCE, THIS FLOWER.
BEAUTIFUL, YET FRAGILE, IT THRUSTS ITS FIRM YOUNG PETALS SKYWARD, TURNING ITS POLLEN-SPLATTERED FACE HOPEFULLY TOWARDS THE SUN!
BUT JUST AS THIS FLOWER COULD NOT GROW IN A BED OF FILTH AND GARBAGE--
-- A YOUNG GIRL CANNOT BLOSSOM INTO HER FULL POTENTIAL WHEN PLANTED IN THIS DREADFUL ENVIRONMENT OF CRIME AND DEPRAVITY YOU'RE CREATING!
??? B-BUT, SIR!
I HAVEN'T CAUSED ANY CRIMES! I'M EXPOSING THEM IN ORDER TO STOP THEM!
chirp chirp
chirp
PERHAPS ANOTHER EXAMPLE.
CONSIDER THIS WASP'S NEST.
STING!
OW! BUGGER!

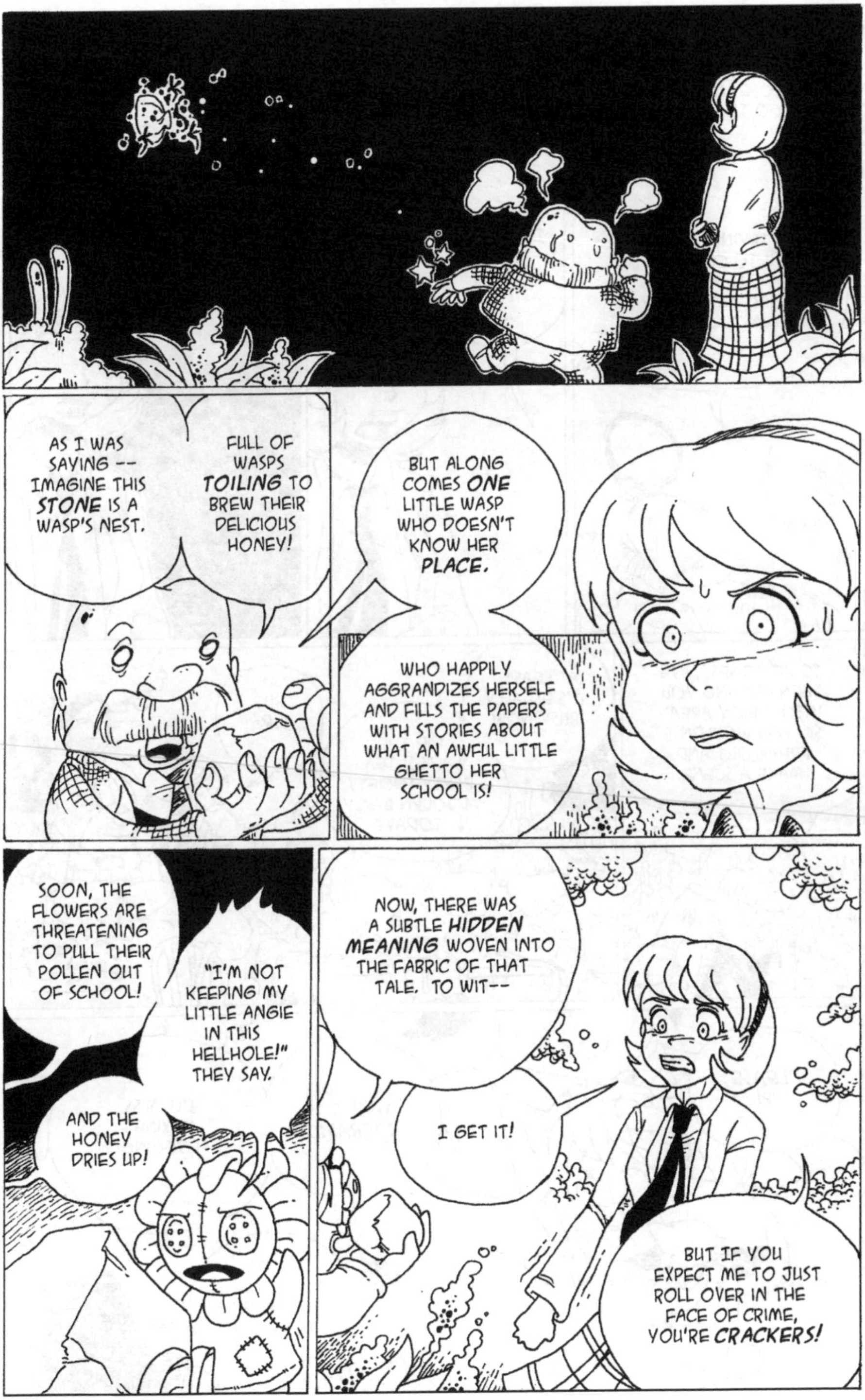
AS I WAS SAYING -- IMAGINE THIS STONE IS A WASP'S NEST.
FULL OF WASPS TOILING TO BREW THEIR DELICIOUS HONEY!
BUT ALONG COMES ONE LITTLE WASP WHO DOESN'T KNOW HER PLACE.
WHO HAPPILY AGGRANDIZES HERSELF AND FILLS THE PAPERS WITH STORIES ABOUT WHAT AN AWFUL LITTLE GHETTO HER SCHOOL IS!
SOON, THE FLOWERS ARE THREATENING TO PULL THEIR POLLEN OUT OF SCHOOL!
"I'M NOT KEEPING MY LITTLE ANGIE IN THIS HELLHOLE!" THEY SAY.
AND THE HONEY DRIES UP!
NOW, THERE WAS A SUBTLE HIDDEN MEANING WOVEN INTO THE FABRIC OF THAT TALE. TO WIT--
I GET IT!
BUT IF YOU EXPECT ME TO JUST ROLL OVER IN THE FACE OF CRIME, YOU'RE CRACKERS!

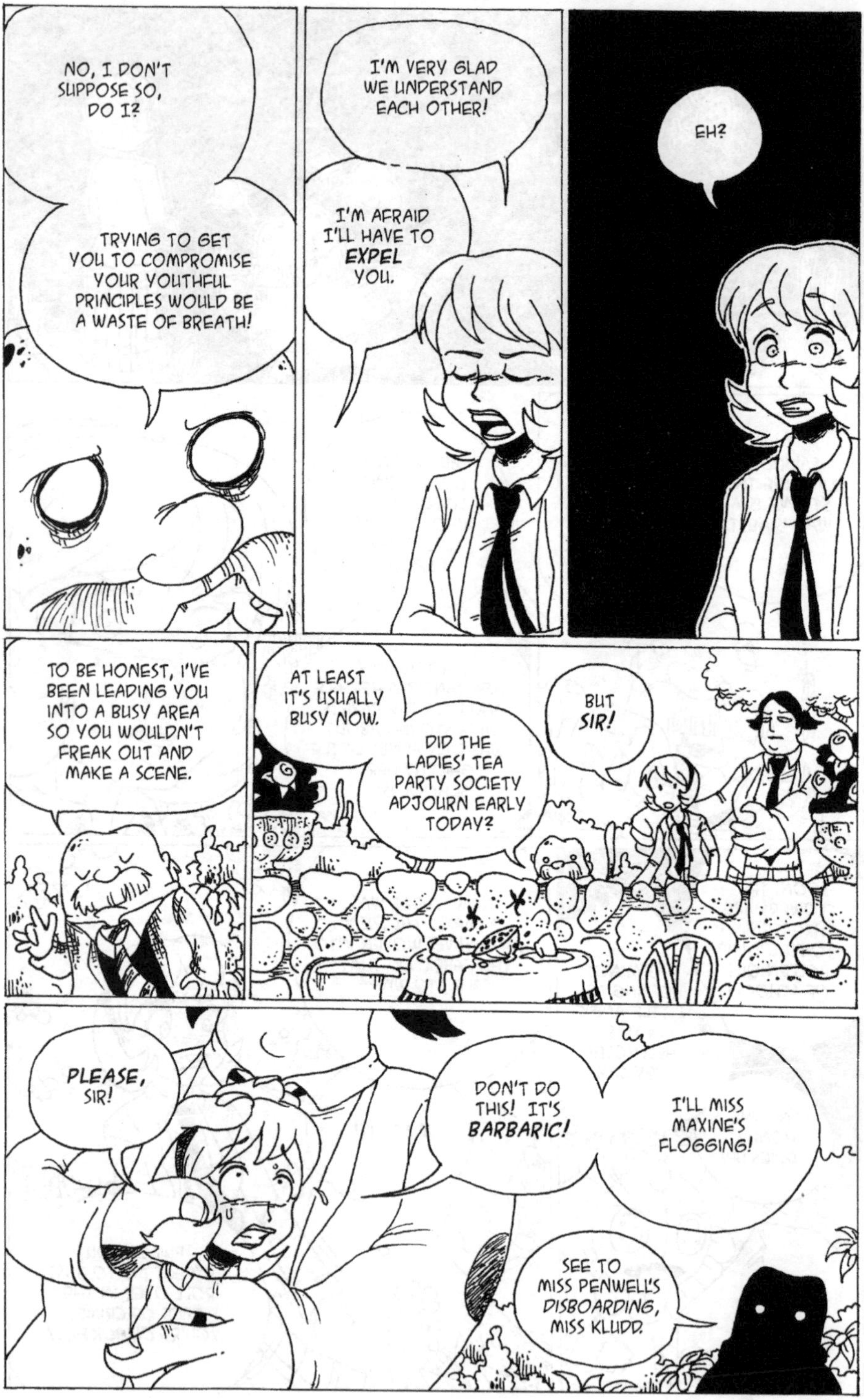
NO, I DON'T SUPPOSE SO, DO I?
TRYING TO GET YOU TO COMPROMISE YOUR YOUTHFUL PRINCIPLES WOULD BE A WASTE OF BREATH!
I'M VERY GLAD WE UNDERSTAND EACH OTHER!
I'M AFRAID I'LL HAVE TO **EXPEL** YOU.
EH?
TO BE HONEST, I'VE BEEN LEADING YOU INTO A BUSY AREA SO YOU WOULDN'T FREAK OUT AND MAKE A SCENE.
AT LEAST IT'S USUALLY BUSY NOW.
DID THE LADIES' TEA PARTY SOCIETY ADJOURN EARLY TODAY?
BUT **SIR!**
PLEASE, SIR!
DON'T DO THIS! IT'S **BARBARIC!**
I'LL MISS MAXINE'S FLOGGING!
SEE TO MISS PENWELL'S *DISBOARDING*, MISS KLUDD.

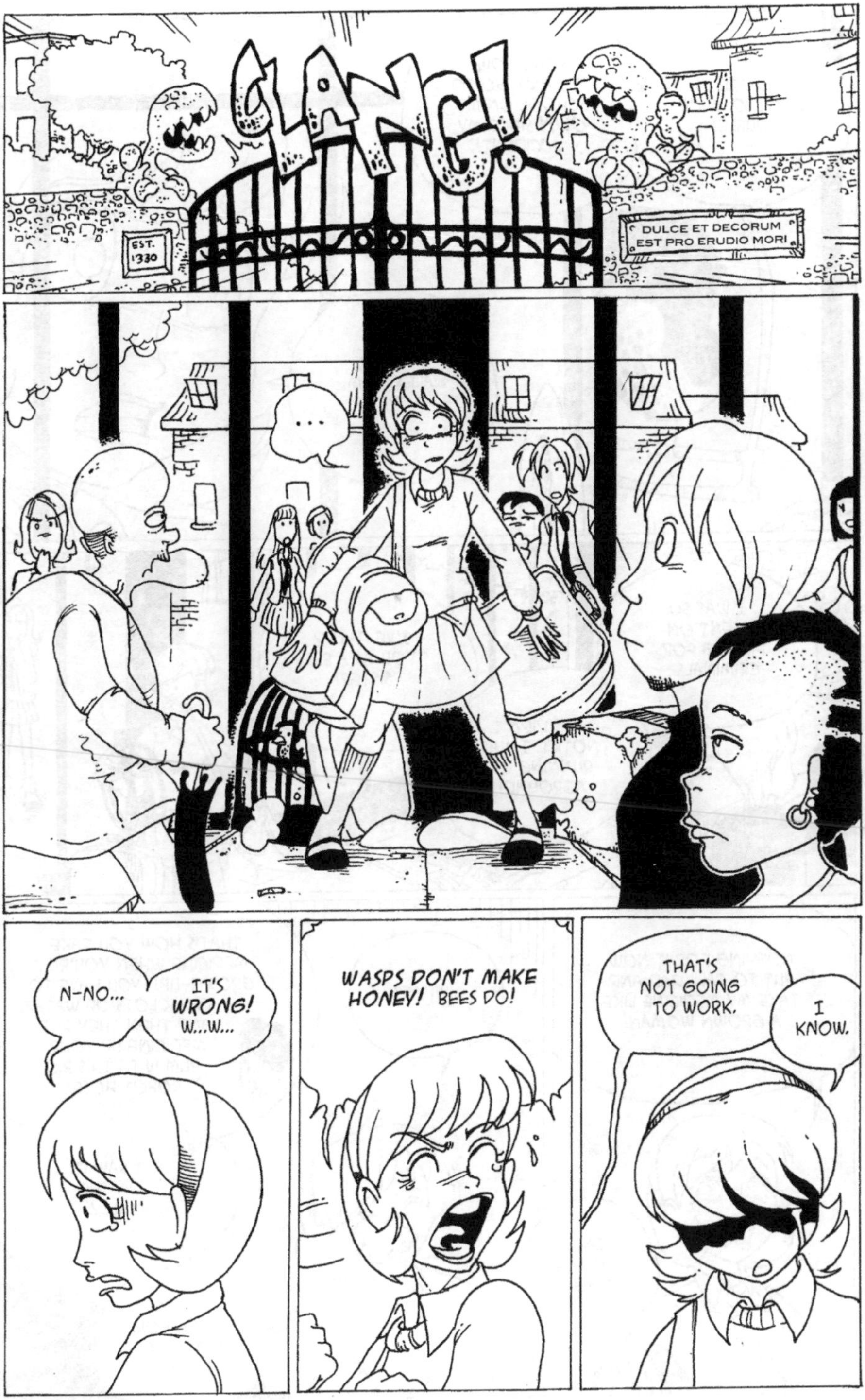
CLANG!
EST. 1330
DULCE ET DECORUM EST PRO ERUDIO MORI
...
N-NO...
IT'S WRONG! W...W...
WASPS DON'T MAKE HONEY! BEES DO!
THAT'S NOT GOING TO WORK.
I KNOW.

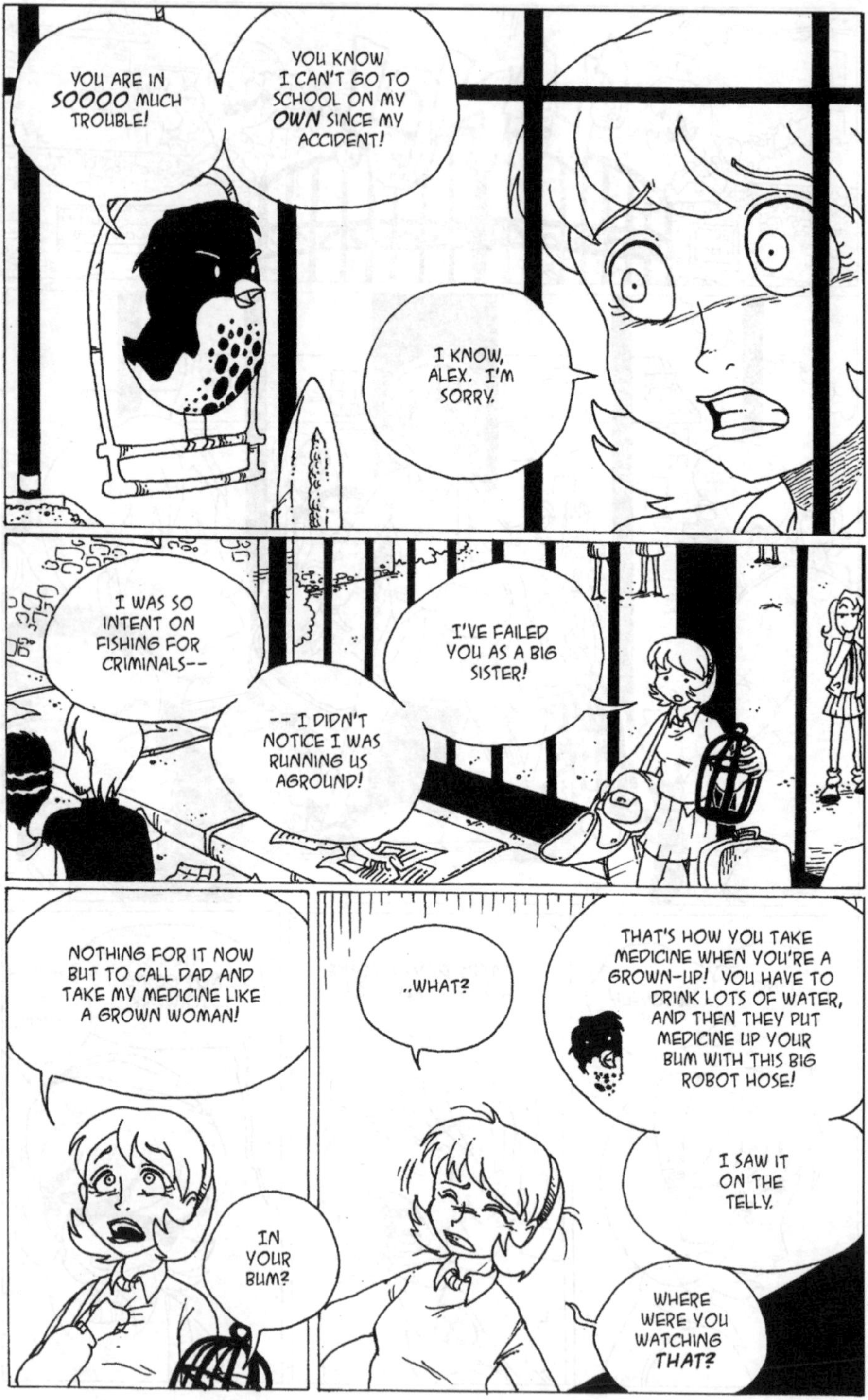
YOU ARE IN SOOOO MUCH TROUBLE!
YOU KNOW I CAN'T GO TO SCHOOL ON MY OWN SINCE MY ACCIDENT!
I KNOW, ALEX. I'M SORRY.
I WAS SO INTENT ON FISHING FOR CRIMINALS--
--I DIDN'T NOTICE I WAS RUNNING US AGROUND!
I'VE FAILED YOU AS A BIG SISTER!
NOTHING FOR IT NOW BUT TO CALL DAD AND TAKE MY MEDICINE LIKE A GROWN WOMAN!
IN YOUR BUM?
..WHAT?
THAT'S HOW YOU TAKE MEDICINE WHEN YOU'RE A GROWN-UP! YOU HAVE TO DRINK LOTS OF WATER, AND THEN THEY PUT MEDICINE UP YOUR BUM WITH THIS BIG ROBOT HOSE!
I SAW IT ON THE TELLY.
WHERE WERE YOU WATCHING THAT?

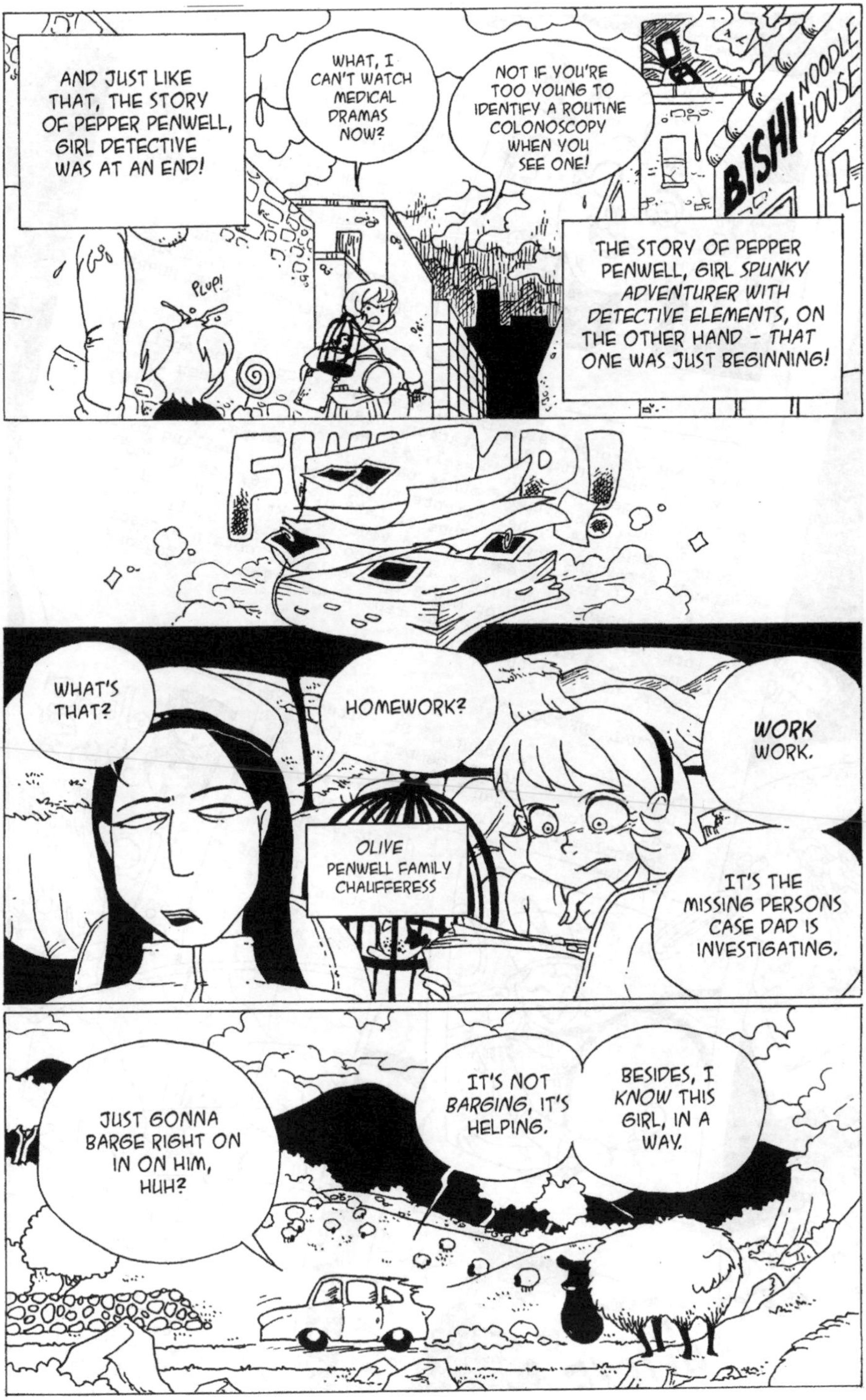
AND JUST LIKE THAT, THE STORY OF PEPPER PENWELL, GIRL DETECTIVE WAS AT AN END!
WHAT, I CAN'T WATCH MEDICAL DRAMAS NOW?
NOT IF YOU'RE TOO YOUNG TO IDENTIFY A ROUTINE COLONOSCOPY WHEN YOU SEE ONE!
BISHI NOODLE HOUSE
PLUP!
THE STORY OF PEPPER PENWELL, GIRL SPUNKY ADVENTURER WITH DETECTIVE ELEMENTS, ON THE OTHER HAND – THAT ONE WAS JUST BEGINNING!
WHAT'S THAT?
HOMEWORK?
WORK WORK.
OLIVE PENWELL FAMILY CHAUFFERESS
IT'S THE MISSING PERSONS CASE DAD IS INVESTIGATING.
JUST GONNA BARGE RIGHT ON IN ON HIM, HUH?
IT'S NOT BARGING, IT'S HELPING.
BESIDES, I KNOW THIS GIRL, IN A WAY.

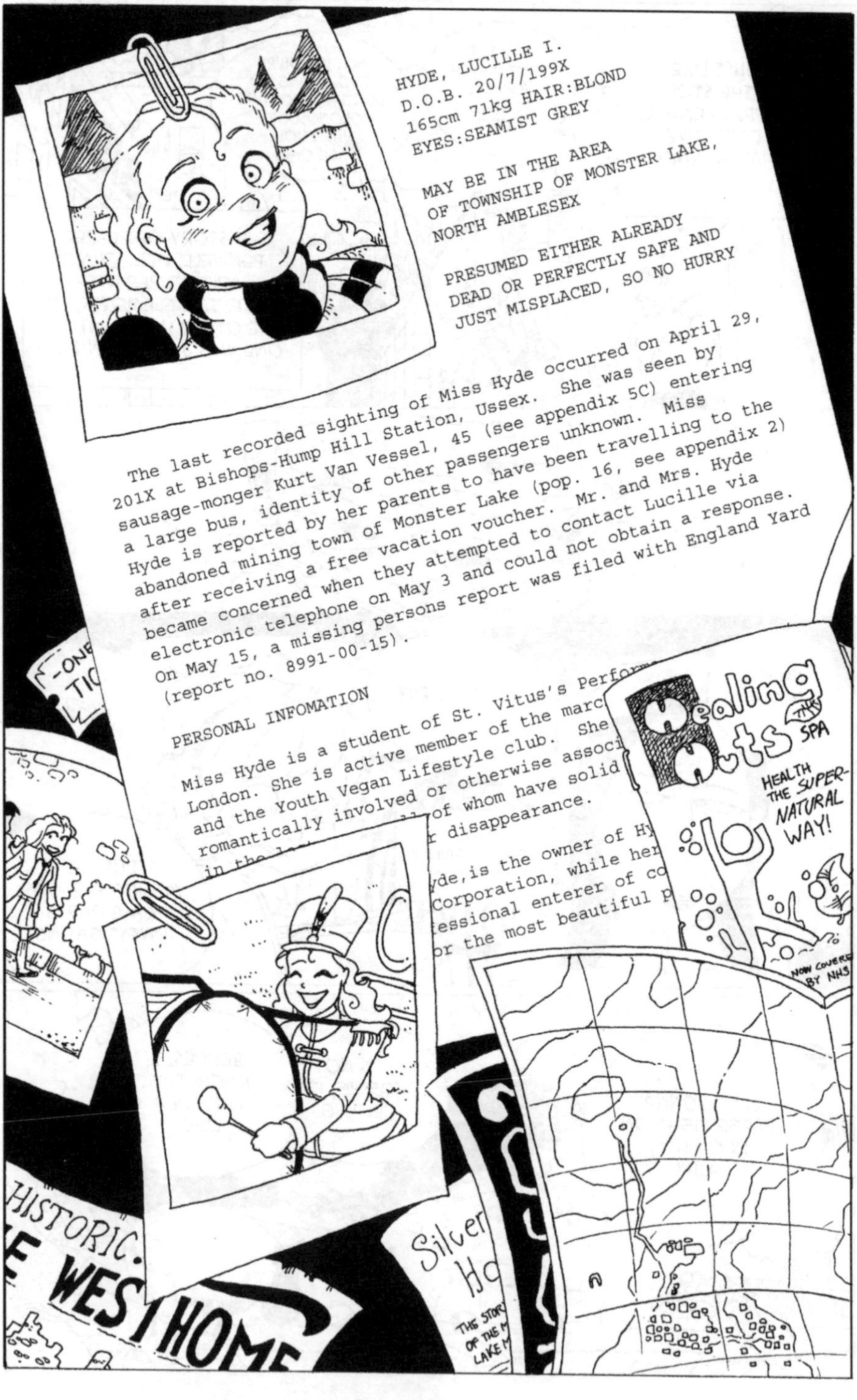

HYDE, LUCILLE I.
D.O.B. 20/7/199X
165cm 71kg HAIR:BLOND
EYES:SEAMIST GREY
MAY BE IN THE AREA
OF TOWNSHIP OF MONSTER LAKE,
NORTH AMBLESEX
PRESUMED EITHER ALREADY
DEAD OR PERFECTLY SAFE AND
JUST MISPLACED, SO NO HURRY
The last recorded sighting of Miss Hyde occurred on April 29, 201X at Bishops-Hump Hill Station, Ussex. She was seen by sausage-monger Kurt Van Vessel, 45 (see appendix 5C) entering a large bus, identity of other passengers unknown. Miss Hyde is reported by her parents to have been travelling to the abandoned mining town of Monster Lake (pop. 16, see appendix 2) after receiving a free vacation voucher. Mr. and Mrs. Hyde became concerned when they attempted to contact Lucille via electronic telephone on May 3 and could not obtain a response. On May 15, a missing persons report was filed with England Yard (report no. 8991-00-15).
PERSONAL INFOMATION
Miss Hyde is a student of St. Vitus's Perform
London. She is active member of the marc
and the Youth Vegan Lifestyle club. She
romantically involved or otherwise associ
of whom have solid
r disappearance.
yde, is the owner of Hy
Corporation, while her
essional enterer of co
or the most beautiful p
Healing Huts
THE SPA
HEALTH THE SUPER-NATURAL WAY!
NOW COVERED BY NHS
HISTORIC
WEST HOME
Silver

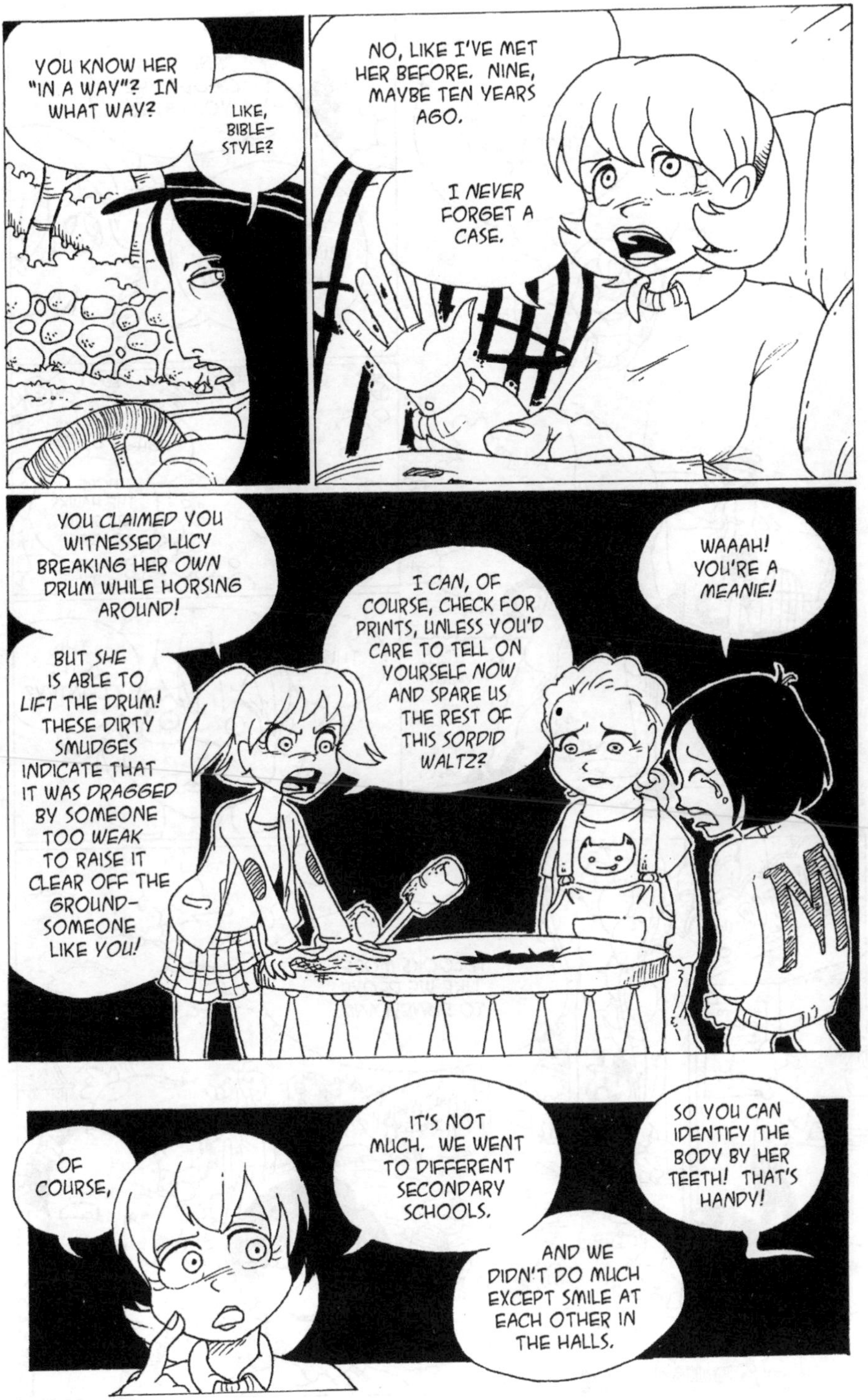
YOU KNOW HER "IN A WAY"? IN WHAT WAY?
LIKE, BIBLE-STYLE?
NO, LIKE I'VE MET HER BEFORE. NINE, MAYBE TEN YEARS AGO.
I NEVER FORGET A CASE.
YOU CLAIMED YOU WITNESSED LUCY BREAKING HER OWN DRUM WHILE HORSING AROUND!
BUT SHE IS ABLE TO LIFT THE DRUM! THESE DIRTY SMUDGES INDICATE THAT IT WAS DRAGGED BY SOMEONE TOO WEAK TO RAISE IT CLEAR OFF THE GROUND- SOMEONE LIKE YOU!
I CAN, OF COURSE, CHECK FOR PRINTS, UNLESS YOU'D CARE TO TELL ON YOURSELF NOW AND SPARE US THE REST OF THIS SORDID WALTZ?
WAAAH! YOU'RE A MEANIE!
OF COURSE,
IT'S NOT MUCH. WE WENT TO DIFFERENT SECONDARY SCHOOLS.
AND WE DIDN'T DO MUCH EXCEPT SMILE AT EACH OTHER IN THE HALLS.
SO YOU CAN IDENTIFY THE BODY BY HER TEETH! THAT'S HANDY!

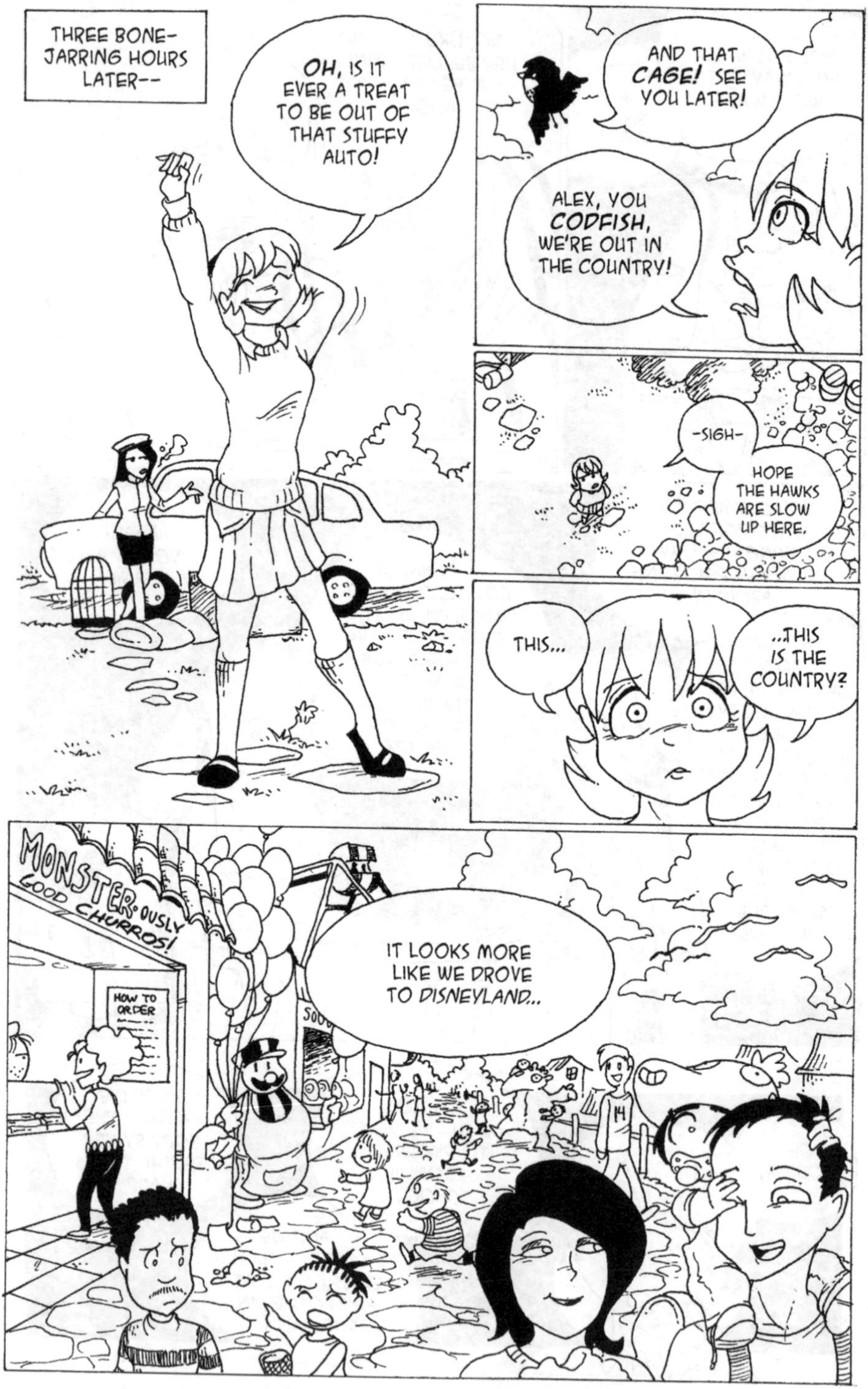
THREE BONE-JARRING HOURS LATER--
OH, IS IT EVER A TREAT TO BE OUT OF THAT STUFFY AUTO!
AND THAT CAGE! SEE YOU LATER!
ALEX, YOU CODFISH, WE'RE OUT IN THE COUNTRY!
-SIGH-
HOPE THE HAWKS ARE SLOW UP HERE.
THIS...
..THIS IS THE COUNTRY?
MONSTER-OUSLY GOOD CHURROS!
HOW TO ORDER
IT LOOKS MORE LIKE WE DROVE TO DISNEYLAND...
14

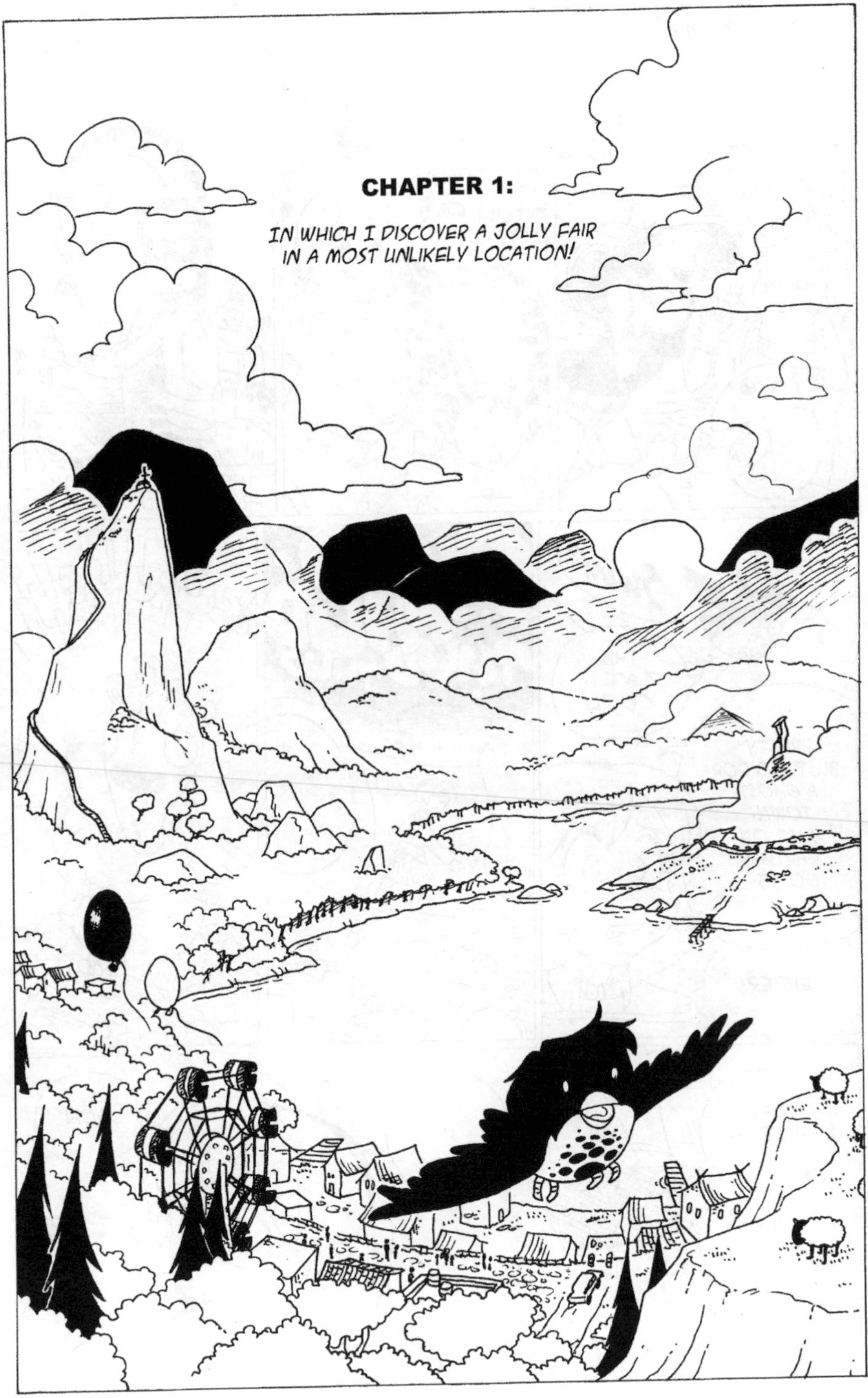
CHAPTER 1:
IN WHICH I DISCOVER A JOLLY FAIR IN A MOST UNLIKELY LOCATION!

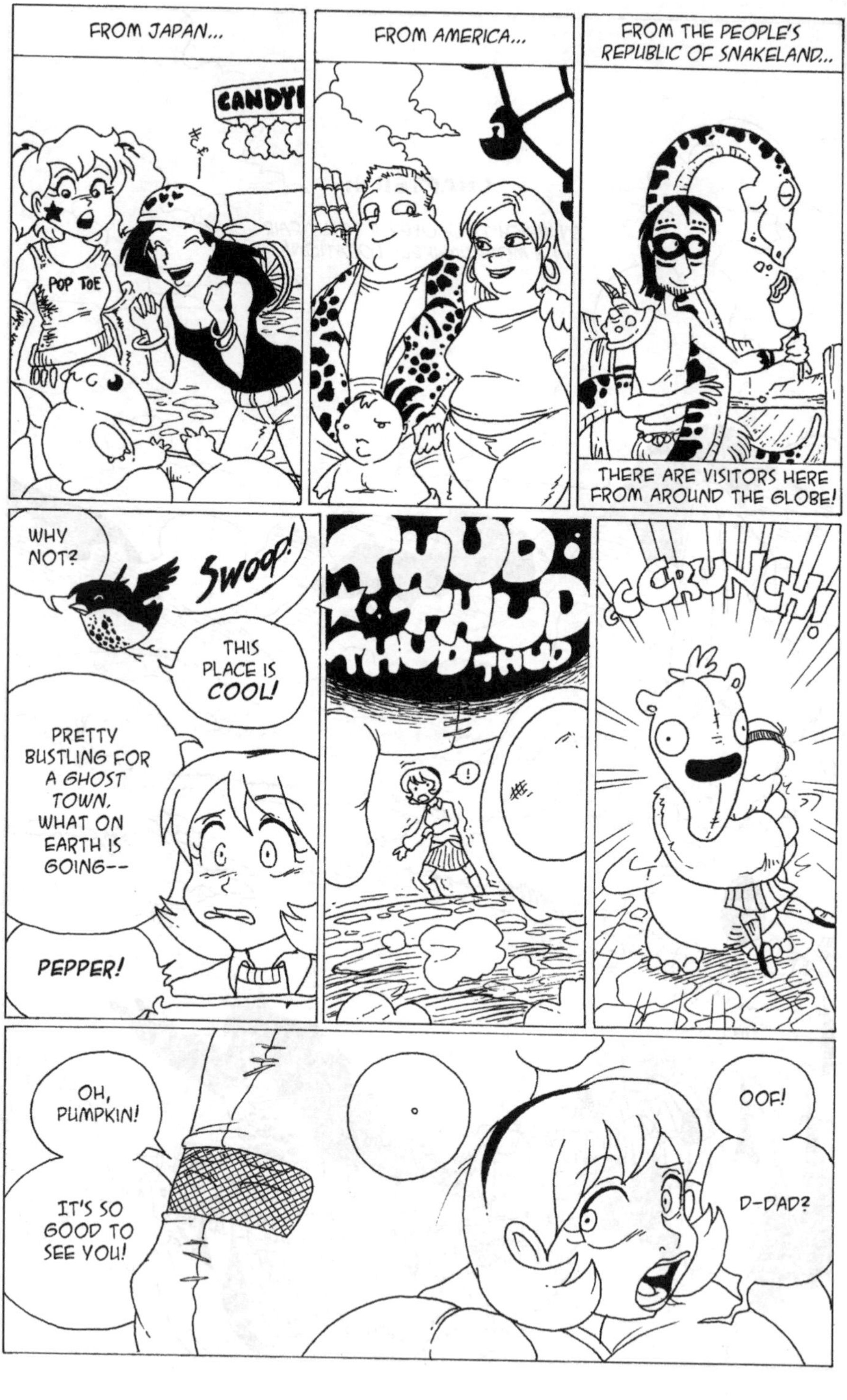

FROM JAPAN...
CANDY
きゃー
POP TOE
FROM AMERICA...
FROM THE PEOPLE'S REPUBLIC OF SNAKELAND...
THERE ARE VISITORS HERE FROM AROUND THE GLOBE!
WHY NOT?
SWOOP!
THIS PLACE IS COOL!
PRETTY BUSTLING FOR A GHOST TOWN. WHAT ON EARTH IS GOING--
PEPPER!
THUD THUD THUD THUD
!
CCRUNCH!
OH, PUMPKIN!
IT'S SO GOOD TO SEE YOU!
OOF!
D-DAD?

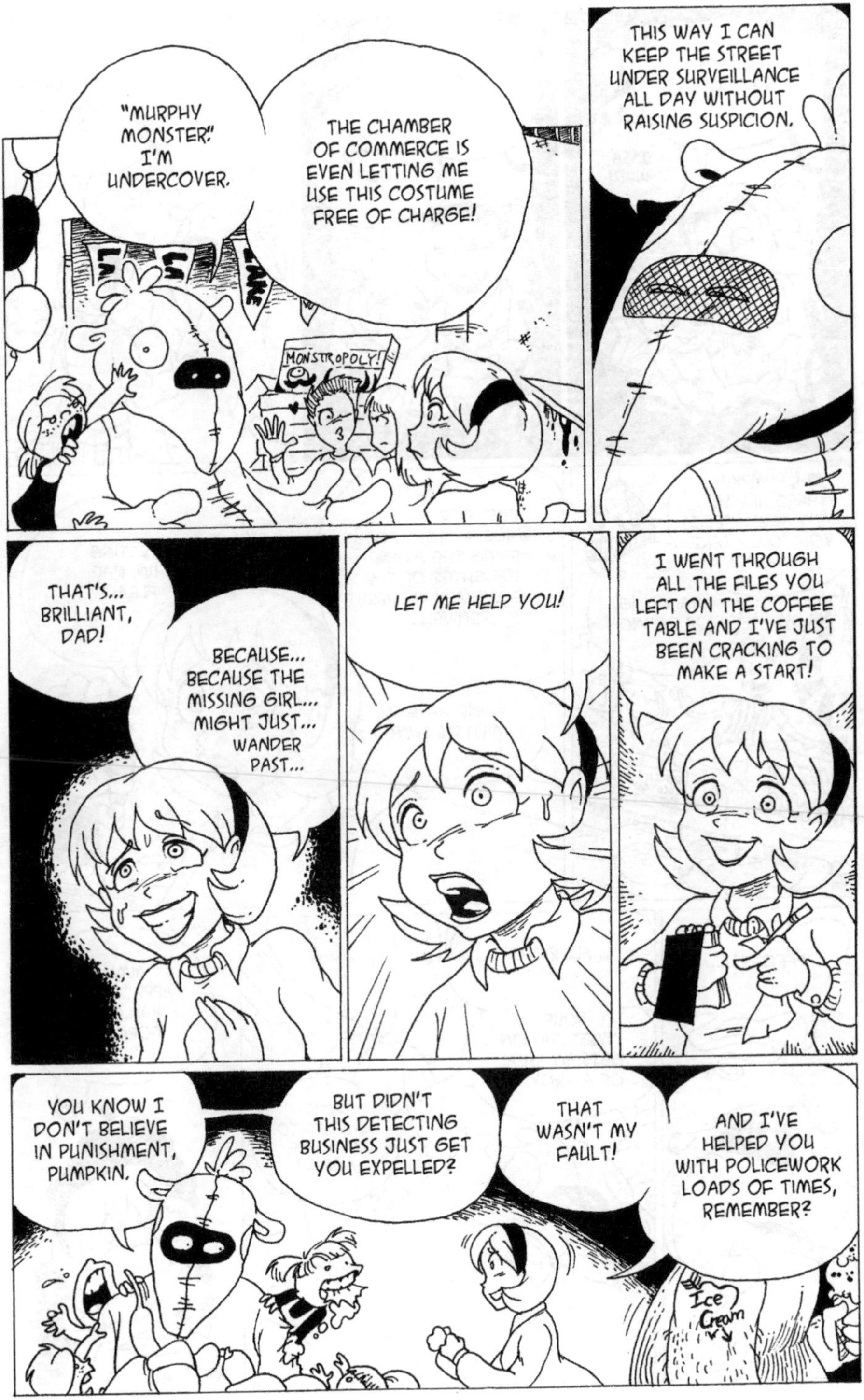
"MURPHY MONSTER." I'M UNDERCOVER.
THE CHAMBER OF COMMERCE IS EVEN LETTING ME USE THIS COSTUME FREE OF CHARGE!
MONSTROPOLY!
THIS WAY I CAN KEEP THE STREET UNDER SURVEILLANCE ALL DAY WITHOUT RAISING SUSPICION.
THAT'S... BRILLIANT, DAD!
BECAUSE... BECAUSE THE MISSING GIRL... MIGHT JUST... WANDER PAST...
LET ME HELP YOU!
I WENT THROUGH ALL THE FILES YOU LEFT ON THE COFFEE TABLE AND I'VE JUST BEEN CRACKING TO MAKE A START!
YOU KNOW I DON'T BELIEVE IN PUNISHMENT, PUMPKIN.
BUT DIDN'T THIS DETECTING BUSINESS JUST GET YOU EXPELLED?
THAT WASN'T MY FAULT!
AND I'VE HELPED YOU WITH POLICEWORK LOADS OF TIMES, REMEMBER?
Ice Cream

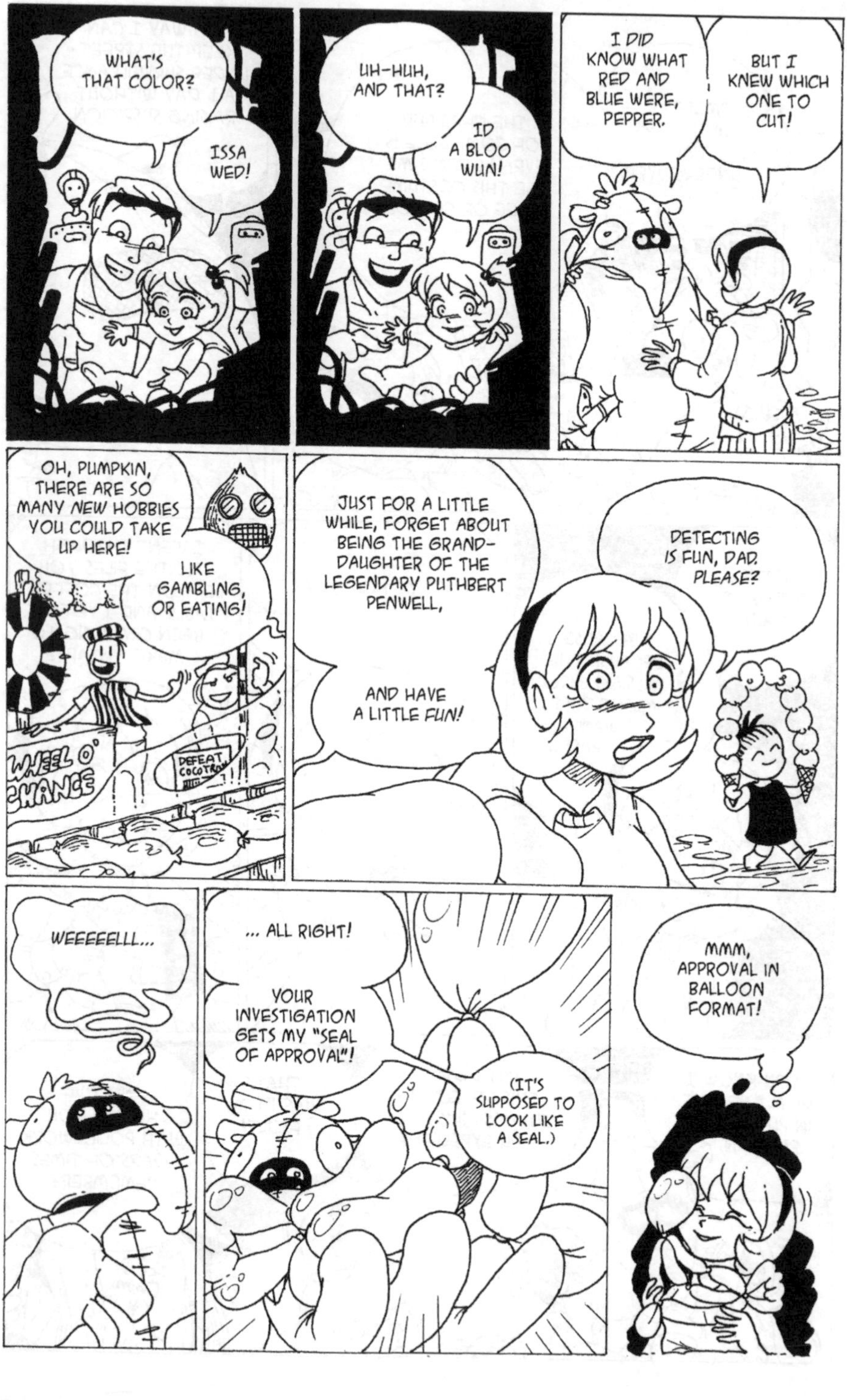
WHAT'S THAT COLOR?
ISSA WED!
UH-HUH, AND THAT?
ID A BLOO WUN!
I DID KNOW WHAT RED AND BLUE WERE, PEPPER.
BUT I KNEW WHICH ONE TO CUT!
OH, PUMPKIN, THERE ARE SO MANY NEW HOBBIES YOU COULD TAKE UP HERE!
LIKE GAMBLING, OR EATING!
WHEEL O' CHANCE
DEFEAT COCOTRON
JUST FOR A LITTLE WHILE, FORGET ABOUT BEING THE GRAND-DAUGHTER OF THE LEGENDARY PUTHBERT PENWELL,
AND HAVE A LITTLE FUN!
DETECTING IS FUN, DAD. PLEASE?
WEEEEELLL...
... ALL RIGHT!
YOUR INVESTIGATION GETS MY "SEAL OF APPROVAL"!
(IT'S SUPPOSED TO LOOK LIKE A SEAL.)
MMM, APPROVAL IN BALLOON FORMAT!

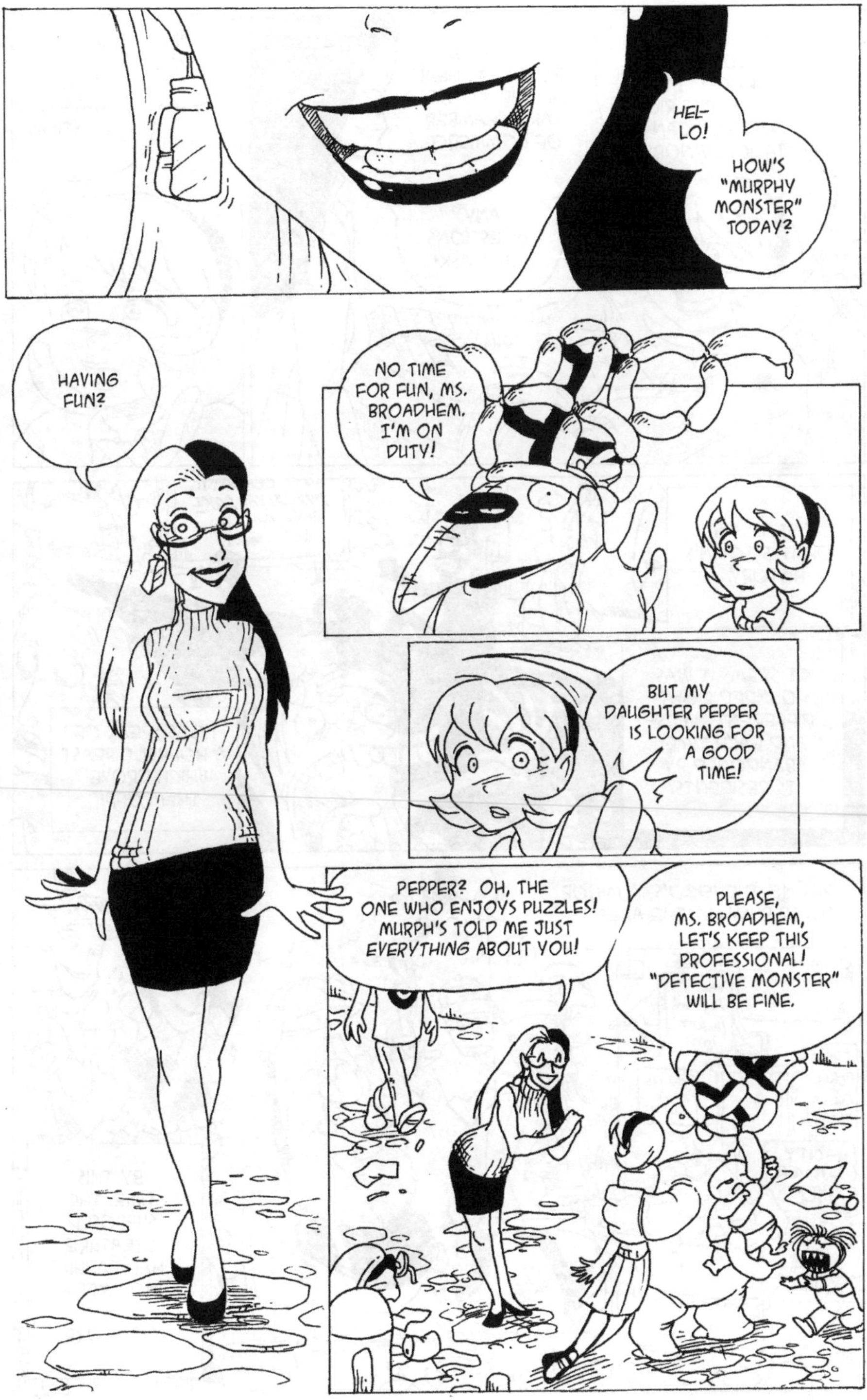
HEL-LO!
HOW'S "MURPHY MONSTER" TODAY?
HAVING FUN?
NO TIME FOR FUN, MS. BROADHEM. I'M ON DUTY!
BUT MY DAUGHTER PEPPER IS LOOKING FOR A GOOD TIME!
PEPPER? OH, THE ONE WHO ENJOYS PUZZLES! MURPH'S TOLD ME JUST EVERYTHING ABOUT YOU!
PLEASE, MS. BROADHEM, LET'S KEEP THIS PROFESSIONAL! "DETECTIVE MONSTER" WILL BE FINE.

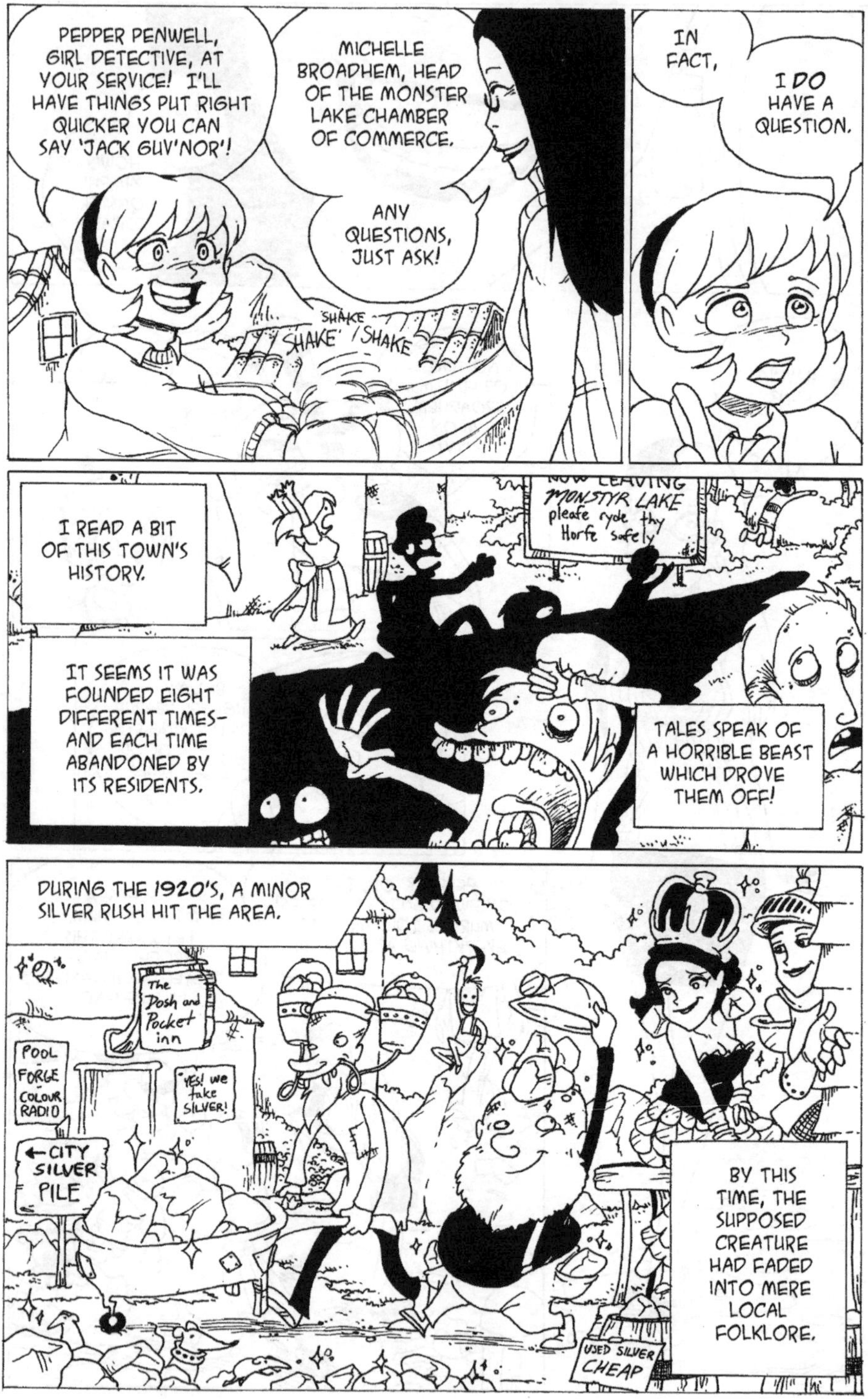

PEPPER PENWELL, GIRL DETECTIVE, AT YOUR SERVICE! I'LL HAVE THINGS PUT RIGHT QUICKER YOU CAN SAY 'JACK GUV'NOR'!
MICHELLE BROADHEM, HEAD OF THE MONSTER LAKE CHAMBER OF COMMERCE.
ANY QUESTIONS, JUST ASK!
SHAKE SHAKE SHAKE
IN FACT,
I DO HAVE A QUESTION.
I READ A BIT OF THIS TOWN'S HISTORY.
MONSTYR LAKE
pleafe ryde thy Horfe fafely
IT SEEMS IT WAS FOUNDED EIGHT DIFFERENT TIMES- AND EACH TIME ABANDONED BY ITS RESIDENTS.
TALES SPEAK OF A HORRIBLE BEAST WHICH DROVE THEM OFF!
DURING THE 1920'S, A MINOR SILVER RUSH HIT THE AREA.
The Dosh and Pocket inn
POOL - FORGE - COLOUR RADIO
YES! we take SILVER!
← CITY SILVER PILE
USED SILVER CHEAP
BY THIS TIME, THE SUPPOSED CREATURE HAD FADED INTO MERE LOCAL FOLKLORE.

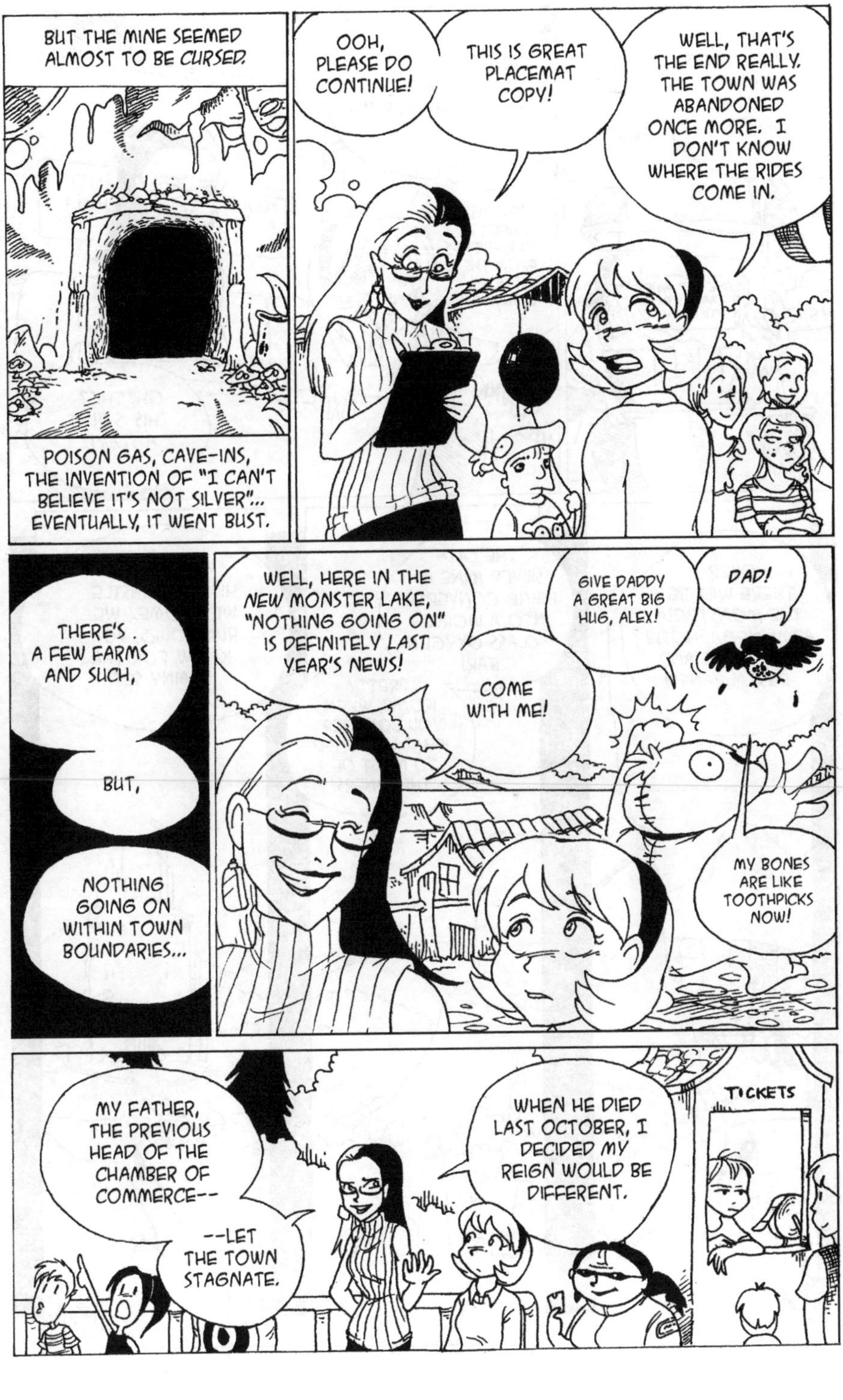
BUT THE MINE SEEMED ALMOST TO BE CURSED.
POISON GAS, CAVE-INS, THE INVENTION OF "I CAN'T BELIEVE IT'S NOT SILVER"... EVENTUALLY, IT WENT BUST.
OOH, PLEASE DO CONTINUE!
THIS IS GREAT PLACEMAT COPY!
WELL, THAT'S THE END REALLY. THE TOWN WAS ABANDONED ONCE MORE. I DON'T KNOW WHERE THE RIDES COME IN.
THERE'S A FEW FARMS AND SUCH,
BUT,
NOTHING GOING ON WITHIN TOWN BOUNDARIES...
WELL, HERE IN THE NEW MONSTER LAKE, "NOTHING GOING ON" IS DEFINITELY LAST YEAR'S NEWS!
COME WITH ME!
GIVE DADDY A GREAT BIG HUG, ALEX!
DAD!
MY BONES ARE LIKE TOOTHPICKS NOW!
MY FATHER, THE PREVIOUS HEAD OF THE CHAMBER OF COMMERCE--
--LET THE TOWN STAGNATE.
WHEN HE DIED LAST OCTOBER, I DECIDED MY REIGN WOULD BE DIFFERENT.
TICKETS

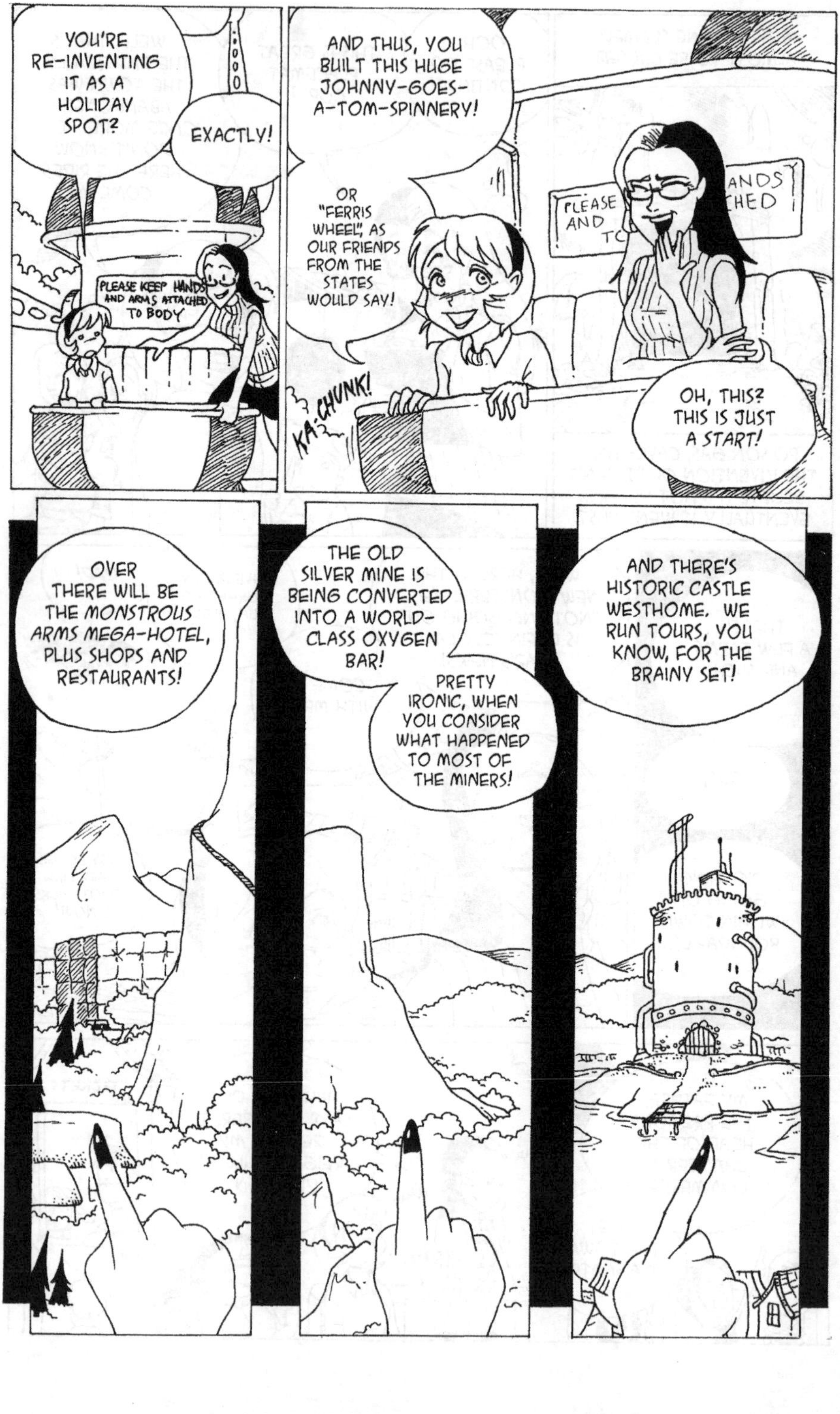
YOU'RE RE-INVENTING IT AS A HOLIDAY SPOT?
EXACTLY!
PLEASE KEEP HANDS AND ARMS ATTACHED TO BODY
AND THUS, YOU BUILT THIS HUGE JOHNNY-GOES-A-TOM-SPINNERY!
OR "FERRIS WHEEL," AS OUR FRIENDS FROM THE STATES WOULD SAY!
KA-CHUNK!
OH, THIS? THIS IS JUST A START!
OVER THERE WILL BE THE *MONSTROUS ARMS MEGA-HOTEL*, PLUS SHOPS AND RESTAURANTS!
THE OLD SILVER MINE IS BEING CONVERTED INTO A WORLD-CLASS OXYGEN BAR!
PRETTY IRONIC, WHEN YOU CONSIDER WHAT HAPPENED TO MOST OF THE MINERS!
AND THERE'S HISTORIC CASTLE WESTHOME. WE RUN TOURS, YOU KNOW, FOR THE BRAINY SET!

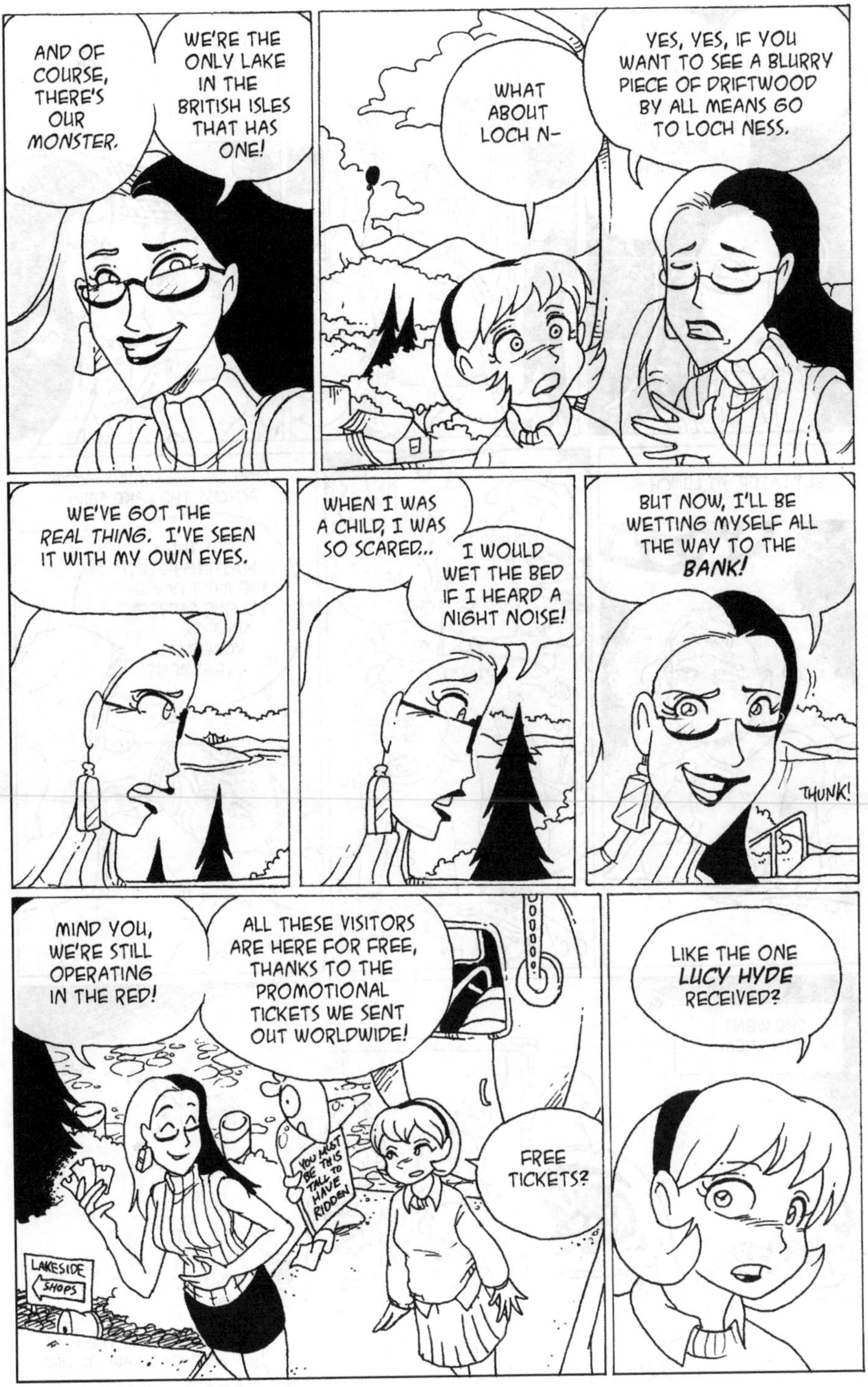

AND OF COURSE, THERE'S OUR MONSTER.
WE'RE THE ONLY LAKE IN THE BRITISH ISLES THAT HAS ONE!
WHAT ABOUT LOCH N-
YES, YES, IF YOU WANT TO SEE A BLURRY PIECE OF DRIFTWOOD BY ALL MEANS GO TO LOCH NESS.
WE'VE GOT THE REAL THING. I'VE SEEN IT WITH MY OWN EYES.
WHEN I WAS A CHILD, I WAS SO SCARED...
I WOULD WET THE BED IF I HEARD A NIGHT NOISE!
BUT NOW, I'LL BE WETTING MYSELF ALL THE WAY TO THE BANK!
THUNK!
MIND YOU, WE'RE STILL OPERATING IN THE RED!
ALL THESE VISITORS ARE HERE FOR FREE, THANKS TO THE PROMOTIONAL TICKETS WE SENT OUT WORLDWIDE!
YOU MUST BE THIS TALL TO HAVE RIDDEN
LAKESIDE
SHOPS
FREE TICKETS?
LIKE THE ONE LUCY HYDE RECEIVED?

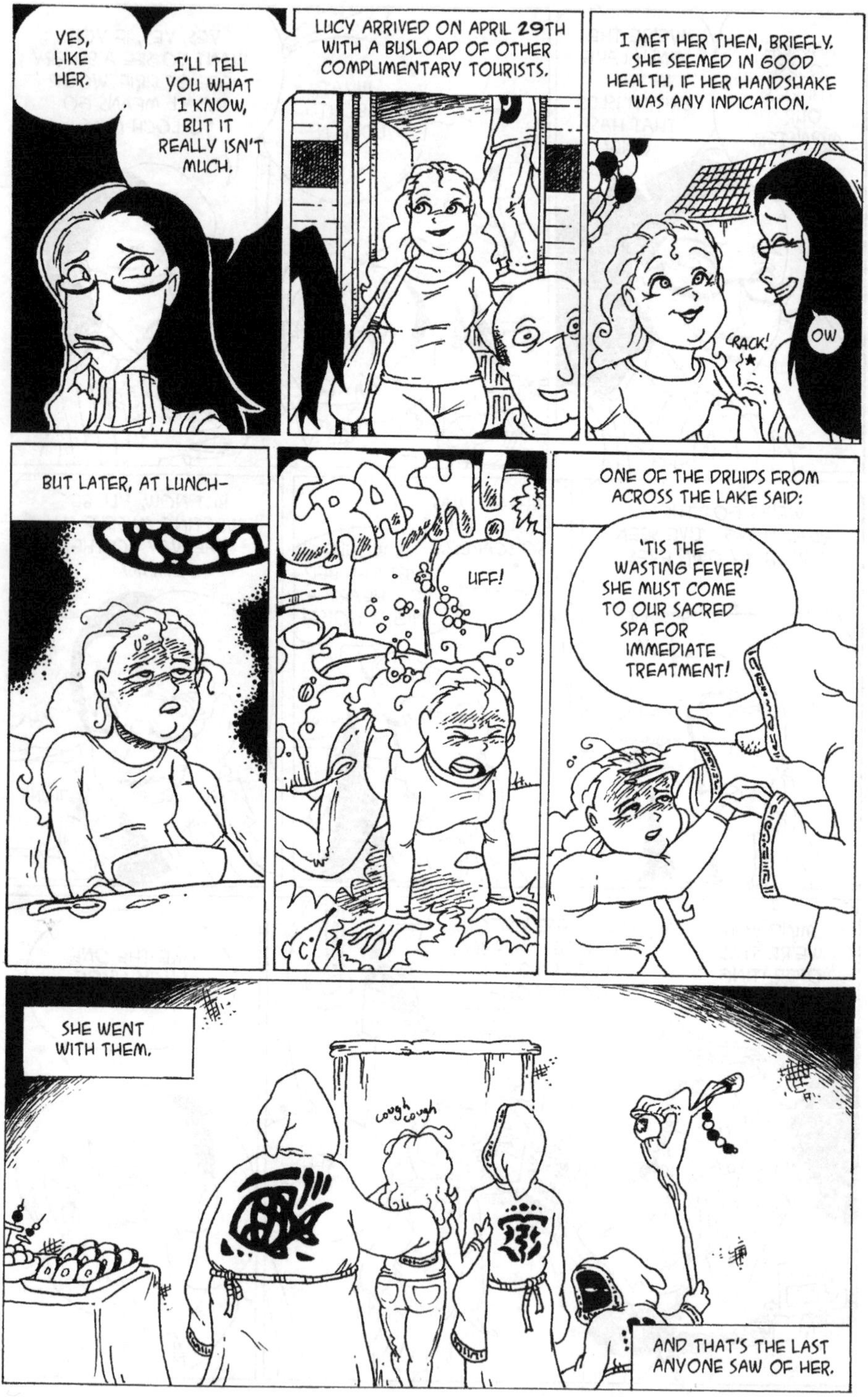
YES, LIKE HER.
I'LL TELL YOU WHAT I KNOW, BUT IT REALLY ISN'T MUCH.
LUCY ARRIVED ON APRIL 29TH WITH A BUSLOAD OF OTHER COMPLIMENTARY TOURISTS.
I MET HER THEN, BRIEFLY. SHE SEEMED IN GOOD HEALTH, IF HER HANDSHAKE WAS ANY INDICATION.
CRACK!
OW
BUT LATER, AT LUNCH-
CRASH!
UFF!
ONE OF THE DRUIDS FROM ACROSS THE LAKE SAID:
'TIS THE WASTING FEVER! SHE MUST COME TO OUR SACRED SPA FOR IMMEDIATE TREATMENT!
SHE WENT WITH THEM.
cough cough
AND THAT'S THE LAST ANYONE SAW OF HER.

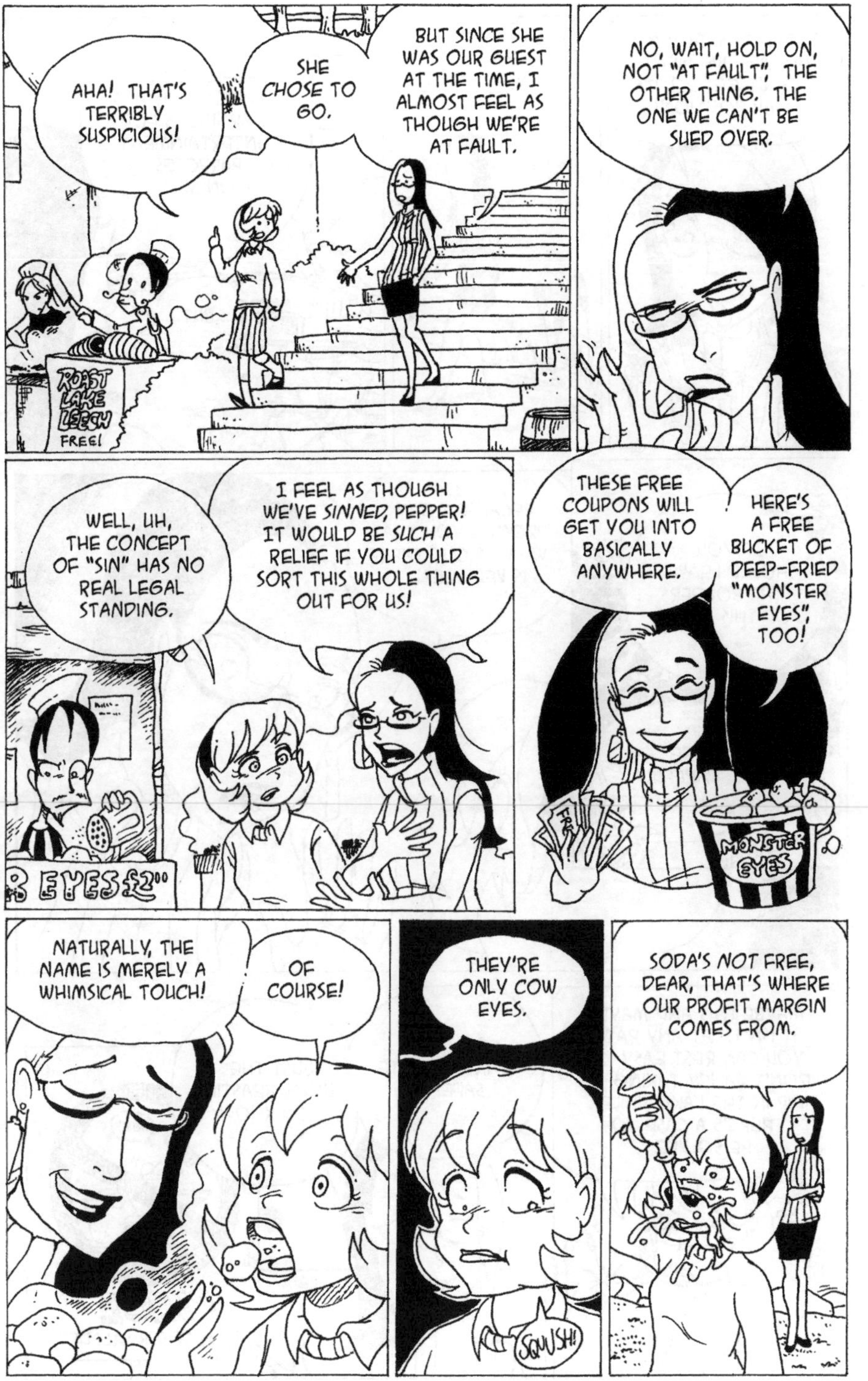
AHA! THAT'S TERRIBLY SUSPICIOUS!
SHE CHOSE TO GO.
BUT SINCE SHE WAS OUR GUEST AT THE TIME, I ALMOST FEEL AS THOUGH WE'RE AT FAULT.
ROAST LAKE LEECH FREE!
NO, WAIT, HOLD ON, NOT "AT FAULT", THE OTHER THING. THE ONE WE CAN'T BE SUED OVER.
WELL, UH, THE CONCEPT OF "SIN" HAS NO REAL LEGAL STANDING.
I FEEL AS THOUGH WE'VE *SINNED*, PEPPER! IT WOULD BE *SUCH* A RELIEF IF YOU COULD SORT THIS WHOLE THING OUT FOR US!
R EYES £2.00
THESE FREE COUPONS WILL GET YOU INTO BASICALLY ANYWHERE.
HERE'S A FREE BUCKET OF DEEP-FRIED "MONSTER EYES", TOO!
MONSTER EYES
NATURALLY, THE NAME IS MERELY A WHIMSICAL TOUCH!
OF COURSE!
THEY'RE ONLY COW EYES.
SQUISH!
SODA'S NOT FREE, DEAR, THAT'S WHERE OUR PROFIT MARGIN COMES FROM.

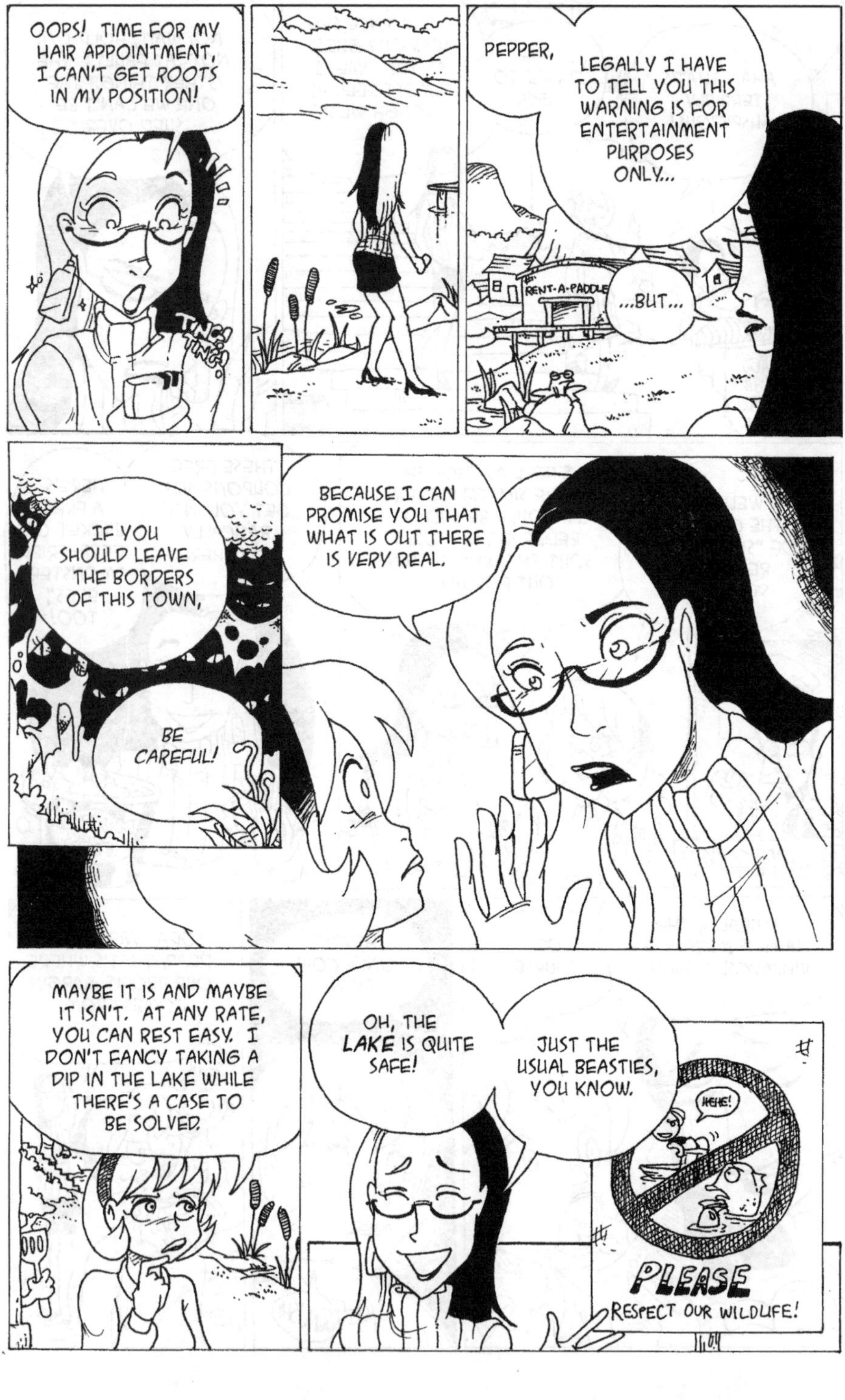
OOPS! TIME FOR MY HAIR APPOINTMENT, I CAN'T GET ROOTS IN MY POSITION!
TING! TING!
PEPPER,
LEGALLY I HAVE TO TELL YOU THIS WARNING IS FOR ENTERTAINMENT PURPOSES ONLY...
RENT-A-PADDLE
...BUT...
IF YOU SHOULD LEAVE THE BORDERS OF THIS TOWN,
BE CAREFUL!
BECAUSE I CAN PROMISE YOU THAT WHAT IS OUT THERE IS VERY REAL.
MAYBE IT IS AND MAYBE IT ISN'T. AT ANY RATE, YOU CAN REST EASY. I DON'T FANCY TAKING A DIP IN THE LAKE WHILE THERE'S A CASE TO BE SOLVED.
OH, THE LAKE IS QUITE SAFE!
JUST THE USUAL BEASTIES, YOU KNOW.
HEHE!
PLEASE
RESPECT OUR WILDLIFE!

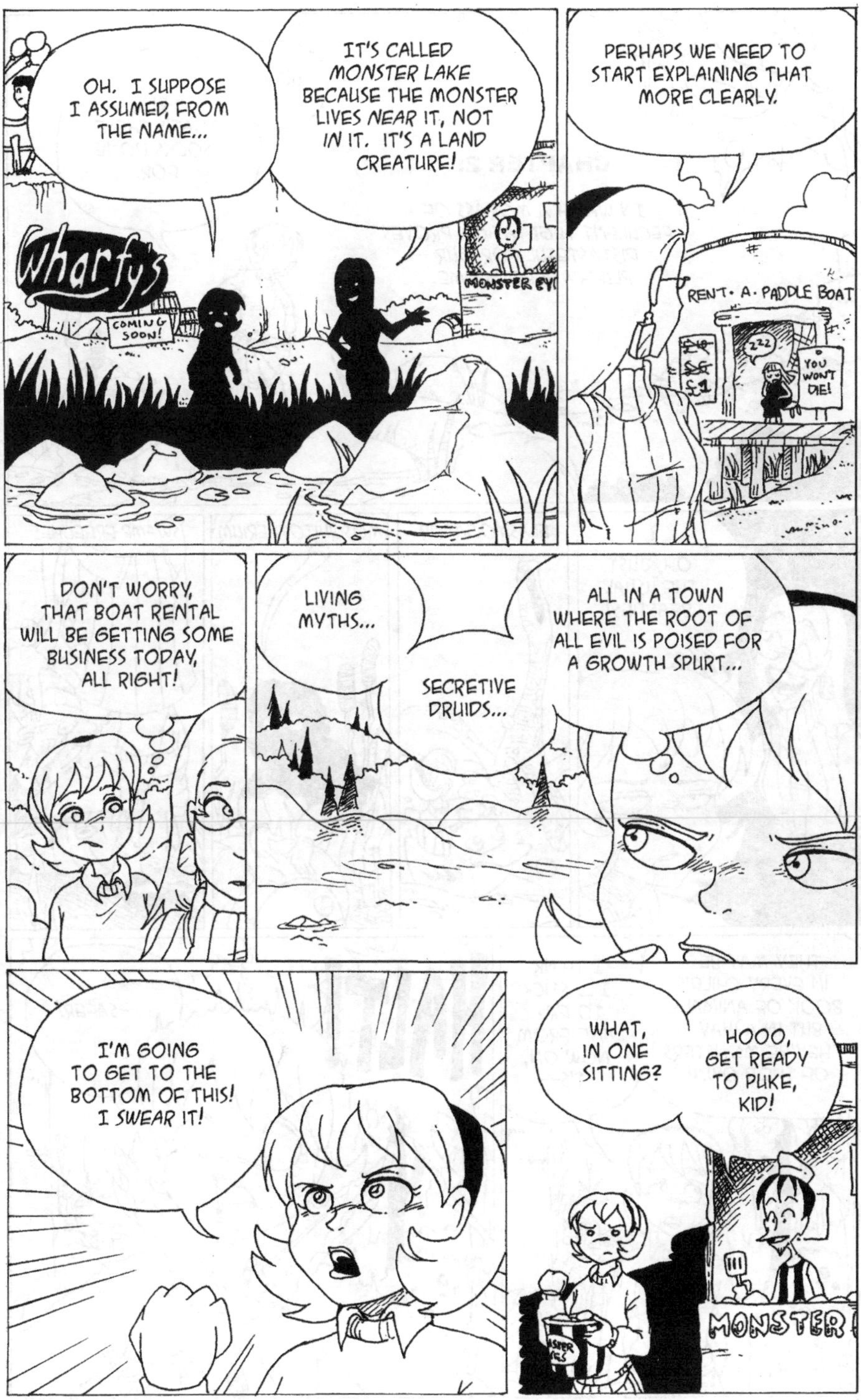
OH. I SUPPOSE I ASSUMED, FROM THE NAME...
IT'S CALLED *MONSTER LAKE* BECAUSE THE MONSTER LIVES *NEAR* IT, NOT *IN* IT. IT'S A LAND CREATURE!
Wharfy's
COMING SOON!
MONSTER EY
PERHAPS WE NEED TO START EXPLAINING THAT MORE CLEARLY.
RENT · A · PADDLE BOAT
ZZZ
YOU WON'T DIE!
DON'T WORRY, THAT BOAT RENTAL WILL BE GETTING SOME BUSINESS TODAY, ALL RIGHT!
LIVING MYTHS...
SECRETIVE DRUIDS...
ALL IN A TOWN WHERE THE ROOT OF ALL EVIL IS POISED FOR A GROWTH SPURT...
I'M GOING TO GET TO THE BOTTOM OF THIS! I SWEAR IT!
WHAT, IN ONE SITTING?
HOOO, GET READY TO PUKE, KID!
MONSTER

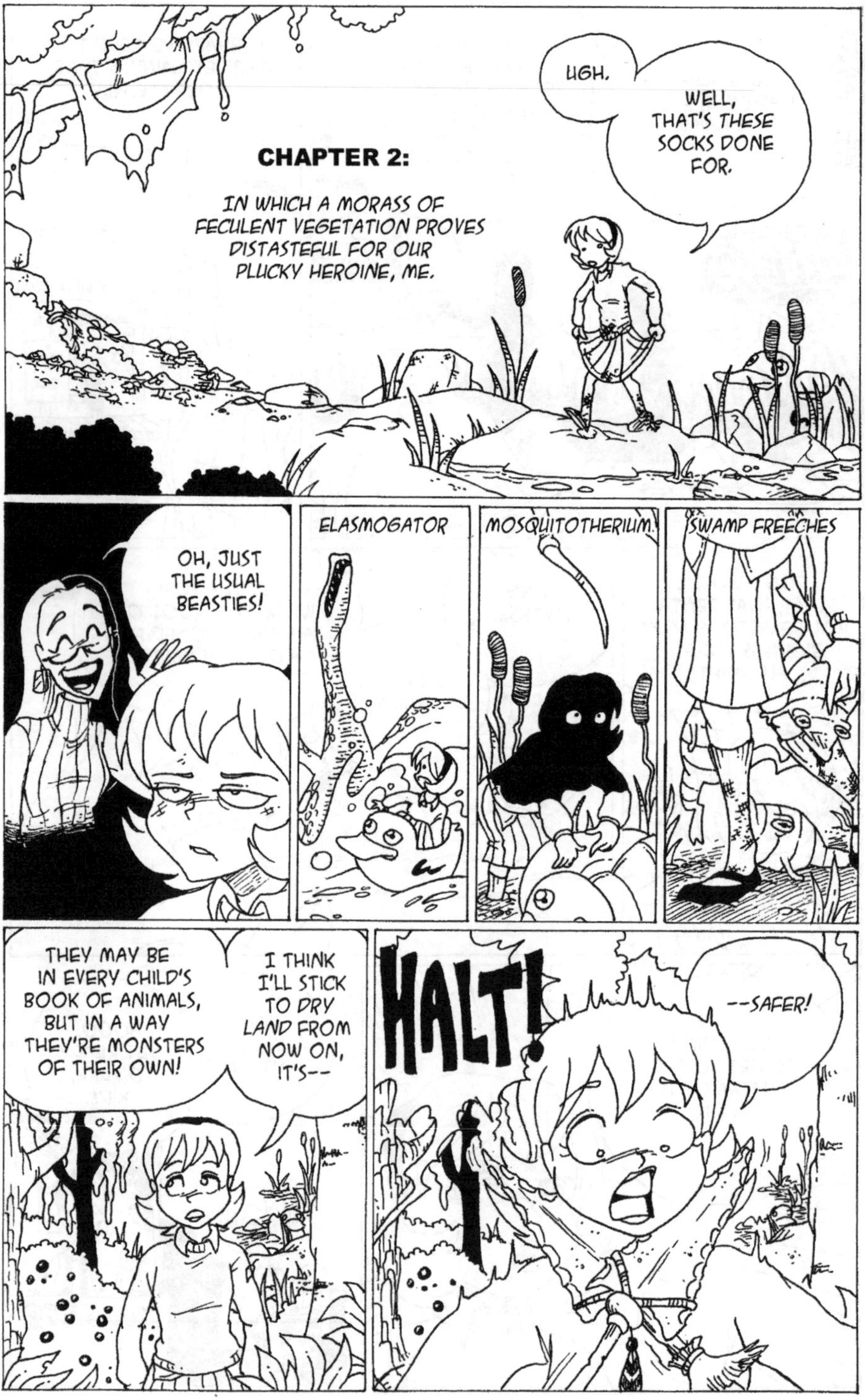
CHAPTER 2:
IN WHICH A MORASS OF FECULENT VEGETATION PROVES DISTASTEFUL FOR OUR PLUCKY HEROINE, ME.
UGH.
WELL, THAT'S THESE SOCKS DONE FOR.
OH, JUST THE USUAL BEASTIES!
ELASMOGATOR
MOSQUITOTHERIUM
SWAMP FREECHES
THEY MAY BE IN EVERY CHILD'S BOOK OF ANIMALS, BUT IN A WAY THEY'RE MONSTERS OF THEIR OWN!
I THINK I'LL STICK TO DRY LAND FROM NOW ON, IT'S--
HALT!
--SAFER!

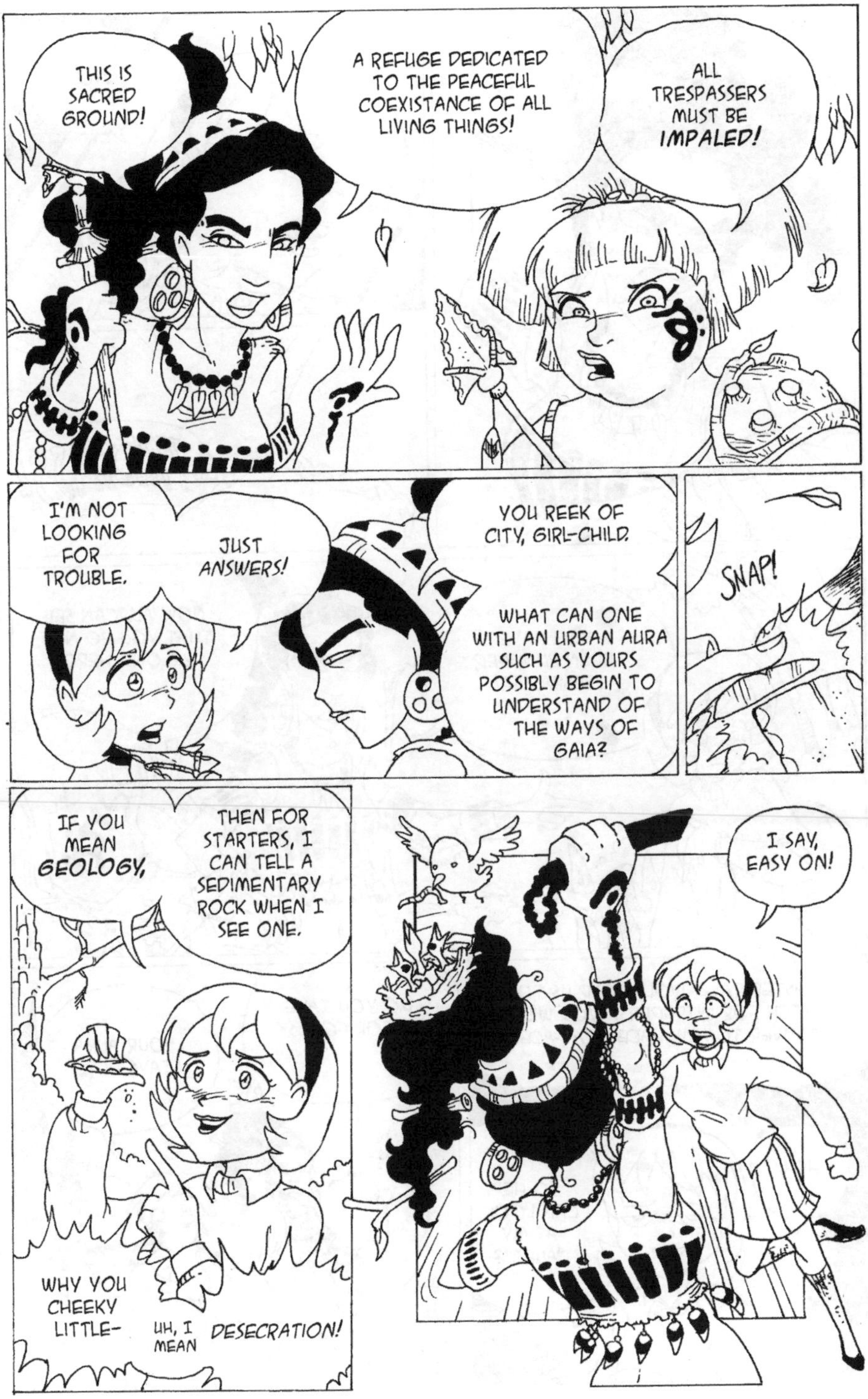

THIS IS SACRED GROUND!
A REFUGE DEDICATED TO THE PEACEFUL COEXISTANCE OF ALL LIVING THINGS!
ALL TRESPASSERS MUST BE IMPALED!
I'M NOT LOOKING FOR TROUBLE.
JUST ANSWERS!
YOU REEK OF CITY, GIRL-CHILD.
WHAT CAN ONE WITH AN URBAN AURA SUCH AS YOURS POSSIBLY BEGIN TO UNDERSTAND OF THE WAYS OF GAIA?
SNAP!
IF YOU MEAN GEOLOGY,
THEN FOR STARTERS, I CAN TELL A SEDIMENTARY ROCK WHEN I SEE ONE.
WHY YOU CHEEKY LITTLE-
UH, I MEAN
DESECRATION!
I SAY, EASY ON!

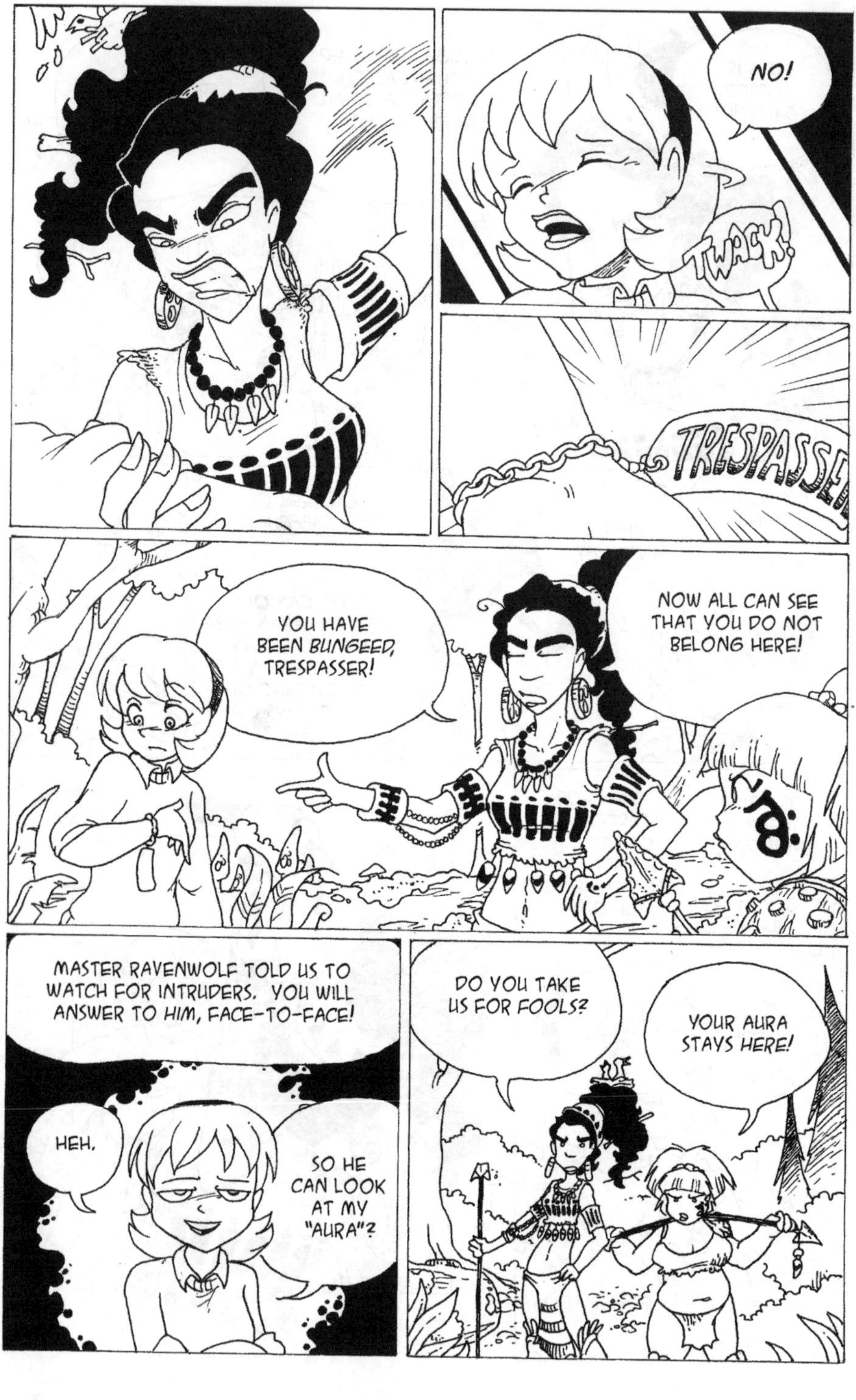

NO!
TWACK!
TRESPASSE
YOU HAVE BEEN *BUNGEED*, TRESPASSER!
NOW ALL CAN SEE THAT YOU DO NOT BELONG HERE!
MASTER RAVENWOLF TOLD US TO WATCH FOR INTRUDERS. YOU WILL ANSWER TO HIM, FACE-TO-FACE!
HEH.
SO HE CAN LOOK AT MY "AURA"?
DO YOU TAKE US FOR FOOLS?
YOUR AURA STAYS HERE!

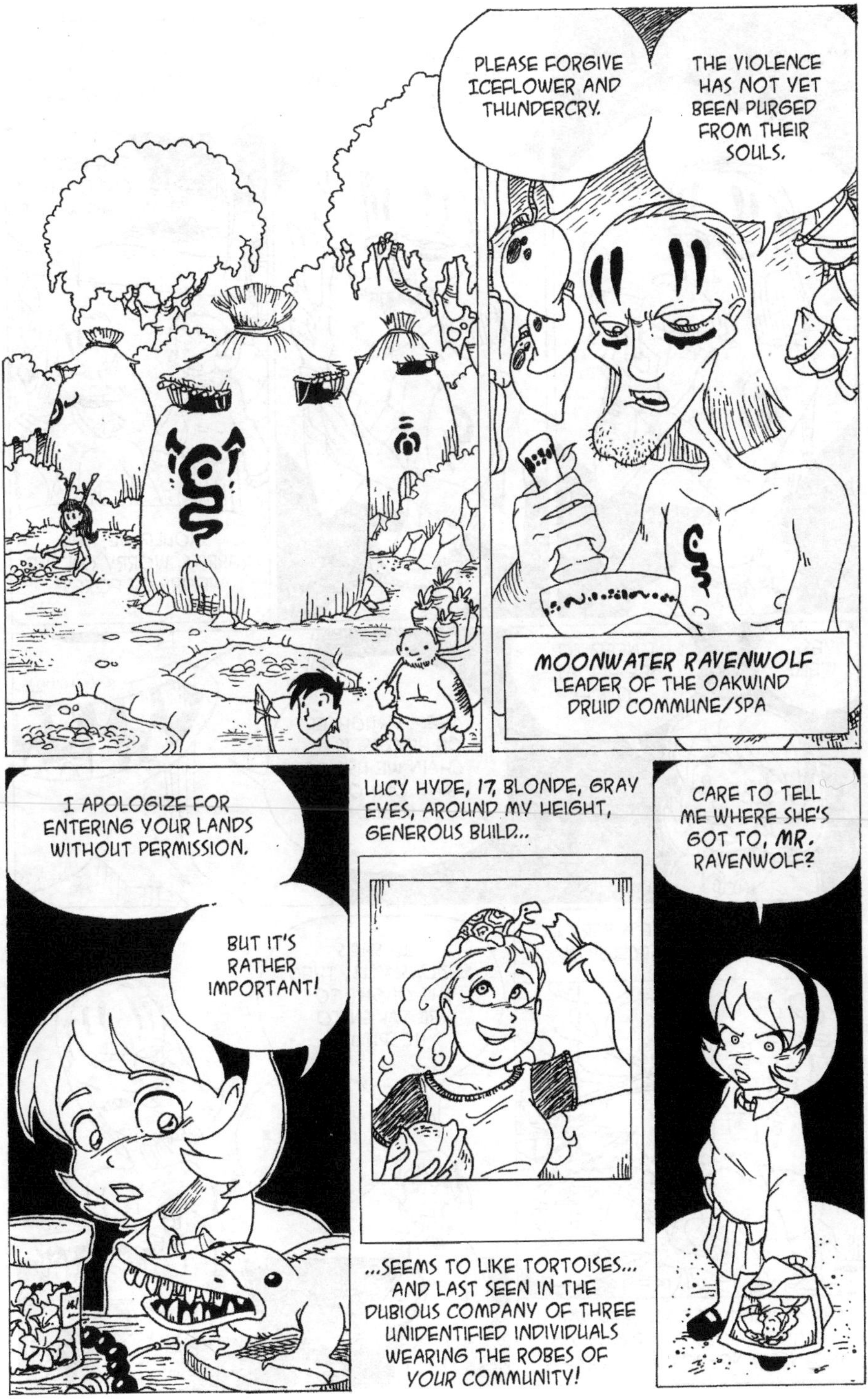
PLEASE FORGIVE ICEFLOWER AND THUNDERCRY.
THE VIOLENCE HAS NOT YET BEEN PURGED FROM THEIR SOULS.
MOONWATER RAVENWOLF
LEADER OF THE OAKWIND DRUID COMMUNE/SPA
I APOLOGIZE FOR ENTERING YOUR LANDS WITHOUT PERMISSION.
BUT IT'S RATHER IMPORTANT!
LUCY HYDE, 17, BLONDE, GRAY EYES, AROUND MY HEIGHT, GENEROUS BUILD...
...SEEMS TO LIKE TORTOISES... AND LAST SEEN IN THE DUBIOUS COMPANY OF THREE UNIDENTIFIED INDIVIDUALS WEARING THE ROBES OF YOUR COMMUNITY!
CARE TO TELL ME WHERE SHE'S GOT TO, MR. RAVENWOLF?

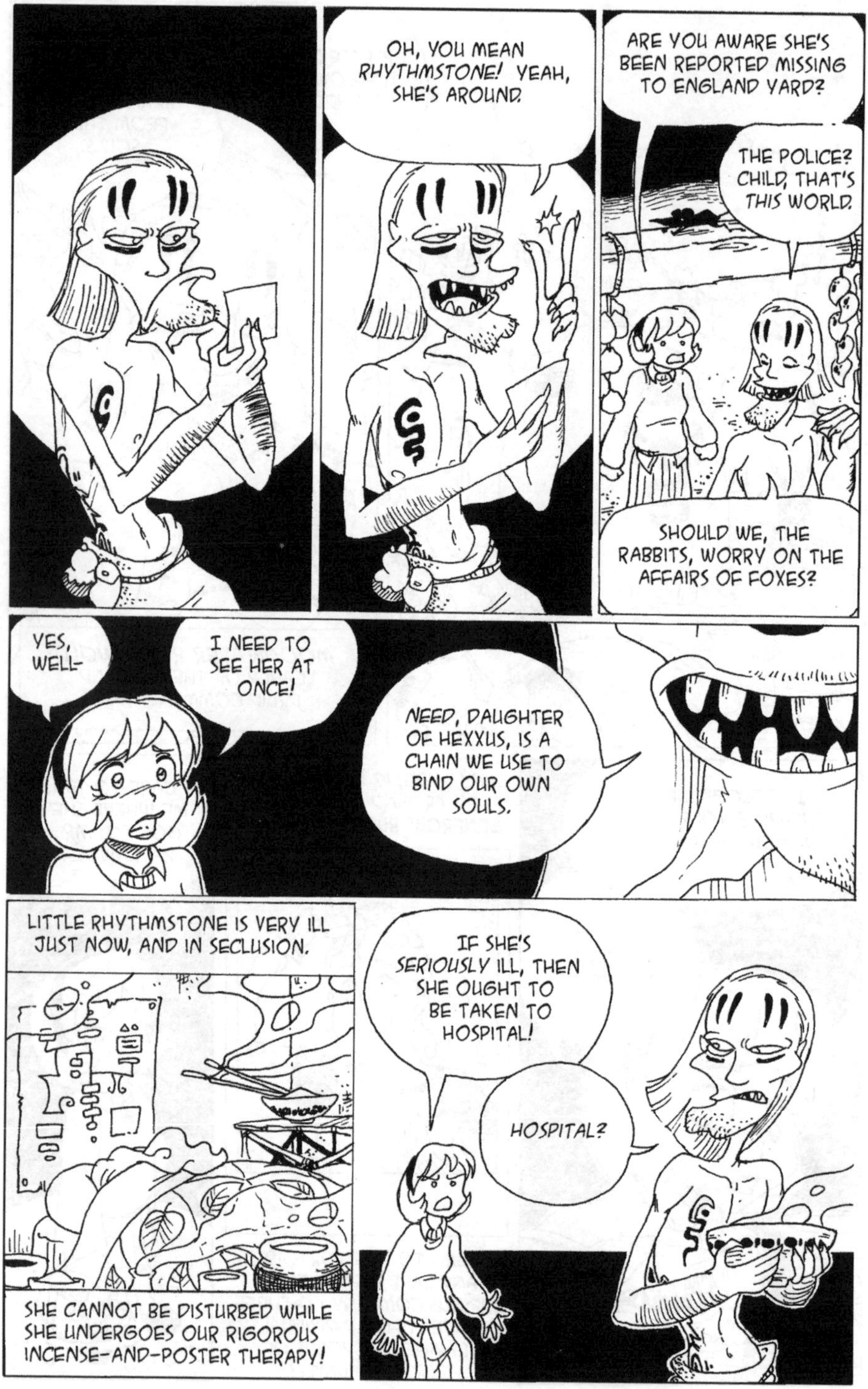
OH, YOU MEAN RHYTHMSTONE! YEAH, SHE'S AROUND.
ARE YOU AWARE SHE'S BEEN REPORTED MISSING TO ENGLAND YARD?
THE POLICE? CHILD, THAT'S THIS WORLD.
SHOULD WE, THE RABBITS, WORRY ON THE AFFAIRS OF FOXES?
YES, WELL-
I NEED TO SEE HER AT ONCE!
NEED, DAUGHTER OF HEXXUS, IS A CHAIN WE USE TO BIND OUR OWN SOULS.
LITTLE RHYTHMSTONE IS VERY ILL JUST NOW, AND IN SECLUSION.
SHE CANNOT BE DISTURBED WHILE SHE UNDERGOES OUR RIGOROUS INCENSE-AND-POSTER THERAPY!
IF SHE'S SERIOUSLY ILL, THEN SHE OUGHT TO BE TAKEN TO HOSPITAL!
HOSPITAL?

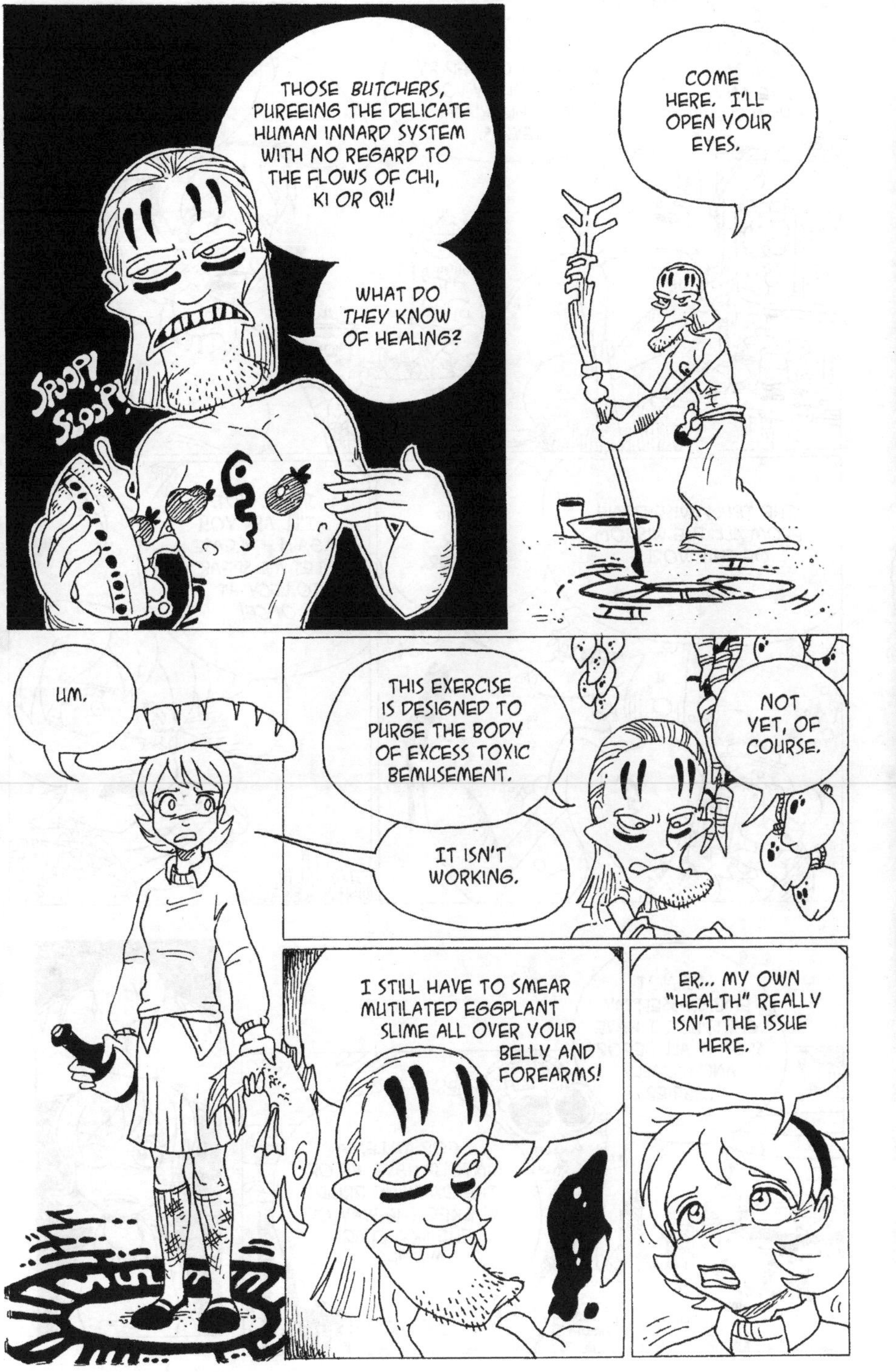
THOSE BUTCHERS, PUREEING THE DELICATE HUMAN INNARD SYSTEM WITH NO REGARD TO THE FLOWS OF CHI, KI OR QI!
WHAT DO THEY KNOW OF HEALING?
SPOOP! SLOOP!
COME HERE. I'LL OPEN YOUR EYES.
UM.
THIS EXERCISE IS DESIGNED TO PURGE THE BODY OF EXCESS TOXIC BEMUSEMENT.
IT ISN'T WORKING.
NOT YET, OF COURSE.
I STILL HAVE TO SMEAR MUTILATED EGGPLANT SLIME ALL OVER YOUR BELLY AND FOREARMS!
ER... MY OWN "HEALTH" REALLY ISN'T THE ISSUE HERE.

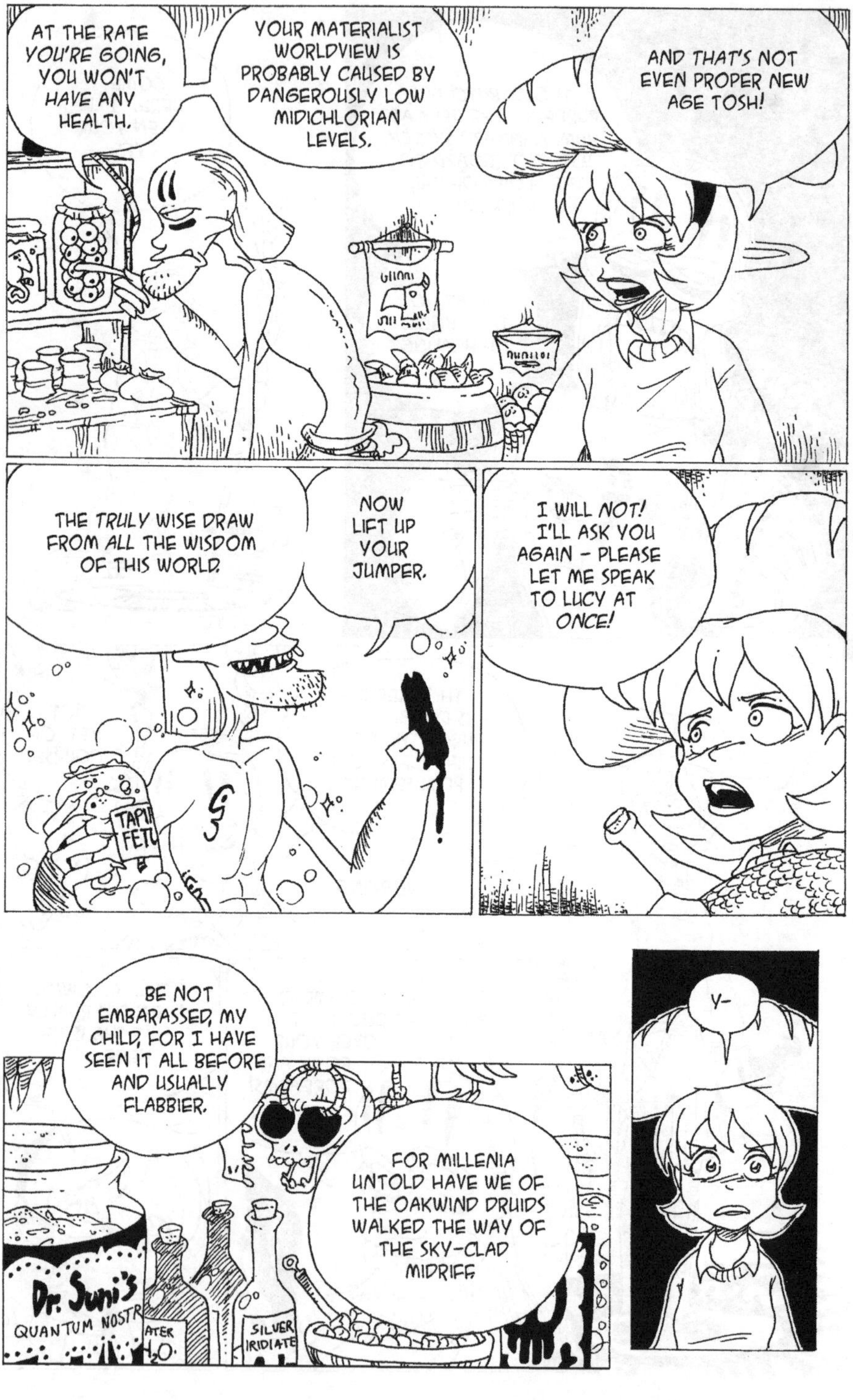
AT THE RATE YOU'RE GOING, YOU WON'T HAVE ANY HEALTH.
YOUR MATERIALIST WORLDVIEW IS PROBABLY CAUSED BY DANGEROUSLY LOW MIDICHLORIAN LEVELS.
AND THAT'S NOT EVEN PROPER NEW AGE TOSH!
THE TRULY WISE DRAW FROM ALL THE WISDOM OF THIS WORLD.
NOW LIFT UP YOUR JUMPER.
TAPI
FETU
I WILL NOT! I'LL ASK YOU AGAIN - PLEASE LET ME SPEAK TO LUCY AT ONCE!
BE NOT EMBARASSED, MY CHILD, FOR I HAVE SEEN IT ALL BEFORE AND USUALLY FLABBIER.
FOR MILLENIA UNTOLD HAVE WE OF THE OAKWIND DRUIDS WALKED THE WAY OF THE SKY-CLAD MIDRIFF.
Dr. Suni's
QUANTUM NOSTR
ATER
SILVER IRIDIATE
Y-

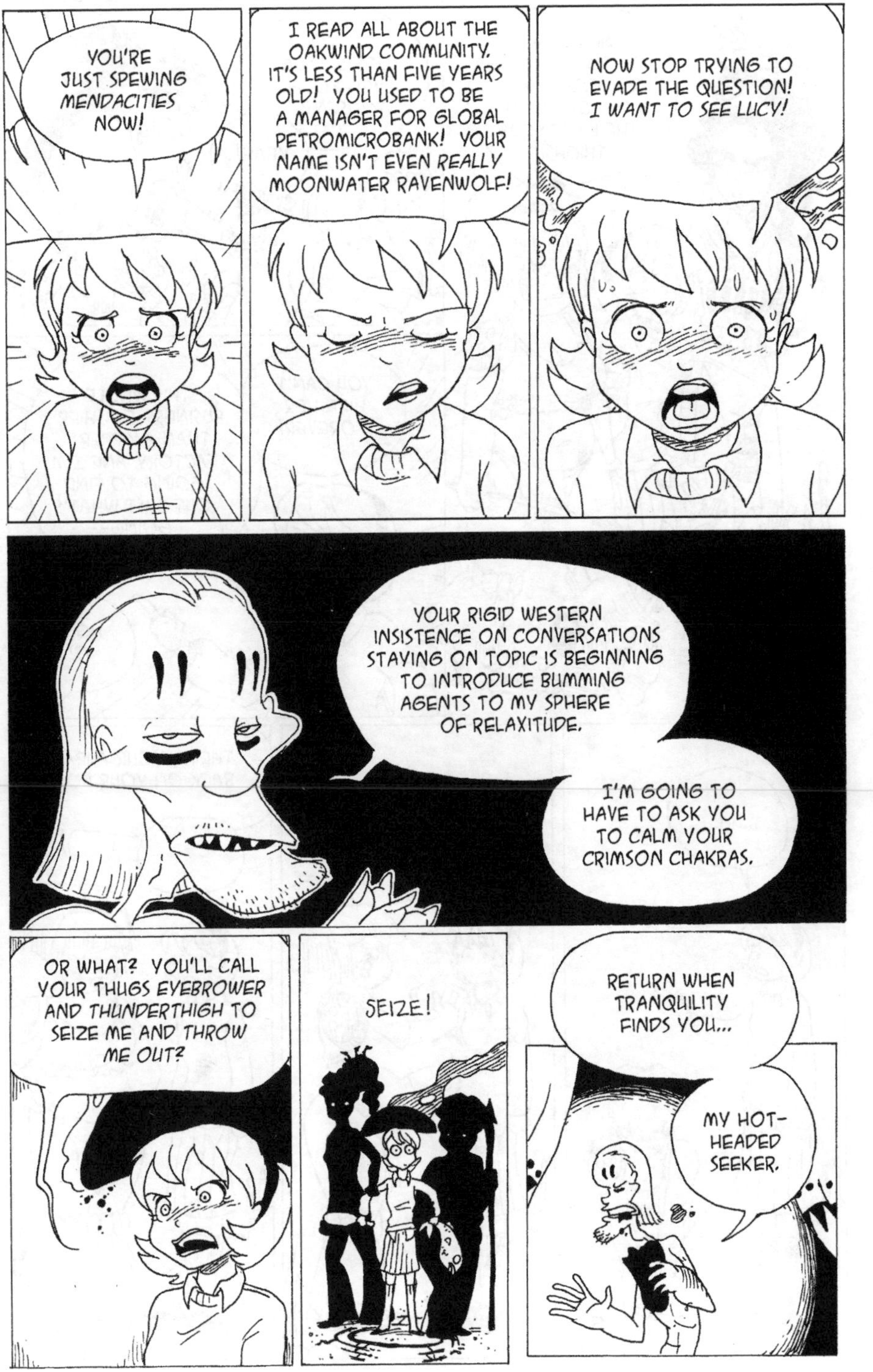
YOU'RE JUST SPEWING MENDACITIES NOW!
I READ ALL ABOUT THE OAKWIND COMMUNITY. IT'S LESS THAN FIVE YEARS OLD! YOU USED TO BE A MANAGER FOR GLOBAL PETROMICROBANK! YOUR NAME ISN'T EVEN *REALLY* MOONWATER RAVENWOLF!
NOW STOP TRYING TO EVADE THE QUESTION! I WANT TO SEE LUCY!
YOUR RIGID WESTERN INSISTENCE ON CONVERSATIONS STAYING ON TOPIC IS BEGINNING TO INTRODUCE BUMMING AGENTS TO MY SPHERE OF RELAXITUDE.
I'M GOING TO HAVE TO ASK YOU TO CALM YOUR CRIMSON CHAKRAS.
OR WHAT? YOU'LL CALL YOUR THUGS *EYEBROWER* AND *THUNDERTHIGH* TO SEIZE ME AND THROW ME OUT?
SEIZE!
RETURN WHEN TRANQUILITY FINDS YOU...
MY HOT-HEADED SEEKER.

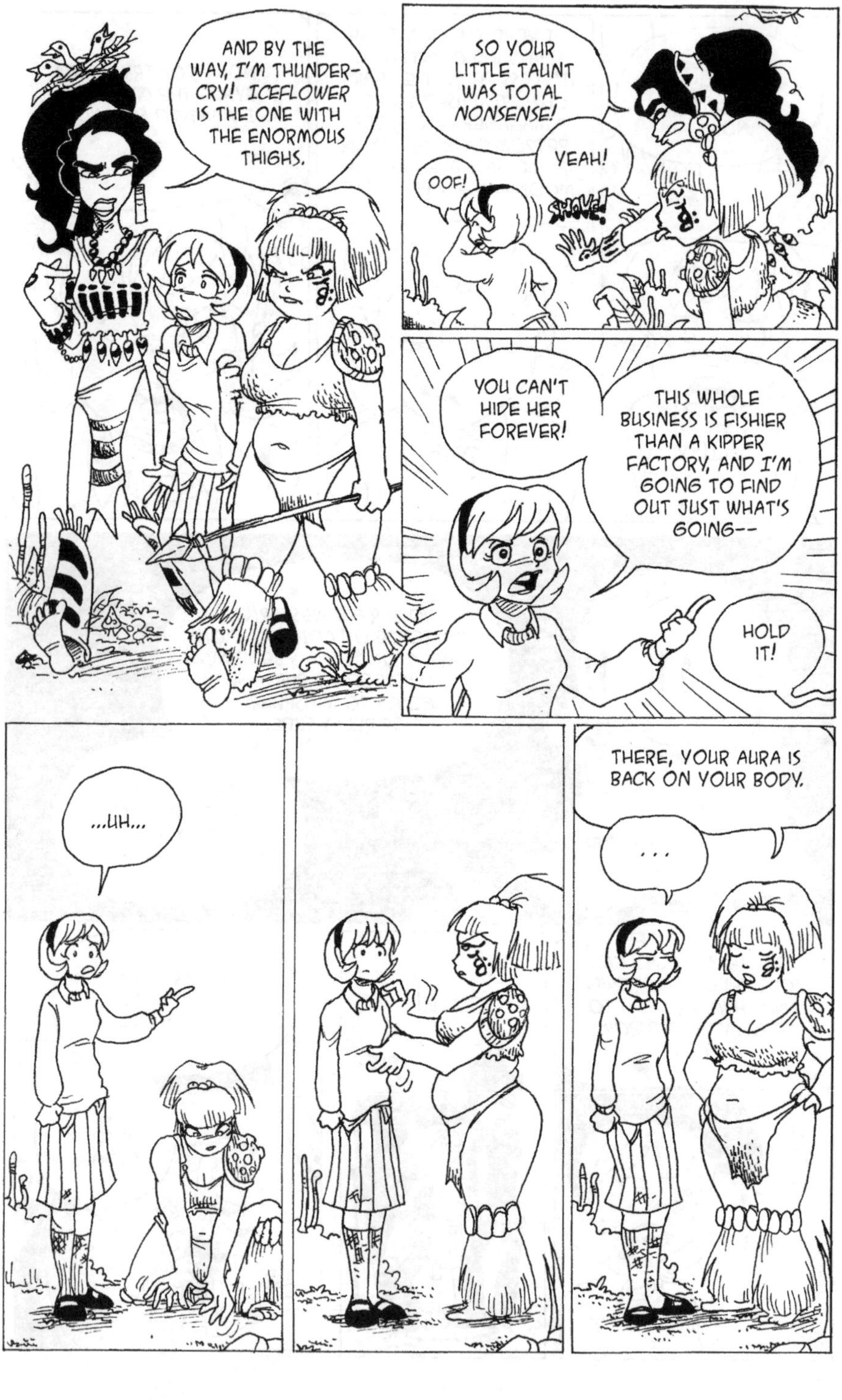
AND BY THE WAY, I'M THUNDER-CRY! ICEFLOWER IS THE ONE WITH THE ENORMOUS THIGHS.
SO YOUR LITTLE TAUNT WAS TOTAL NONSENSE!
YEAH!
OOF!
SHOVE!
YOU CAN'T HIDE HER FOREVER!
THIS WHOLE BUSINESS IS FISHIER THAN A KIPPER FACTORY, AND I'M GOING TO FIND OUT JUST WHAT'S GOING--
HOLD IT!
...UH...
THERE, YOUR AURA IS BACK ON YOUR BODY.
. . .

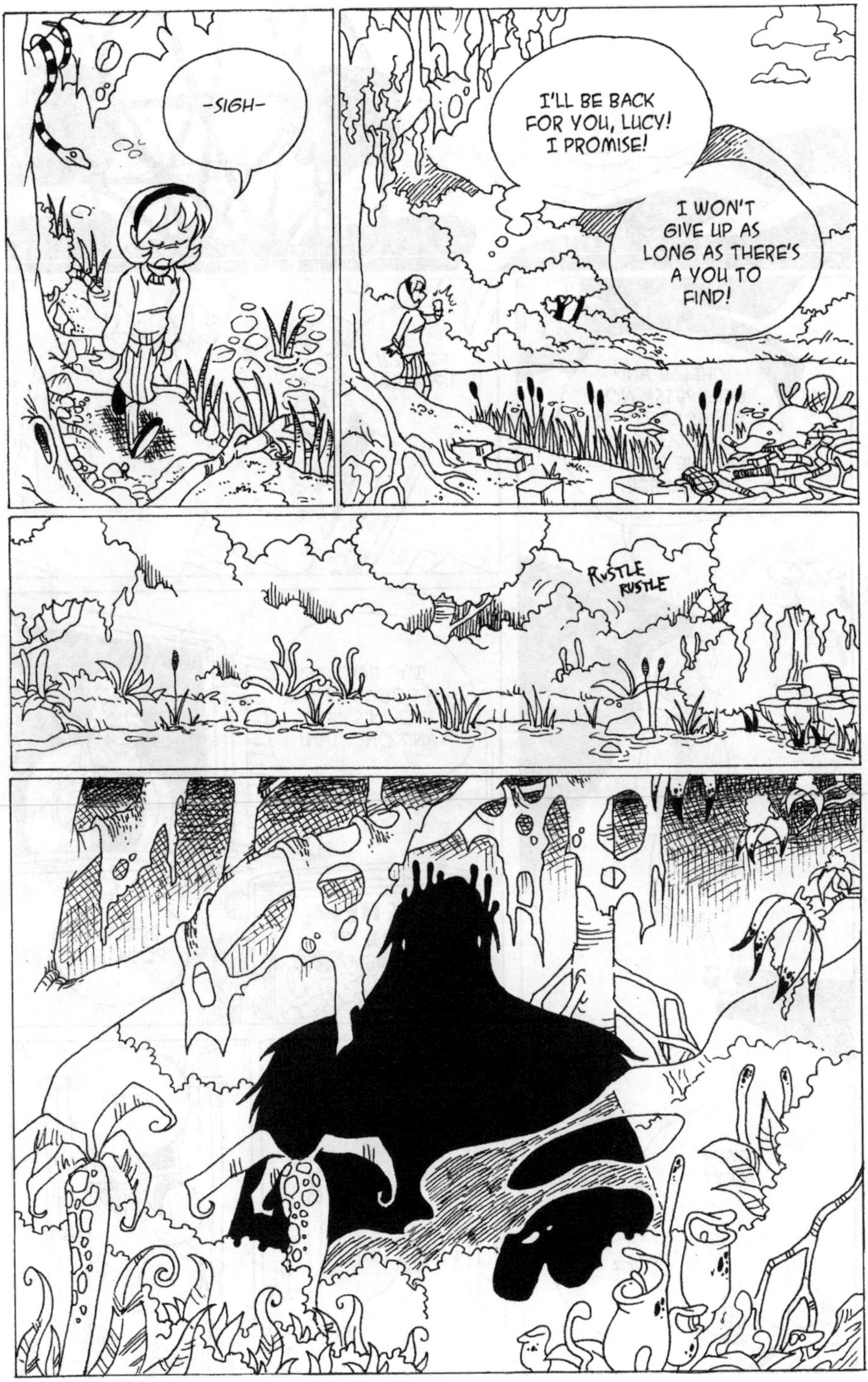
-SIGH-
I'LL BE BACK FOR YOU, LUCY! I PROMISE!
I WON'T GIVE UP AS LONG AS THERE'S A YOU TO FIND!
RUSTLE RUSTLE

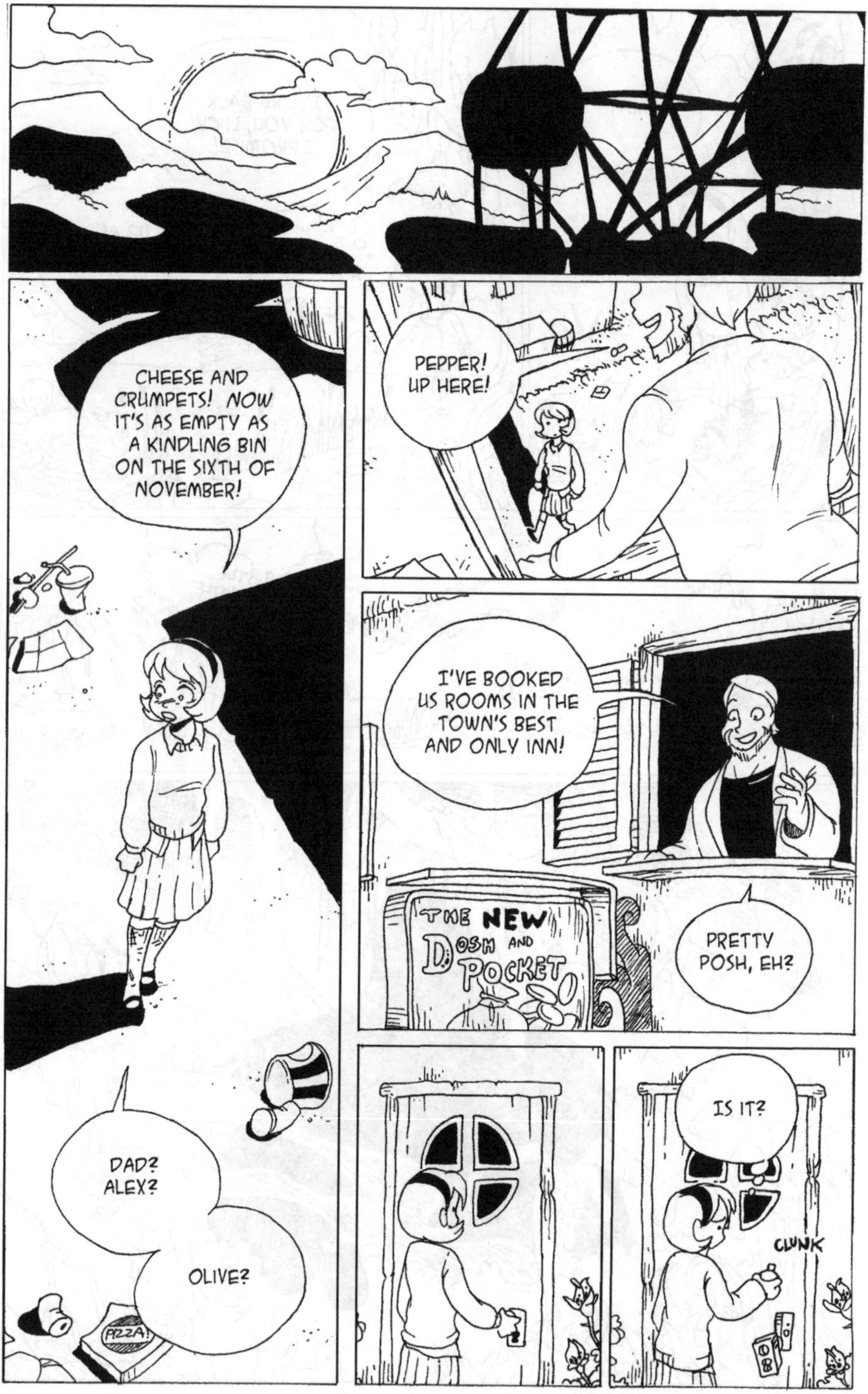
CHEESE AND CRUMPETS! NOW IT'S AS EMPTY AS A KINDLING BIN ON THE SIXTH OF NOVEMBER!
PEPPER! UP HERE!
I'VE BOOKED US ROOMS IN THE TOWN'S BEST AND ONLY INN!
THE NEW DOSH AND POCKET
PRETTY POSH, EH?
DAD? ALEX?
OLIVE?
PIZZA!
IS IT?
CLUNK

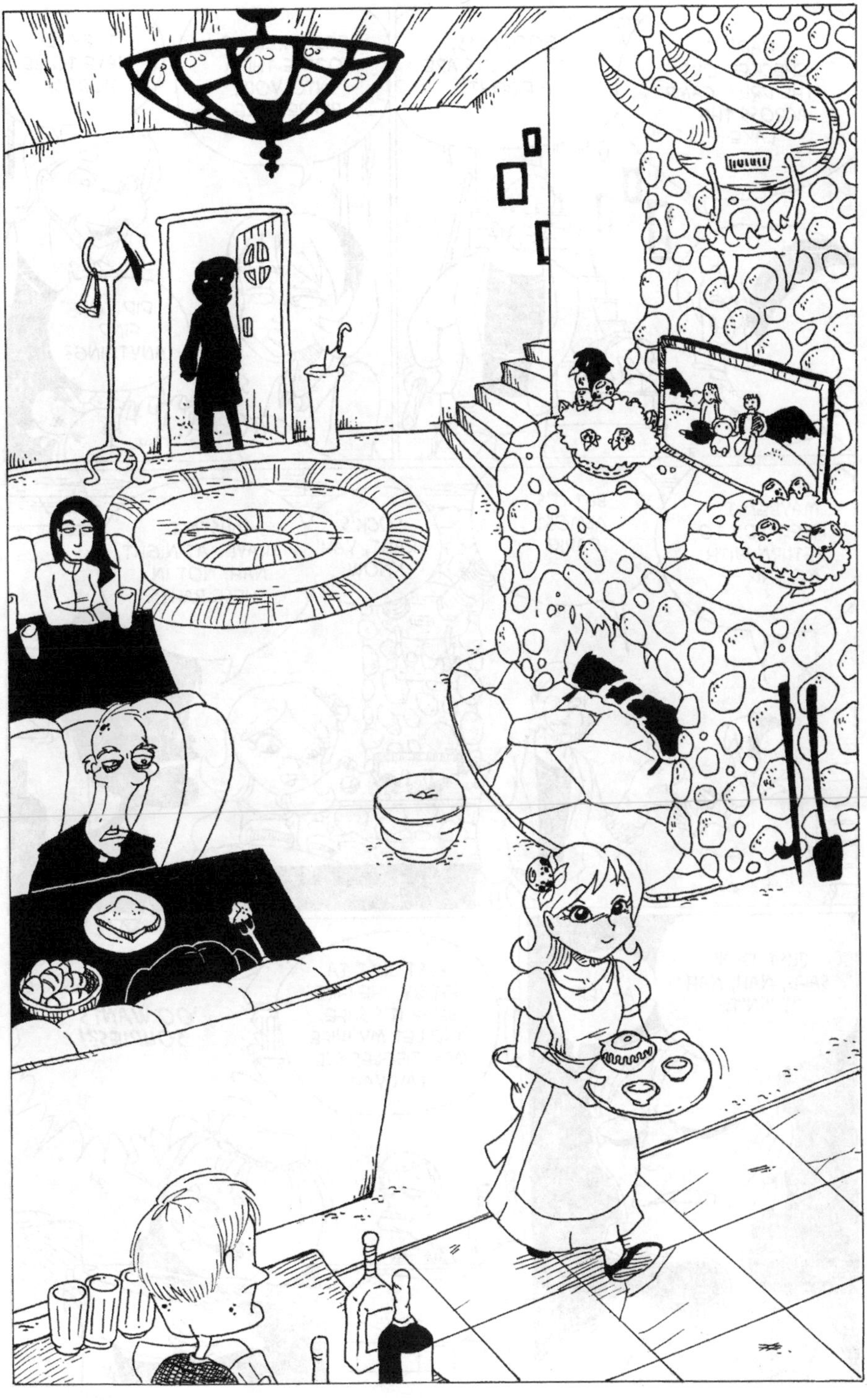

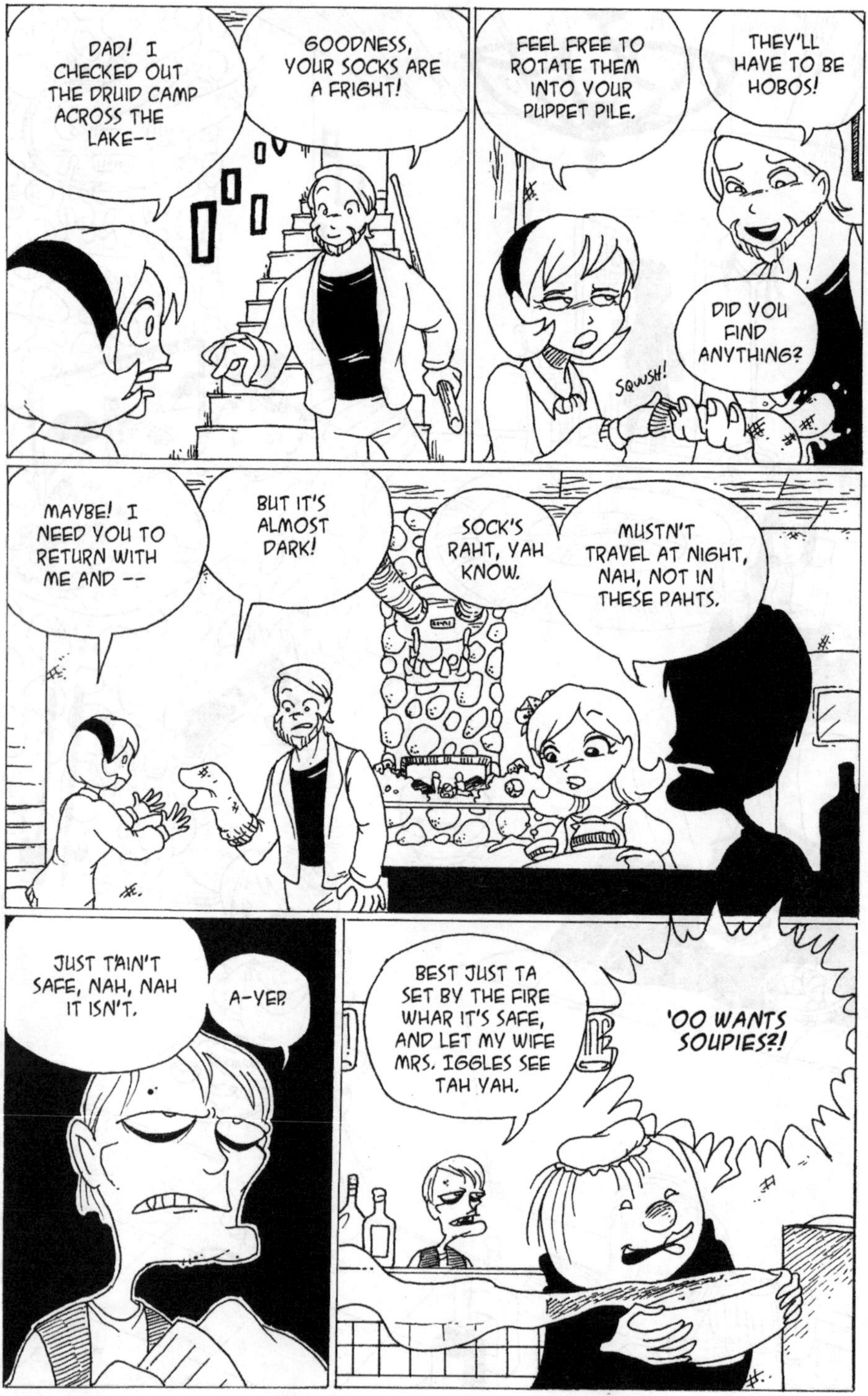
DAD! I CHECKED OUT THE DRUID CAMP ACROSS THE LAKE--
GOODNESS, YOUR SOCKS ARE A FRIGHT!
FEEL FREE TO ROTATE THEM INTO YOUR PUPPET PILE.
THEY'LL HAVE TO BE HOBOS!
SQUUSH!
DID YOU FIND ANYTHING?
MAYBE! I NEED YOU TO RETURN WITH ME AND --
BUT IT'S ALMOST DARK!
SOCK'S RAHT, YAH KNOW.
MUSTN'T TRAVEL AT NIGHT, NAH, NOT IN THESE PAHTS.
JUST T'AIN'T SAFE, NAH, NAH IT ISN'T.
A-YEP.
BEST JUST TA SET BY THE FIRE WHAR IT'S SAFE, AND LET MY WIFE MRS. IGGLES SEE TAH YAH.
'OO WANTS SOUPIES?!

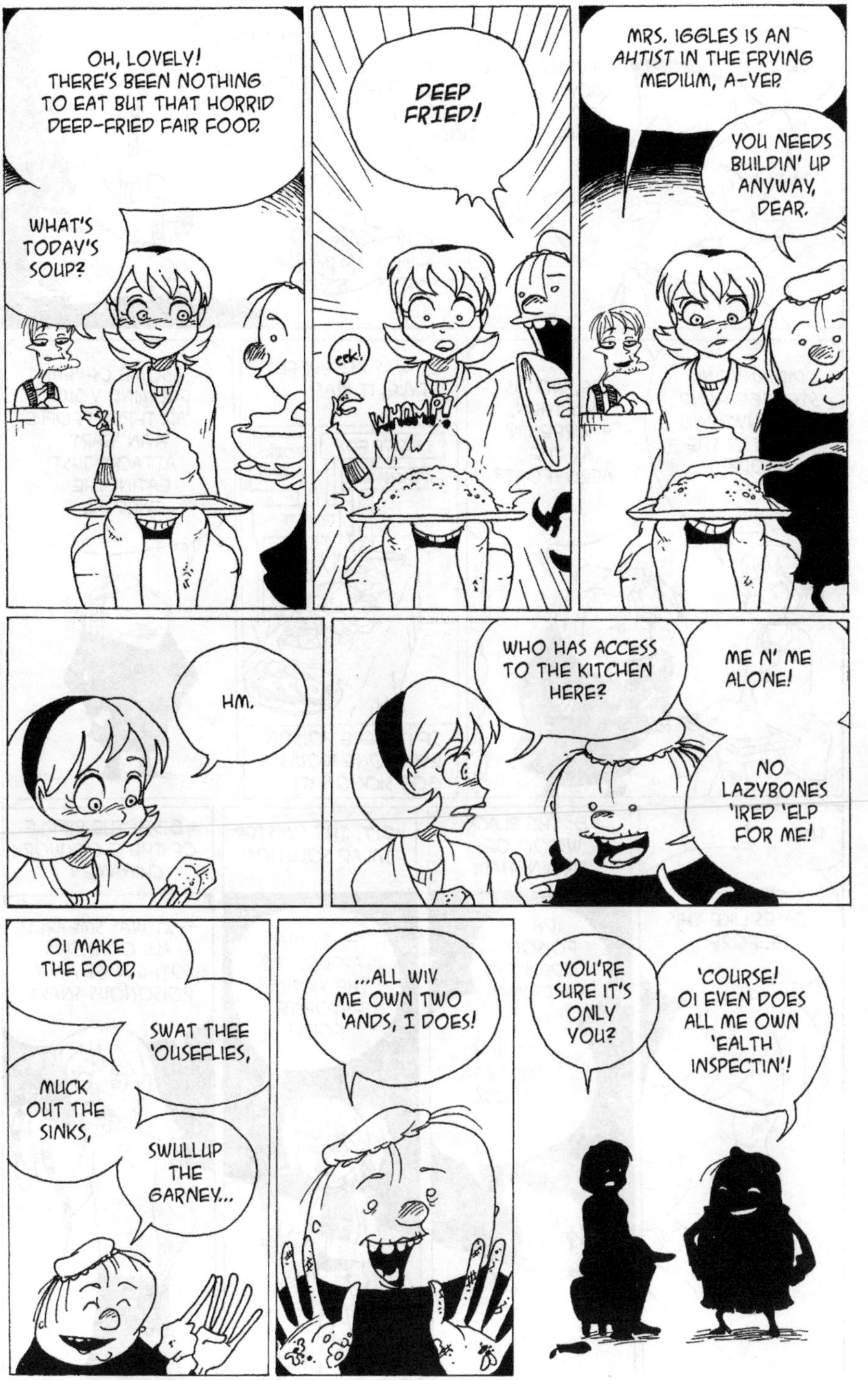
OH, LOVELY! THERE'S BEEN NOTHING TO EAT BUT THAT HORRID DEEP-FRIED FAIR FOOD.
WHAT'S TODAY'S SOUP?
DEEP FRIED!
eek!
WHOMP!
MRS. IGGLES IS AN AHTIST IN THE FRYING MEDIUM, A-YEP.
YOU NEEDS BUILDIN' UP ANYWAY, DEAR.
HM.
WHO HAS ACCESS TO THE KITCHEN HERE?
ME N' ME ALONE!
NO LAZYBONES 'IRED 'ELP FOR ME!
OI MAKE THE FOOD,
SWAT THEE 'OUSEFLIES,
MUCK OUT THE SINKS,
SWULLUP THE GARNEY...
...ALL WIV ME OWN TWO 'ANDS, I DOES!
YOU'RE SURE IT'S ONLY YOU?
'COURSE! OI EVEN DOES ALL ME OWN 'EALTH INSPECTIN'!

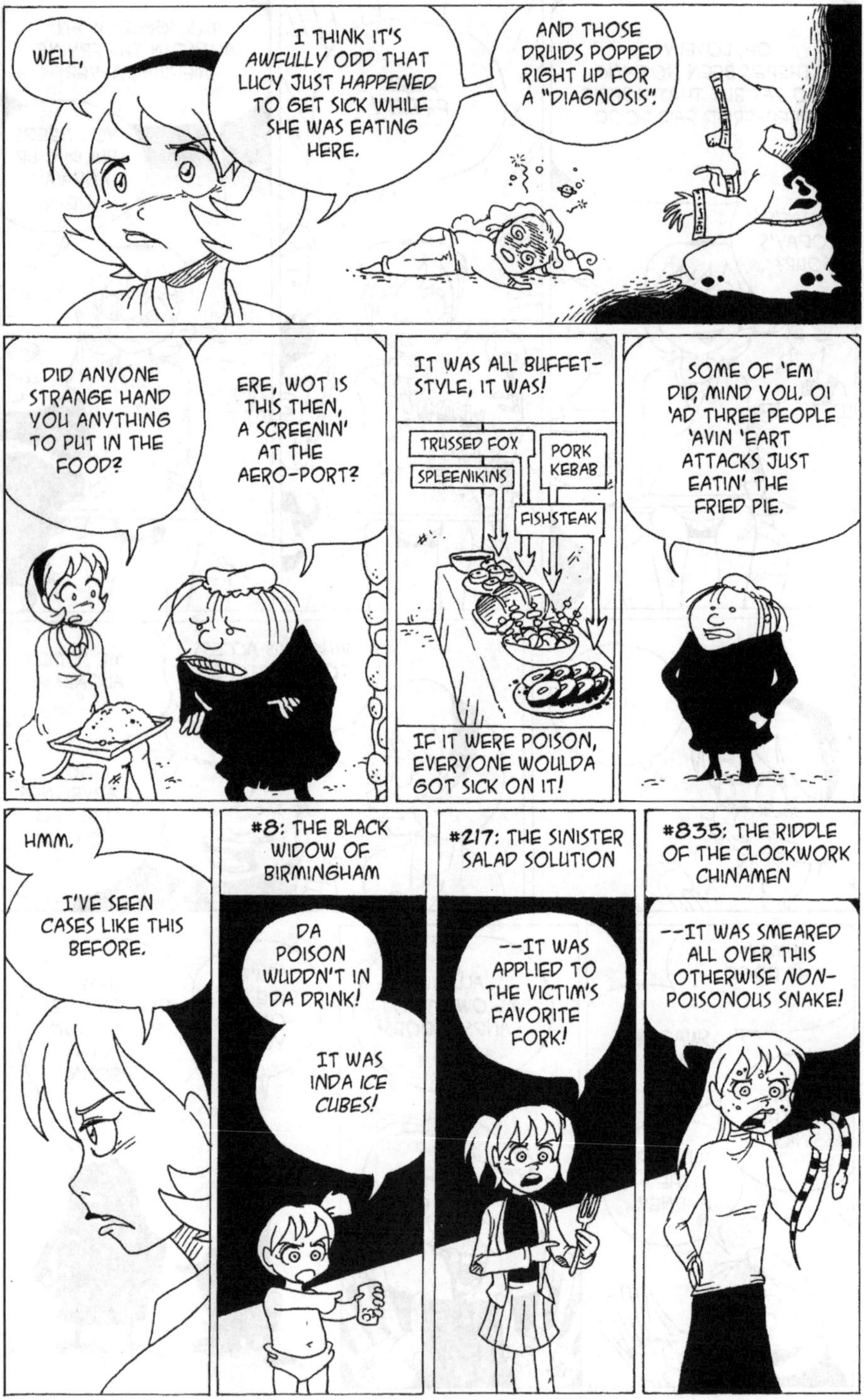
WELL,
I THINK IT'S AWFULLY ODD THAT LUCY JUST HAPPENED TO GET SICK WHILE SHE WAS EATING HERE.
AND THOSE DRUIDS POPPED RIGHT UP FOR A "DIAGNOSIS".
DID ANYONE STRANGE HAND YOU ANYTHING TO PUT IN THE FOOD?
ERE, WOT IS THIS THEN, A SCREENIN' AT THE AERO-PORT?
IT WAS ALL BUFFET-STYLE, IT WAS!
TRUSSED FOX
SPLEENIKINS
PORK KEBAB
FISHSTEAK
IF IT WERE POISON, EVERYONE WOULDA GOT SICK ON IT!
SOME OF 'EM DID, MIND YOU. OI 'AD THREE PEOPLE 'AVIN 'EART ATTACKS JUST EATIN' THE FRIED PIE.
HMM.
I'VE SEEN CASES LIKE THIS BEFORE.
#8: THE BLACK WIDOW OF BIRMINGHAM
DA POISON WUDDN'T IN DA DRINK!
IT WAS INDA ICE CUBES!
#217: THE SINISTER SALAD SOLUTION
--IT WAS APPLIED TO THE VICTIM'S FAVORITE FORK!
#835: THE RIDDLE OF THE CLOCKWORK CHINAMEN
--IT WAS SMEARED ALL OVER THIS OTHERWISE NON-POISONOUS SNAKE!

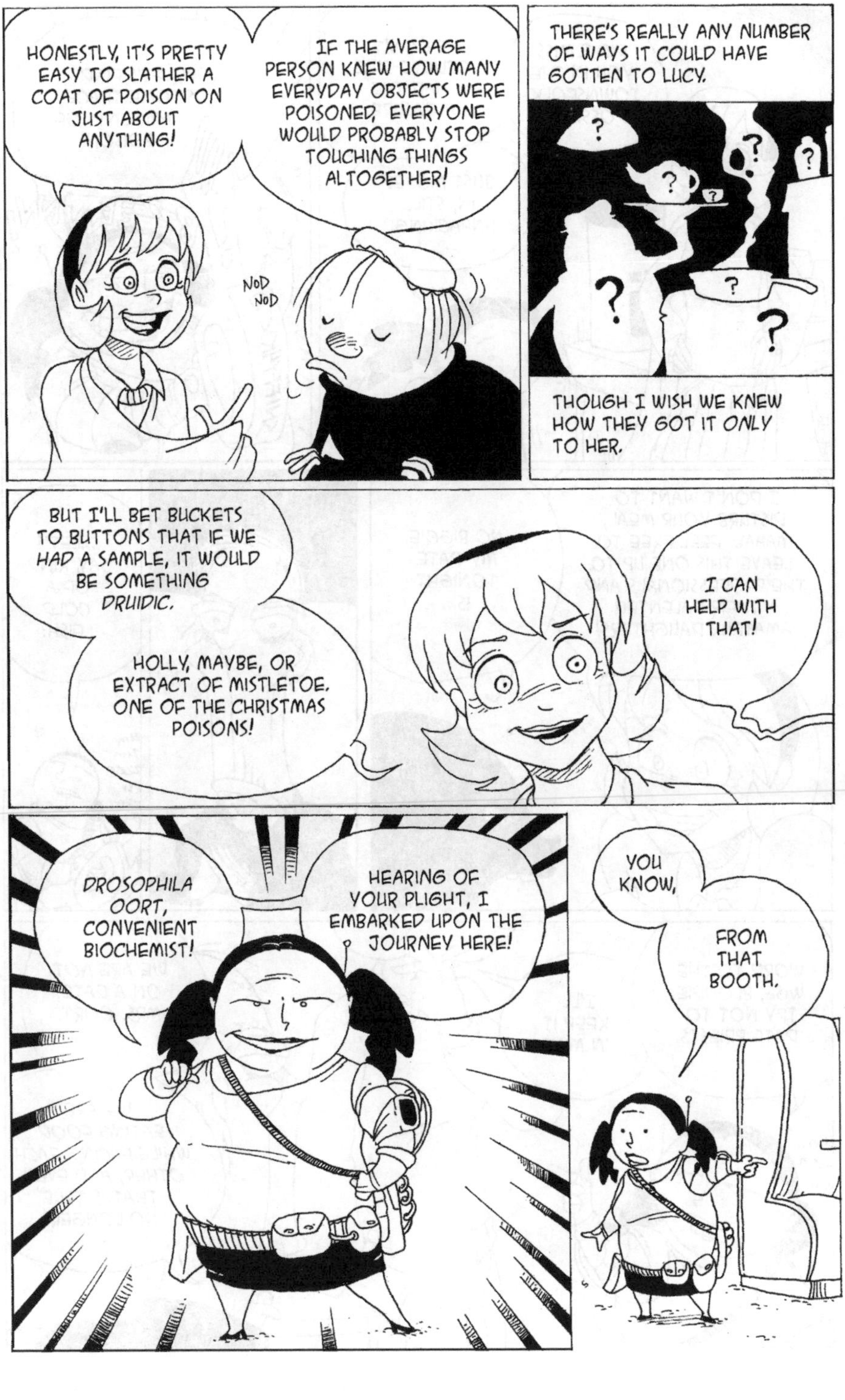

HONESTLY, IT'S PRETTY EASY TO SLATHER A COAT OF POISON ON JUST ABOUT ANYTHING!
IF THE AVERAGE PERSON KNEW HOW MANY EVERYDAY OBJECTS WERE POISONED, EVERYONE WOULD PROBABLY STOP TOUCHING THINGS ALTOGETHER!
NOD NOD
THERE'S REALLY ANY NUMBER OF WAYS IT COULD HAVE GOTTEN TO LUCY.
THOUGH I WISH WE KNEW HOW THEY GOT IT *ONLY* TO HER.
BUT I'LL BET BUCKETS TO BUTTONS THAT IF WE *HAD* A SAMPLE, IT WOULD BE SOMETHING *DRUIDIC*.
HOLLY, MAYBE, OR EXTRACT OF MISTLETOE. ONE OF THE CHRISTMAS POISONS!
I CAN HELP WITH THAT!
DROSOPHILA OORT, CONVENIENT BIOCHEMIST!
HEARING OF YOUR PLIGHT, I EMBARKED UPON THE JOURNEY HERE!
YOU KNOW,
FROM THAT BOOTH.

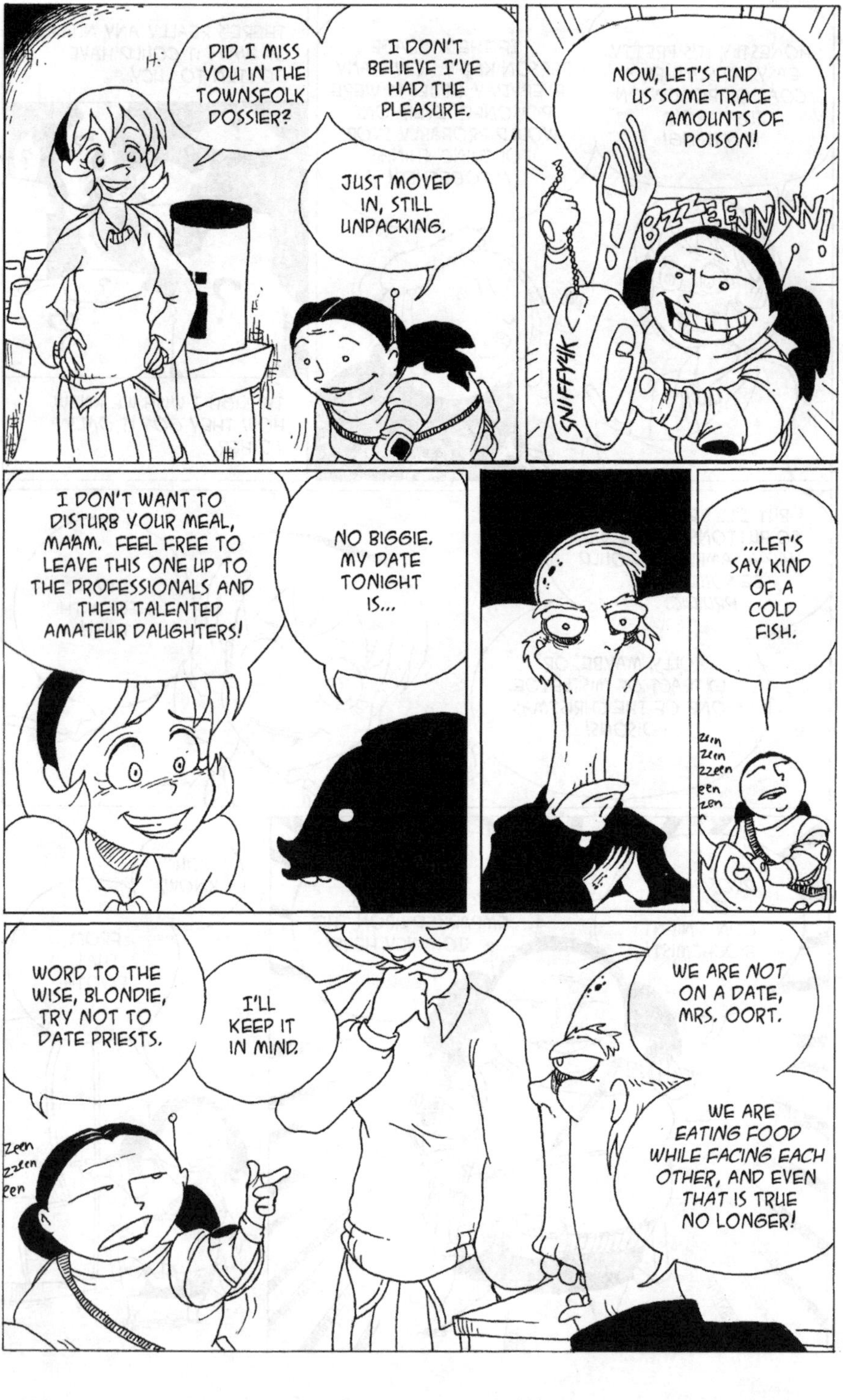
DID I MISS YOU IN THE TOWNSFOLK DOSSIER?
I DON'T BELIEVE I'VE HAD THE PLEASURE.
JUST MOVED IN, STILL UNPACKING.
NOW, LET'S FIND US SOME TRACE AMOUNTS OF POISON!
BZZZEEJNNNN!
SNIFFY4K
I DON'T WANT TO DISTURB YOUR MEAL, MA'AM. FEEL FREE TO LEAVE THIS ONE UP TO THE PROFESSIONALS AND THEIR TALENTED AMATEUR DAUGHTERS!
NO BIGGIE. MY DATE TONIGHT IS...
...LET'S SAY, KIND OF A COLD FISH.
WORD TO THE WISE, BLONDIE, TRY NOT TO DATE PRIESTS.
I'LL KEEP IT IN MIND.
WE ARE NOT ON A DATE, MRS. OORT.
WE ARE EATING FOOD WHILE FACING EACH OTHER, AND EVEN THAT IS TRUE NO LONGER!

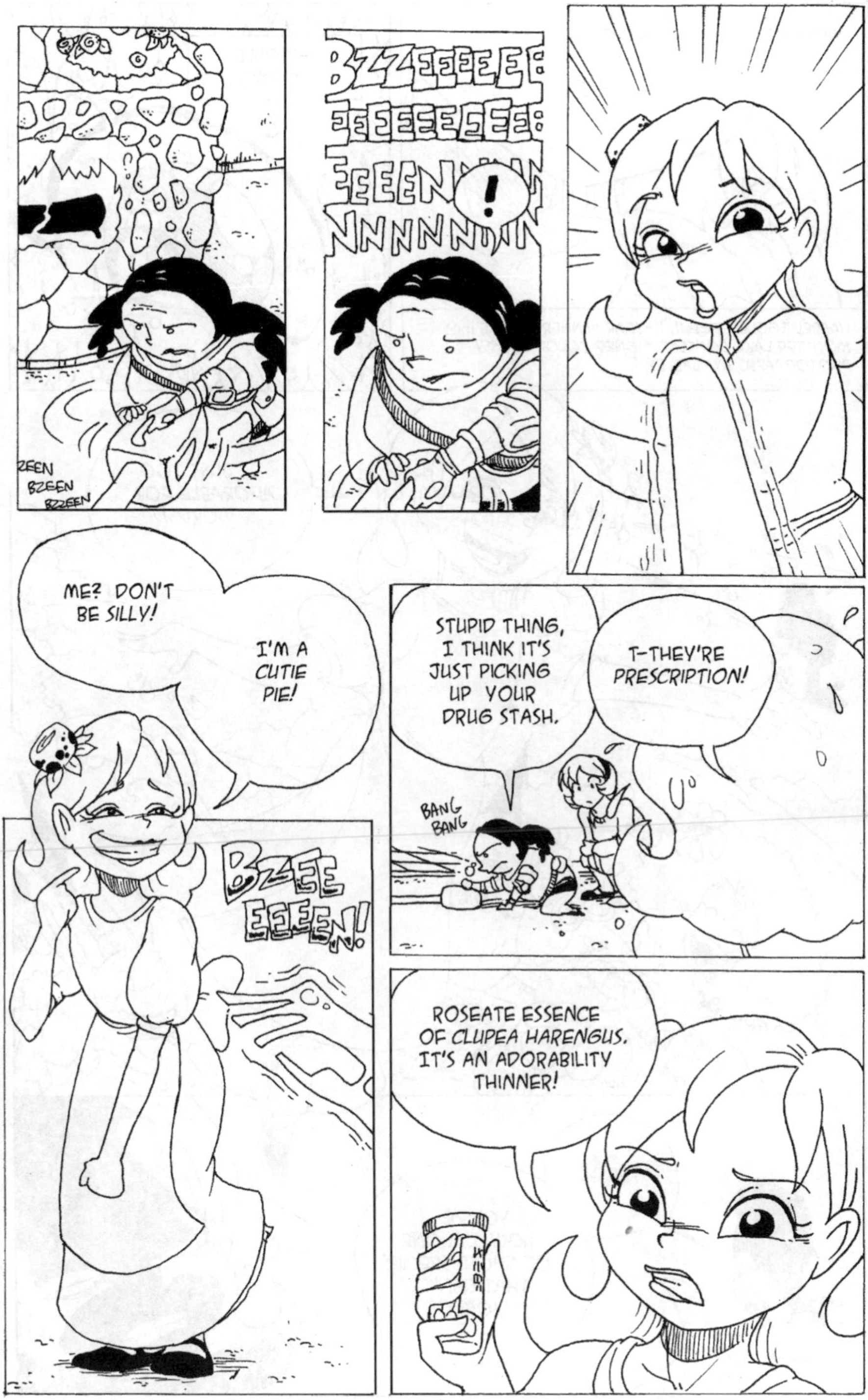
BZEEN
BZEEN
BZEEN
BZZEEEEEEEEEEEEEEEEEEENNNNNNNN
!
ME? DON'T BE SILLY!
I'M A CUTIE PIE!
BZEEEEEEN!
BANG BANG
STUPID THING, I THINK IT'S JUST PICKING UP YOUR DRUG STASH.
T-THEY'RE PRESCRIPTION!
ROSEATE ESSENCE OF CLUPEA HARENGUS. IT'S AN ADORABILITY THINNER!

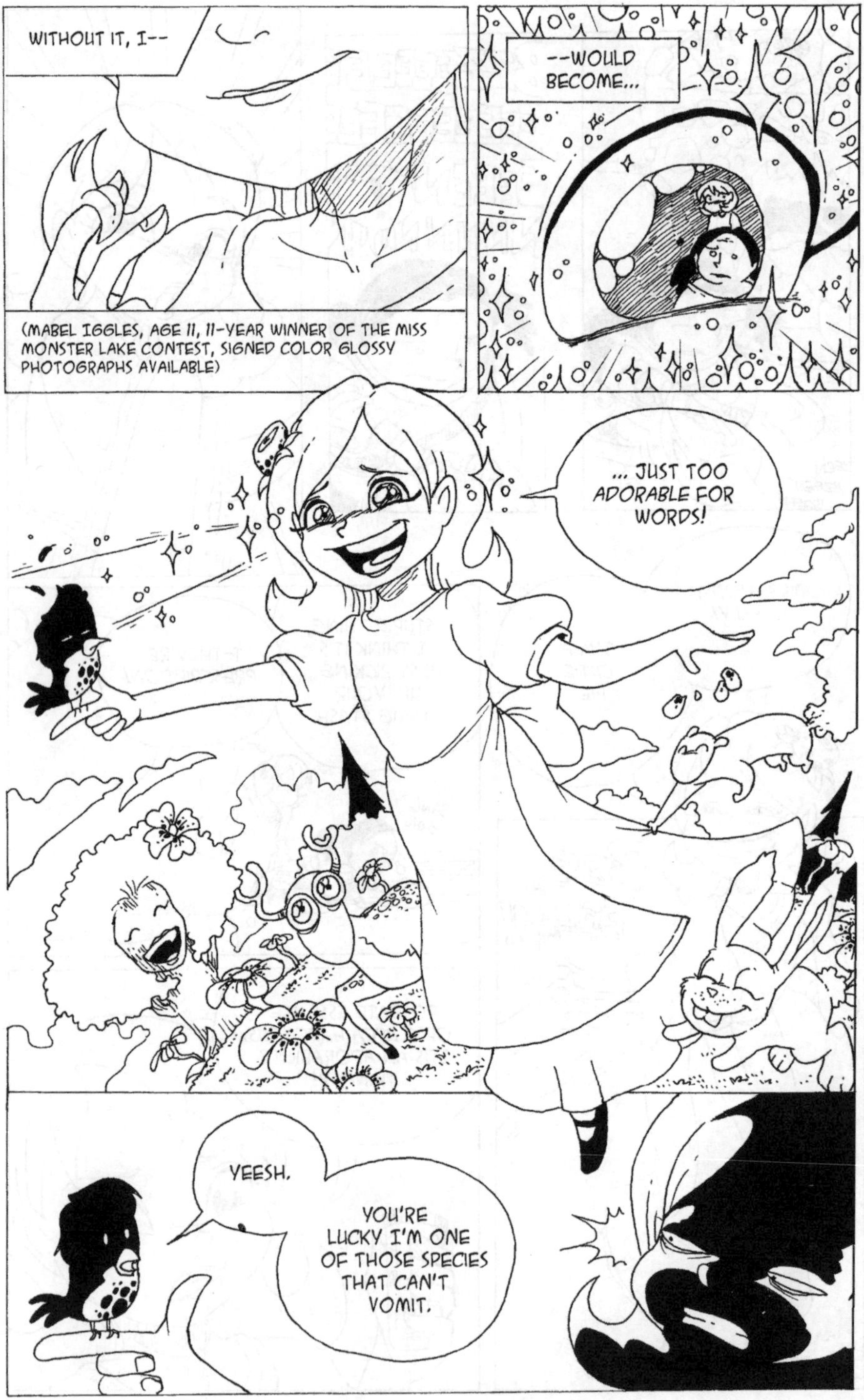
WITHOUT IT, I--
(MABEL IGGLES, AGE 11, 11-YEAR WINNER OF THE MISS MONSTER LAKE CONTEST, SIGNED COLOR GLOSSY PHOTOGRAPHS AVAILABLE)
--WOULD BECOME...
... JUST TOO ADORABLE FOR WORDS!
YEESH.
YOU'RE LUCKY I'M ONE OF THOSE SPECIES THAT CAN'T VOMIT.

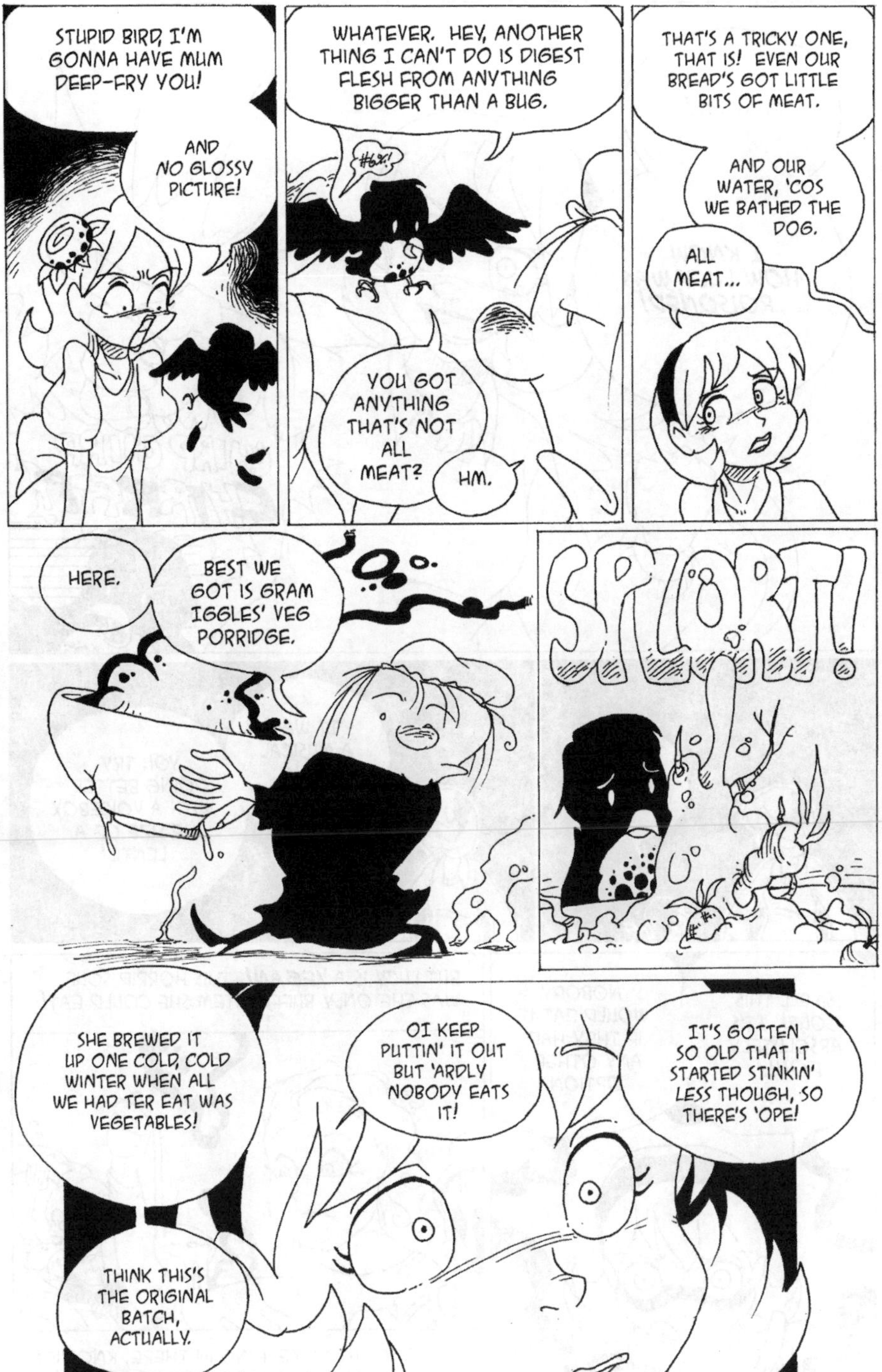
STUPID BIRD, I'M GONNA HAVE MUM DEEP-FRY YOU!
AND NO GLOSSY PICTURE!
WHATEVER. HEY, ANOTHER THING I CAN'T DO IS DIGEST FLESH FROM ANYTHING BIGGER THAN A BUG.
#6%!
YOU GOT ANYTHING THAT'S NOT ALL MEAT?
HM.
THAT'S A TRICKY ONE, THAT IS! EVEN OUR BREAD'S GOT LITTLE BITS OF MEAT.
AND OUR WATER, 'COS WE BATHED THE DOG.
ALL MEAT...
HERE.
BEST WE GOT IS GRAM IGGLES' VEG PORRIDGE.
SPLORT!
SHE BREWED IT UP ONE COLD, COLD WINTER WHEN ALL WE HAD TER EAT WAS VEGETABLES!
THINK THIS'S THE ORIGINAL BATCH, ACTUALLY.
OI KEEP PUTTIN' IT OUT BUT 'ARDLY NOBODY EATS IT!
IT'S GOTTEN SO OLD THAT IT STARTED STINKIN' LESS THOUGH, SO THERE'S 'OPE!

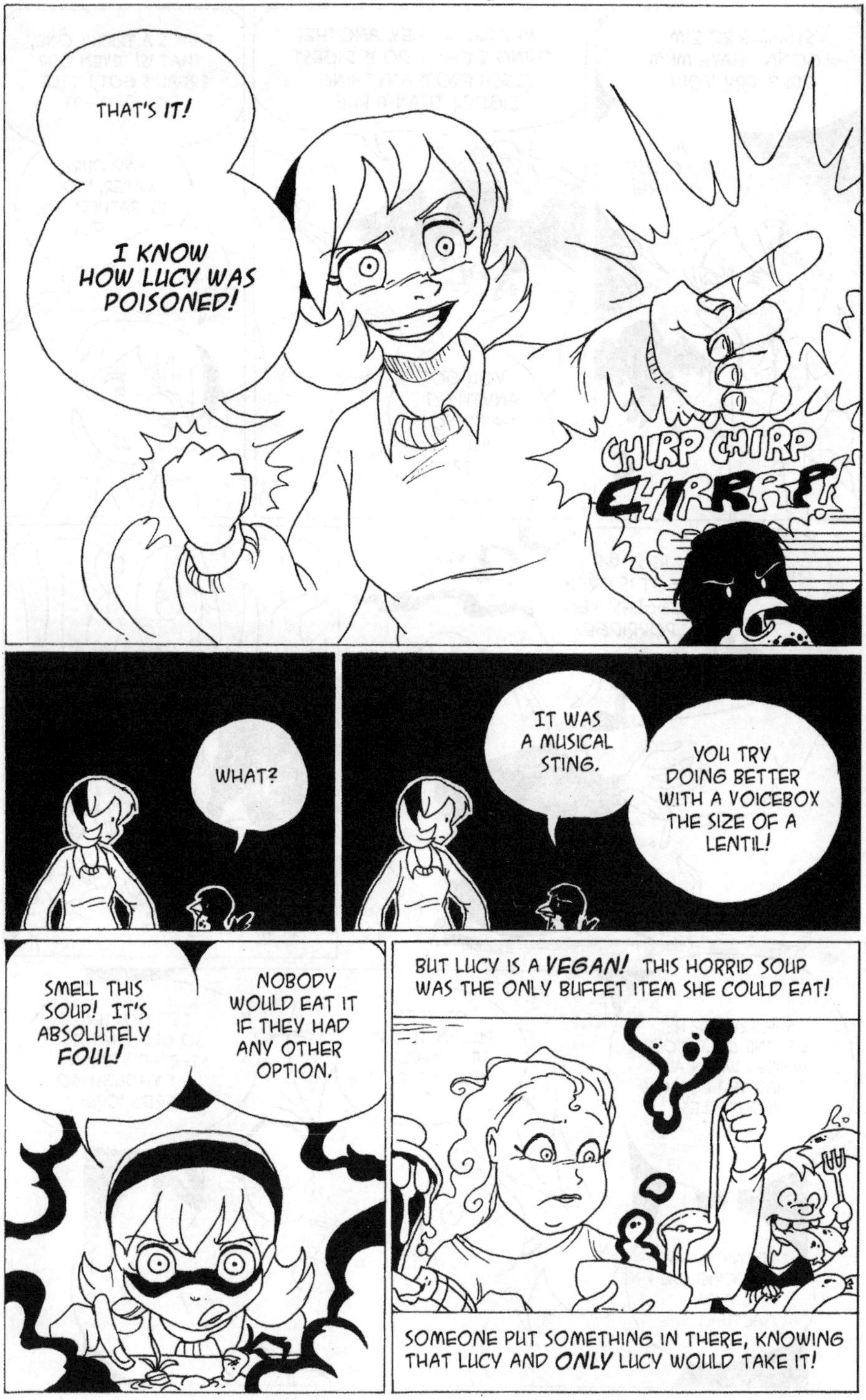
THAT'S IT!
I KNOW HOW LUCY WAS POISONED!
CHIRP CHIRP CHIRRP!
WHAT?
IT WAS A MUSICAL STING.
YOU TRY DOING BETTER WITH A VOICEBOX THE SIZE OF A LENTIL!
SMELL THIS SOUP! IT'S ABSOLUTELY FOUL!
NOBODY WOULD EAT IT IF THEY HAD ANY OTHER OPTION.
BUT LUCY IS A VEGAN! THIS HORRID SOUP WAS THE ONLY BUFFET ITEM SHE COULD EAT!
SOMEONE PUT SOMETHING IN THERE, KNOWING THAT LUCY AND ONLY LUCY WOULD TAKE IT!

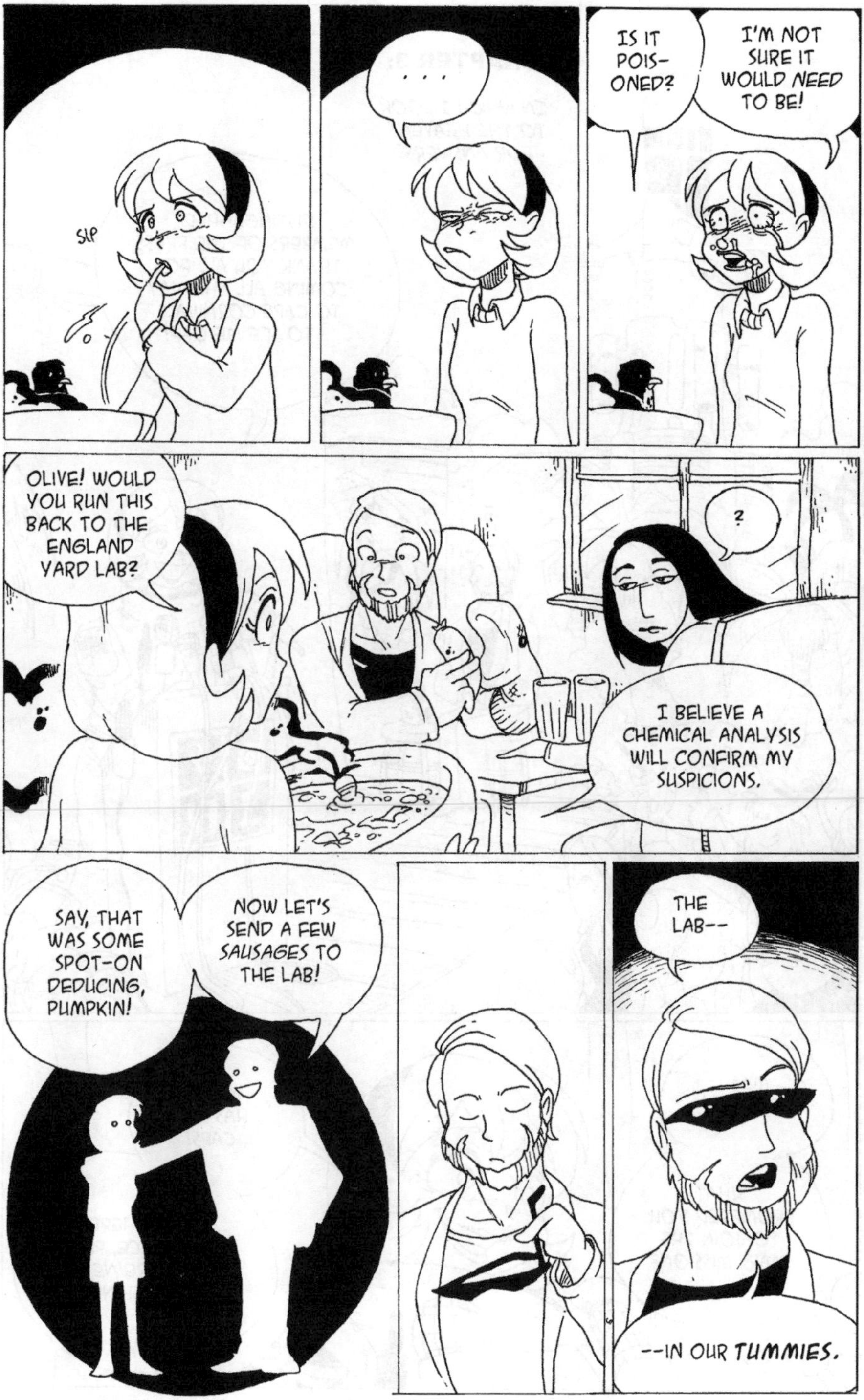

SIP
...
IS IT POIS-ONED?
I'M NOT SURE IT WOULD NEED TO BE!
OLIVE! WOULD YOU RUN THIS BACK TO THE ENGLAND YARD LAB?
?
I BELIEVE A CHEMICAL ANALYSIS WILL CONFIRM MY SUSPICIONS.
SAY, THAT WAS SOME SPOT-ON DEDUCING, PUMPKIN!
NOW LET'S SEND A FEW SAUSAGES TO THE LAB!
THE LAB--
--IN OUR TUMMIES.

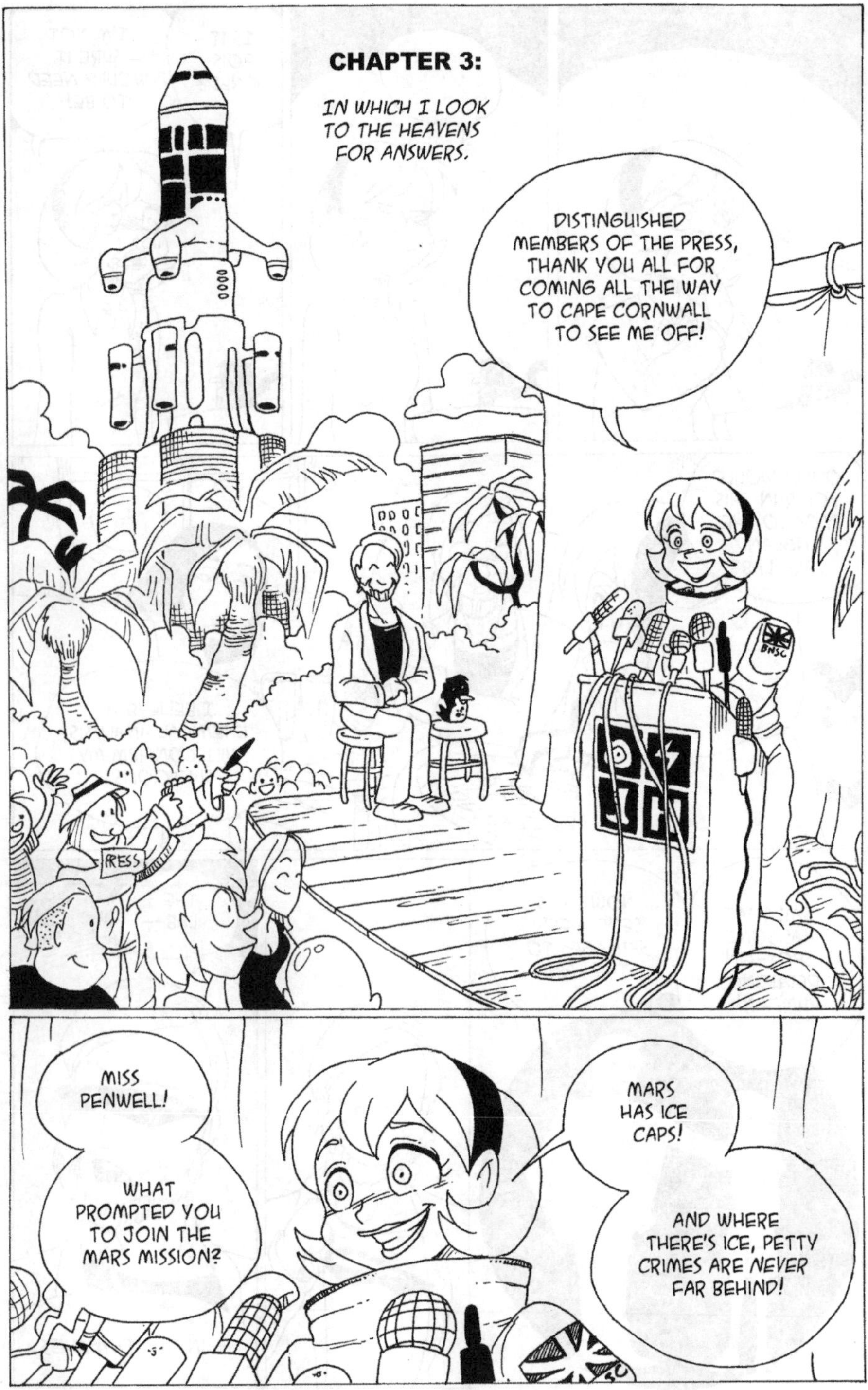
CHAPTER 3:
IN WHICH I LOOK TO THE HEAVENS FOR ANSWERS.
DISTINGUISHED MEMBERS OF THE PRESS, THANK YOU ALL FOR COMING ALL THE WAY TO CAPE CORNWALL TO SEE ME OFF!
BNSC
PRESS
MISS PENWELL!
WHAT PROMPTED YOU TO JOIN THE MARS MISSION?
MARS HAS ICE CAPS!
AND WHERE THERE'S ICE, PETTY CRIMES ARE NEVER FAR BEHIND!

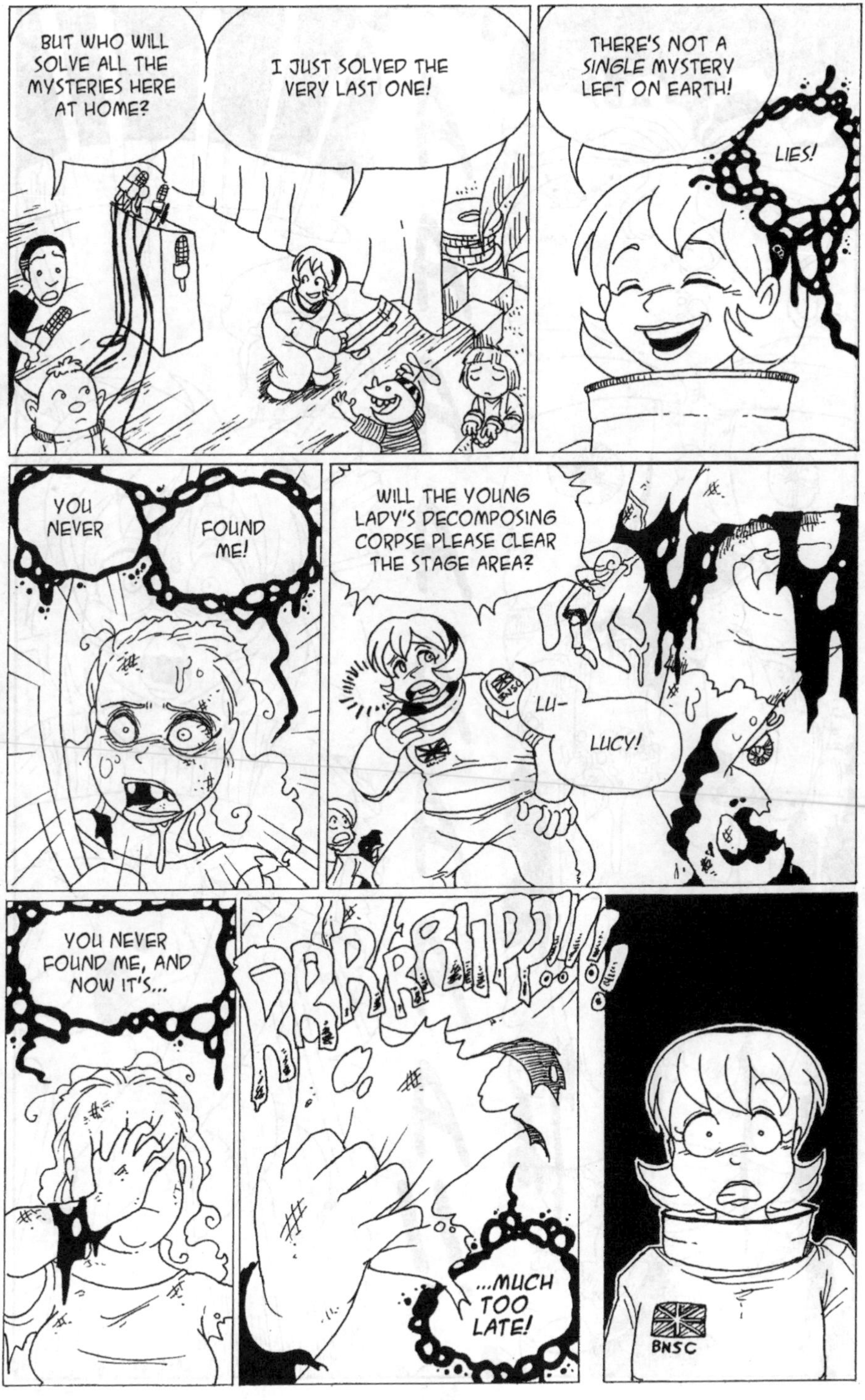
BUT WHO WILL SOLVE ALL THE MYSTERIES HERE AT HOME?
I JUST SOLVED THE VERY LAST ONE!
THERE'S NOT A SINGLE MYSTERY LEFT ON EARTH!
LIES!
YOU NEVER
FOUND ME!
WILL THE YOUNG LADY'S DECOMPOSING CORPSE PLEASE CLEAR THE STAGE AREA?
LU-
LUCY!
YOU NEVER FOUND ME, AND NOW IT'S...
DRRRRIIP!!!
...MUCH TOO LATE!
BNSC

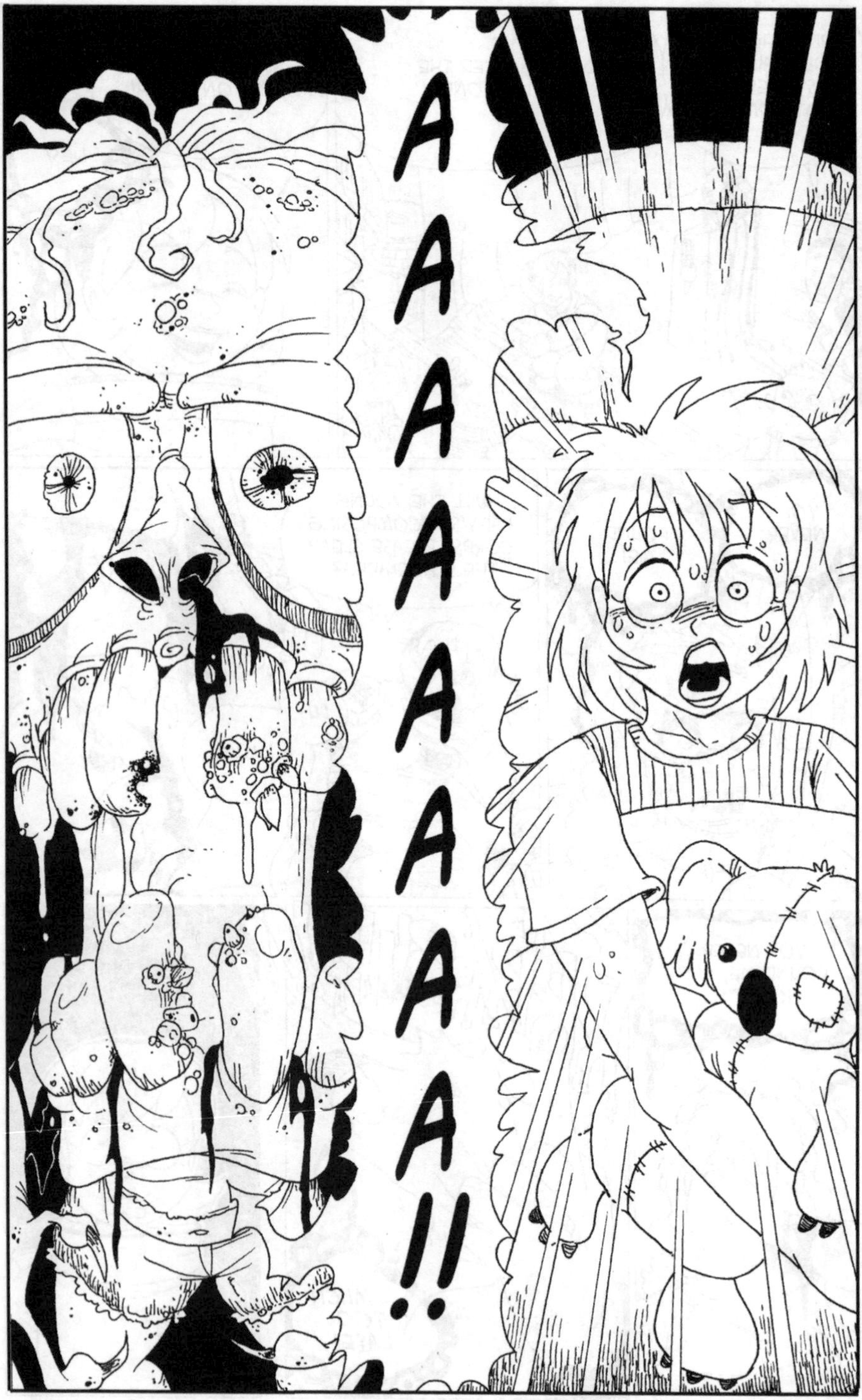
AAAAAAAA!!

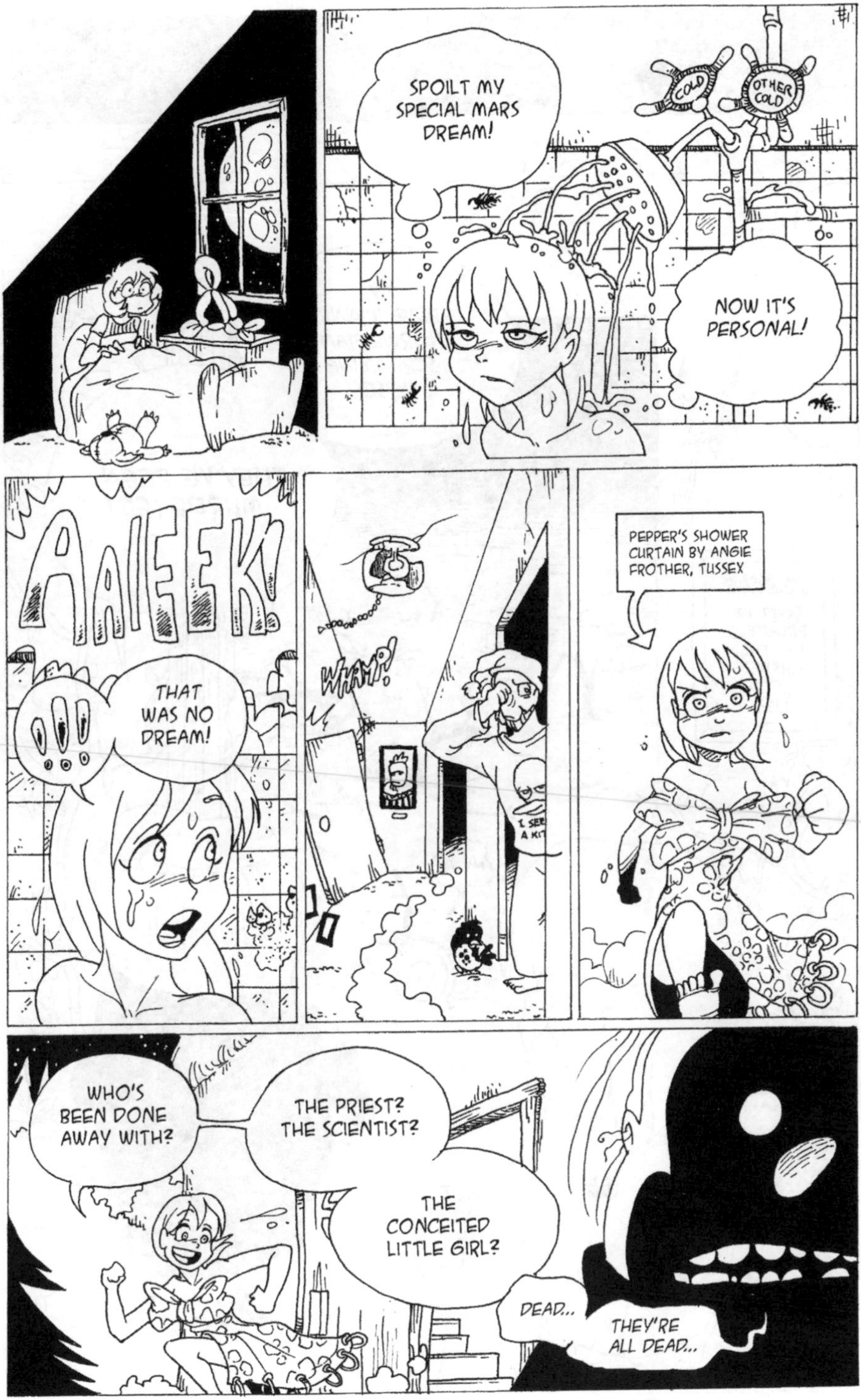
SPOILT MY SPECIAL MARS DREAM!
COLD
OTHER COLD
NOW IT'S PERSONAL!
AAIEEK!
THAT WAS NO DREAM!
WHAM!
PEPPER'S SHOWER CURTAIN BY ANGIE FROTHER, TUSSEX
WHO'S BEEN DONE AWAY WITH?
THE PRIEST? THE SCIENTIST?
THE CONCEITED LITTLE GIRL?
DEAD...
THEY'RE ALL DEAD...

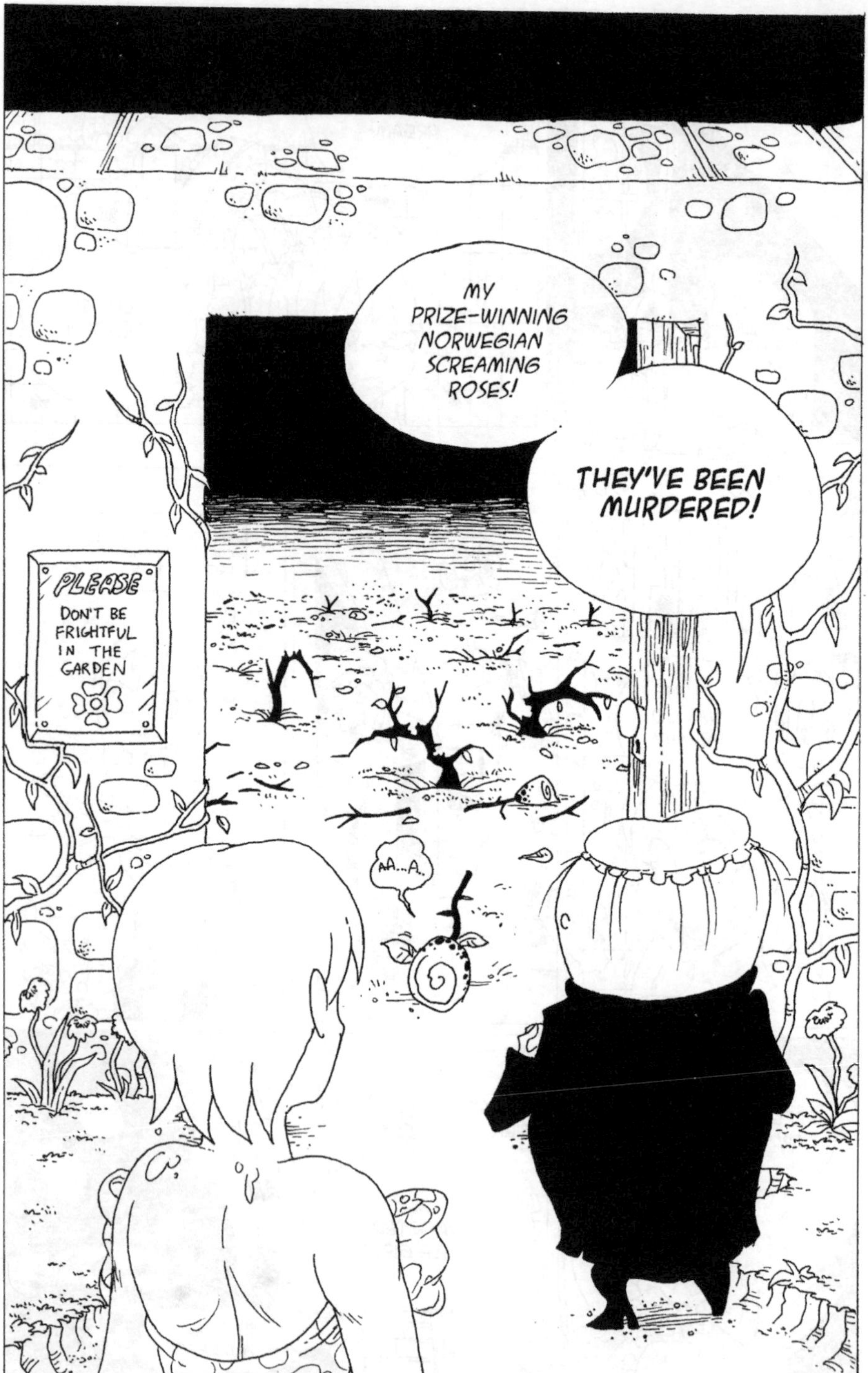
PLEASE
DON'T BE FRIGHTFUL IN THE GARDEN
MY PRIZE-WINNING NORWEGIAN SCREAMING ROSES!
THEY'VE BEEN MURDERED!
AA...A..

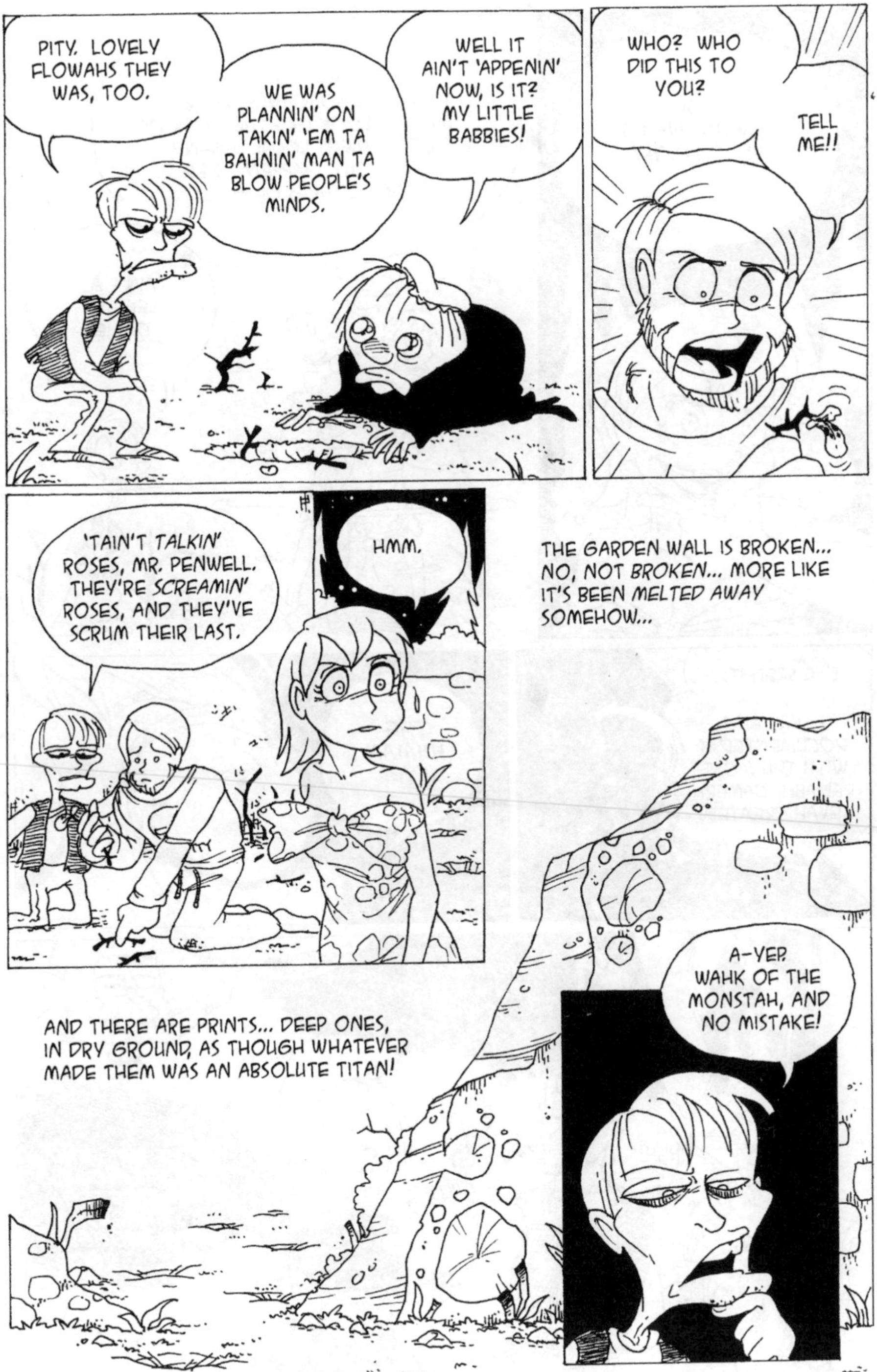
PITY. LOVELY FLOWAHS THEY WAS, TOO.
WE WAS PLANNIN' ON TAKIN' 'EM TA BAHNIN' MAN TA BLOW PEOPLE'S MINDS.
WELL IT AIN'T 'APPENIN' NOW, IS IT? MY LITTLE BABBIES!
WHO? WHO DID THIS TO YOU?
TELL ME!!
'TAIN'T *TALKIN'* ROSES, MR. PENWELL. THEY'RE *SCREAMIN'* ROSES, AND THEY'VE SCRUM THEIR LAST.
HMM.
THE GARDEN WALL IS BROKEN... NO, NOT *BROKEN*... MORE LIKE IT'S BEEN *MELTED AWAY* SOMEHOW...
AND THERE ARE PRINTS... DEEP ONES, IN DRY GROUND, AS THOUGH WHATEVER MADE THEM WAS AN ABSOLUTE TITAN!
A-YEP. WAHK OF THE MONSTAH, AND NO MISTAKE!

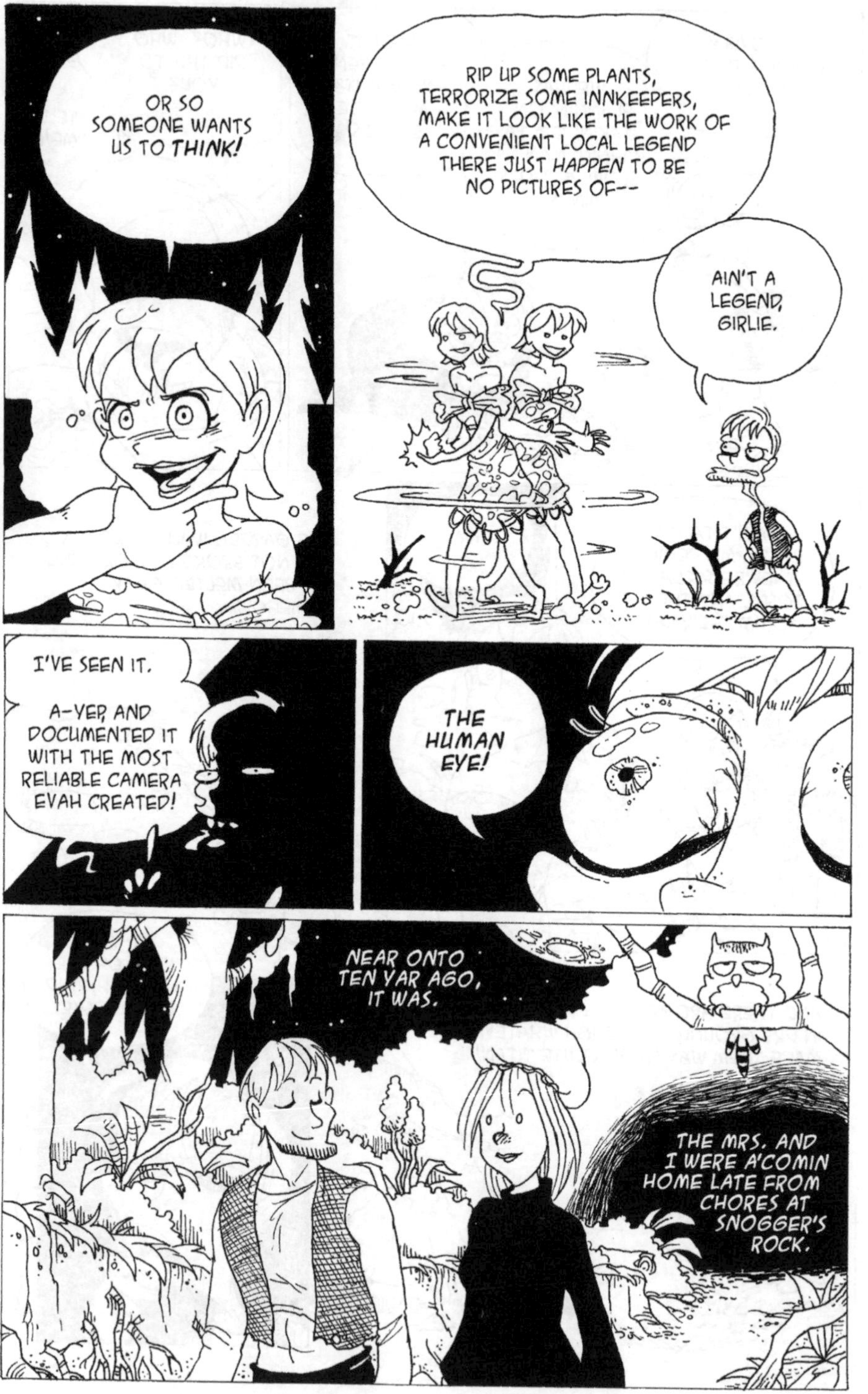
OR SO SOMEONE WANTS US TO THINK!
RIP UP SOME PLANTS, TERRORIZE SOME INNKEEPERS, MAKE IT LOOK LIKE THE WORK OF A CONVENIENT LOCAL LEGEND THERE JUST HAPPEN TO BE NO PICTURES OF--
AIN'T A LEGEND, GIRLIE.
I'VE SEEN IT.
A-YEP, AND DOCUMENTED IT WITH THE MOST RELIABLE CAMERA EVAH CREATED!
THE HUMAN EYE!
NEAR ONTO TEN YAR AGO, IT WAS.
THE MRS. AND I WERE A'COMIN HOME LATE FROM CHORES AT SNOGGER'S ROCK.

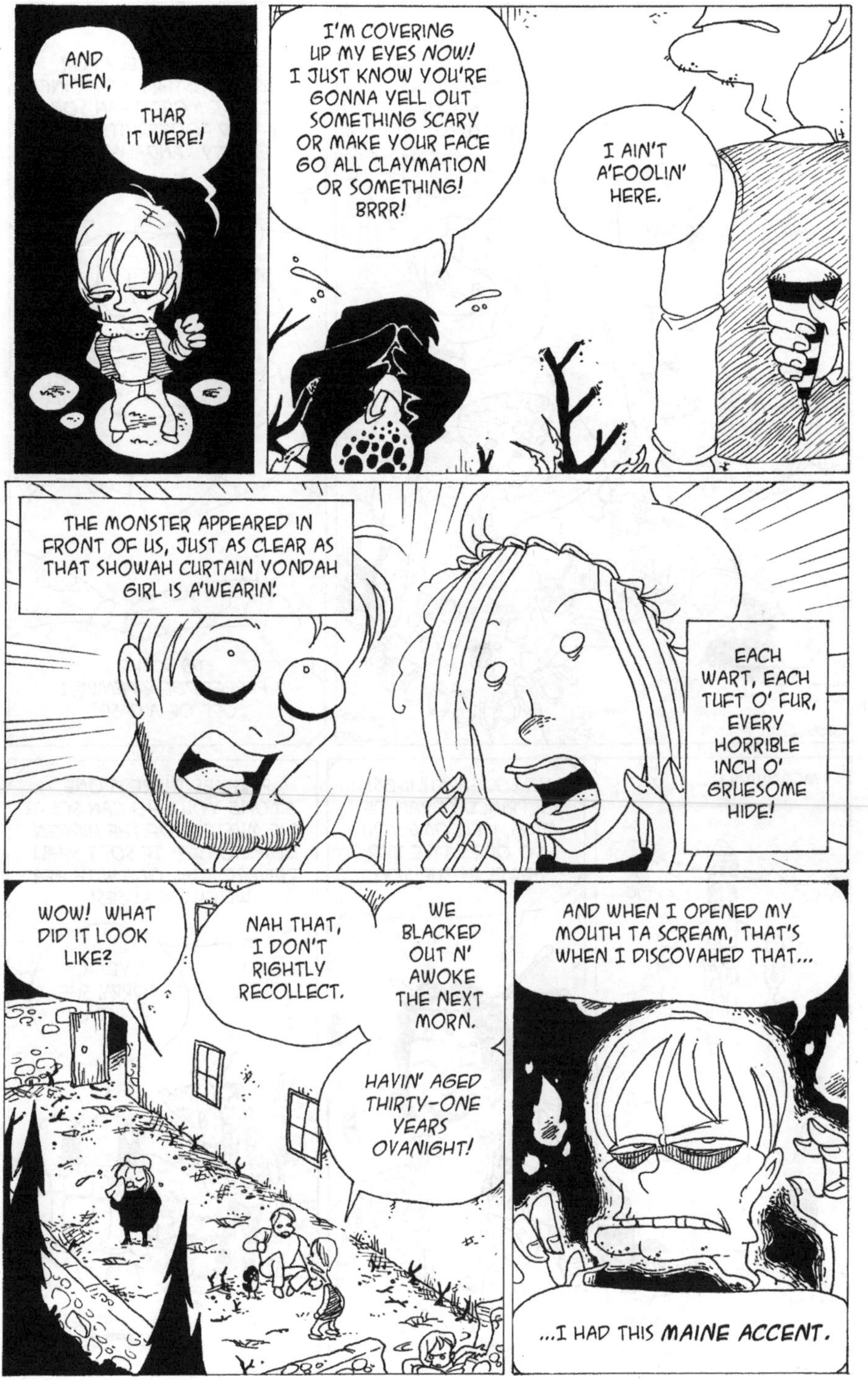
AND THEN,
THAR IT WERE!
I'M COVERING UP MY EYES *NOW!* I JUST KNOW YOU'RE GONNA YELL OUT SOMETHING SCARY OR MAKE YOUR FACE GO ALL CLAYMATION OR SOMETHING! BRRR!
I AIN'T A'FOOLIN' HERE.
THE MONSTER APPEARED IN FRONT OF US, JUST AS CLEAR AS THAT SHOWAH CURTAIN YONDAH GIRL IS A'WEARIN'.
EACH WART, EACH TUFT O' FUR, EVERY HORRIBLE INCH O' GRUESOME HIDE!
WOW! WHAT DID IT LOOK LIKE?
NAH THAT, I DON'T RIGHTLY RECOLLECT.
WE BLACKED OUT N' AWOKE THE NEXT MORN.
HAVIN' AGED THIRTY-ONE YEARS OVANIGHT!
AND WHEN I OPENED MY MOUTH TA SCREAM, THAT'S WHEN I DISCOVAHED THAT...
...I HAD THIS **MAINE ACCENT.**

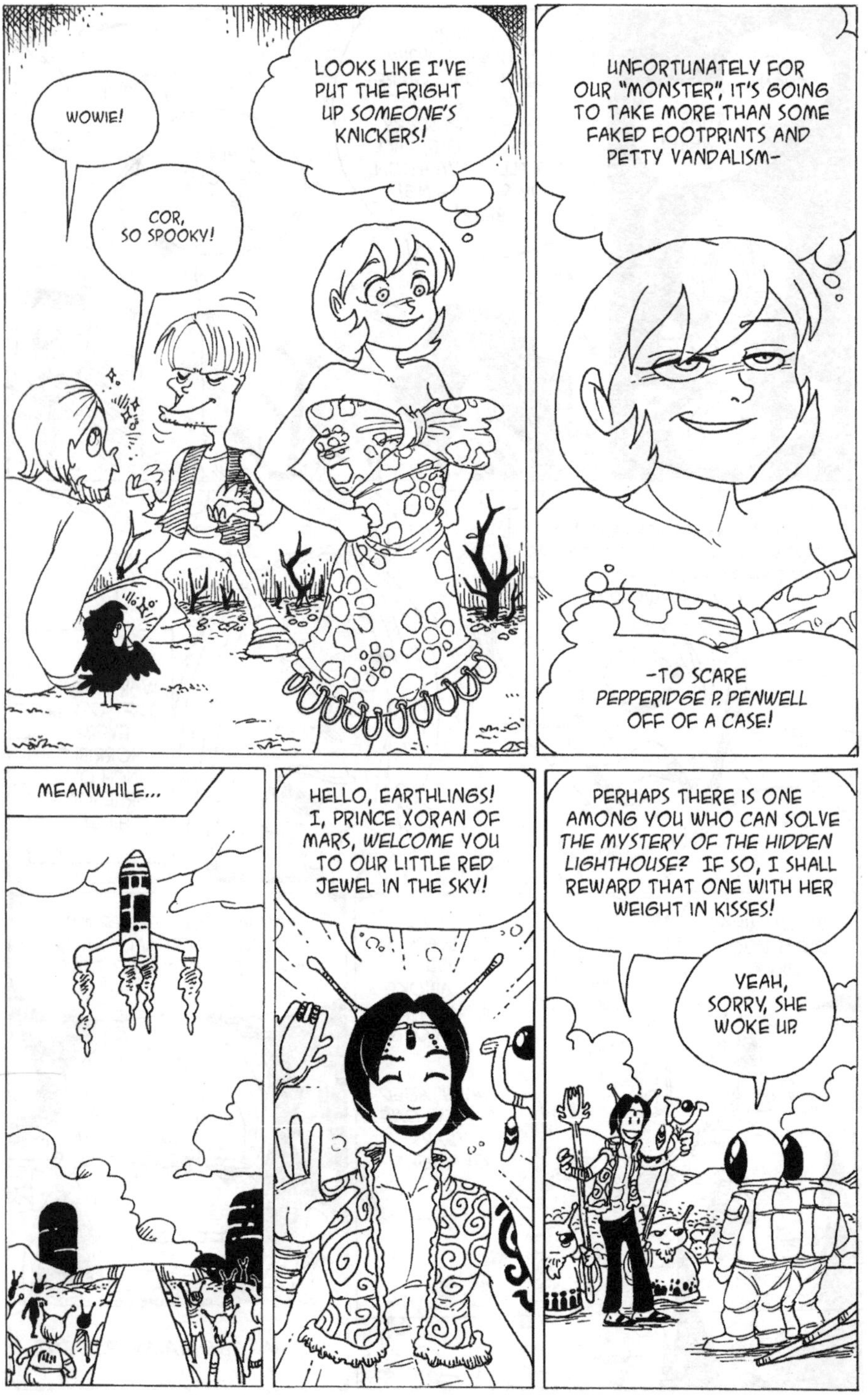
WOWIE!
COR, SO SPOOKY!
LOOKS LIKE I'VE PUT THE FRIGHT UP *SOMEONE'S* KNICKERS!
UNFORTUNATELY FOR OUR "MONSTER", IT'S GOING TO TAKE MORE THAN SOME FAKED FOOTPRINTS AND PETTY VANDALISM-
-TO SCARE *PEPPERIDGE P. PENWELL* OFF OF A CASE!
MEANWHILE...
HELLO, EARTHLINGS! I, PRINCE XORAN OF MARS, *WELCOME YOU* TO OUR LITTLE RED JEWEL IN THE SKY!
PERHAPS THERE IS ONE AMONG YOU WHO CAN SOLVE *THE MYSTERY OF THE HIDDEN LIGHTHOUSE?* IF SO, I SHALL REWARD THAT ONE WITH HER WEIGHT IN KISSES!
YEAH, SORRY, SHE WOKE UP.

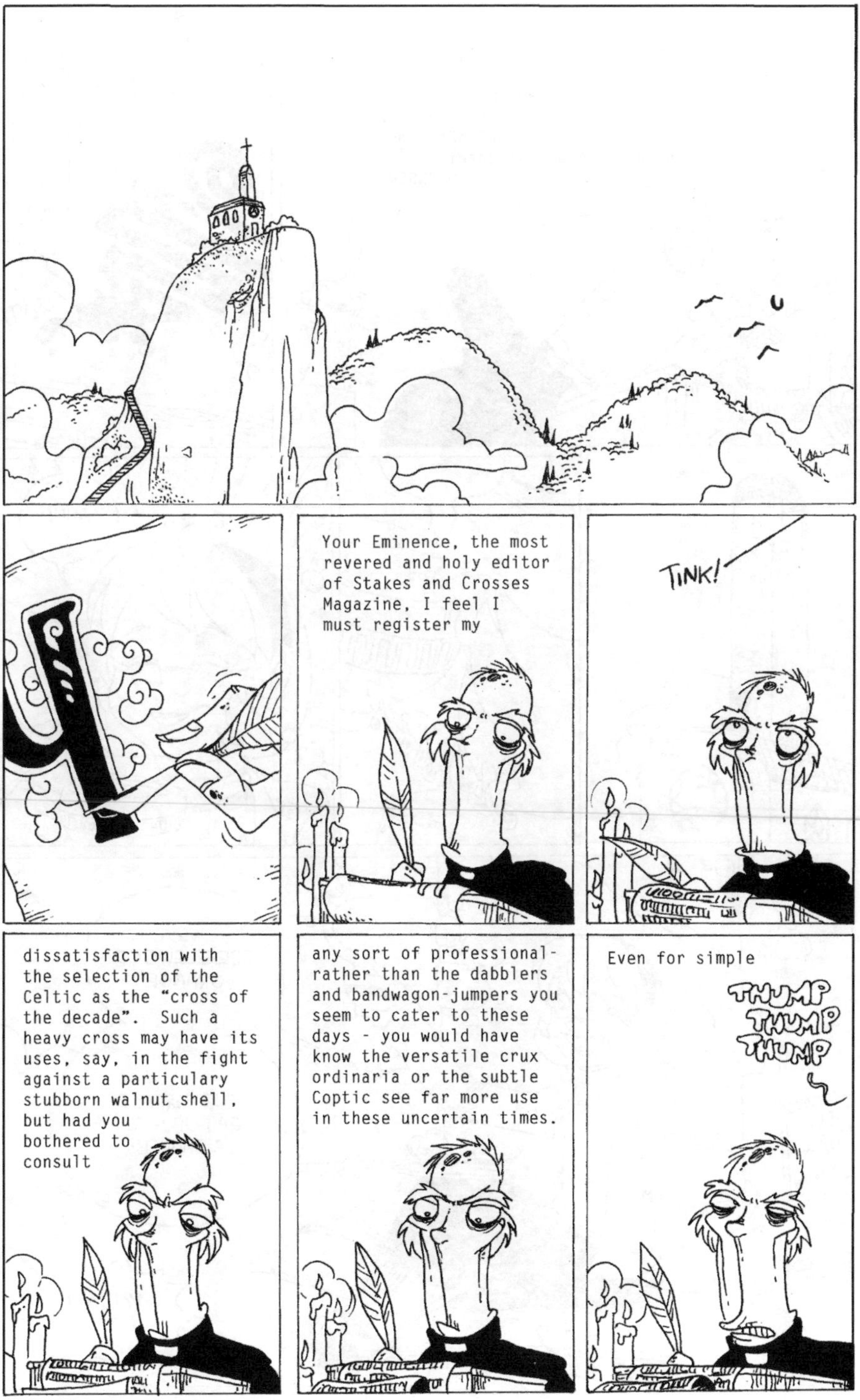
Your Eminence, the most revered and holy editor of Stakes and Crosses Magazine, I feel I must register my
TINK!
dissatisfaction with the selection of the Celtic as the "cross of the decade". Such a heavy cross may have its uses, say, in the fight against a particulary stubborn walnut shell, but had you bothered to consult
any sort of professional- rather than the dabblers and bandwagon-jumpers you seem to cater to these days - you would have know the versatile crux ordinaria or the subtle Coptic see far more use in these uncertain times.
Even for simple
THUMP THUMP THUMP

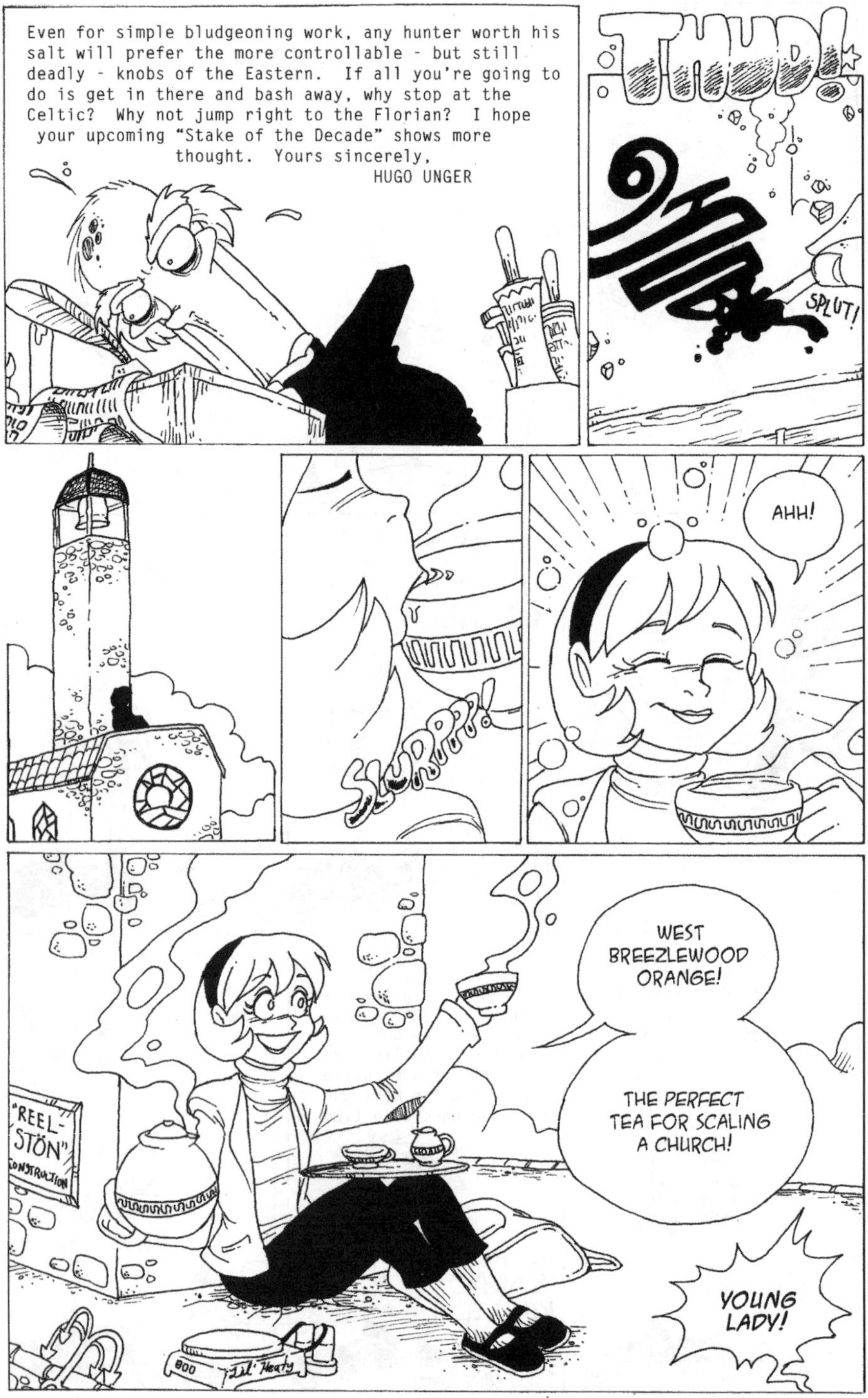
Even for simple bludgeoning work, any hunter worth his salt will prefer the more controllable - but still deadly - knobs of the Eastern. If all you're going to do is get in there and bash away, why stop at the Celtic? Why not jump right to the Florian? I hope your upcoming "Stake of the Decade" shows more thought. Yours sincerely,
HUGO UNGER
THUD!
SPLUT!
SLURPPP!
AHH!
WEST BREEZLEWOOD ORANGE!
THE PERFECT TEA FOR SCALING A CHURCH!
YOUNG LADY!
"REEL-STÖN" CONSTRUCTION
Lil' Heaty

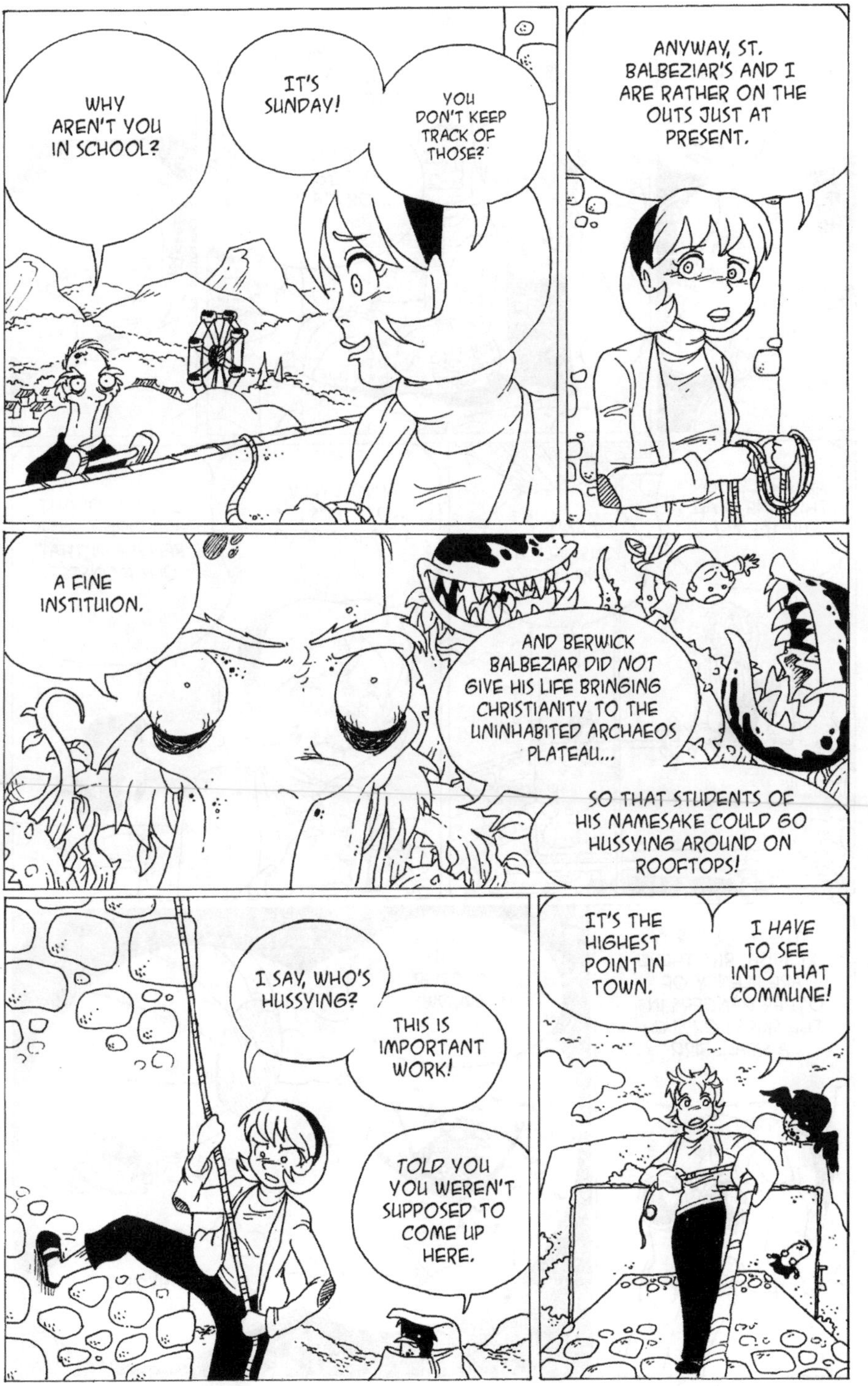
WHY AREN'T YOU IN SCHOOL?
IT'S SUNDAY!
YOU DON'T KEEP TRACK OF THOSE?
ANYWAY, ST. BALBEZIAR'S AND I ARE RATHER ON THE OUTS JUST AT PRESENT.
A FINE INSTITUION.
AND BERWICK BALBEZIAR DID NOT GIVE HIS LIFE BRINGING CHRISTIANITY TO THE UNINHABITED ARCHAEOS PLATEAU...
SO THAT STUDENTS OF HIS NAMESAKE COULD GO HUSSYING AROUND ON ROOFTOPS!
I SAY, WHO'S HUSSYING?
THIS IS IMPORTANT WORK!
TOLD YOU YOU WEREN'T SUPPOSED TO COME UP HERE.
IT'S THE HIGHEST POINT IN TOWN.
I HAVE TO SEE INTO THAT COMMUNE!

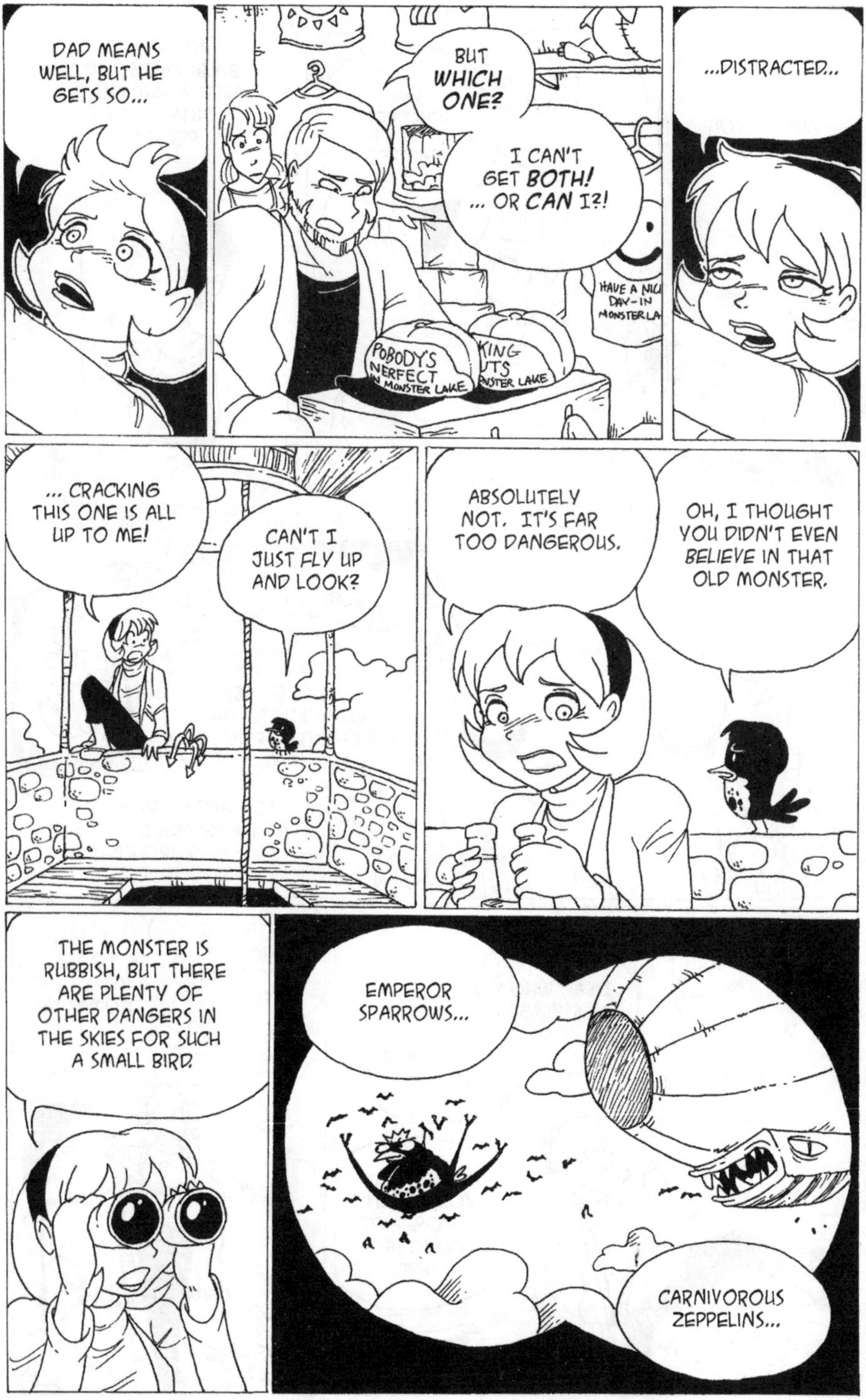
DAD MEANS WELL, BUT HE GETS SO...
BUT WHICH ONE?
I CAN'T GET BOTH! ... OR CAN I?!
HAVE A NICE DAY-IN MONSTER LAKE
POBODY'S NERFECT IN MONSTER LAKE
...DISTRACTED...
... CRACKING THIS ONE IS ALL UP TO ME!
CAN'T I JUST FLY UP AND LOOK?
ABSOLUTELY NOT. IT'S FAR TOO DANGEROUS.
OH, I THOUGHT YOU DIDN'T EVEN BELIEVE IN THAT OLD MONSTER.
THE MONSTER IS RUBBISH, BUT THERE ARE PLENTY OF OTHER DANGERS IN THE SKIES FOR SUCH A SMALL BIRD.
EMPEROR SPARROWS...
CARNIVOROUS ZEPPELINS...

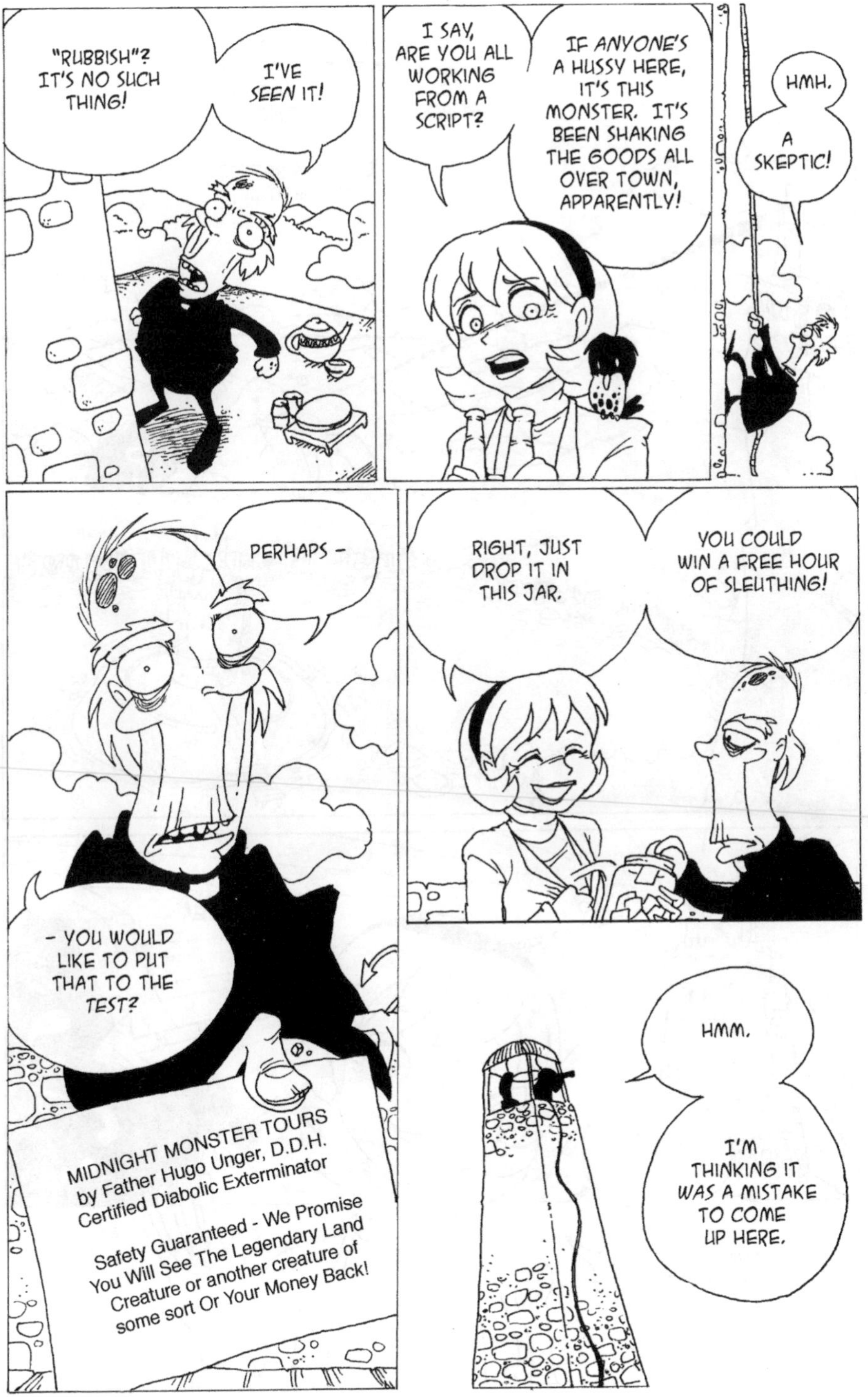
"RUBBISH"? IT'S NO SUCH THING!
I'VE SEEN IT!
I SAY, ARE YOU ALL WORKING FROM A SCRIPT?
IF ANYONE'S A HUSSY HERE, IT'S THIS MONSTER. IT'S BEEN SHAKING THE GOODS ALL OVER TOWN, APPARENTLY!
HMH.
A SKEPTIC!
PERHAPS -
- YOU WOULD LIKE TO PUT THAT TO THE TEST?
MIDNIGHT MONSTER TOURS
by Father Hugo Unger, D.D.H.
Certified Diabolic Exterminator
Safety Guaranteed - We Promise You Will See The Legendary Land Creature or another creature of some sort Or Your Money Back!
RIGHT, JUST DROP IT IN THIS JAR.
YOU COULD WIN A FREE HOUR OF SLEUTHING!
HMM.
I'M THINKING IT WAS A MISTAKE TO COME UP HERE.

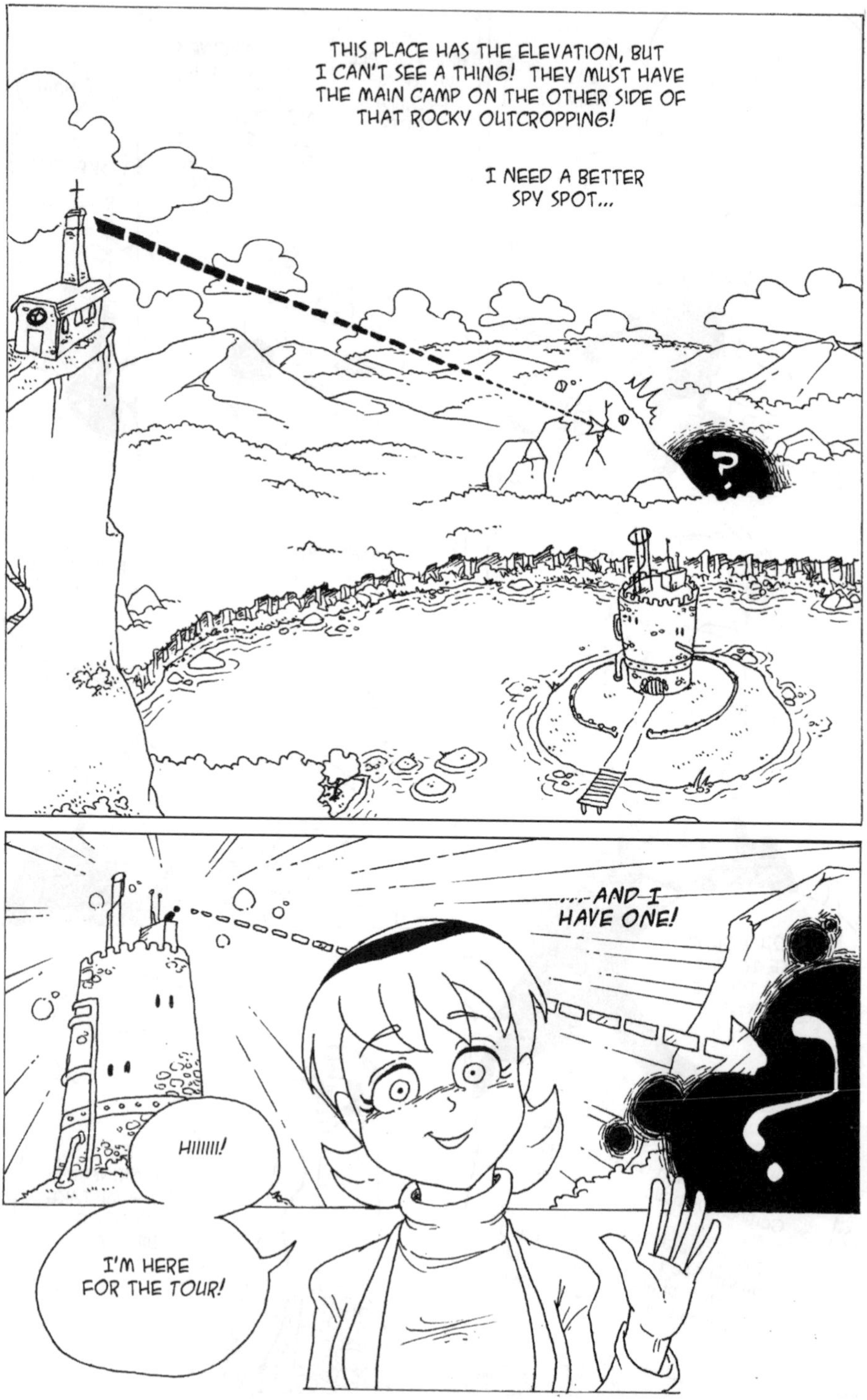
THIS PLACE HAS THE ELEVATION, BUT I CAN'T SEE A THING! THEY MUST HAVE THE MAIN CAMP ON THE OTHER SIDE OF THAT ROCKY OUTCROPPING!
I NEED A BETTER SPY SPOT...
?
...AND I HAVE ONE!
?
HIIIIII!
I'M HERE FOR THE TOUR!

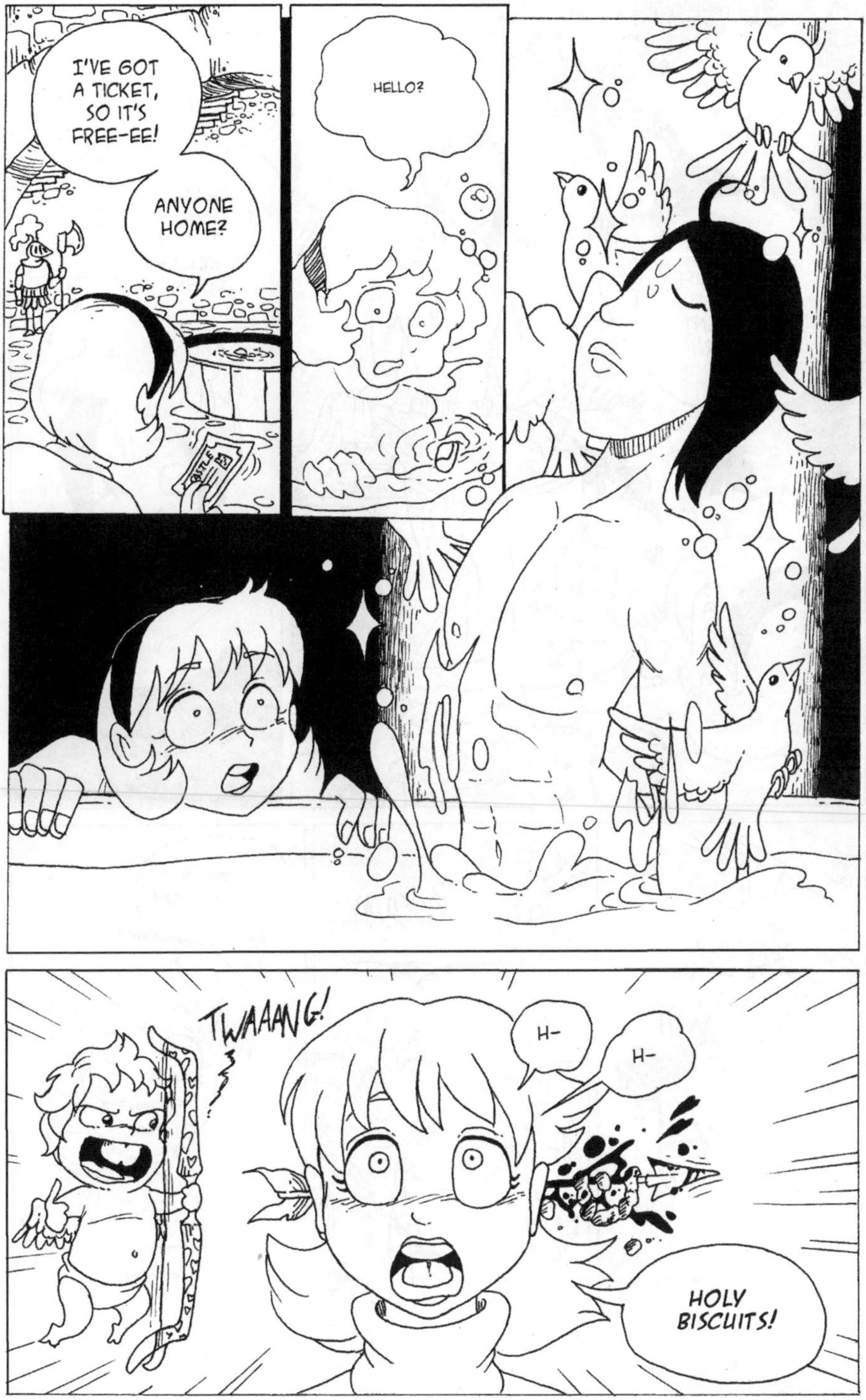
I'VE GOT A TICKET, SO IT'S FREE-EE!
ANYONE HOME?
CASTLE
HELLO?
TWAAANG!
H-
H-
HOLY BISCUITS!

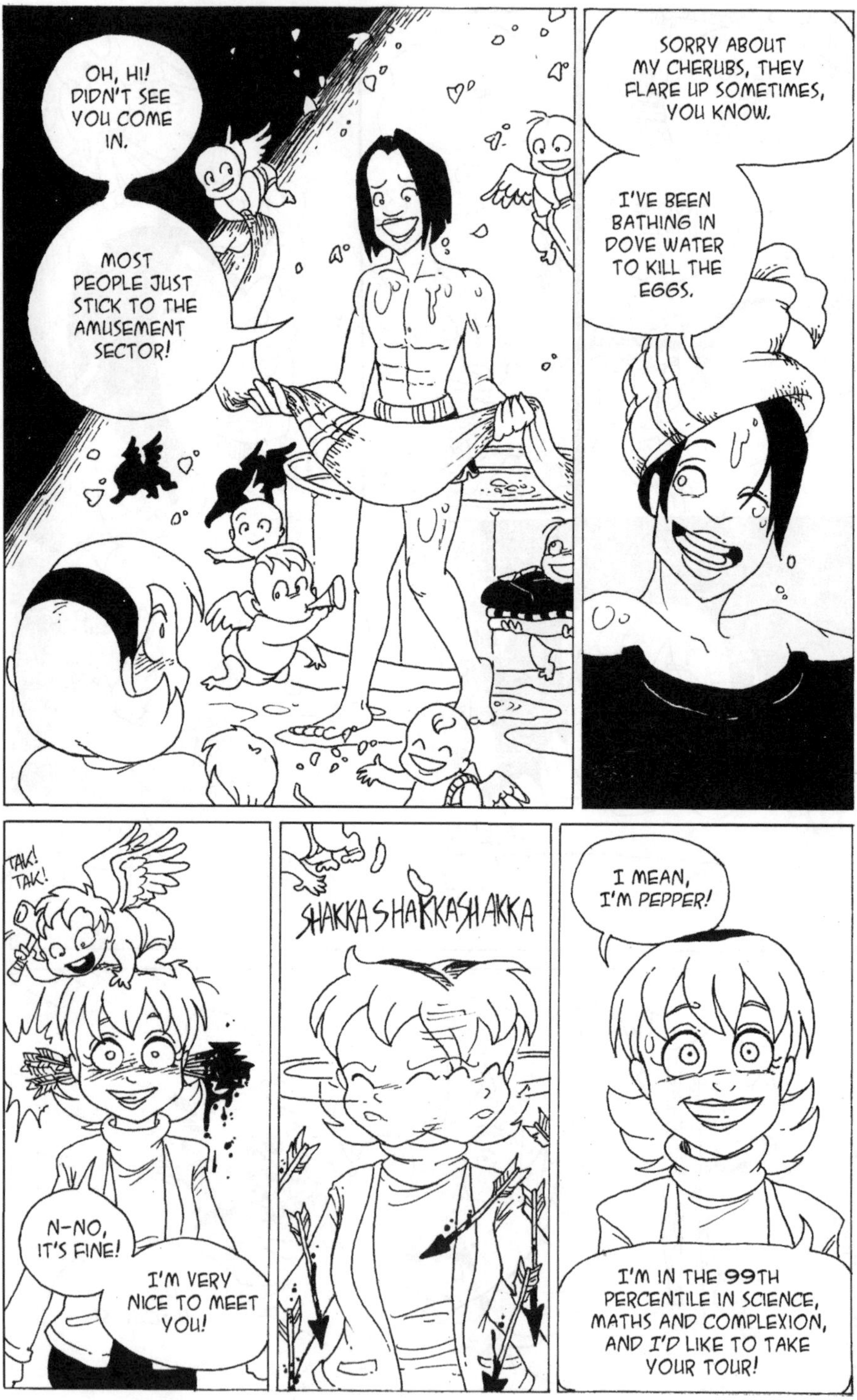
OH, HI! DIDN'T SEE YOU COME IN.
MOST PEOPLE JUST STICK TO THE AMUSEMENT SECTOR!
SORRY ABOUT MY CHERUBS, THEY FLARE UP SOMETIMES, YOU KNOW.
I'VE BEEN BATHING IN DOVE WATER TO KILL THE EGGS.
TAK! TAK!
N-NO, IT'S FINE!
I'M VERY NICE TO MEET YOU!
SHAKKA SHAKKA SHAKKA
I MEAN, I'M PEPPER!
I'M IN THE 99TH PERCENTILE IN SCIENCE, MATHS AND COMPLEXION, AND I'D LIKE TO TAKE YOUR TOUR!

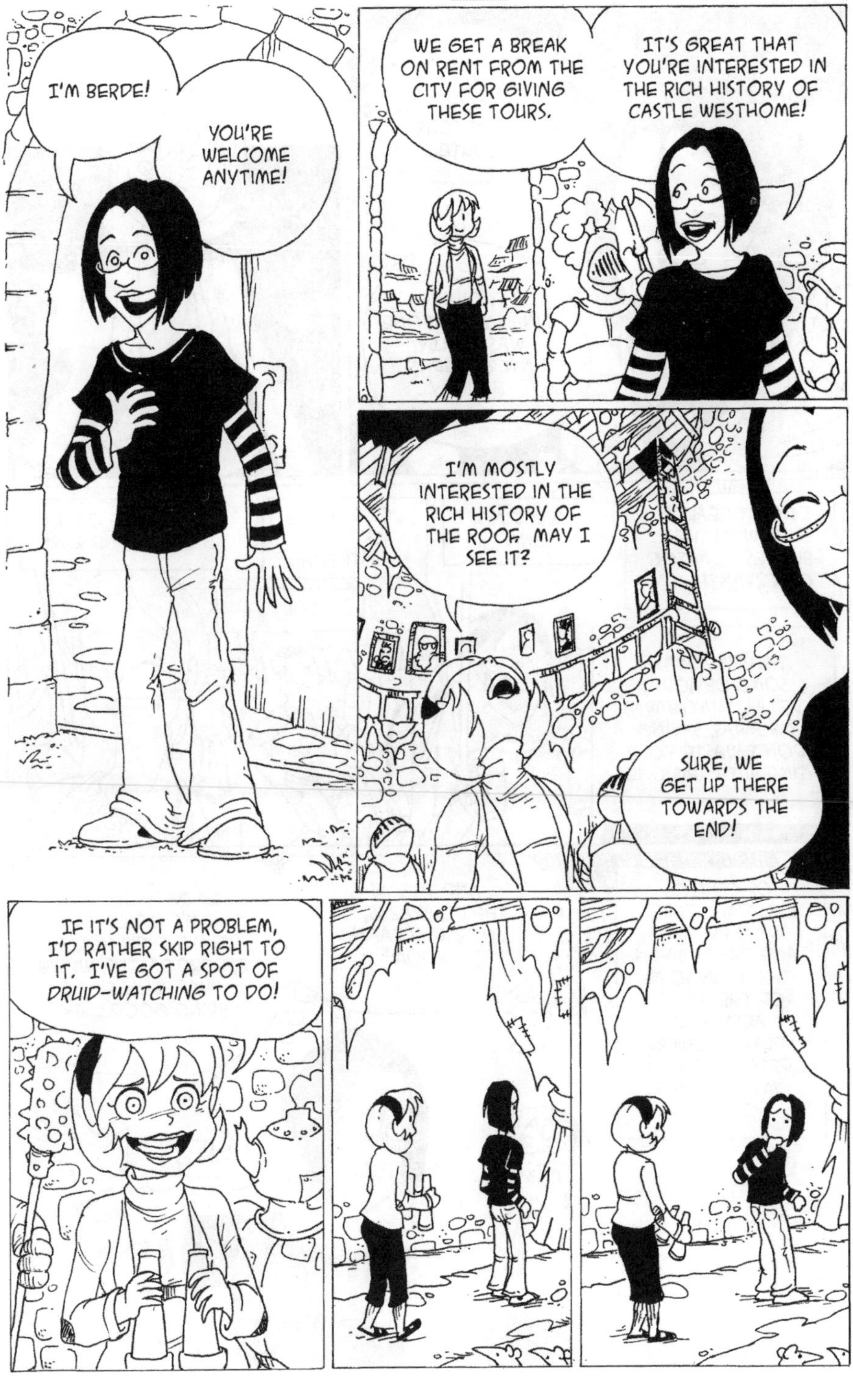
I'M BERDE!
YOU'RE WELCOME ANYTIME!
WE GET A BREAK ON RENT FROM THE CITY FOR GIVING THESE TOURS.
IT'S GREAT THAT YOU'RE INTERESTED IN THE RICH HISTORY OF CASTLE WESTHOME!
I'M MOSTLY INTERESTED IN THE RICH HISTORY OF THE ROOF. MAY I SEE IT?
SURE, WE GET UP THERE TOWARDS THE END!
IF IT'S NOT A PROBLEM, I'D RATHER SKIP RIGHT TO IT. I'VE GOT A SPOT OF *DRUID-WATCHING* TO DO!

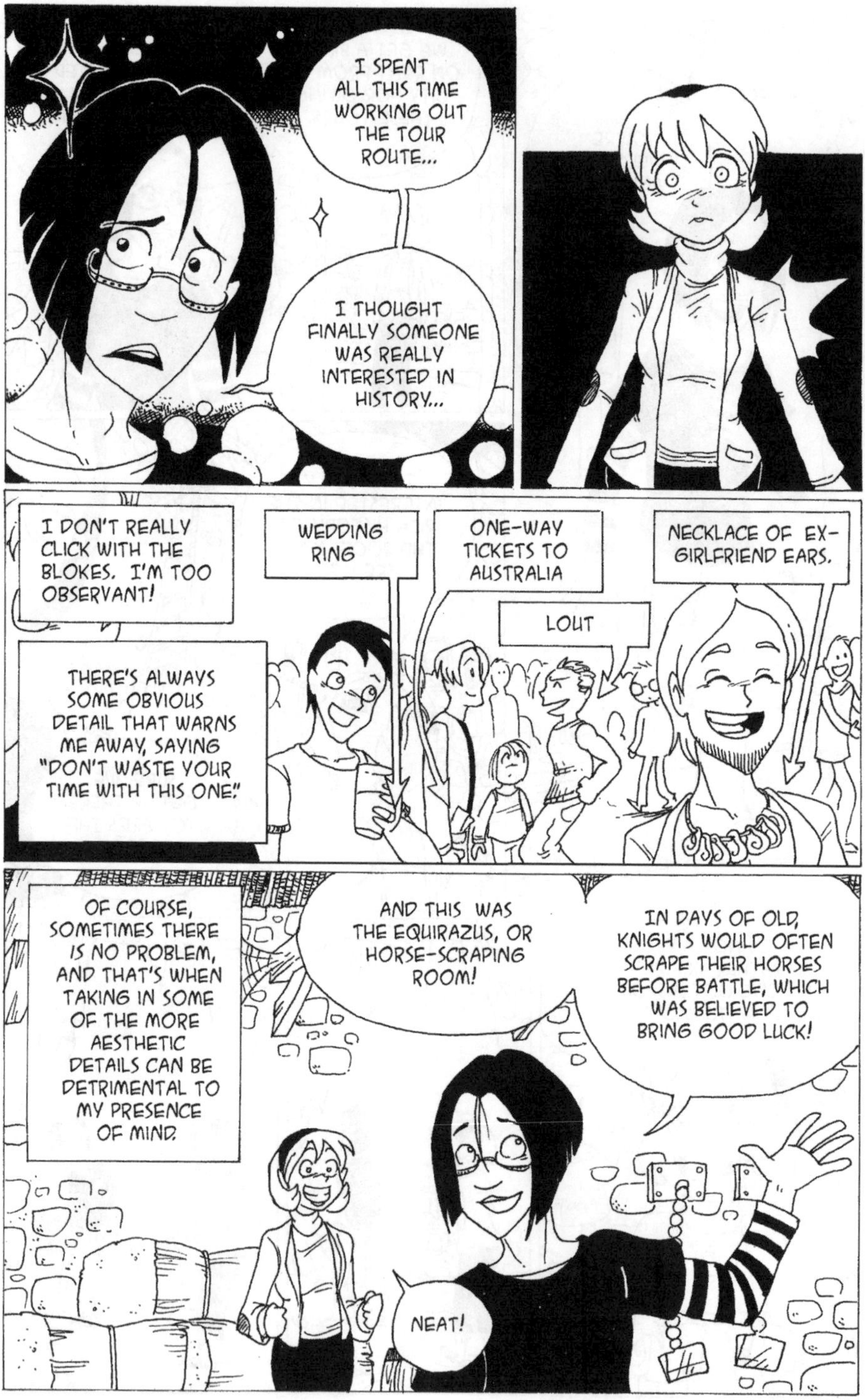

I SPENT ALL THIS TIME WORKING OUT THE TOUR ROUTE...
I THOUGHT FINALLY SOMEONE WAS REALLY INTERESTED IN HISTORY...
I DON'T REALLY CLICK WITH THE BLOKES. I'M TOO OBSERVANT!
THERE'S ALWAYS SOME OBVIOUS DETAIL THAT WARNS ME AWAY, SAYING "DON'T WASTE YOUR TIME WITH THIS ONE."
WEDDING RING
ONE-WAY TICKETS TO AUSTRALIA
LOUT
NECKLACE OF EX-GIRLFRIEND EARS.
OF COURSE, SOMETIMES THERE IS NO PROBLEM, AND THAT'S WHEN TAKING IN SOME OF THE MORE AESTHETIC DETAILS CAN BE DETRIMENTAL TO MY PRESENCE OF MIND.
AND THIS WAS THE EQUIRAZUS, OR HORSE-SCRAPING ROOM!
IN DAYS OF OLD, KNIGHTS WOULD OFTEN SCRAPE THEIR HORSES BEFORE BATTLE, WHICH WAS BELIEVED TO BRING GOOD LUCK!
NEAT!

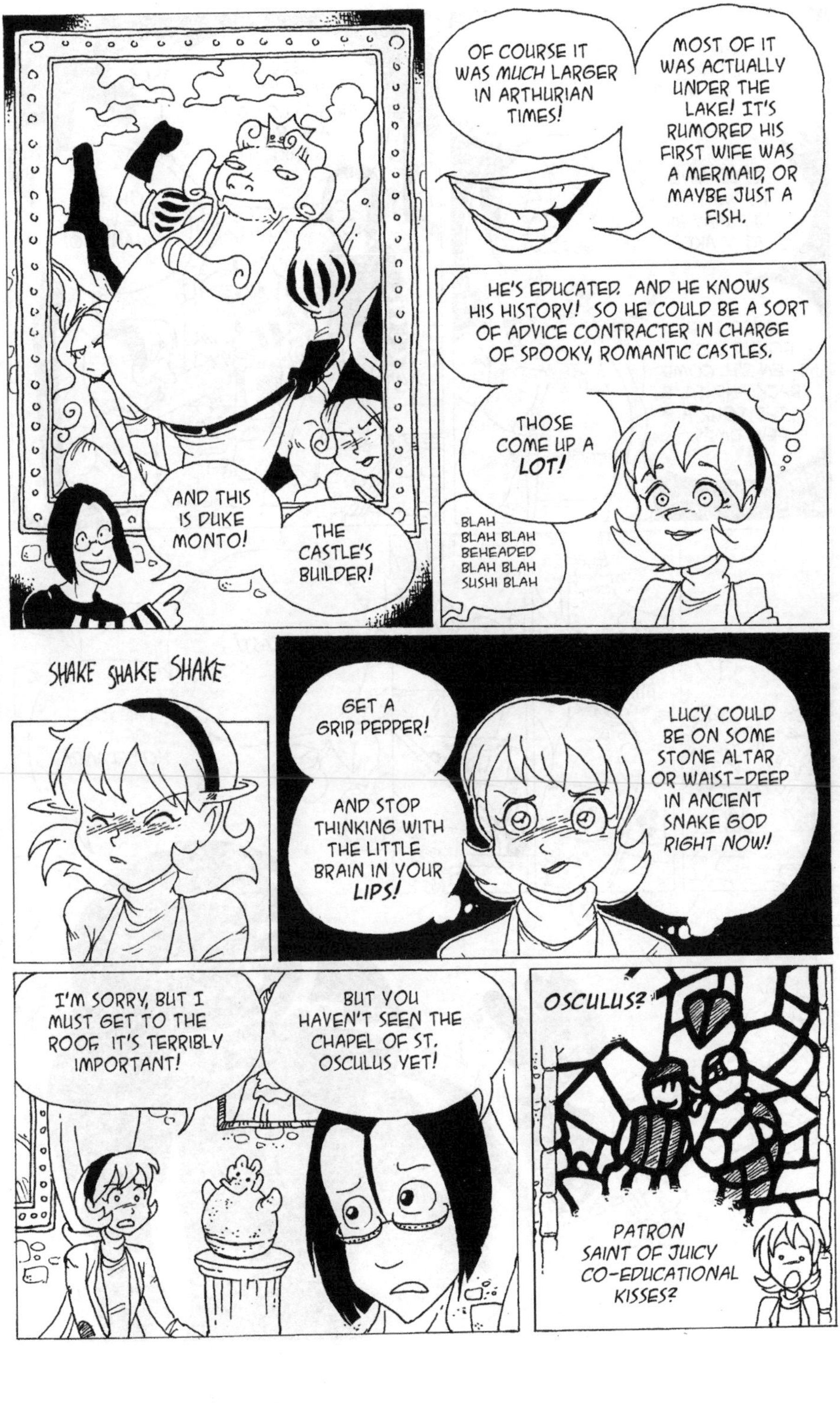
AND THIS IS DUKE MONTO!
THE CASTLE'S BUILDER!
OF COURSE IT WAS *MUCH* LARGER IN ARTHURIAN TIMES!
MOST OF IT WAS ACTUALLY UNDER THE LAKE! IT'S RUMORED HIS FIRST WIFE WAS A MERMAID, OR MAYBE JUST A FISH.
HE'S EDUCATED. AND HE KNOWS HIS HISTORY! SO HE COULD BE A SORT OF ADVICE CONTRACTER IN CHARGE OF SPOOKY, ROMANTIC CASTLES.
THOSE COME UP A **LOT!**
BLAH BLAH BLAH BEHEADED BLAH BLAH SUSHI BLAH
SHAKE SHAKE SHAKE
GET A GRIP, PEPPER!
AND STOP THINKING WITH THE LITTLE BRAIN IN YOUR ***LIPS!***
LUCY COULD BE ON SOME STONE ALTAR OR WAIST-DEEP IN ANCIENT SNAKE GOD RIGHT NOW!
I'M SORRY, BUT I MUST GET TO THE ROOF. IT'S TERRIBLY IMPORTANT!
BUT YOU HAVEN'T SEEN THE CHAPEL OF ST. OSCULUS YET!
OSCULUS?
PATRON SAINT OF JUICY CO-EDUCATIONAL KISSES?

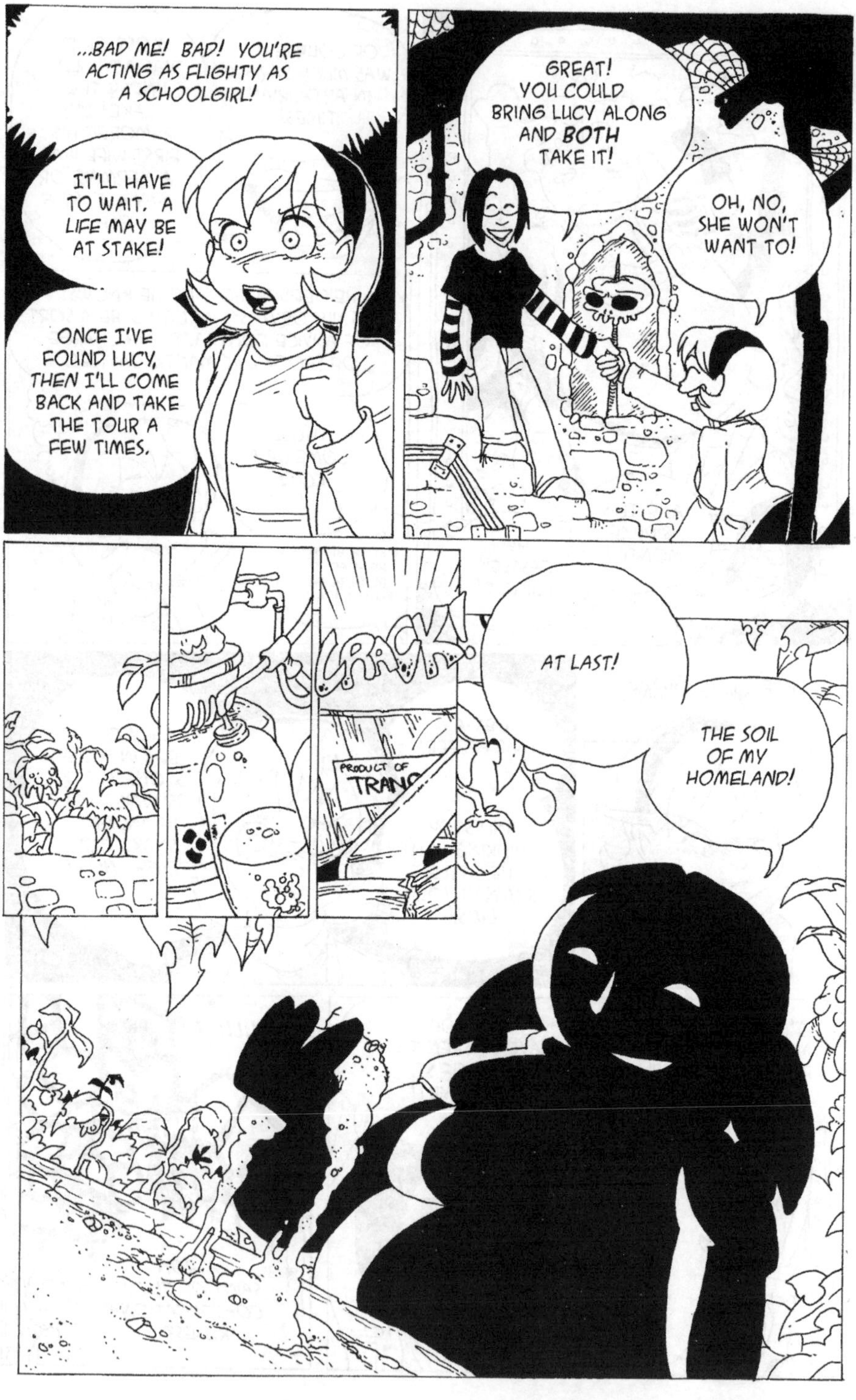
...BAD ME! BAD! YOU'RE ACTING AS FLIGHTY AS A SCHOOLGIRL!
IT'LL HAVE TO WAIT. A LIFE MAY BE AT STAKE!
ONCE I'VE FOUND LUCY, THEN I'LL COME BACK AND TAKE THE TOUR A FEW TIMES.
GREAT! YOU COULD BRING LUCY ALONG AND BOTH TAKE IT!
OH, NO, SHE WON'T WANT TO!
CRACK!
PRODUCT OF
TRANS
AT LAST!
THE SOIL OF MY HOMELAND!

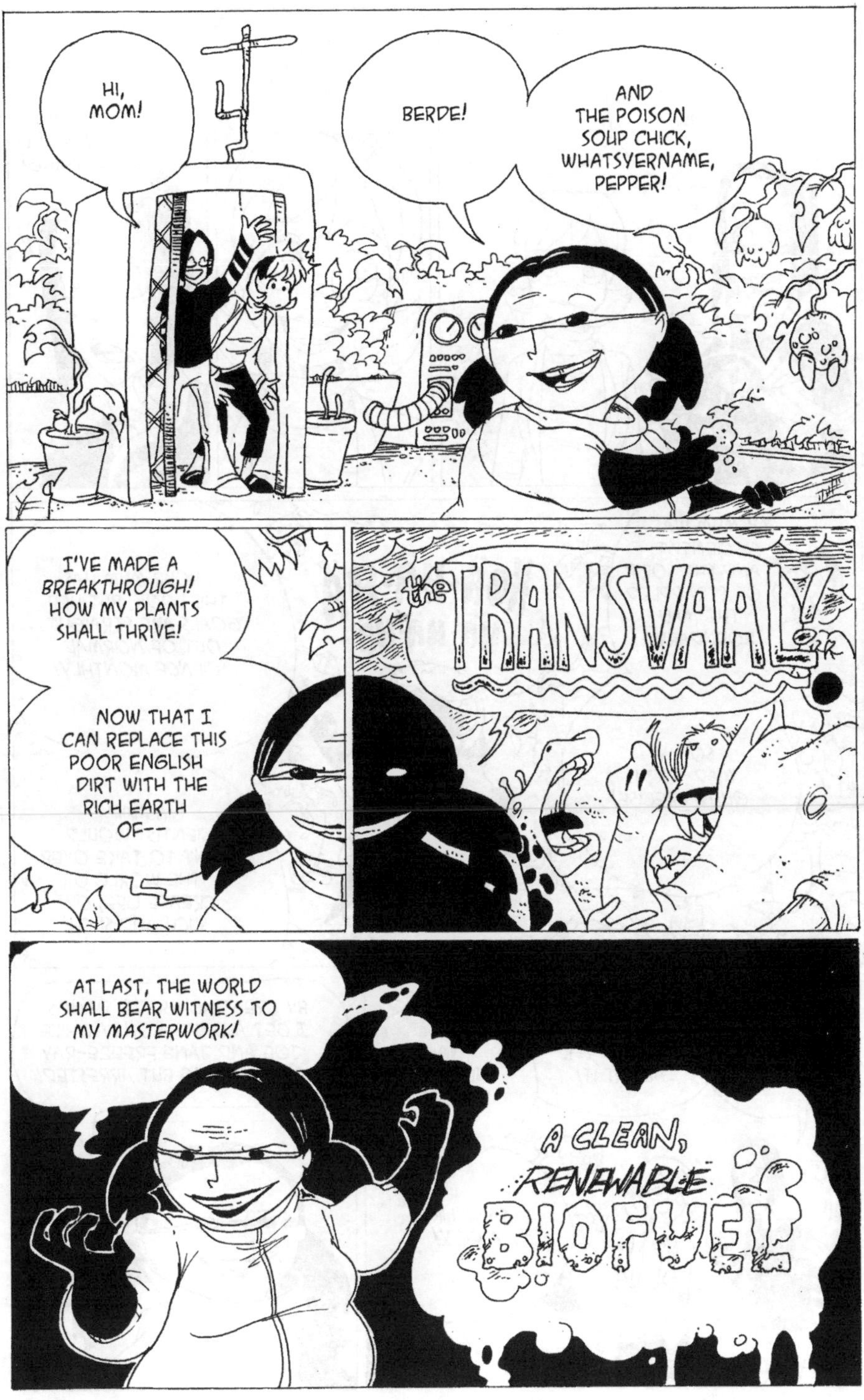
HI, MOM!
BERDE!
AND THE POISON SOUP CHICK, WHATSYERNAME, PEPPER!
I'VE MADE A BREAKTHROUGH! HOW MY PLANTS SHALL THRIVE!
NOW THAT I CAN REPLACE THIS POOR ENGLISH DIRT WITH THE RICH EARTH OF--
the TRANSVAAL!
AT LAST, THE WORLD SHALL BEAR WITNESS TO MY MASTERWORK!
A CLEAN, RENEWABLE BIOFUEL

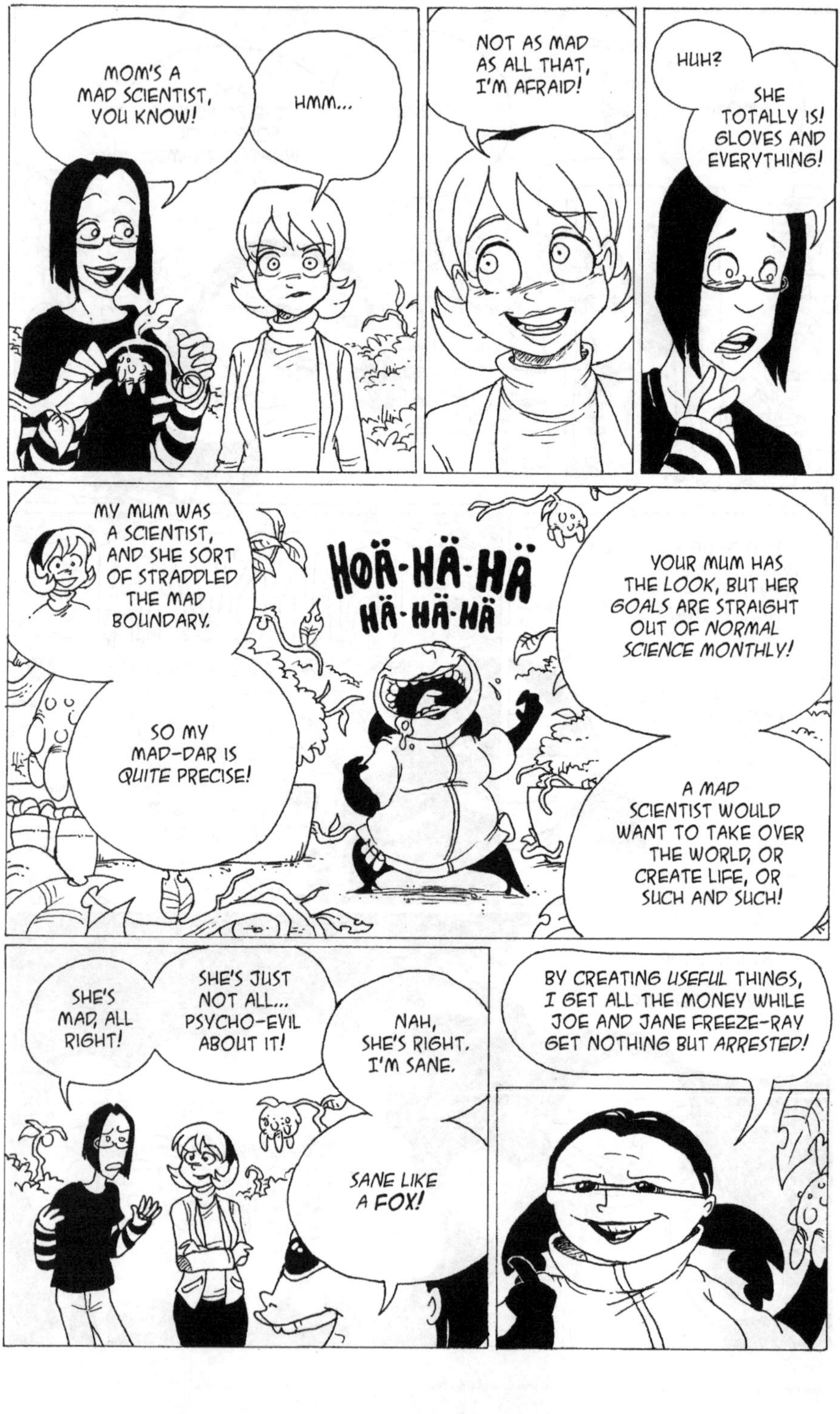
MOM'S A MAD SCIENTIST, YOU KNOW!
HMM...
NOT AS MAD AS ALL THAT, I'M AFRAID!
HUH?
SHE TOTALLY IS! GLOVES AND EVERYTHING!
MY MUM WAS A SCIENTIST, AND SHE SORT OF STRADDLED THE MAD BOUNDARY.
SO MY MAD-DAR IS QUITE PRECISE!
HOÄ-HÄ-HÄ HÄ-HÄ-HÄ
YOUR MUM HAS THE LOOK, BUT HER GOALS ARE STRAIGHT OUT OF NORMAL SCIENCE MONTHLY!
A MAD SCIENTIST WOULD WANT TO TAKE OVER THE WORLD, OR CREATE LIFE, OR SUCH AND SUCH!
SHE'S MAD, ALL RIGHT!
SHE'S JUST NOT ALL... PSYCHO-EVIL ABOUT IT!
NAH, SHE'S RIGHT. I'M SANE.
SANE LIKE A FOX!
BY CREATING USEFUL THINGS, I GET ALL THE MONEY WHILE JOE AND JANE FREEZE-RAY GET NOTHING BUT ARRESTED!

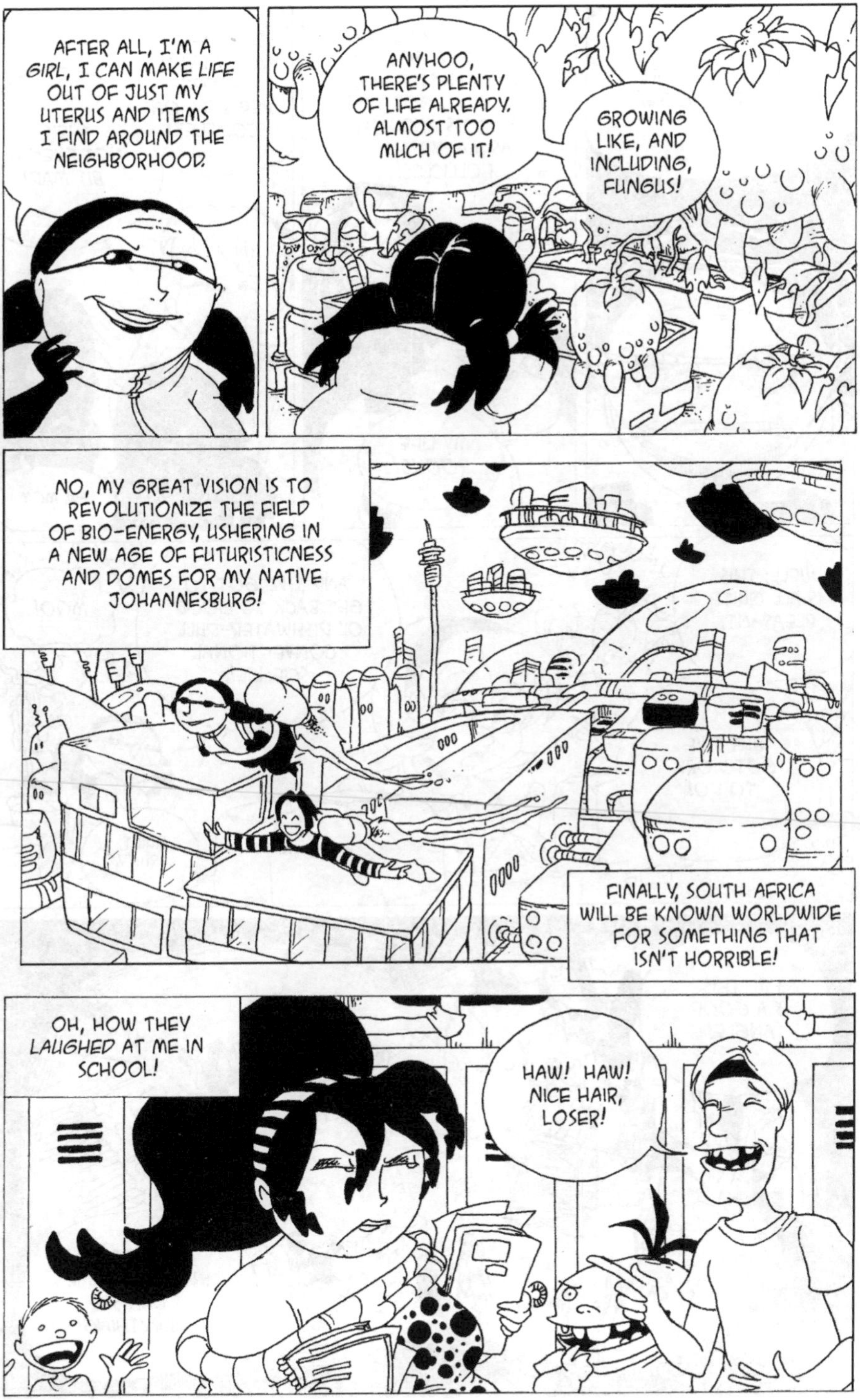
AFTER ALL, I'M A GIRL, I CAN MAKE LIFE OUT OF JUST MY UTERUS AND ITEMS I FIND AROUND THE NEIGHBORHOOD.
ANYHOO, THERE'S PLENTY OF LIFE ALREADY. ALMOST TOO MUCH OF IT!
GROWING LIKE, AND INCLUDING, FUNGUS!
NO, MY GREAT VISION IS TO REVOLUTIONIZE THE FIELD OF BIO-ENERGY, USHERING IN A NEW AGE OF FUTURISTICNESS AND DOMES FOR MY NATIVE JOHANNESBURG!
FINALLY, SOUTH AFRICA WILL BE KNOWN WORLDWIDE FOR SOMETHING THAT ISN'T HORRIBLE!
OH, HOW THEY LAUGHED AT ME IN SCHOOL!
HAW! HAW! NICE HAIR, LOSER!

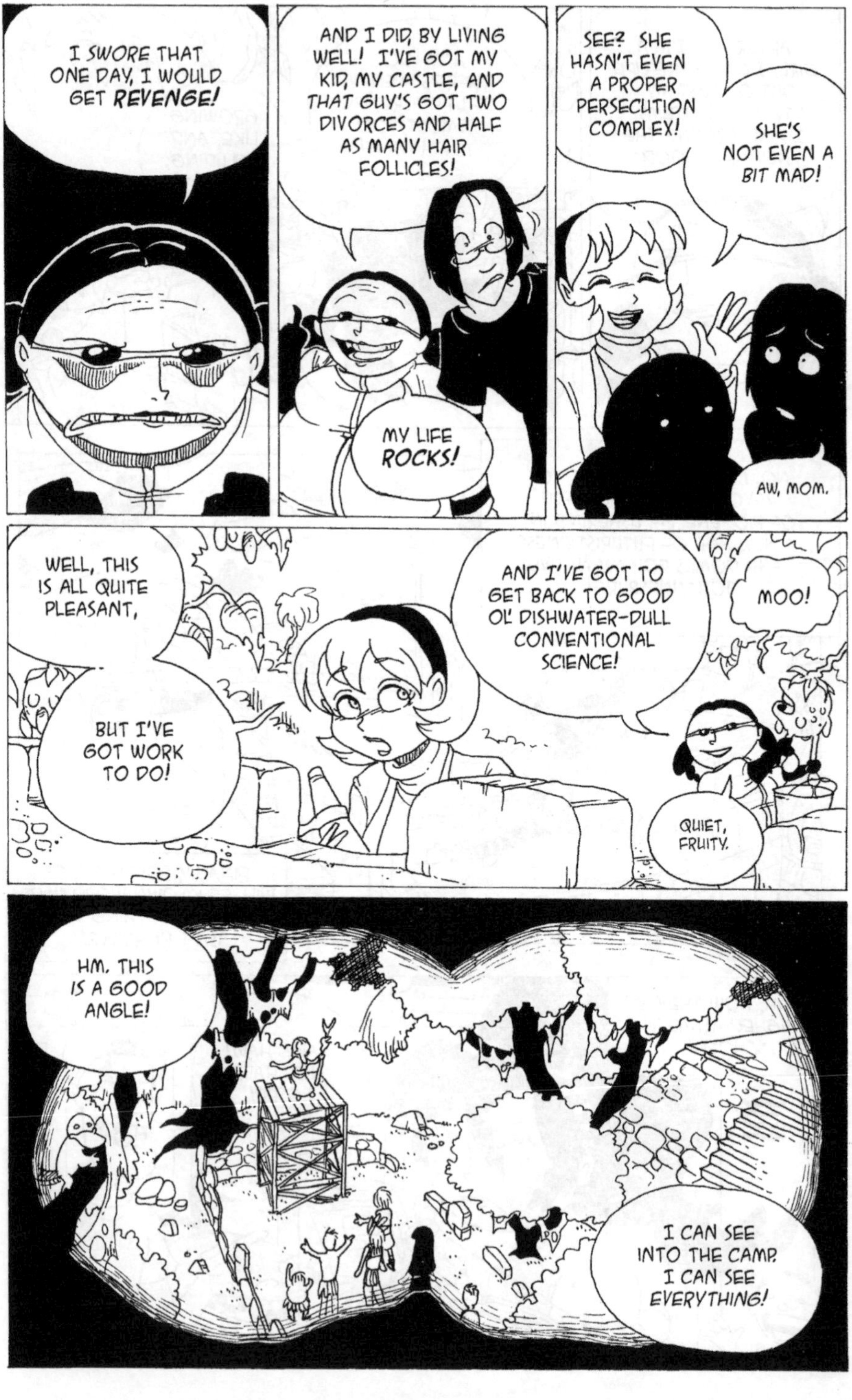
I SWORE THAT ONE DAY, I WOULD GET **REVENGE!**
AND I DID, BY LIVING WELL! I'VE GOT MY KID, MY CASTLE, AND THAT GUY'S GOT TWO DIVORCES AND HALF AS MANY HAIR FOLLICLES!
MY LIFE **ROCKS!**
SEE? SHE HASN'T EVEN A PROPER PERSECUTION COMPLEX!
SHE'S NOT EVEN A BIT MAD!
AW, MOM.
WELL, THIS IS ALL QUITE PLEASANT,
BUT I'VE GOT WORK TO DO!
AND I'VE GOT TO GET BACK TO GOOD OL' DISHWATER-DULL CONVENTIONAL SCIENCE!
MOO!
QUIET, FRUITY.
HM. THIS IS A GOOD ANGLE!
I CAN SEE INTO THE CAMP. I CAN SEE EVERYTHING!

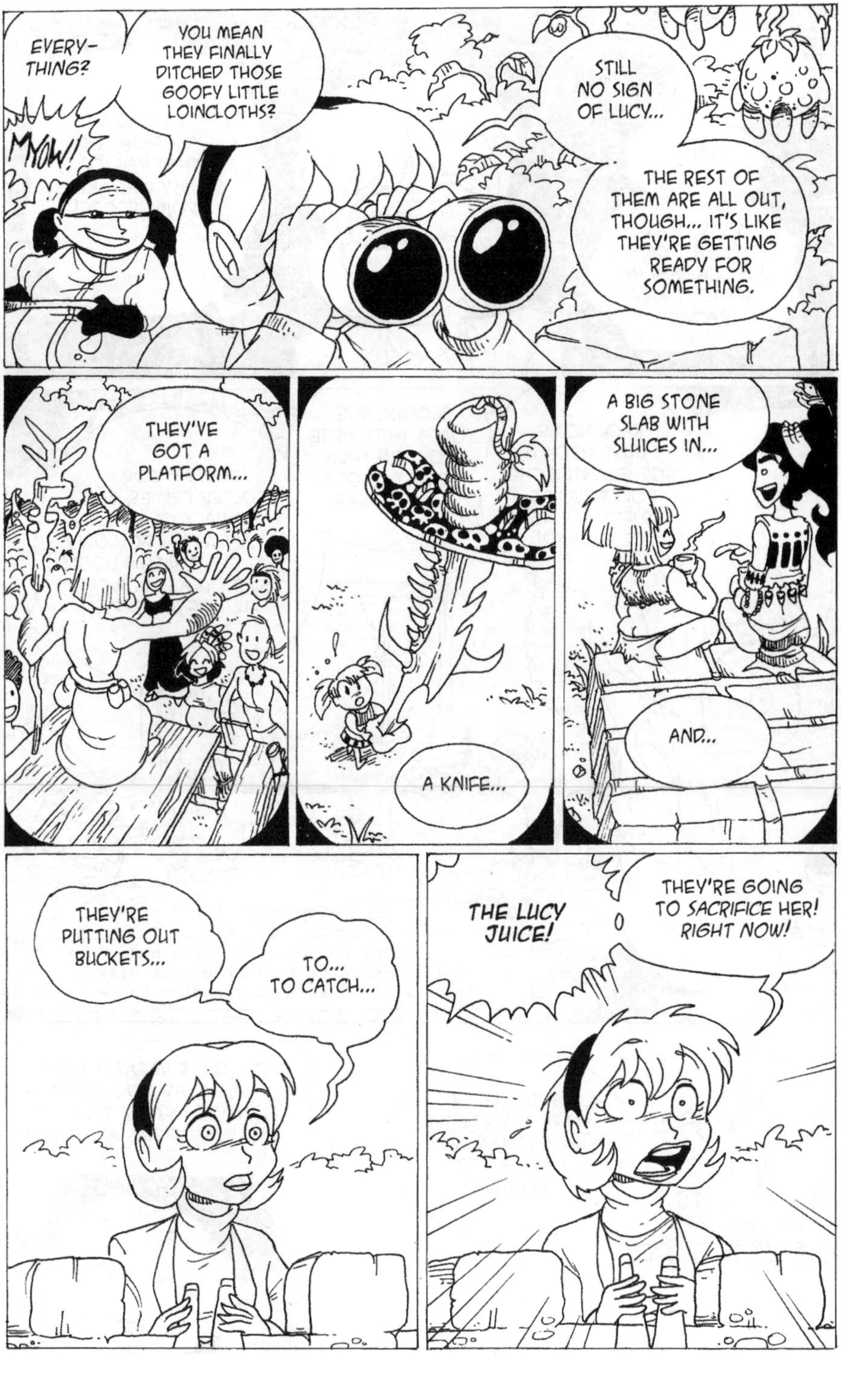

EVERY-THING?
MYOW!
YOU MEAN THEY FINALLY DITCHED THOSE GOOFY LITTLE LOINCLOTHS?
STILL NO SIGN OF LUCY...
THE REST OF THEM ARE ALL OUT, THOUGH... IT'S LIKE THEY'RE GETTING READY FOR SOMETHING.
THEY'VE GOT A PLATFORM...
A KNIFE...
A BIG STONE SLAB WITH SLUICES IN...
AND...
THEY'RE PUTTING OUT BUCKETS...
TO... TO CATCH...
THE LUCY JUICE!
THEY'RE GOING TO SACRIFICE HER! RIGHT NOW!

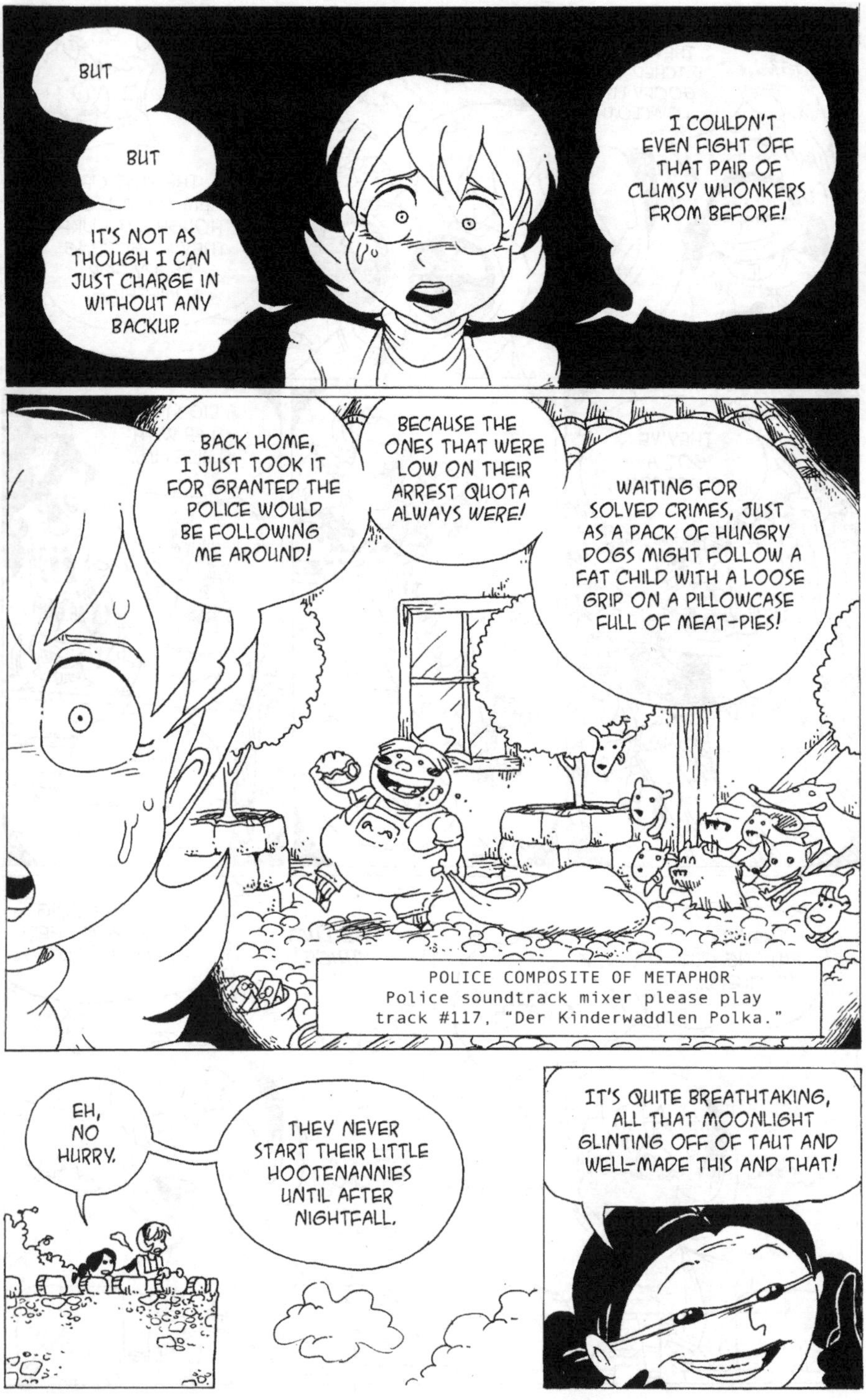
BUT
BUT
IT'S NOT AS THOUGH I CAN JUST CHARGE IN WITHOUT ANY BACKUP.
I COULDN'T EVEN FIGHT OFF THAT PAIR OF CLUMSY WHONKERS FROM BEFORE!
BACK HOME, I JUST TOOK IT FOR GRANTED THE POLICE WOULD BE FOLLOWING ME AROUND!
BECAUSE THE ONES THAT WERE LOW ON THEIR ARREST QUOTA ALWAYS WERE!
WAITING FOR SOLVED CRIMES, JUST AS A PACK OF HUNGRY DOGS MIGHT FOLLOW A FAT CHILD WITH A LOOSE GRIP ON A PILLOWCASE FULL OF MEAT-PIES!
POLICE COMPOSITE OF METAPHOR
Police soundtrack mixer please play track #117, "Der Kinderwaddlen Polka."
EH, NO HURRY.
THEY NEVER START THEIR LITTLE HOOTENANNIES UNTIL AFTER NIGHTFALL.
IT'S QUITE BREATHTAKING, ALL THAT MOONLIGHT GLINTING OFF OF TAUT AND WELL-MADE THIS AND THAT!

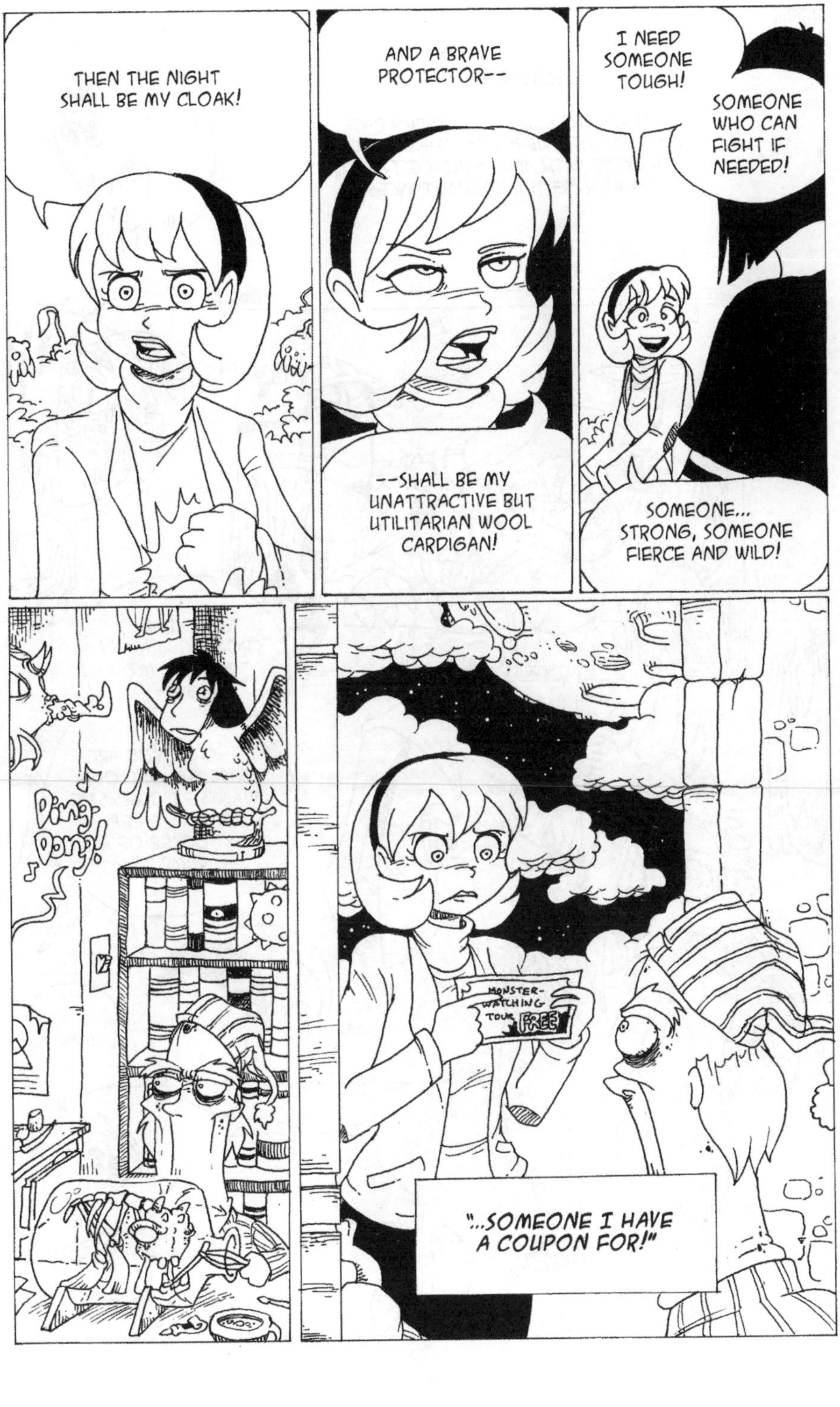
THEN THE NIGHT SHALL BE MY CLOAK!
AND A BRAVE PROTECTOR--
--SHALL BE MY UNATTRACTIVE BUT UTILITARIAN WOOL CARDIGAN!
I NEED SOMEONE TOUGH!
SOMEONE WHO CAN FIGHT IF NEEDED!
SOMEONE... STRONG, SOMEONE FIERCE AND WILD!
Ding-Dong!
MONSTER-WATCHING TOUR FREE
"...SOMEONE I HAVE A COUPON FOR!"

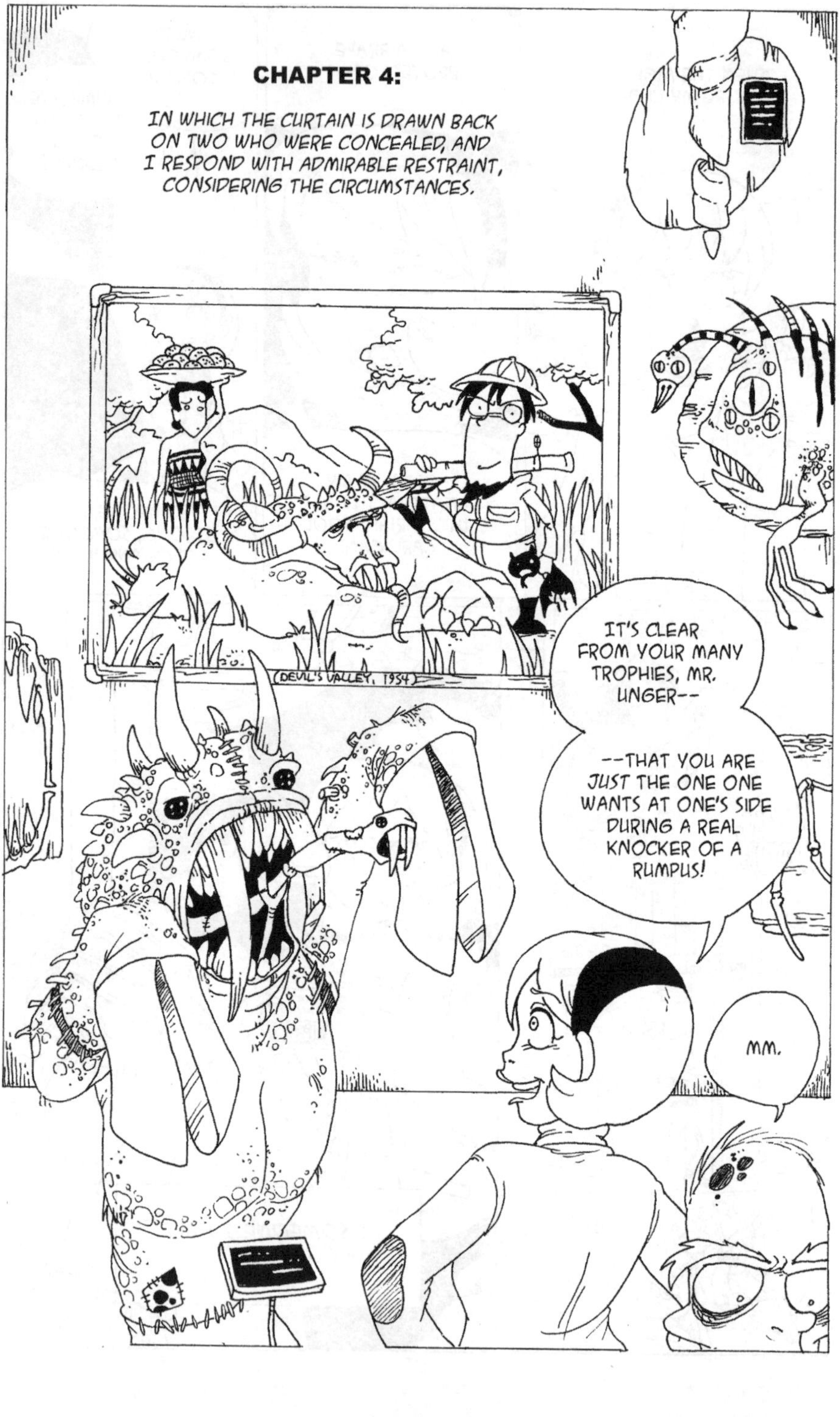
CHAPTER 4:
IN WHICH THE CURTAIN IS DRAWN BACK ON TWO WHO WERE CONCEALED, AND I RESPOND WITH ADMIRABLE RESTRAINT, CONSIDERING THE CIRCUMSTANCES.
(DEVIL'S VALLEY, 1954)
IT'S CLEAR FROM YOUR MANY TROPHIES, MR. UNGER--
--THAT YOU ARE JUST THE ONE ONE WANTS AT ONE'S SIDE DURING A REAL KNOCKER OF A RUMPUS!
MM.

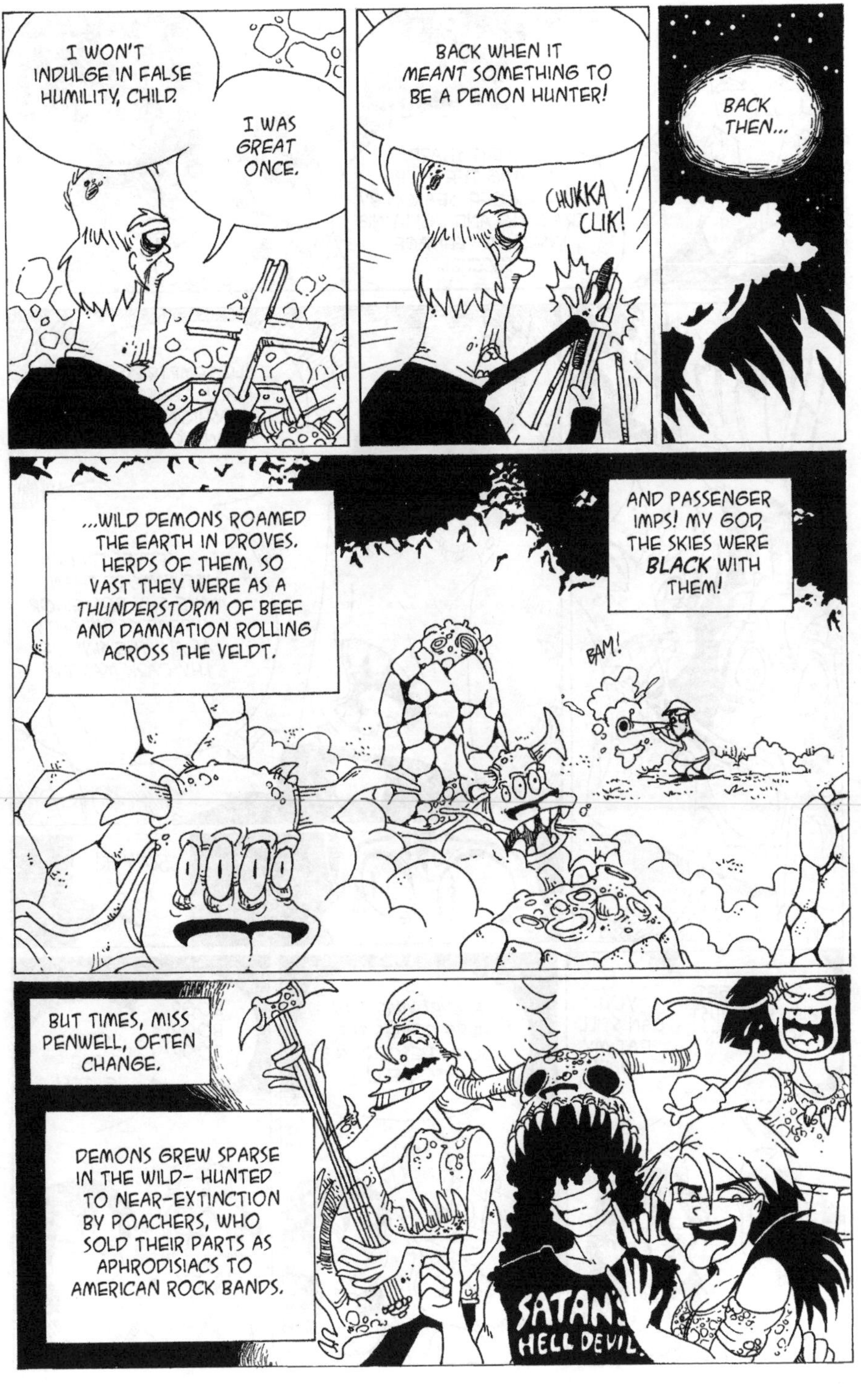
I WON'T INDULGE IN FALSE HUMILITY, CHILD.
I WAS GREAT ONCE.
BACK WHEN IT MEANT SOMETHING TO BE A DEMON HUNTER!
CHUKKA CLIK!
BACK THEN...
...WILD DEMONS ROAMED THE EARTH IN DROVES. HERDS OF THEM, SO VAST THEY WERE AS A *THUNDERSTORM* OF BEEF AND DAMNATION ROLLING ACROSS THE VELDT.
AND PASSENGER IMPS! MY GOD, THE SKIES WERE ***BLACK*** WITH THEM!
BAM!
BUT TIMES, MISS PENWELL, OFTEN CHANGE.
DEMONS GREW SPARSE IN THE WILD- HUNTED TO NEAR-EXTINCTION BY POACHERS, WHO SOLD THEIR PARTS AS APHRODISIACS TO AMERICAN ROCK BANDS.
SATAN'S HELL DEVIL

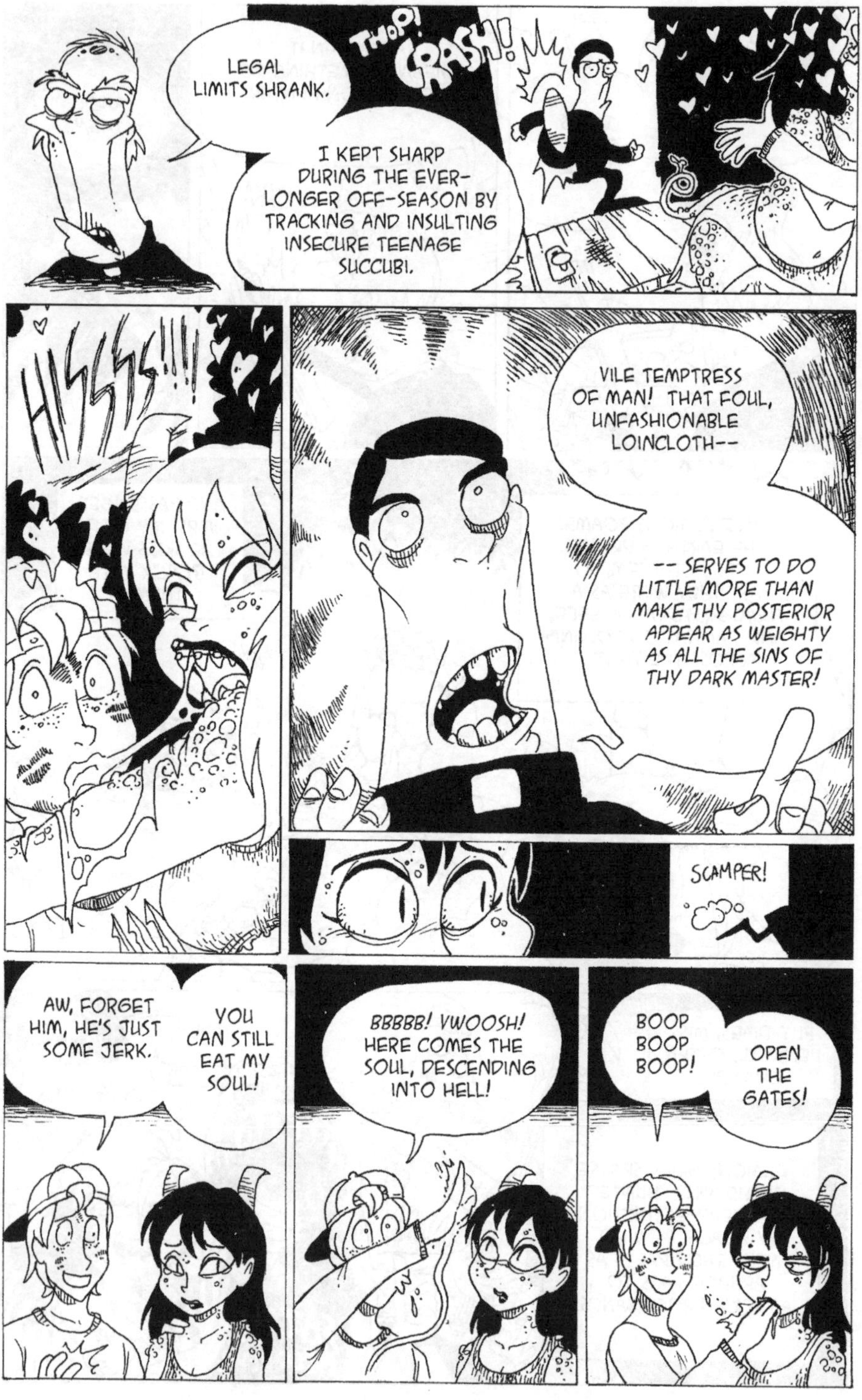
LEGAL LIMITS SHRANK.
I KEPT SHARP DURING THE EVER-LONGER OFF-SEASON BY TRACKING AND INSULTING INSECURE TEENAGE SUCCUBI.
THOP! CRASH!
HISSSS!!!!
VILE TEMPTRESS OF MAN! THAT FOUL, UNFASHIONABLE LOINCLOTH--
-- SERVES TO DO LITTLE MORE THAN MAKE THY POSTERIOR APPEAR AS WEIGHTY AS ALL THE SINS OF THY DARK MASTER!
SCAMPER!
AW, FORGET HIM, HE'S JUST SOME JERK.
YOU CAN STILL EAT MY SOUL!
BBBBB! VWOOSH! HERE COMES THE SOUL, DESCENDING INTO HELL!
BOOP BOOP BOOP!
OPEN THE GATES!

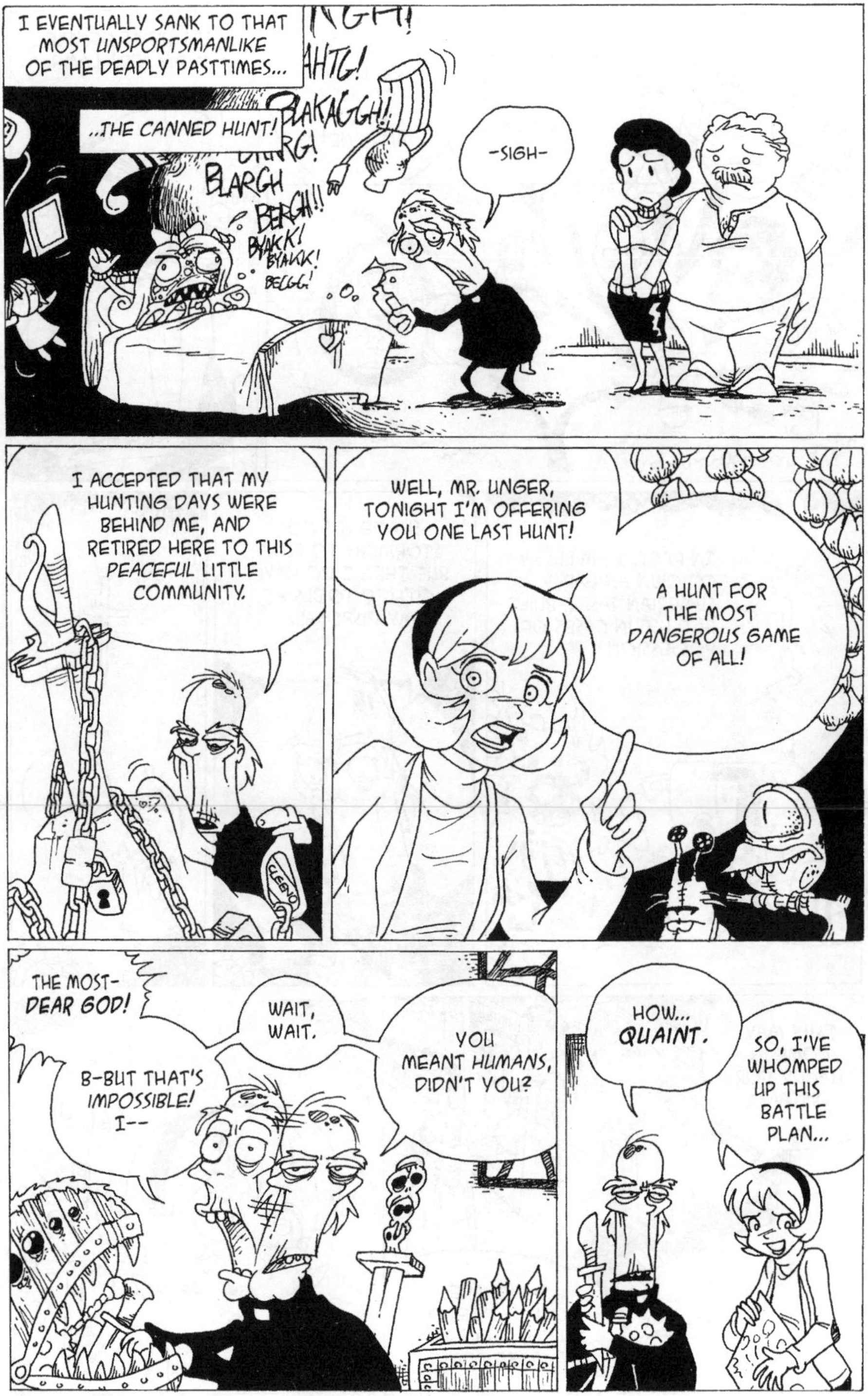
I EVENTUALLY SANK TO THAT MOST UNSPORTSMANLIKE OF THE DEADLY PASTTIMES...
...THE CANNED HUNT!
BLAKAGGH!
BLARGH
BERGH!!
BYAKK!
BYAKK!
BEGG!
-SIGH-
I ACCEPTED THAT MY HUNTING DAYS WERE BEHIND ME, AND RETIRED HERE TO THIS PEACEFUL LITTLE COMMUNITY.
WELL, MR. UNGER, TONIGHT I'M OFFERING YOU ONE LAST HUNT!
A HUNT FOR THE MOST DANGEROUS GAME OF ALL!
THE MOST- DEAR GOD!
B-BUT THAT'S IMPOSSIBLE! I--
WAIT, WAIT.
YOU MEANT HUMANS, DIDN'T YOU?
HOW... QUAINT.
SO, I'VE WHOMPED UP THIS BATTLE PLAN...

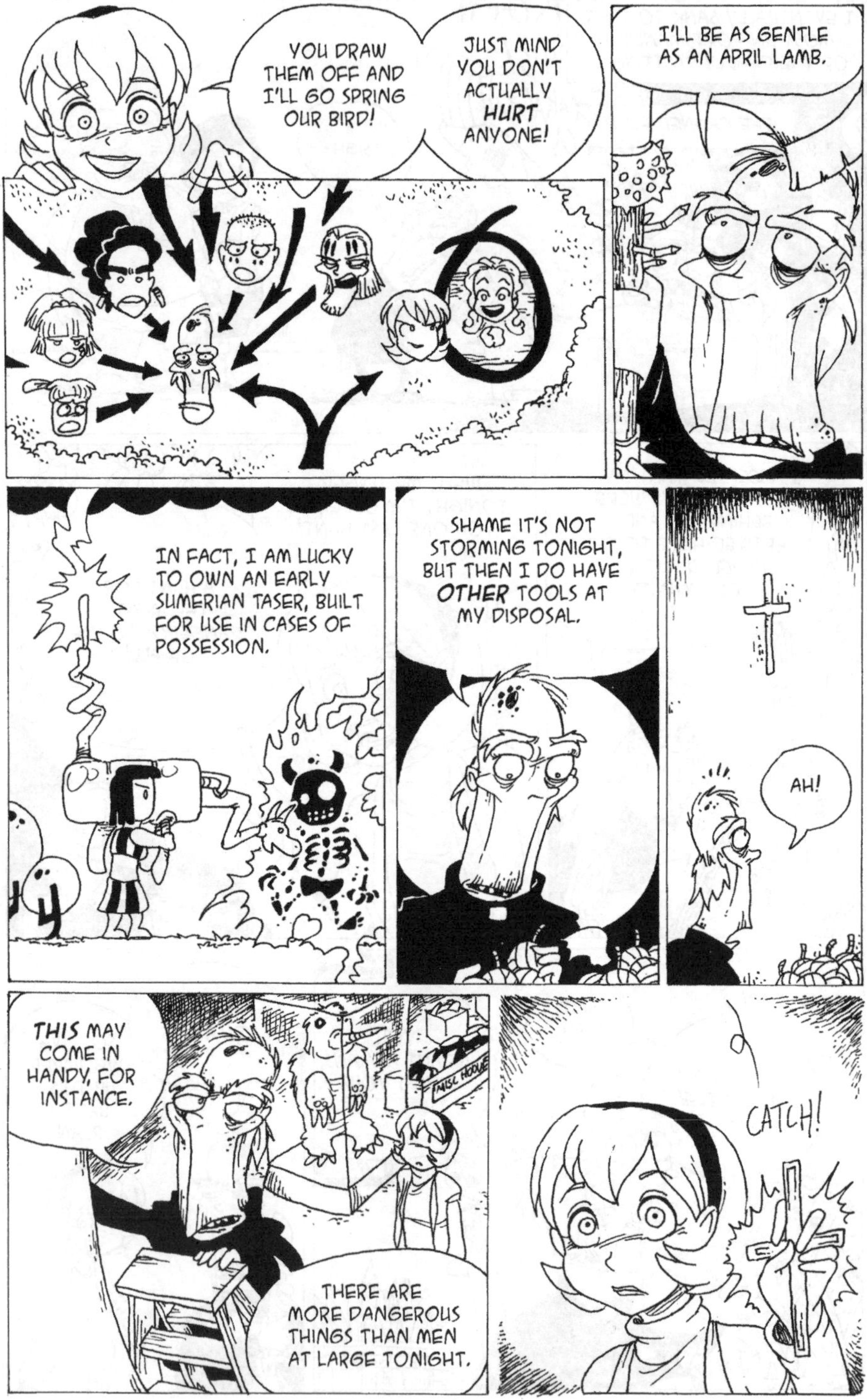
YOU DRAW THEM OFF AND I'LL GO SPRING OUR BIRD!
JUST MIND YOU DON'T ACTUALLY HURT ANYONE!
I'LL BE AS GENTLE AS AN APRIL LAMB.
IN FACT, I AM LUCKY TO OWN AN EARLY SUMERIAN TASER, BUILT FOR USE IN CASES OF POSSESSION.
SHAME IT'S NOT STORMING TONIGHT, BUT THEN I DO HAVE OTHER TOOLS AT MY DISPOSAL.
AH!
THIS MAY COME IN HANDY, FOR INSTANCE.
THERE ARE MORE DANGEROUS THINGS THAN MEN AT LARGE TONIGHT.
CATCH!

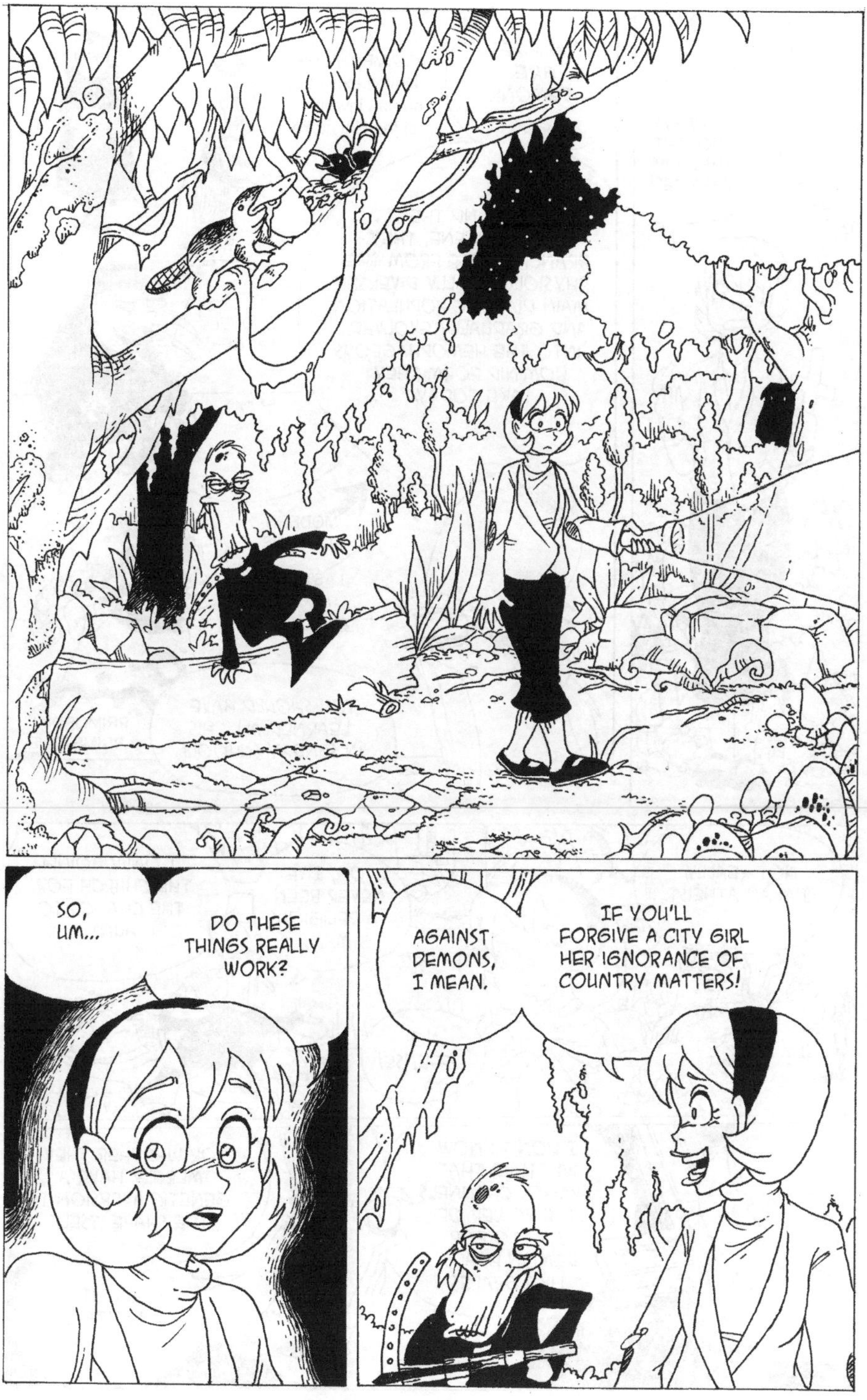
SO, UM...
DO THESE THINGS REALLY WORK?
AGAINST DEMONS, I MEAN.
IF YOU'LL FORGIVE A CITY GIRL HER IGNORANCE OF COUNTRY MATTERS!

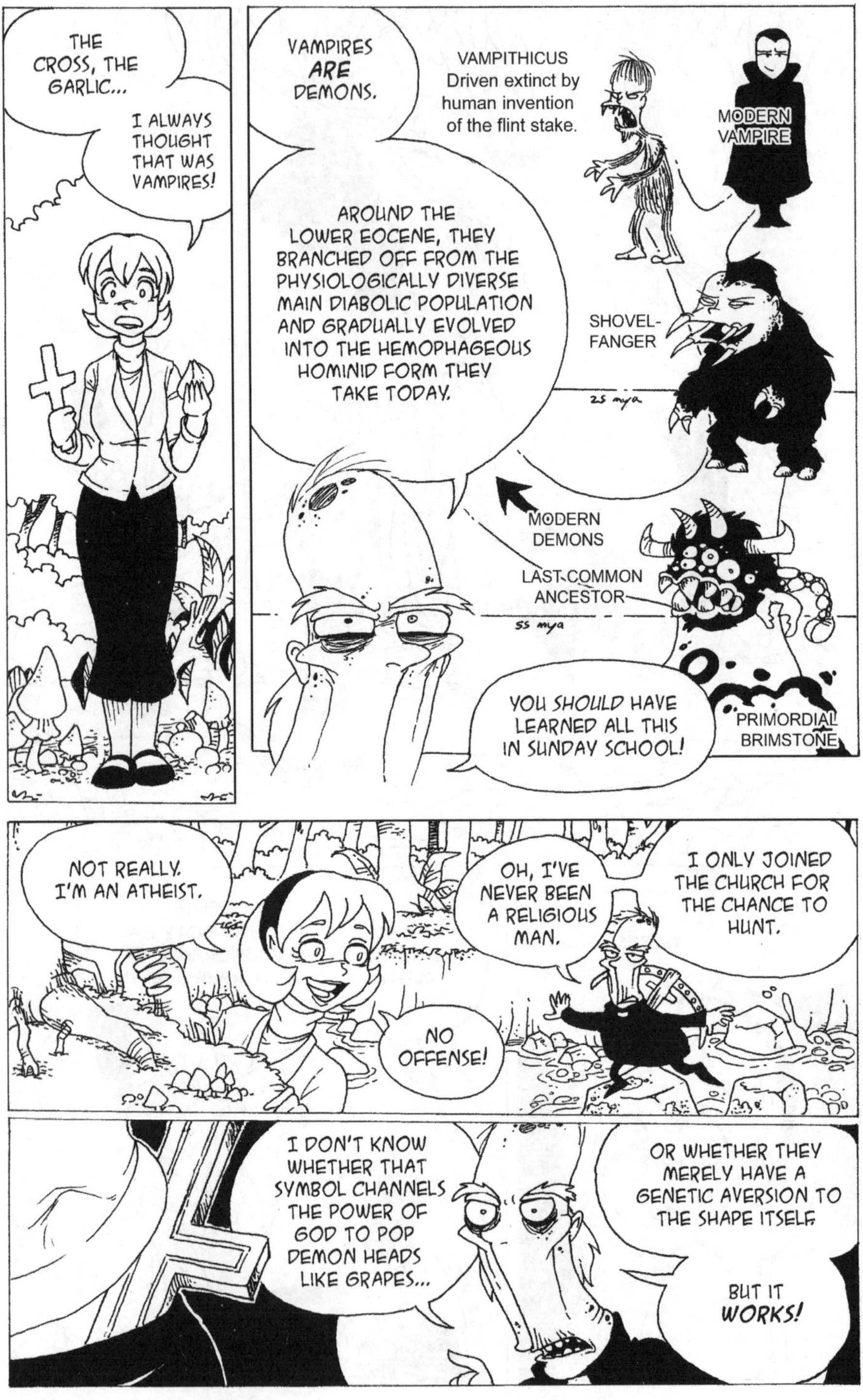
THE CROSS, THE GARLIC...
I ALWAYS THOUGHT THAT WAS VAMPIRES!
VAMPIRES ARE DEMONS.
VAMPITHICUS
Driven extinct by human invention of the flint stake.
MODERN VAMPIRE
AROUND THE LOWER EOCENE, THEY BRANCHED OFF FROM THE PHYSIOLOGICALLY DIVERSE MAIN DIABOLIC POPULATION AND GRADUALLY EVOLVED INTO THE HEMOPHAGEOUS HOMINID FORM THEY TAKE TODAY.
SHOVEL-FANGER
25 mya
MODERN DEMONS
LAST COMMON ANCESTOR
55 mya
YOU SHOULD HAVE LEARNED ALL THIS IN SUNDAY SCHOOL!
PRIMORDIAL BRIMSTONE
NOT REALLY. I'M AN ATHEIST.
NO OFFENSE!
OH, I'VE NEVER BEEN A RELIGIOUS MAN.
I ONLY JOINED THE CHURCH FOR THE CHANCE TO HUNT.
I DON'T KNOW WHETHER THAT SYMBOL CHANNELS THE POWER OF GOD TO POP DEMON HEADS LIKE GRAPES...
OR WHETHER THEY MERELY HAVE A GENETIC AVERSION TO THE SHAPE ITSELF.
BUT IT WORKS!

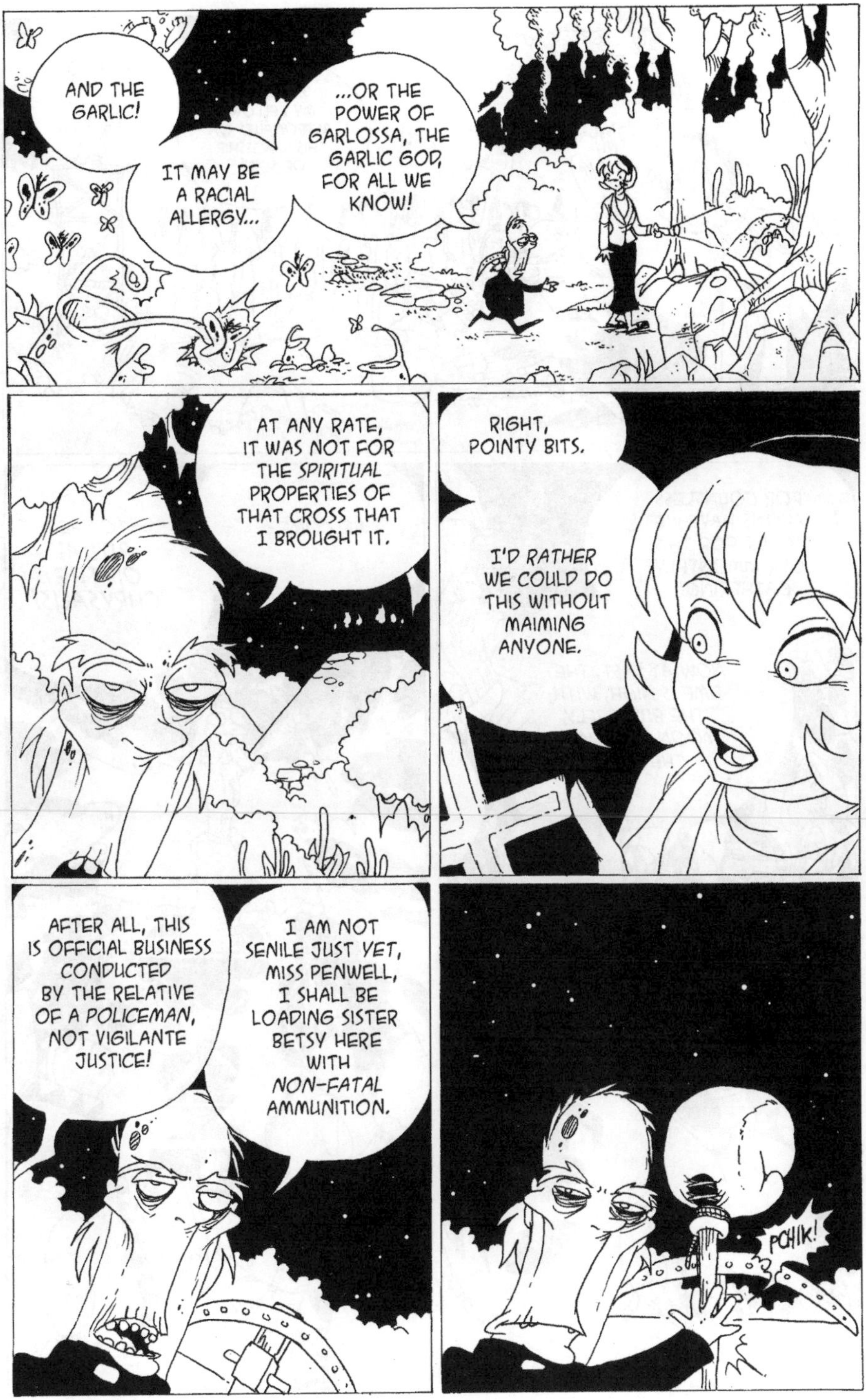
AND THE GARLIC!
IT MAY BE A RACIAL ALLERGY...
...OR THE POWER OF GARLOSSA, THE GARLIC GOD, FOR ALL WE KNOW!
AT ANY RATE, IT WAS NOT FOR THE SPIRITUAL PROPERTIES OF THAT CROSS THAT I BROUGHT IT.
RIGHT, POINTY BITS.
I'D RATHER WE COULD DO THIS WITHOUT MAIMING ANYONE.
AFTER ALL, THIS IS OFFICIAL BUSINESS CONDUCTED BY THE RELATIVE OF A POLICEMAN, NOT VIGILANTE JUSTICE!
I AM NOT SENILE JUST YET, MISS PENWELL, I SHALL BE LOADING SISTER BETSY HERE WITH NON-FATAL AMMUNITION.
PCHIK!

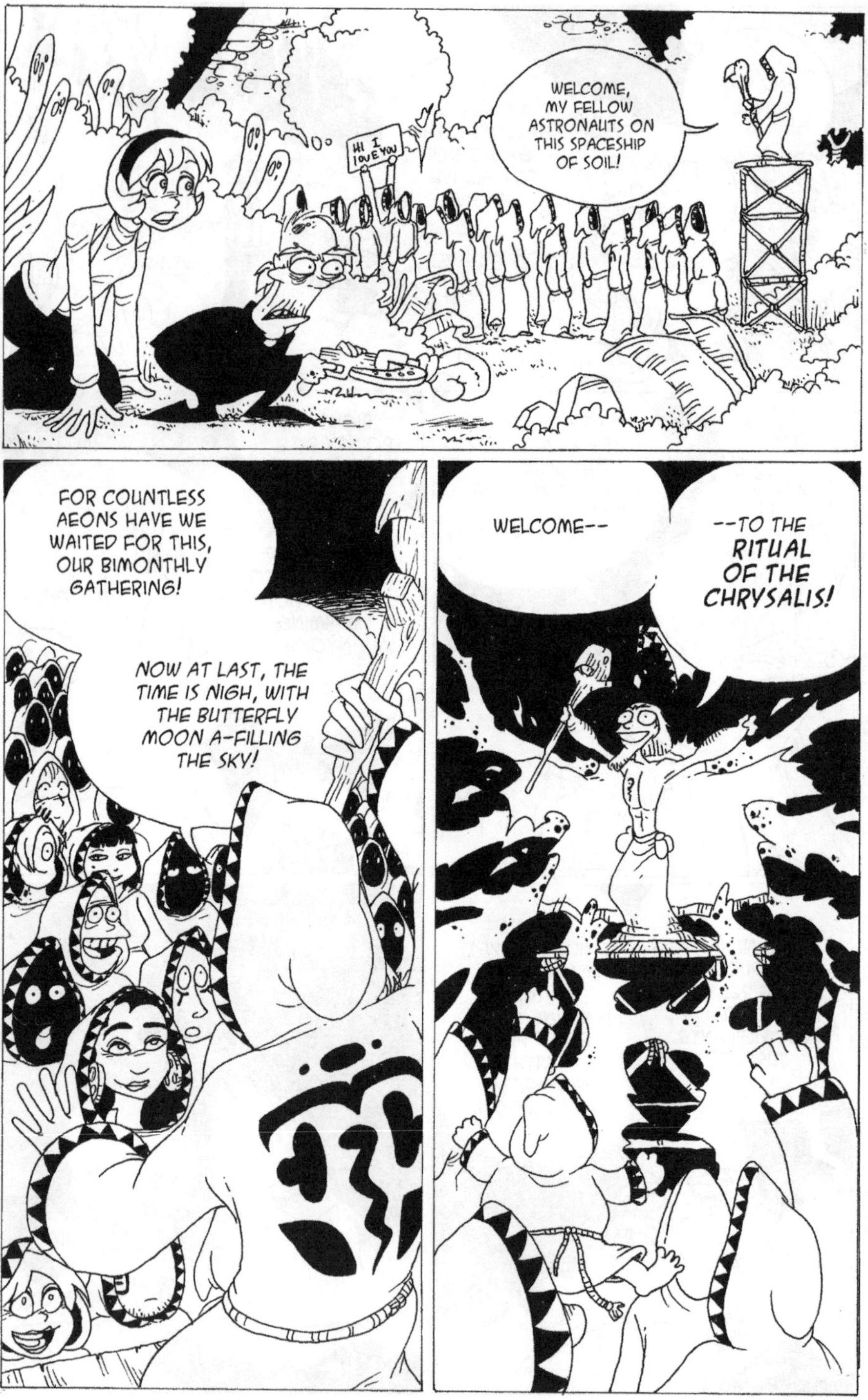
HI I LOVE YOU
WELCOME, MY FELLOW ASTRONAUTS ON THIS SPACESHIP OF SOIL!
FOR COUNTLESS AEONS HAVE WE WAITED FOR THIS, OUR BIMONTHLY GATHERING!
NOW AT LAST, THE TIME IS NIGH, WITH THE BUTTERFLY MOON A-FILLING THE SKY!
WELCOME--
--TO THE RITUAL OF THE CHRYSALIS!

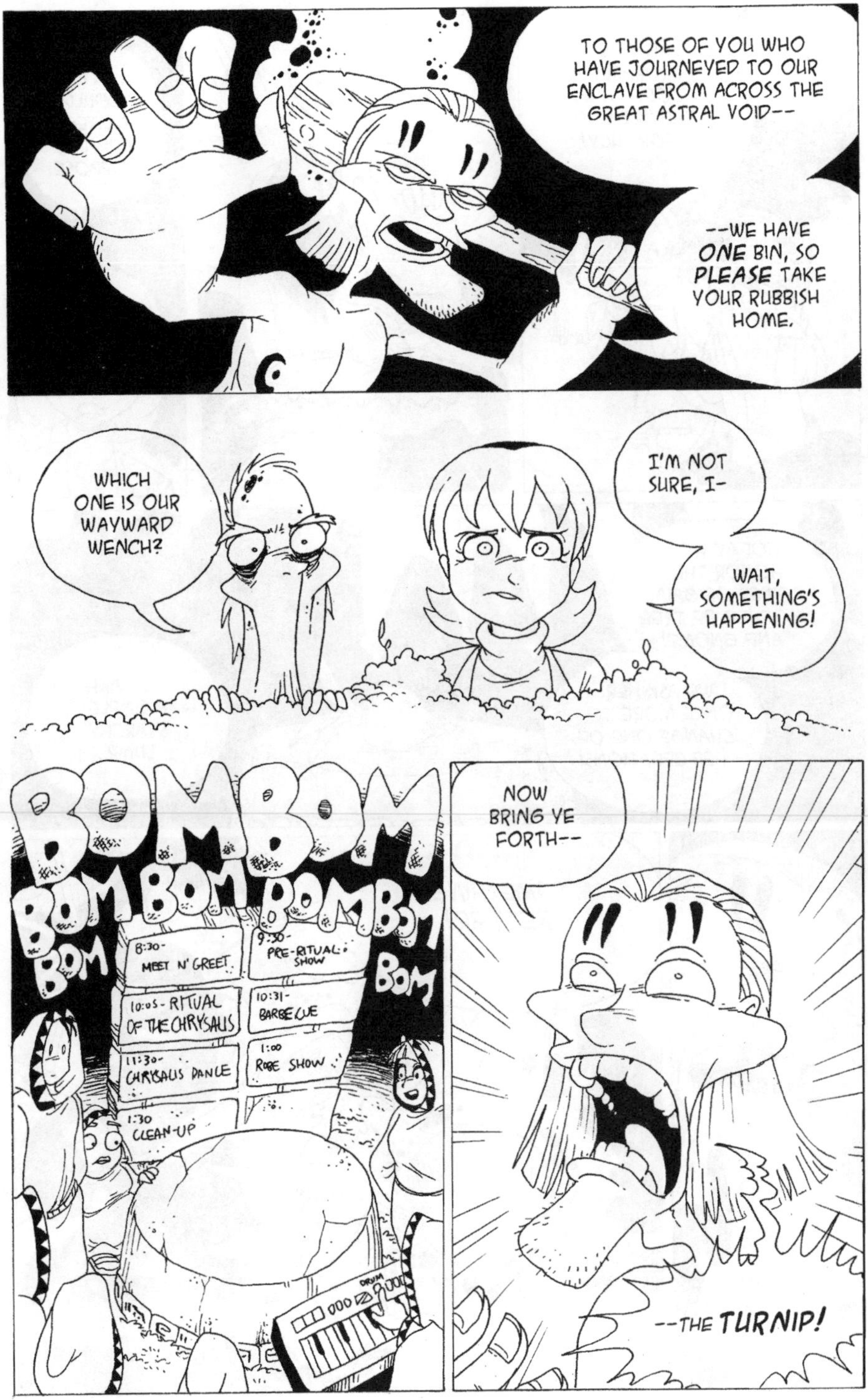
TO THOSE OF YOU WHO HAVE JOURNEYED TO OUR ENCLAVE FROM ACROSS THE GREAT ASTRAL VOID--
--WE HAVE ONE BIN, SO PLEASE TAKE YOUR RUBBISH HOME.
WHICH ONE IS OUR WAYWARD WENCH?
I'M NOT SURE, I-
WAIT, SOMETHING'S HAPPENING!
BOM BOM
BOM BOM BOM BOM
BOM BOM
8:30- MEET N' GREET
9:30- PRE-RITUAL SHOW
10:05- RITUAL OF THE CHRYSALIS
10:31- BARBECUE
11:30- CHRYSALIS DANCE
1:00 ROBE SHOW
1:30 CLEAN-UP
DRUM
NOW BRING YE FORTH--
--THE TURNIP!

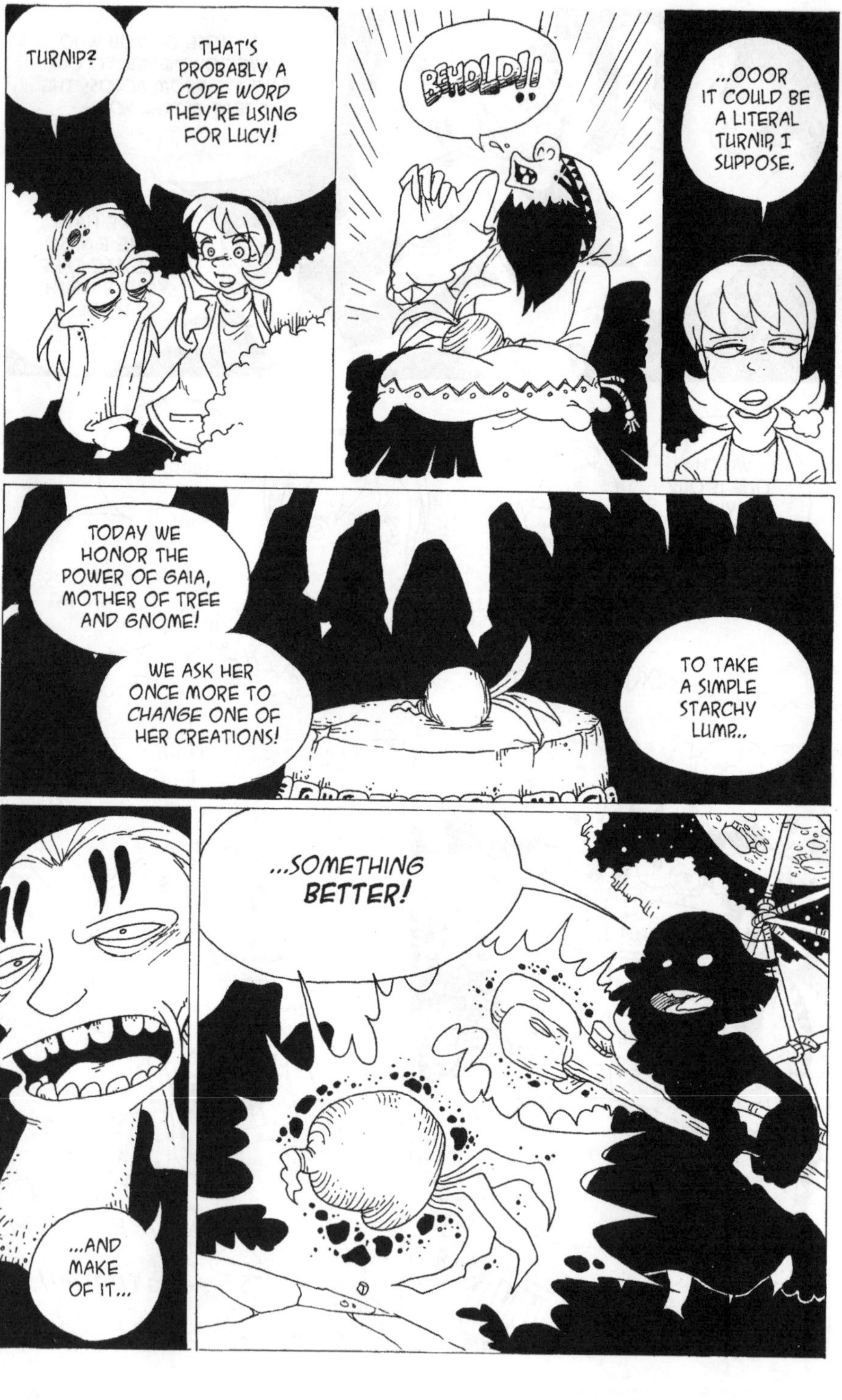
TURNIP?
THAT'S PROBABLY A CODE WORD THEY'RE USING FOR LUCY!
BEHOLD!!
...OOOR IT COULD BE A LITERAL TURNIP, I SUPPOSE.
TODAY WE HONOR THE POWER OF GAIA, MOTHER OF TREE AND GNOME!
WE ASK HER ONCE MORE TO CHANGE ONE OF HER CREATIONS!
TO TAKE A SIMPLE STARCHY LUMP..
...AND MAKE OF IT...
...SOMETHING BETTER!

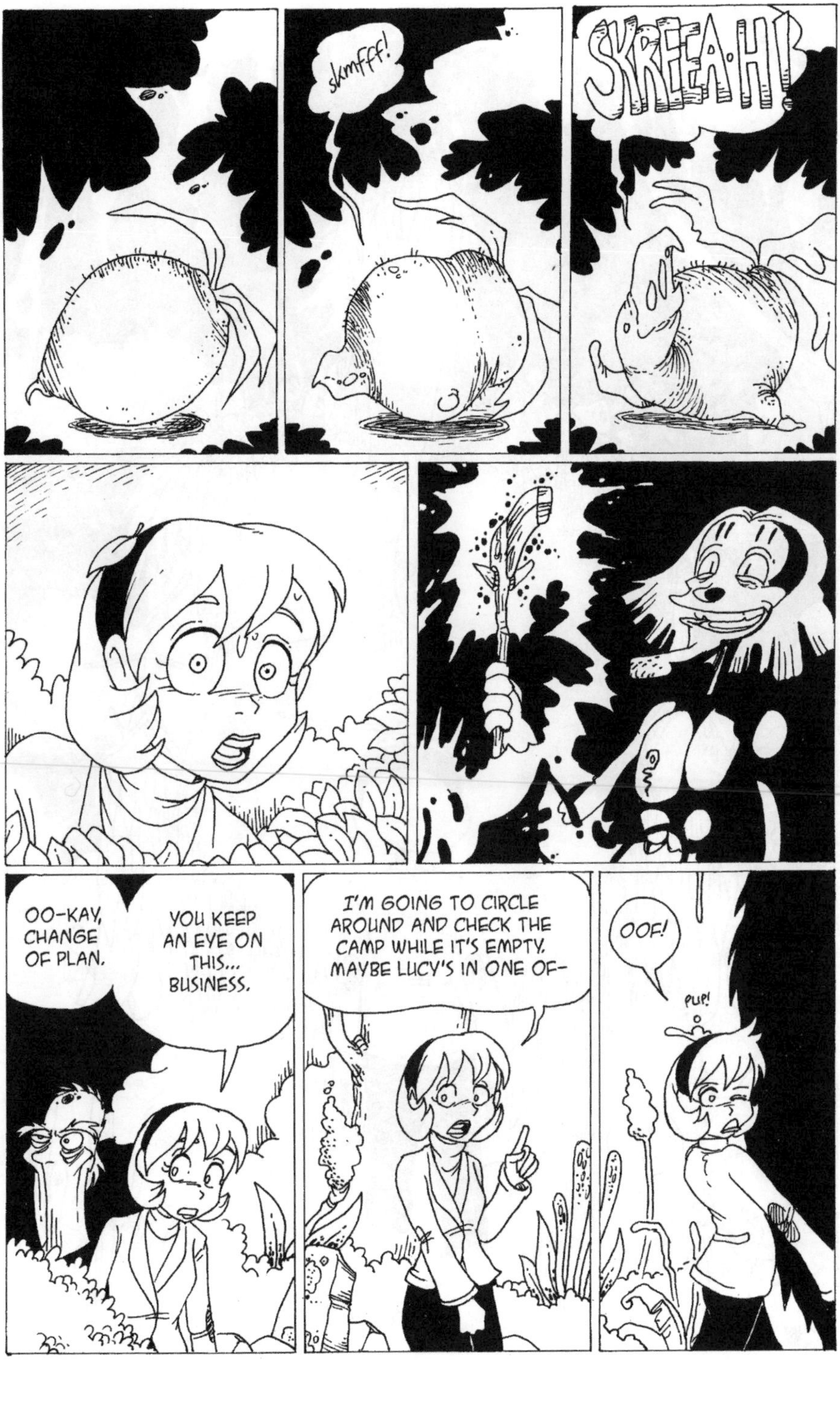
skmfff!
SKREEA-H!
OO-KAY, CHANGE OF PLAN.
YOU KEEP AN EYE ON THIS... BUSINESS.
I'M GOING TO CIRCLE AROUND AND CHECK THE CAMP WHILE IT'S EMPTY. MAYBE LUCY'S IN ONE OF-
OOF!
PLIP!

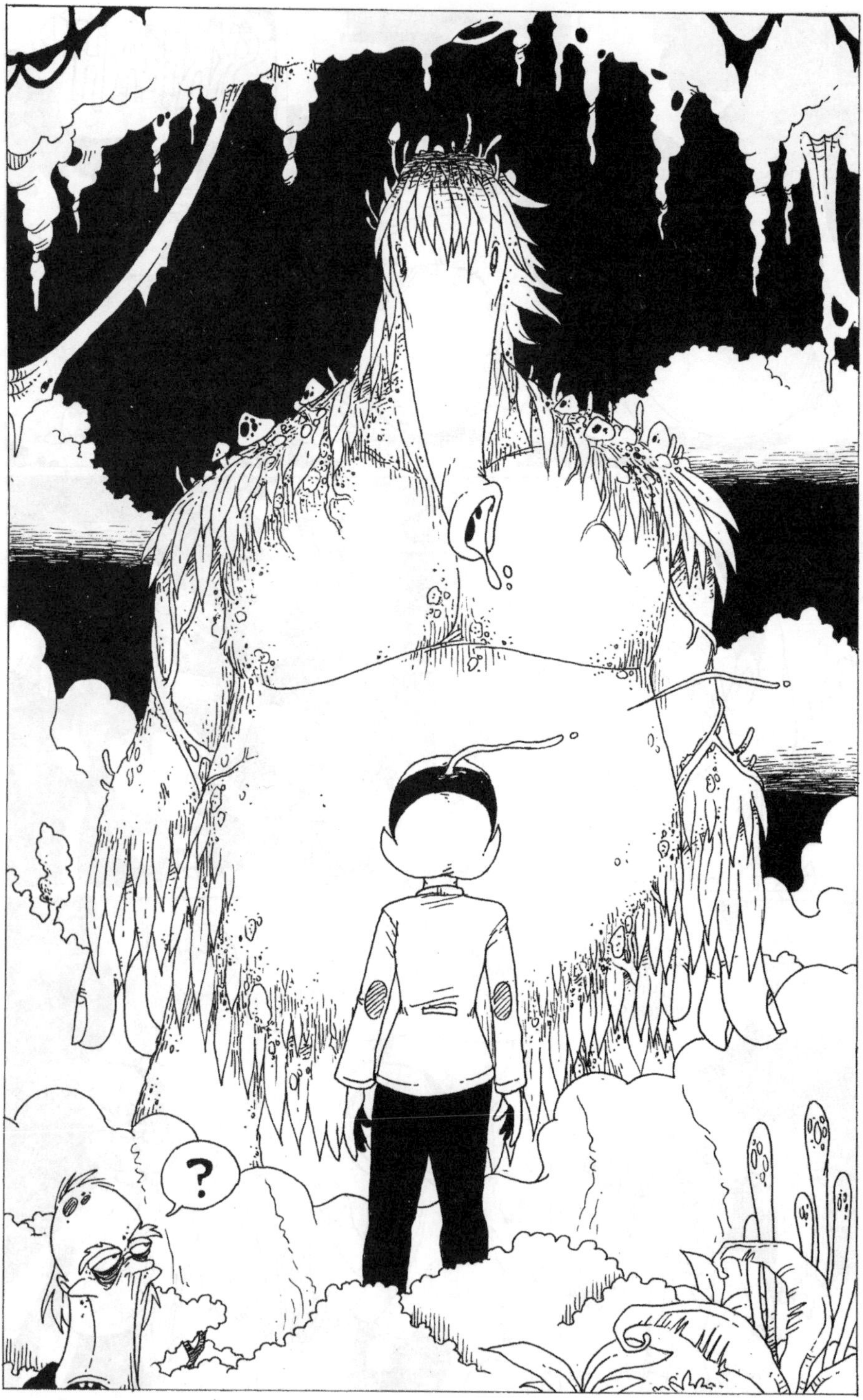
?

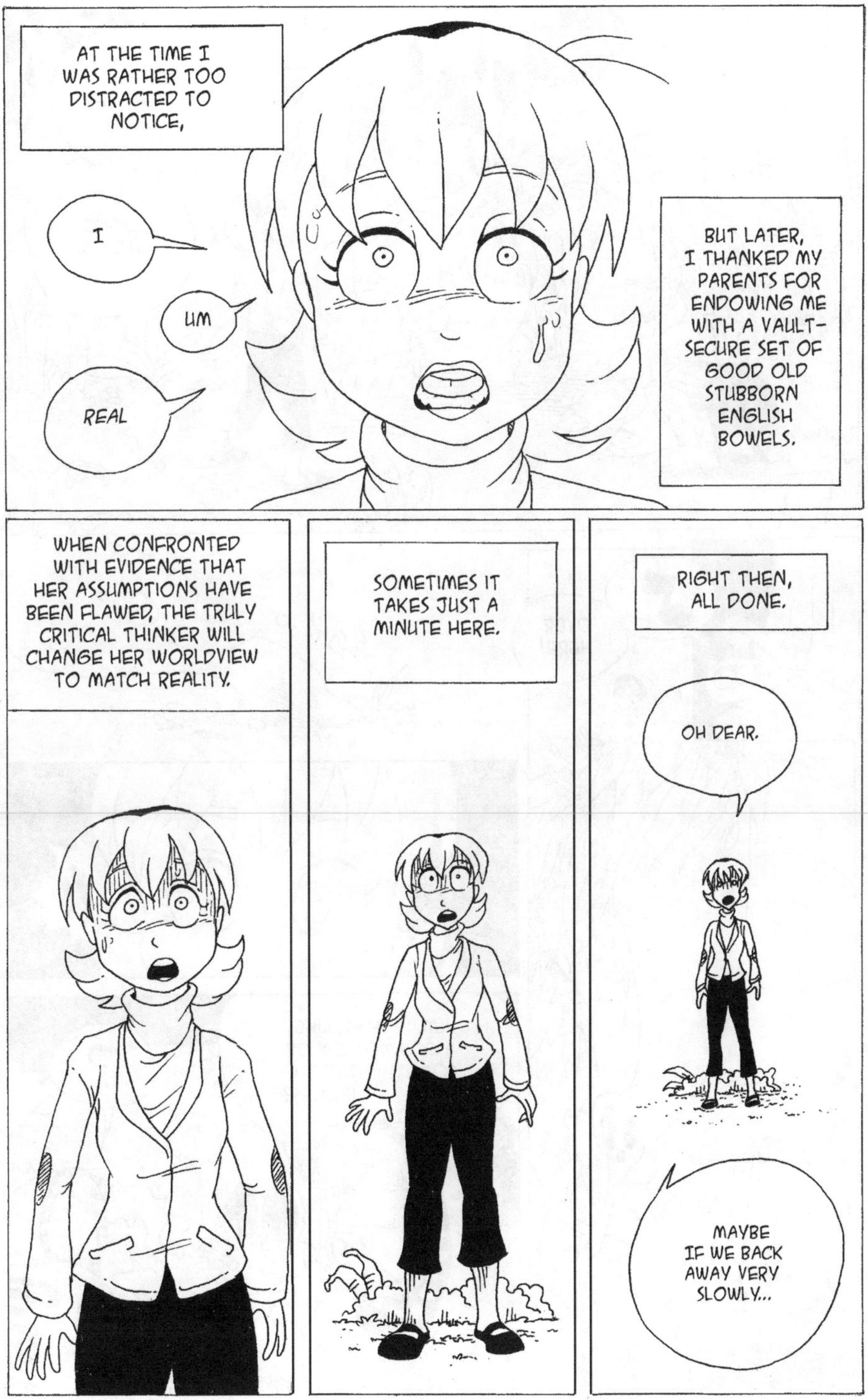

AT THE TIME I WAS RATHER TOO DISTRACTED TO NOTICE,
I
UM
REAL
BUT LATER, I THANKED MY PARENTS FOR ENDOWING ME WITH A VAULT-SECURE SET OF GOOD OLD STUBBORN ENGLISH BOWELS.
WHEN CONFRONTED WITH EVIDENCE THAT HER ASSUMPTIONS HAVE BEEN FLAWED, THE TRULY CRITICAL THINKER WILL CHANGE HER WORLDVIEW TO MATCH REALITY.
SOMETIMES IT TAKES JUST A MINUTE HERE.
RIGHT THEN, ALL DONE.
OH DEAR.
MAYBE IF WE BACK AWAY VERY SLOWLY...

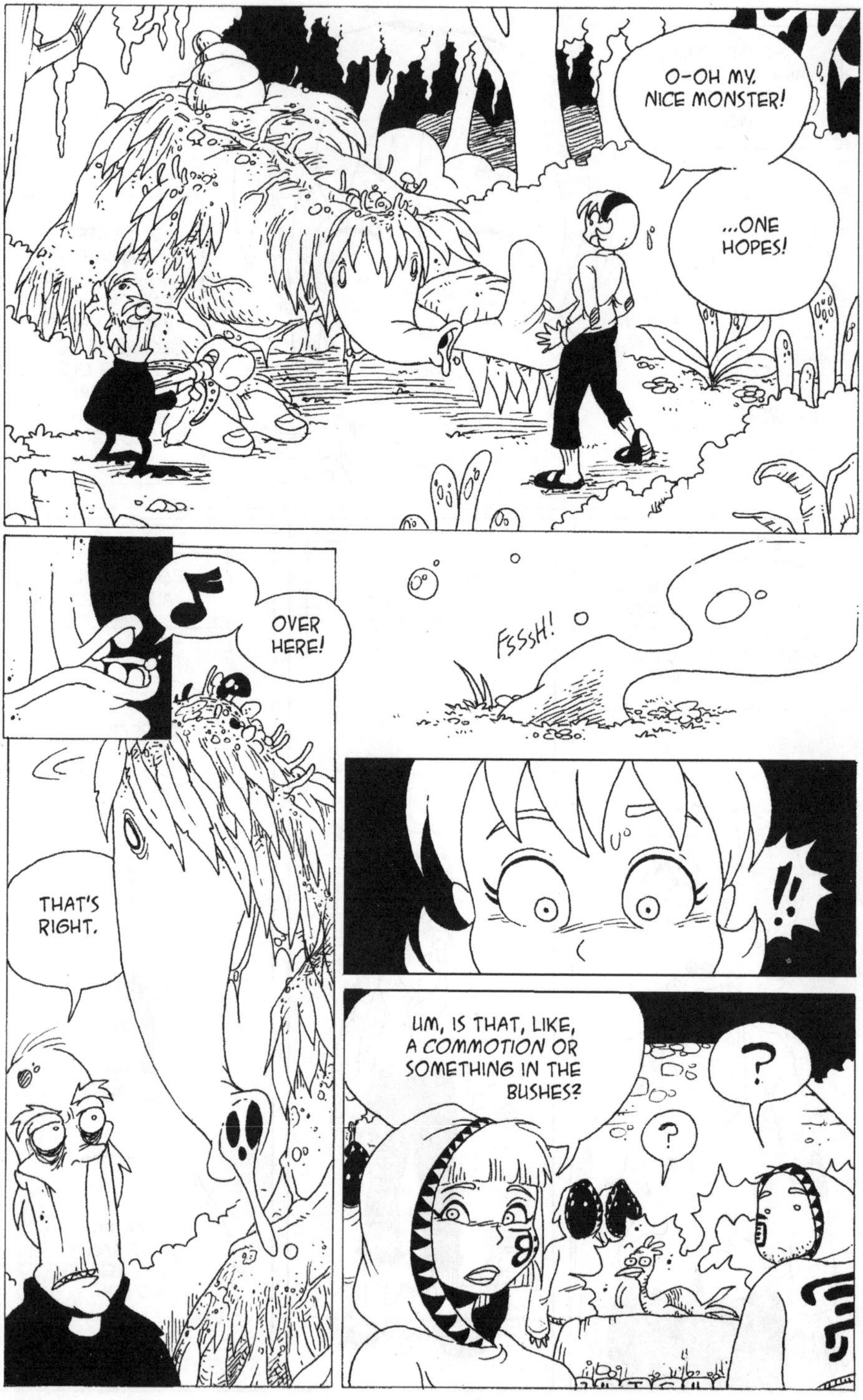
O-OH MY. NICE MONSTER!
...ONE HOPES!
OVER HERE!
FSSSH!
THAT'S RIGHT.
!!
UM, IS THAT, LIKE, A *COMMOTION* OR SOMETHING IN THE BUSHES?
?
?

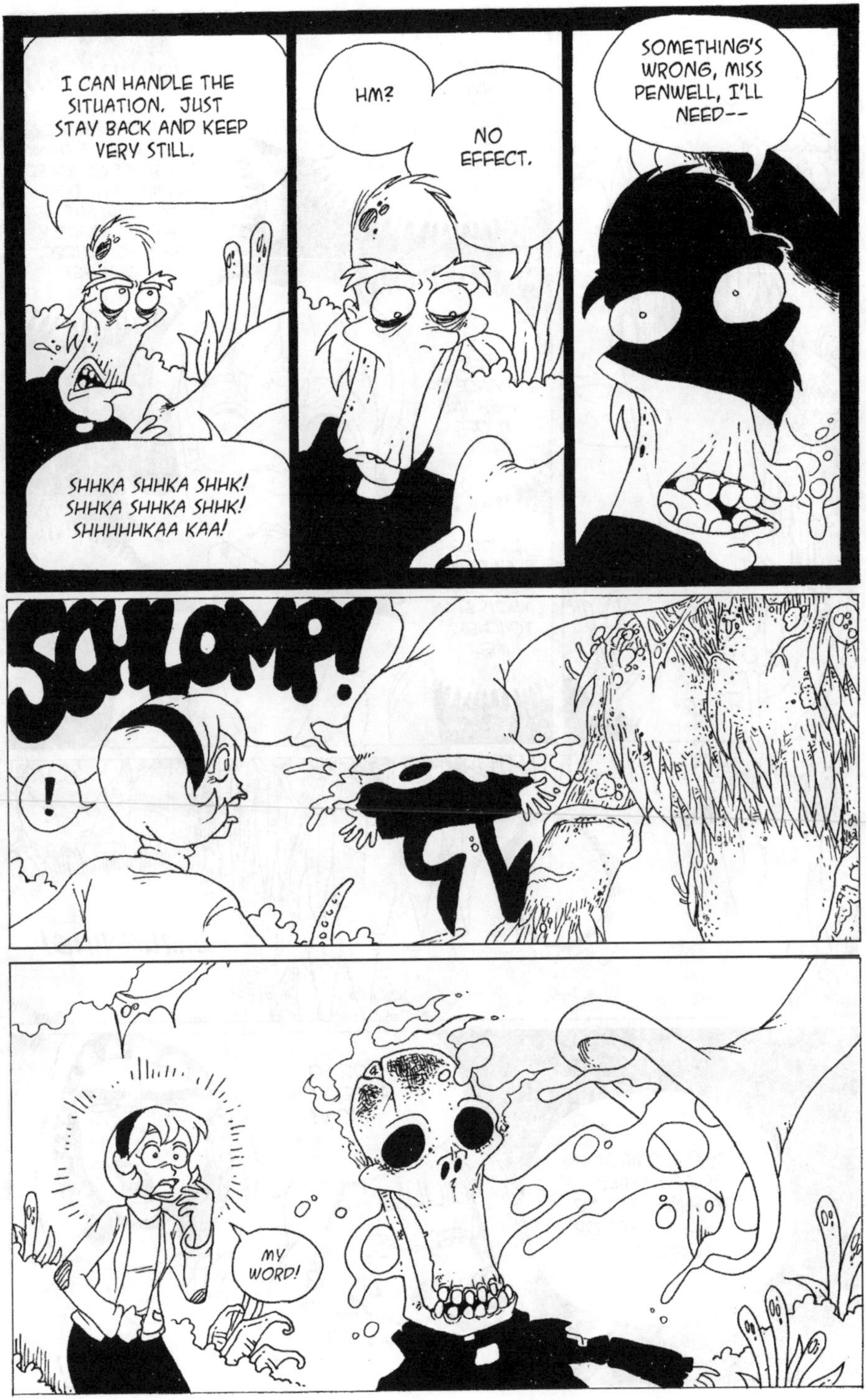
I CAN HANDLE THE SITUATION. JUST STAY BACK AND KEEP VERY STILL.
SHHKA SHHKA SHHK! SHHKA SHHKA SHHK! SHHHHHKAA KAA!
HM?
NO EFFECT.
SOMETHING'S WRONG, MISS PENWELL, I'LL NEED--
SCHLOMP!
!
MY WORD!

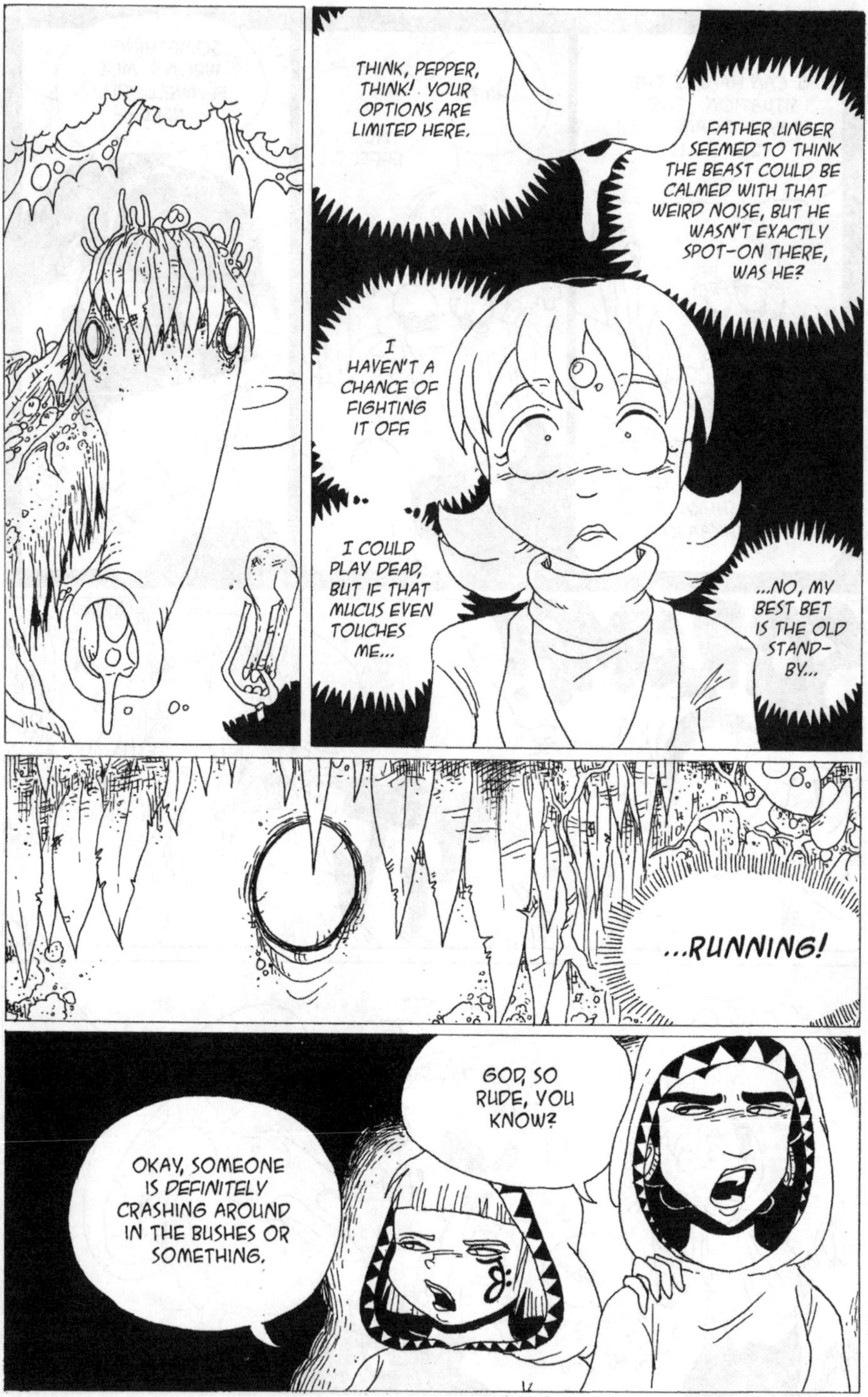

THINK, PEPPER, THINK! YOUR OPTIONS ARE LIMITED HERE.
FATHER UNGER SEEMED TO THINK THE BEAST COULD BE CALMED WITH THAT WEIRD NOISE, BUT HE WASN'T EXACTLY SPOT-ON THERE, WAS HE?
I HAVEN'T A CHANCE OF FIGHTING IT OFF.
I COULD PLAY DEAD, BUT IF THAT MUCUS EVEN TOUCHES ME...
...NO, MY BEST BET IS THE OLD STAND-BY...
...RUNNING!
OKAY, SOMEONE IS DEFINITELY CRASHING AROUND IN THE BUSHES OR SOMETHING.
GOD, SO RUDE, YOU KNOW?

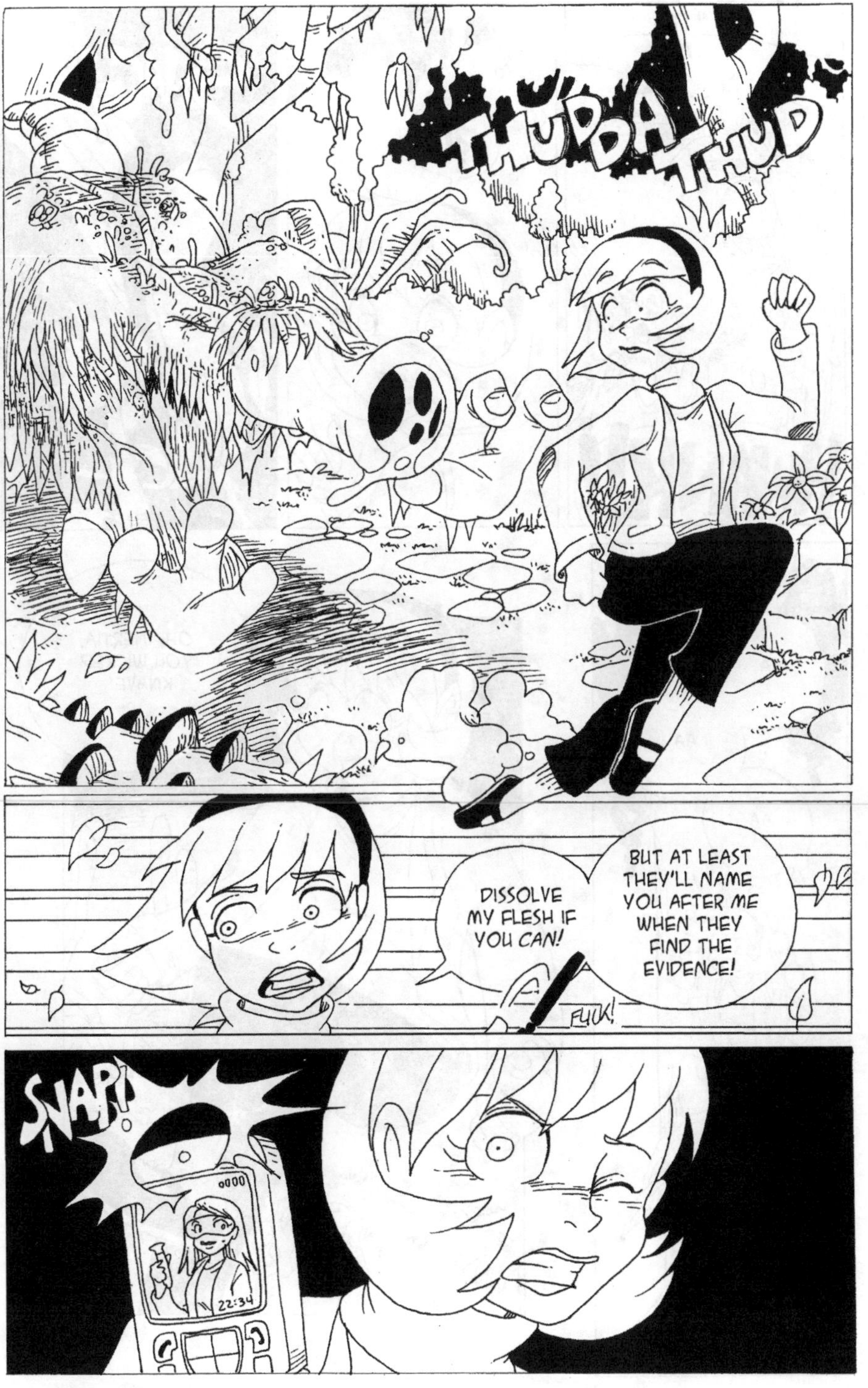

THUDDA THUD
DISSOLVE MY FLESH IF YOU CAN!
BUT AT LEAST THEY'LL NAME YOU AFTER ME WHEN THEY FIND THE EVIDENCE!
FLICK!
SNAP!
22:34

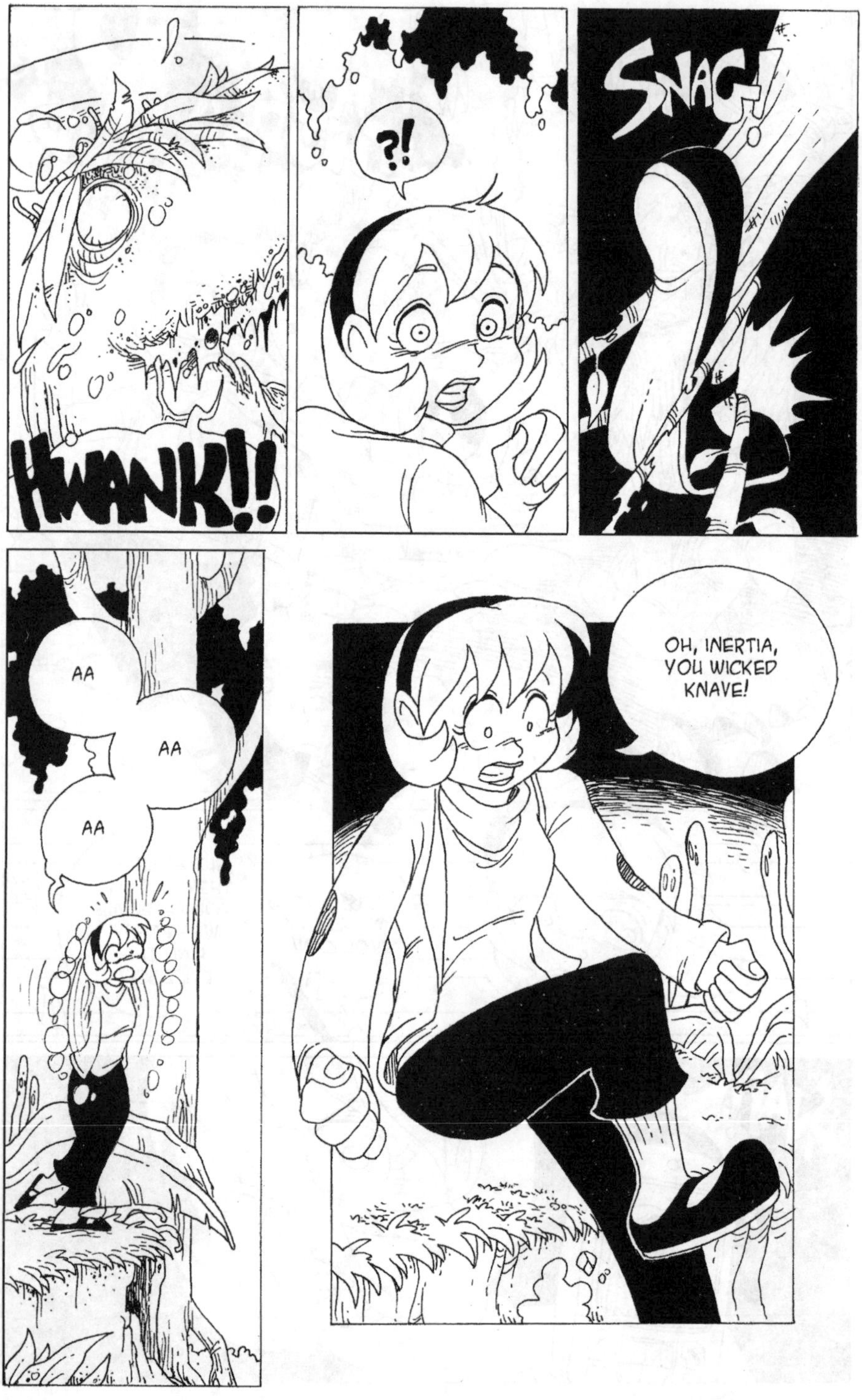
HWANK!!
?!
SNAG!
AA
AA
AA
OH, INERTIA, YOU WICKED KNAVE!

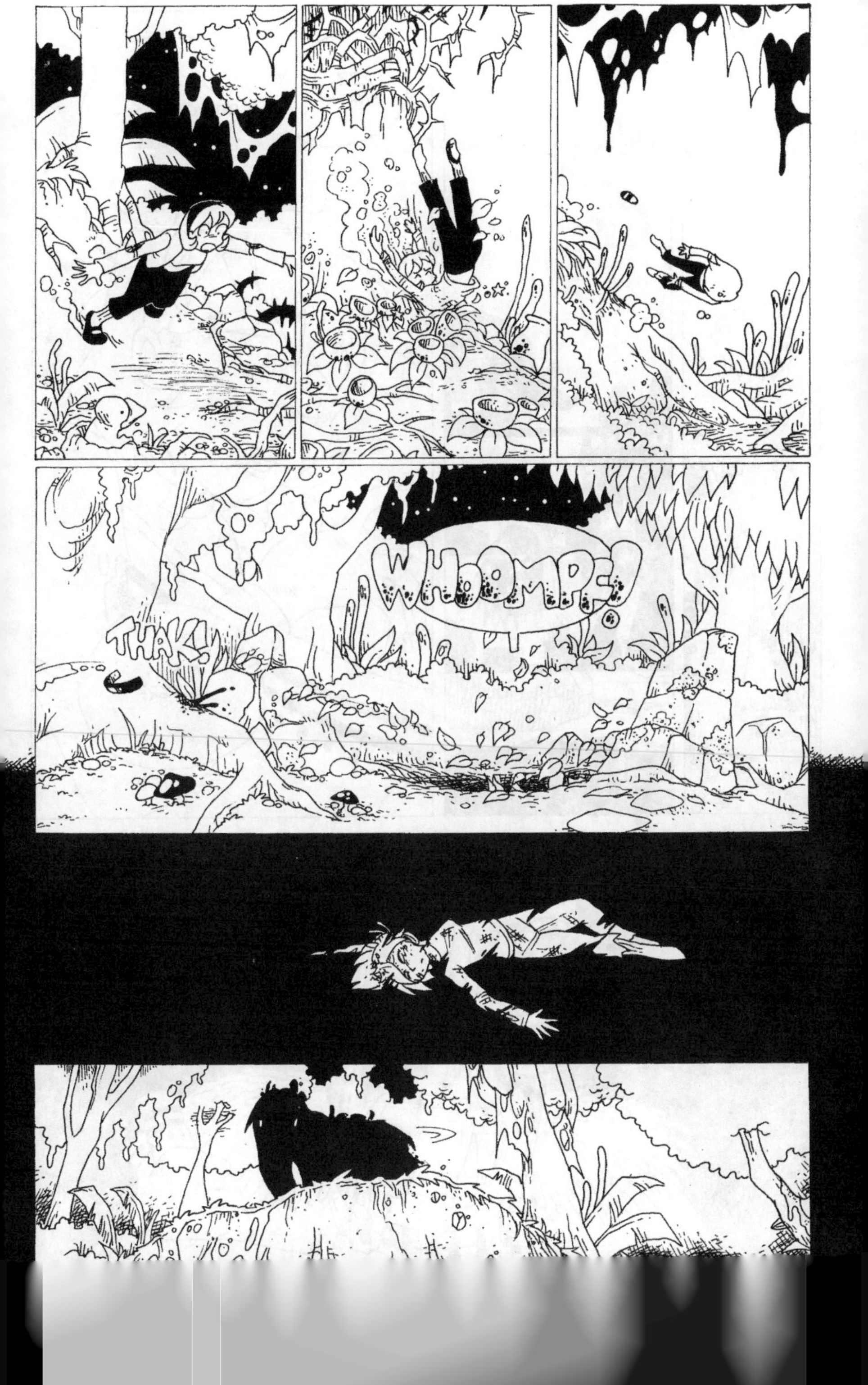
WHOMPF!
THAK!

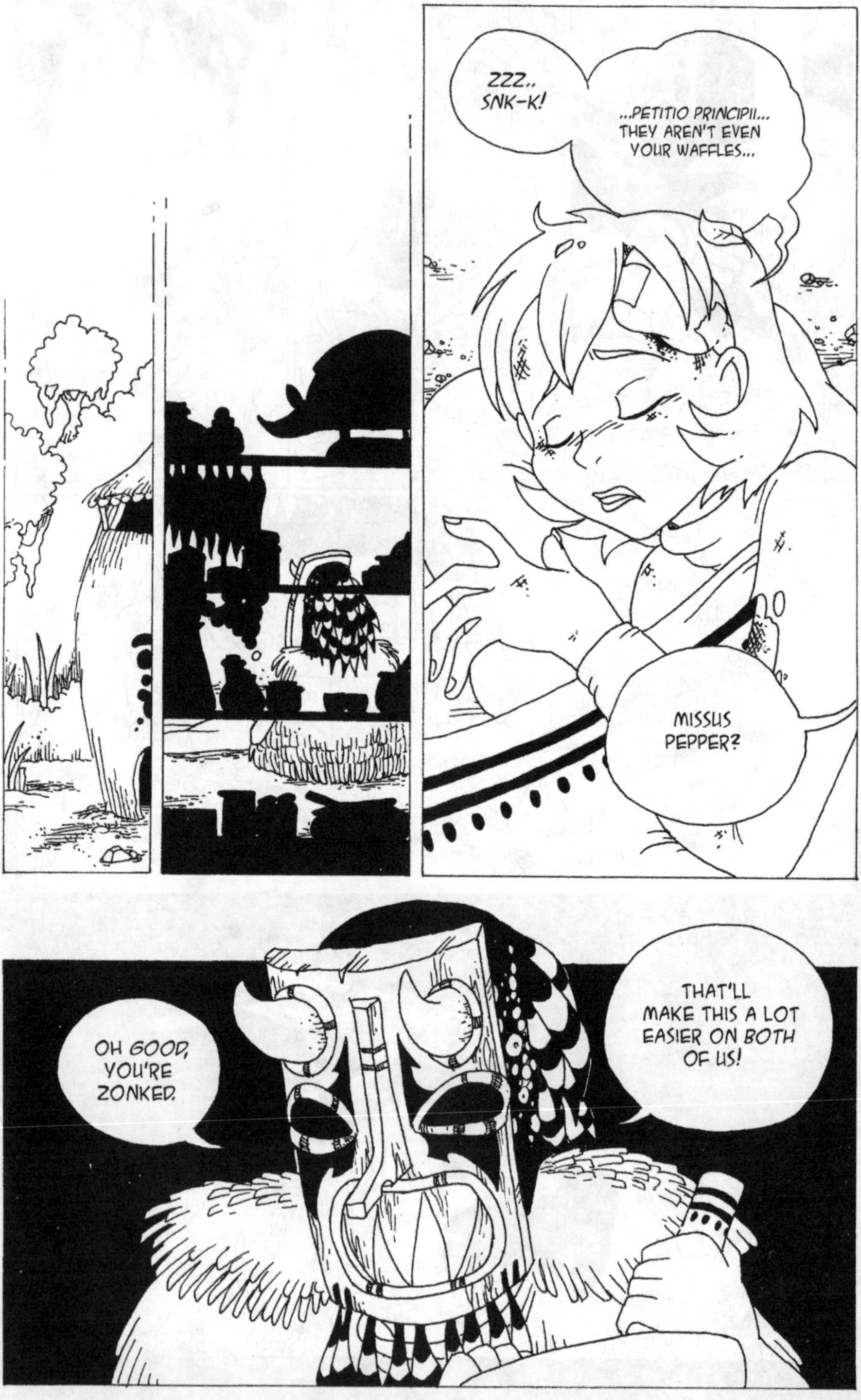
ZZZ..
SNK-K!
...PETITIO PRINCIPII... THEY AREN'T EVEN YOUR WAFFLES...
MISSUS PEPPER?
OH GOOD, YOU'RE ZONKED.
THAT'LL MAKE THIS A LOT EASIER ON BOTH OF US!

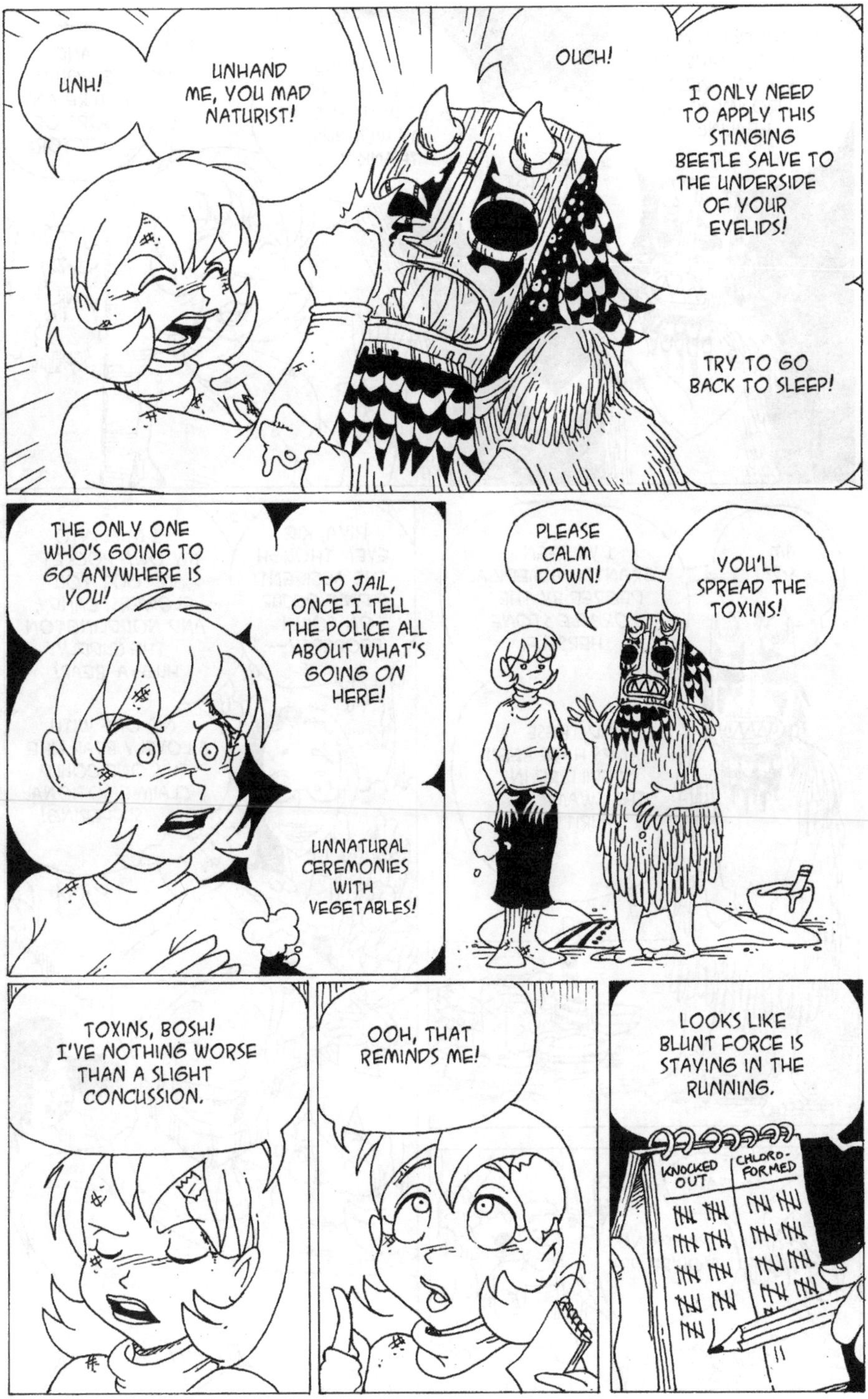
UNH!
UNHAND ME, YOU MAD NATURIST!
OUCH!
I ONLY NEED TO APPLY THIS STINGING BEETLE SALVE TO THE UNDERSIDE OF YOUR EYELIDS!
TRY TO GO BACK TO SLEEP!
THE ONLY ONE WHO'S GOING TO GO ANYWHERE IS YOU!
TO JAIL, ONCE I TELL THE POLICE ALL ABOUT WHAT'S GOING ON HERE!
UNNATURAL CEREMONIES WITH VEGETABLES!
PLEASE CALM DOWN!
YOU'LL SPREAD THE TOXINS!
TOXINS, BOSH! I'VE NOTHING WORSE THAN A SLIGHT CONCUSSION.
OOH, THAT REMINDS ME!
LOOKS LIKE BLUNT FORCE IS STAYING IN THE RUNNING.
KNOCKED OUT
CHLORO-FORMED

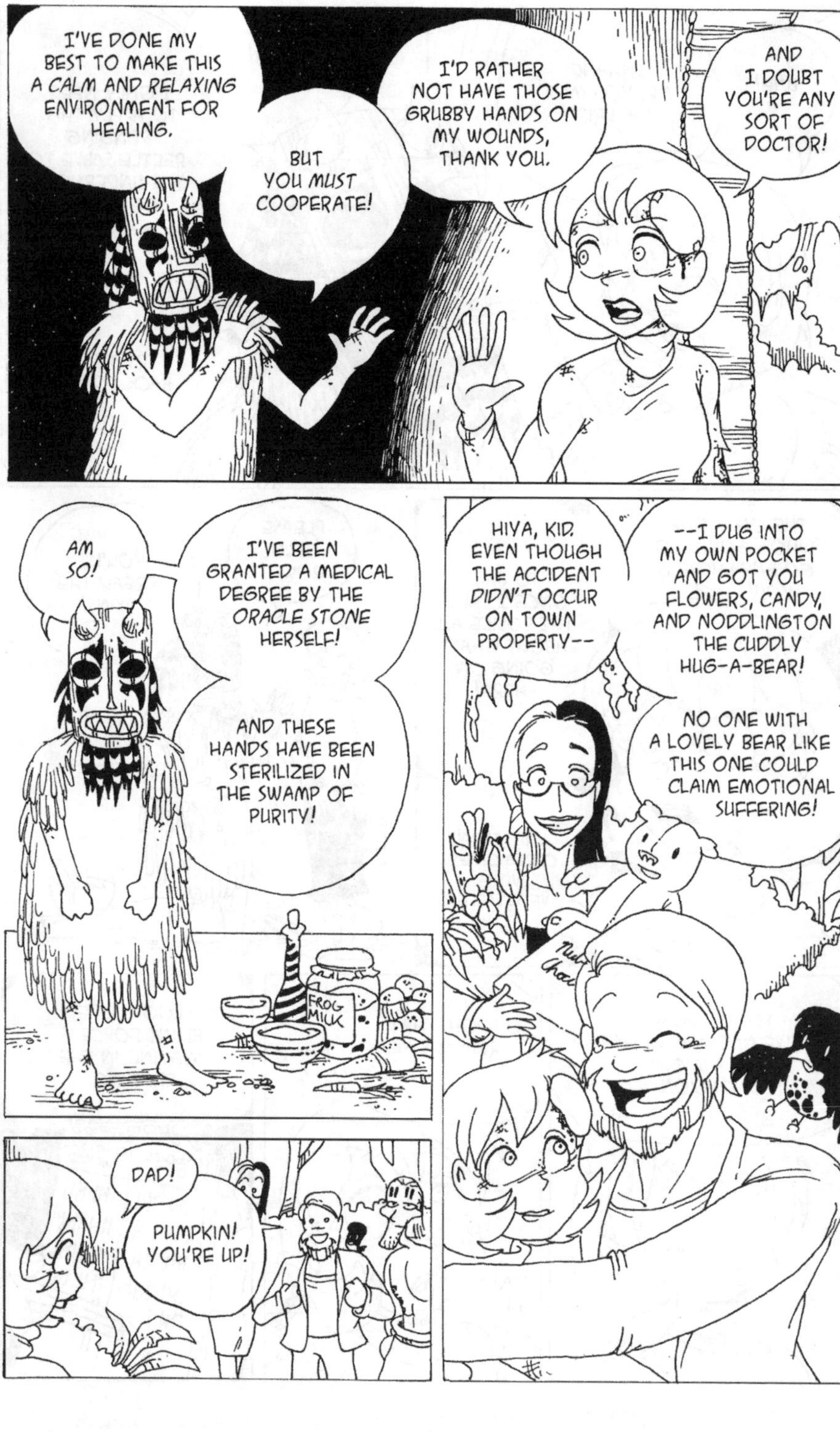
I'VE DONE MY BEST TO MAKE THIS A CALM AND RELAXING ENVIRONMENT FOR HEALING.
BUT YOU MUST COOPERATE!
I'D RATHER NOT HAVE THOSE GRUBBY HANDS ON MY WOUNDS, THANK YOU.
AND I DOUBT YOU'RE ANY SORT OF DOCTOR!
AM SO!
I'VE BEEN GRANTED A MEDICAL DEGREE BY THE ORACLE STONE HERSELF!
AND THESE HANDS HAVE BEEN STERILIZED IN THE SWAMP OF PURITY!
FROG MILK
DAD!
PUMPKIN! YOU'RE UP!
HIYA, KID. EVEN THOUGH THE ACCIDENT DIDN'T OCCUR ON TOWN PROPERTY--
--I DUG INTO MY OWN POCKET AND GOT YOU FLOWERS, CANDY, AND NODDLINGTON THE CUDDLY HUG-A-BEAR!
NO ONE WITH A LOVELY BEAR LIKE THIS ONE COULD CLAIM EMOTIONAL SUFFERING!

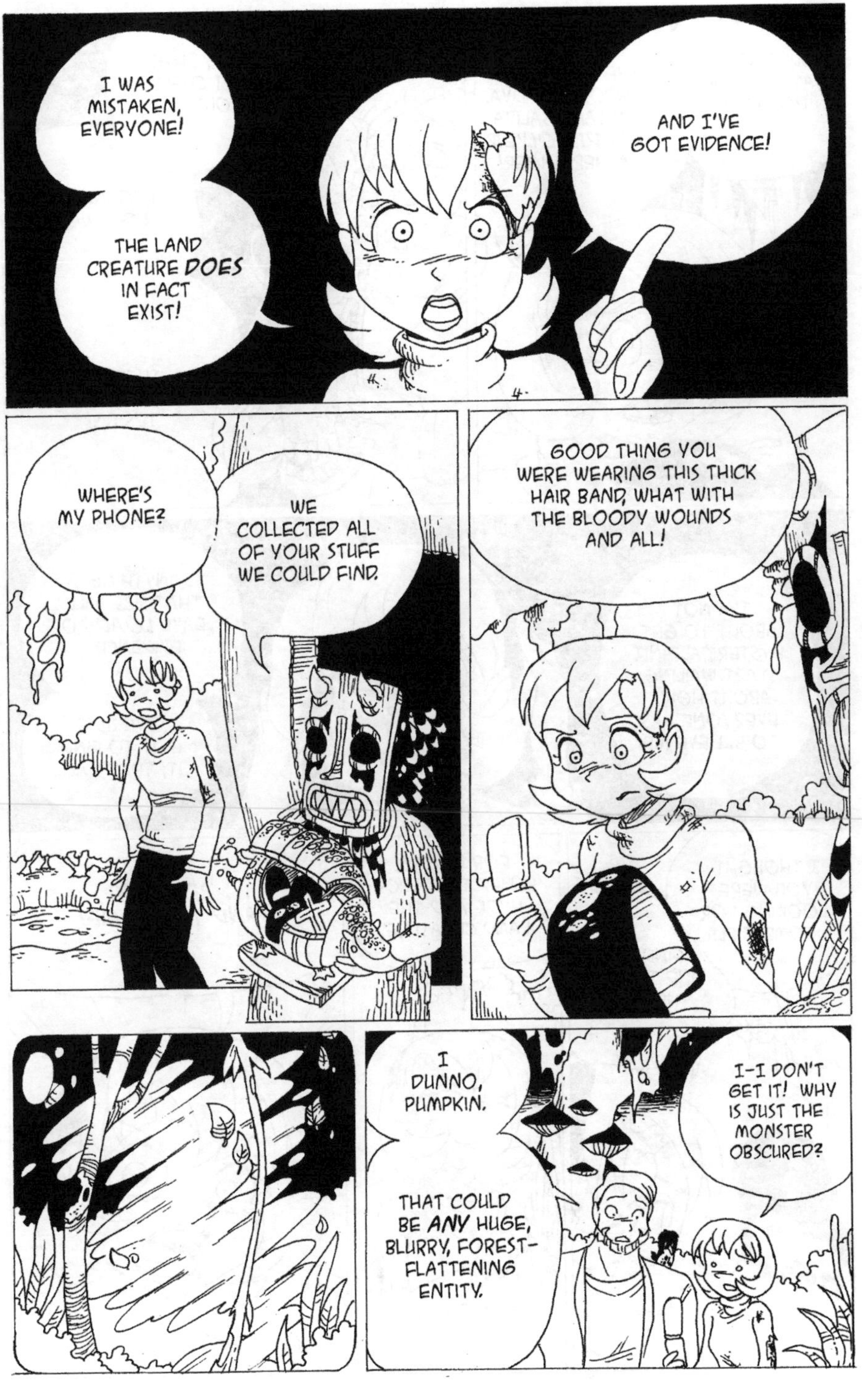
I WAS MISTAKEN, EVERYONE!
THE LAND CREATURE DOES IN FACT EXIST!
AND I'VE GOT EVIDENCE!
4.
WHERE'S MY PHONE?
WE COLLECTED ALL OF YOUR STUFF WE COULD FIND.
GOOD THING YOU WERE WEARING THIS THICK HAIR BAND, WHAT WITH THE BLOODY WOUNDS AND ALL!
I-I DON'T GET IT! WHY IS JUST THE MONSTER OBSCURED?
I DUNNO, PUMPKIN.
THAT COULD BE ANY HUGE, BLURRY, FOREST-FLATTENING ENTITY.

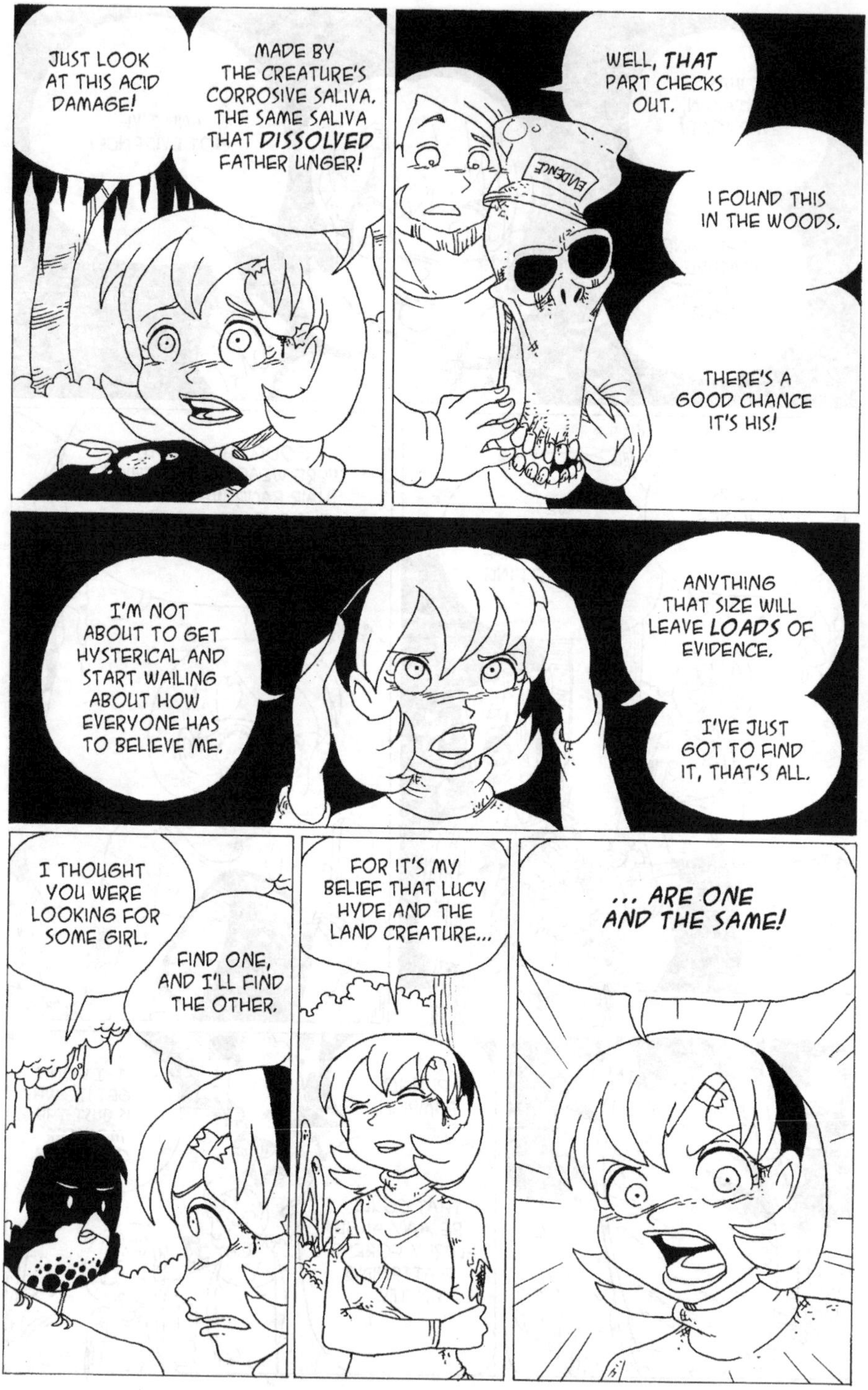
JUST LOOK AT THIS ACID DAMAGE!
MADE BY THE CREATURE'S CORROSIVE SALIVA. THE SAME SALIVA THAT DISSOLVED FATHER UNGER!
WELL, THAT PART CHECKS OUT.
EVIDENCE
I FOUND THIS IN THE WOODS.
THERE'S A GOOD CHANCE IT'S HIS!
I'M NOT ABOUT TO GET HYSTERICAL AND START WAILING ABOUT HOW EVERYONE HAS TO BELIEVE ME.
ANYTHING THAT SIZE WILL LEAVE LOADS OF EVIDENCE.
I'VE JUST GOT TO FIND IT, THAT'S ALL.
I THOUGHT YOU WERE LOOKING FOR SOME GIRL.
FIND ONE, AND I'LL FIND THE OTHER.
FOR IT'S MY BELIEF THAT LUCY HYDE AND THE LAND CREATURE...
... ARE ONE AND THE SAME!

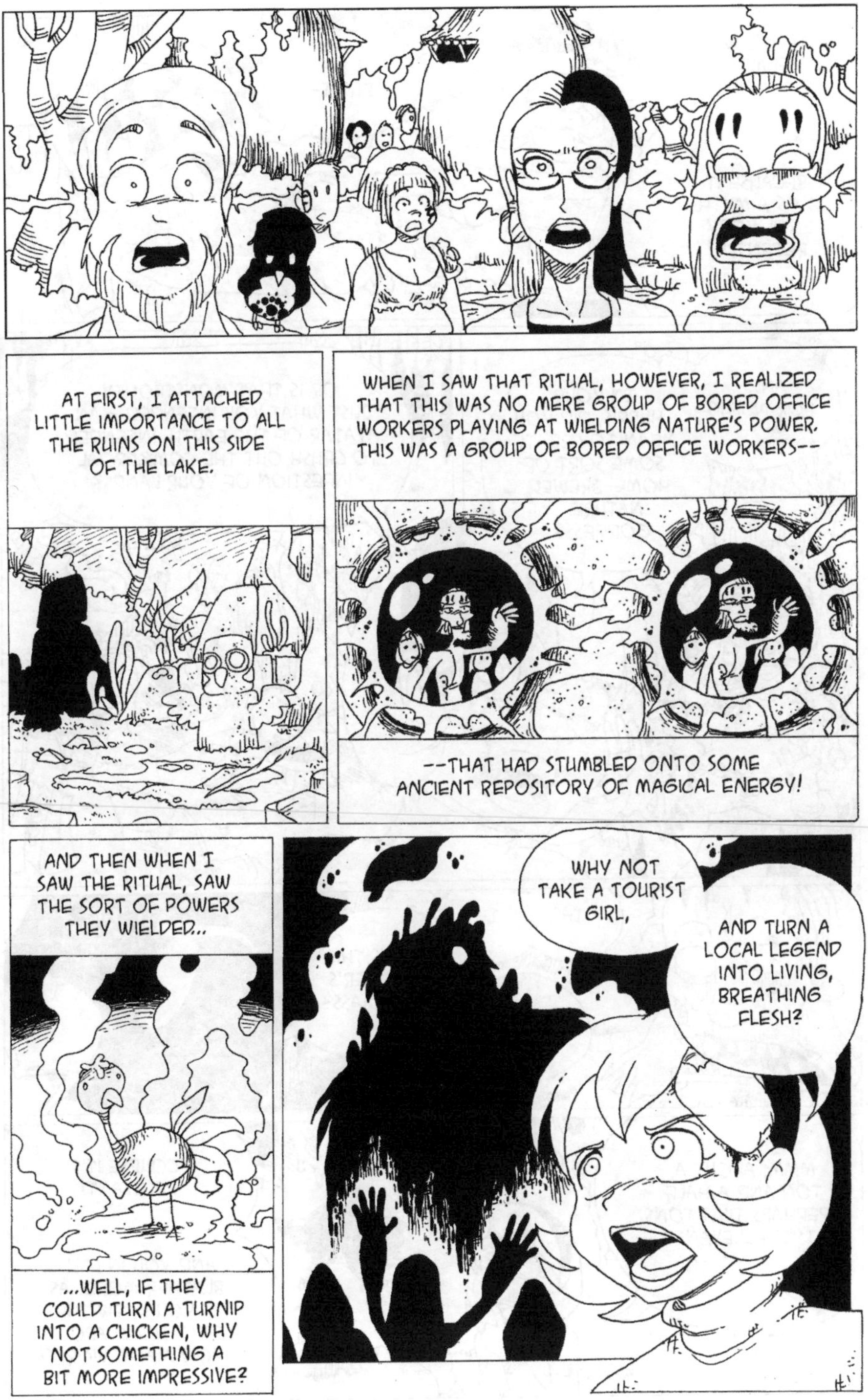
AT FIRST, I ATTACHED LITTLE IMPORTANCE TO ALL THE RUINS ON THIS SIDE OF THE LAKE.
WHEN I SAW THAT RITUAL, HOWEVER, I REALIZED THAT THIS WAS NO MERE GROUP OF BORED OFFICE WORKERS PLAYING AT WIELDING NATURE'S POWER. THIS WAS A GROUP OF BORED OFFICE WORKERS--
--THAT HAD STUMBLED ONTO SOME ANCIENT REPOSITORY OF MAGICAL ENERGY!
AND THEN WHEN I SAW THE RITUAL, SAW THE SORT OF POWERS THEY WIELDED...
...WELL, IF THEY COULD TURN A TURNIP INTO A CHICKEN, WHY NOT SOMETHING A BIT MORE IMPRESSIVE?
WHY NOT TAKE A TOURIST GIRL,
AND TURN A LOCAL LEGEND INTO LIVING, BREATHING FLESH?

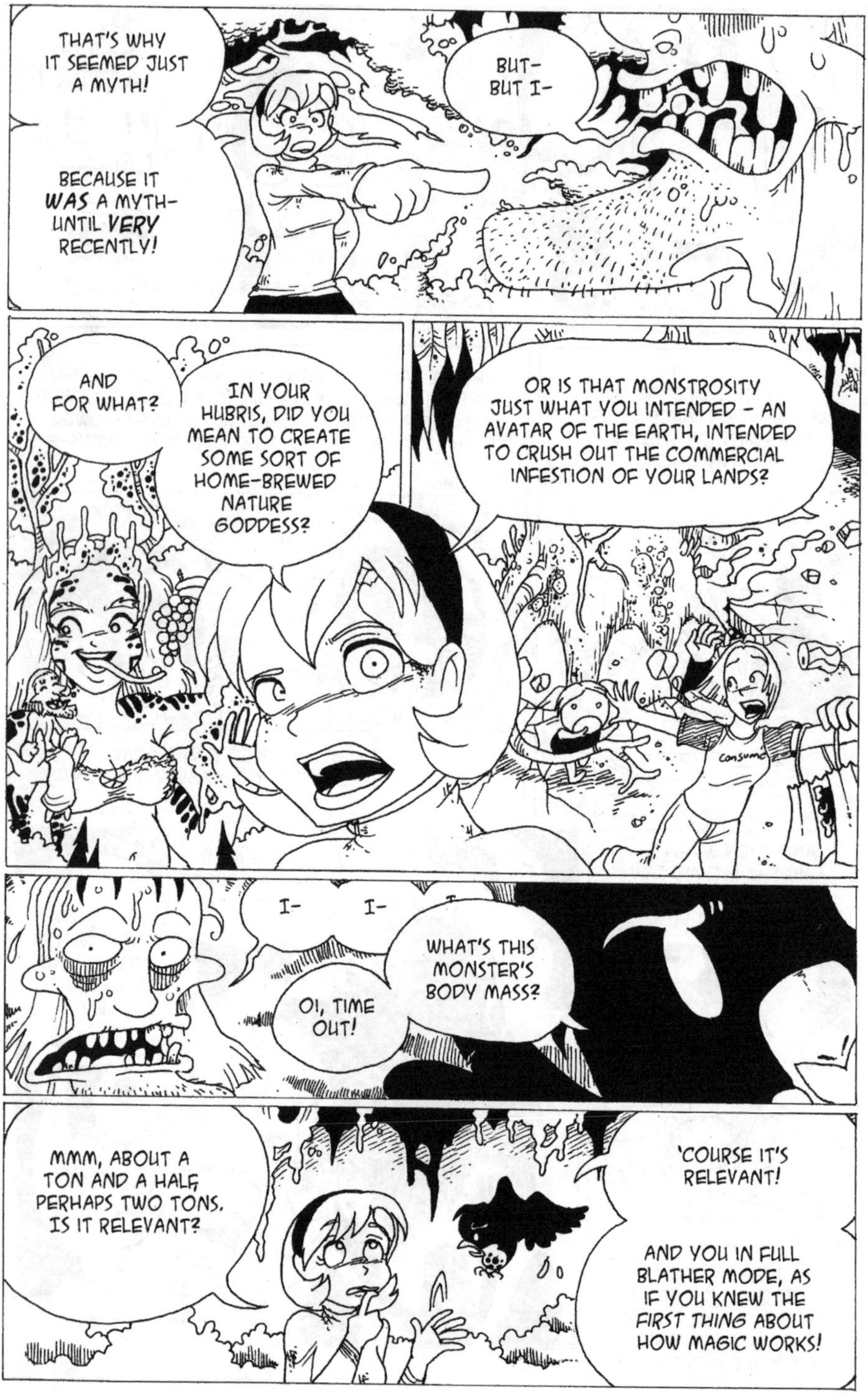
THAT'S WHY IT SEEMED JUST A MYTH!
BECAUSE IT *WAS* A MYTH- UNTIL *VERY* RECENTLY!
BUT- BUT I-
AND FOR WHAT?
IN YOUR HUBRIS, DID YOU MEAN TO CREATE SOME SORT OF HOME-BREWED NATURE GODDESS?
OR IS THAT MONSTROSITY JUST WHAT YOU INTENDED - AN AVATAR OF THE EARTH, INTENDED TO CRUSH OUT THE COMMERCIAL INFESTION OF YOUR LANDS?
I- I-
OI, TIME OUT!
WHAT'S THIS MONSTER'S BODY MASS?
MMM, ABOUT A TON AND A HALF, PERHAPS TWO TONS. IS IT RELEVANT?
'COURSE IT'S RELEVANT!
AND YOU IN FULL BLATHER MODE, AS IF YOU KNEW THE *FIRST THING* ABOUT HOW MAGIC WORKS!

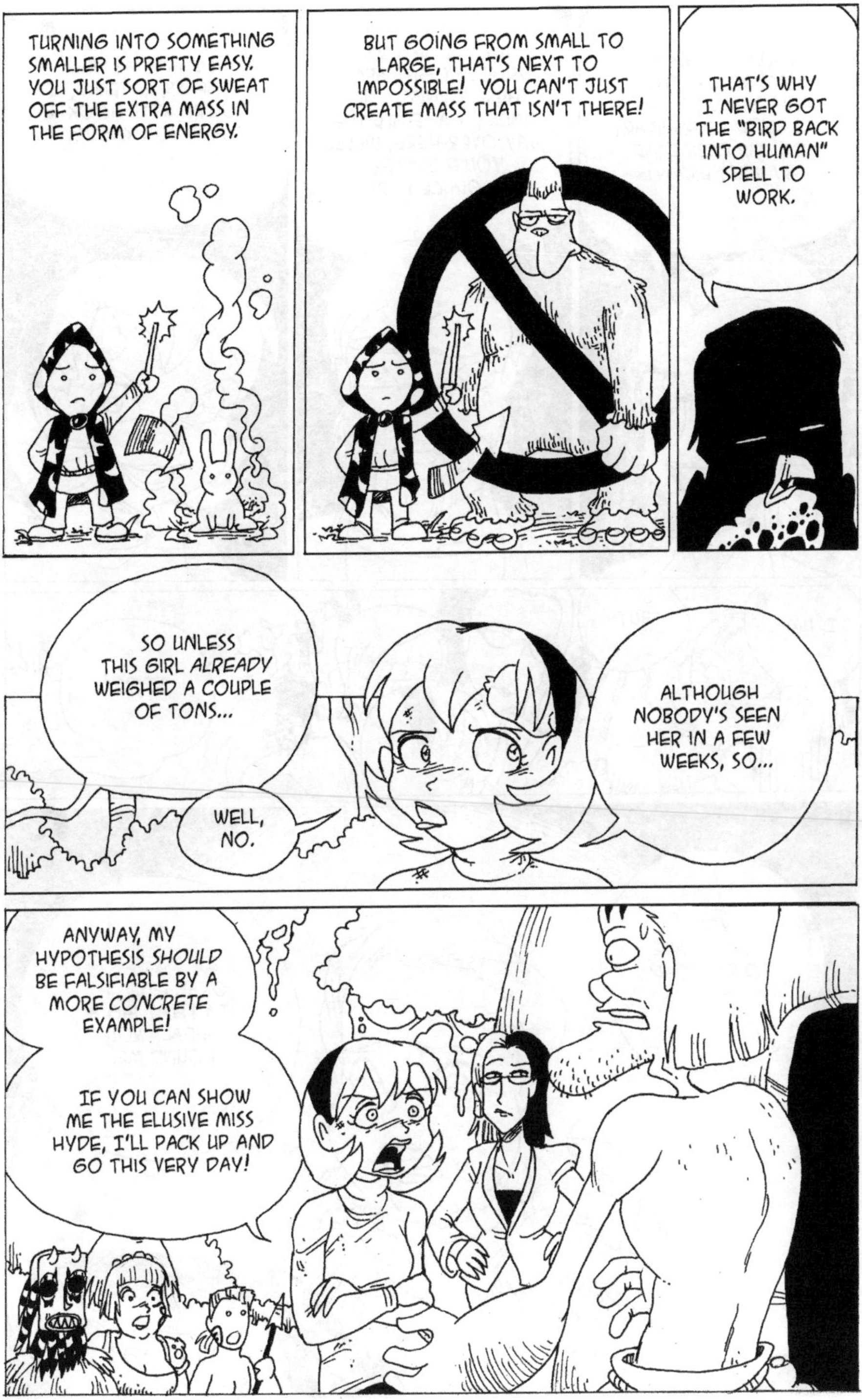
TURNING INTO SOMETHING SMALLER IS PRETTY EASY. YOU JUST SORT OF SWEAT OFF THE EXTRA MASS IN THE FORM OF ENERGY.
BUT GOING FROM SMALL TO LARGE, THAT'S NEXT TO IMPOSSIBLE! YOU CAN'T JUST CREATE MASS THAT ISN'T THERE!
THAT'S WHY I NEVER GOT THE "BIRD BACK INTO HUMAN" SPELL TO WORK.
SO UNLESS THIS GIRL ALREADY WEIGHED A COUPLE OF TONS...
WELL, NO.
ALTHOUGH NOBODY'S SEEN HER IN A FEW WEEKS, SO...
ANYWAY, MY HYPOTHESIS SHOULD BE FALSIFIABLE BY A MORE CONCRETE EXAMPLE!
IF YOU CAN SHOW ME THE ELUSIVE MISS HYDE, I'LL PACK UP AND GO THIS VERY DAY!

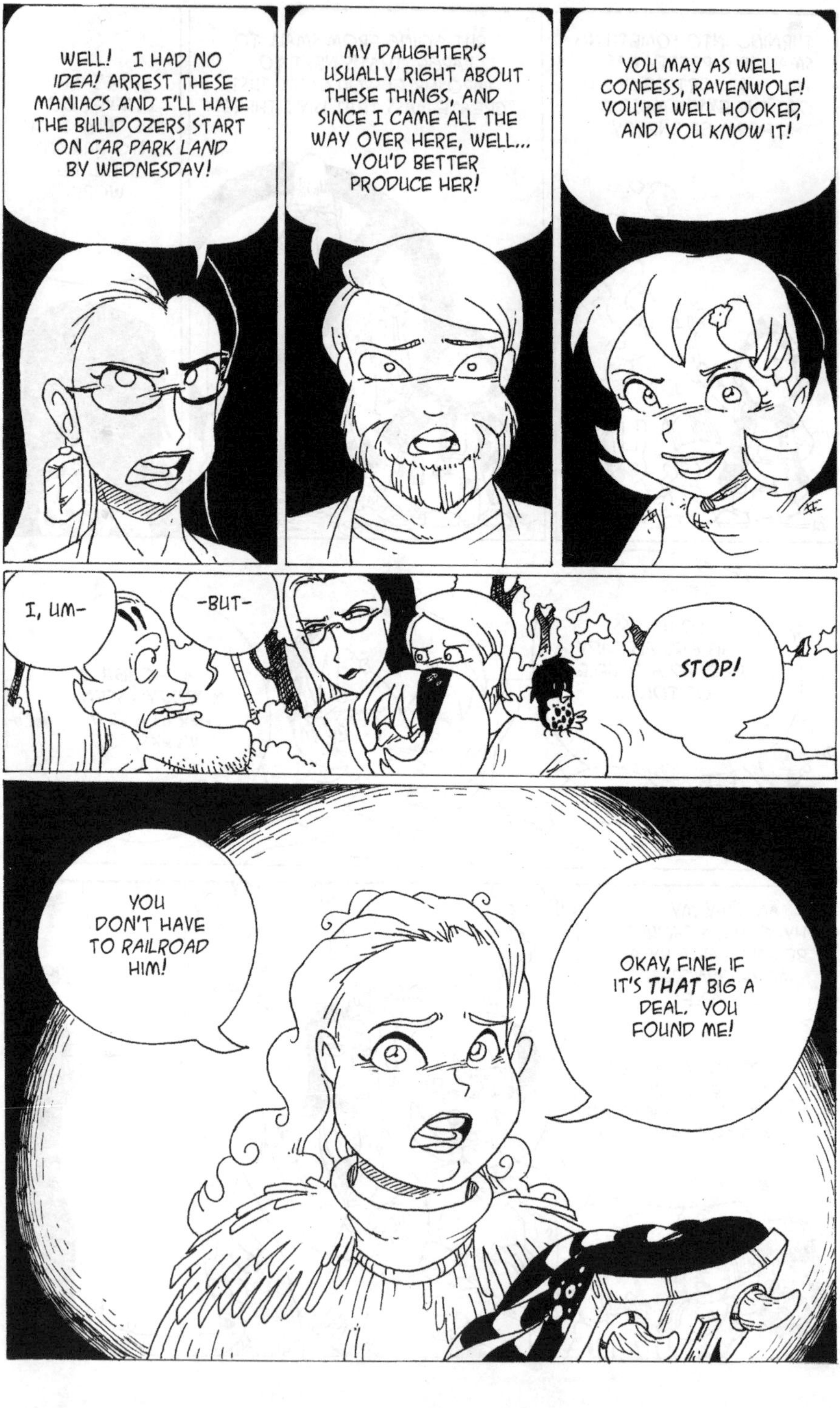
WELL! I HAD NO IDEA! ARREST THESE MANIACS AND I'LL HAVE THE BULLDOZERS START ON CAR PARK LAND BY WEDNESDAY!
MY DAUGHTER'S USUALLY RIGHT ABOUT THESE THINGS, AND SINCE I CAME ALL THE WAY OVER HERE, WELL... YOU'D BETTER PRODUCE HER!
YOU MAY AS WELL CONFESS, RAVENWOLF! YOU'RE WELL HOOKED, AND YOU KNOW IT!
I, UM-
-BUT-
STOP!
YOU DON'T HAVE TO RAILROAD HIM!
OKAY, FINE, IF IT'S THAT BIG A DEAL. YOU FOUND ME!

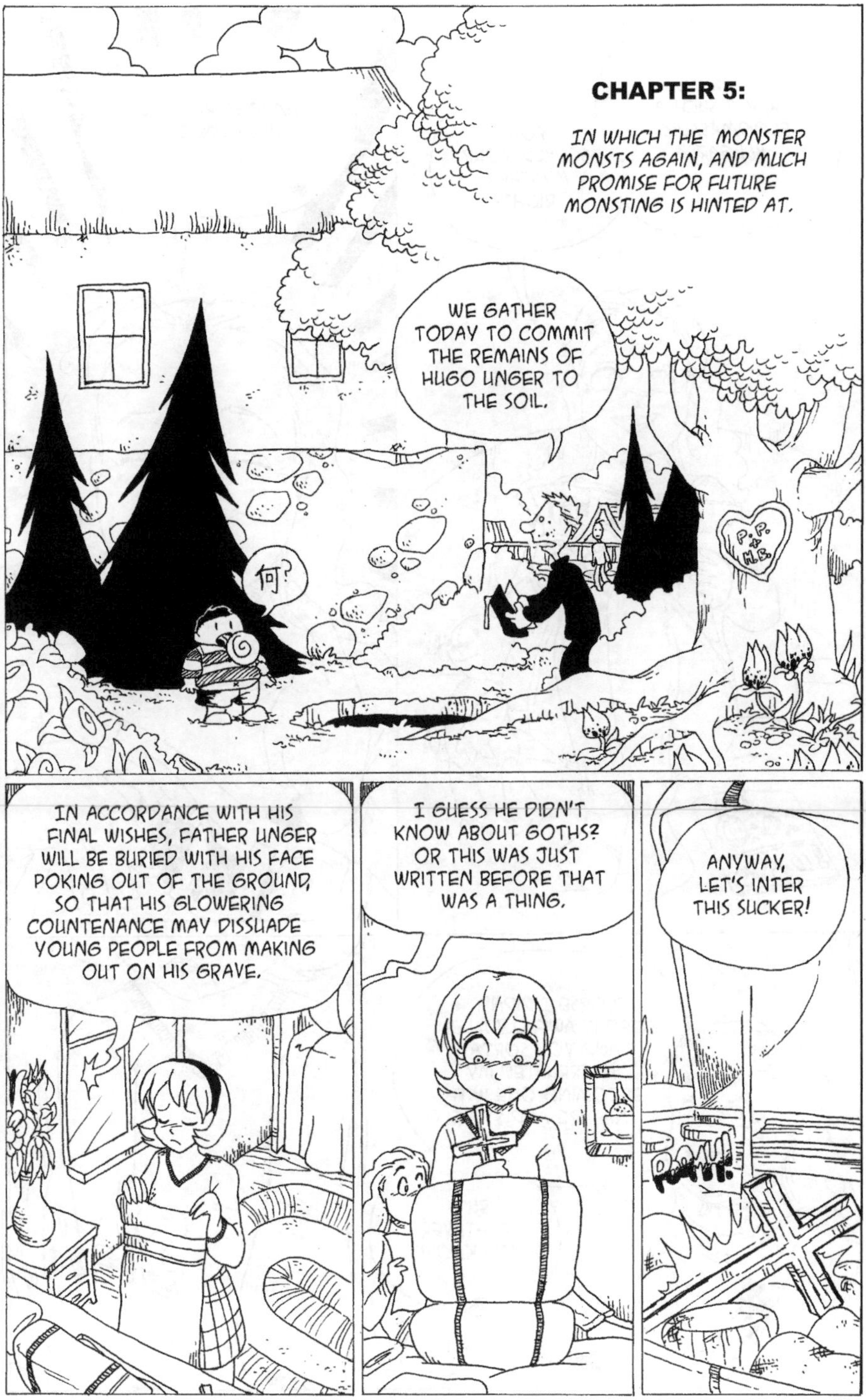
CHAPTER 5:
IN WHICH THE MONSTER MONSTS AGAIN, AND MUCH PROMISE FOR FUTURE MONSTING IS HINTED AT.
WE GATHER TODAY TO COMMIT THE REMAINS OF HUGO UNGER TO THE SOIL.
何?
IN ACCORDANCE WITH HIS FINAL WISHES, FATHER UNGER WILL BE BURIED WITH HIS FACE POKING OUT OF THE GROUND, SO THAT HIS GLOWERING COUNTENANCE MAY DISSUADE YOUNG PEOPLE FROM MAKING OUT ON HIS GRAVE.
I GUESS HE DIDN'T KNOW ABOUT GOTHS? OR THIS WAS JUST WRITTEN BEFORE THAT WAS A THING.
ANYWAY, LET'S INTER THIS SUCKER!

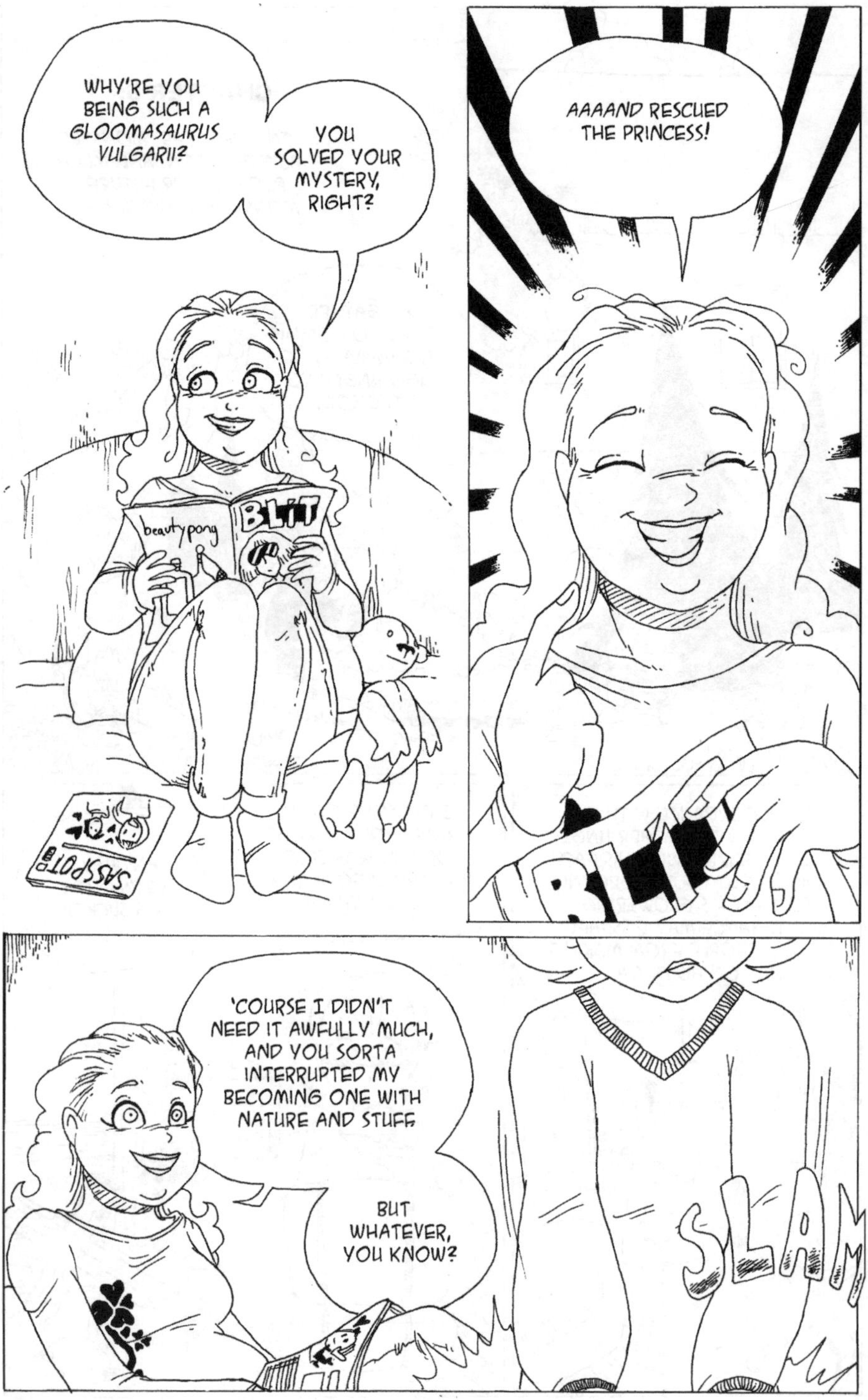
WHY'RE YOU BEING SUCH A GLOOMASAURUS VULGARII?
YOU SOLVED YOUR MYSTERY, RIGHT?
beautypong
BLIT
SASSPOT
AAAAND RESCUED THE PRINCESS!
BLIT
'COURSE I DIDN'T NEED IT AWFULLY MUCH, AND YOU SORTA INTERRUPTED MY BECOMING ONE WITH NATURE AND STUFF
BUT WHATEVER, YOU KNOW?
SLAM

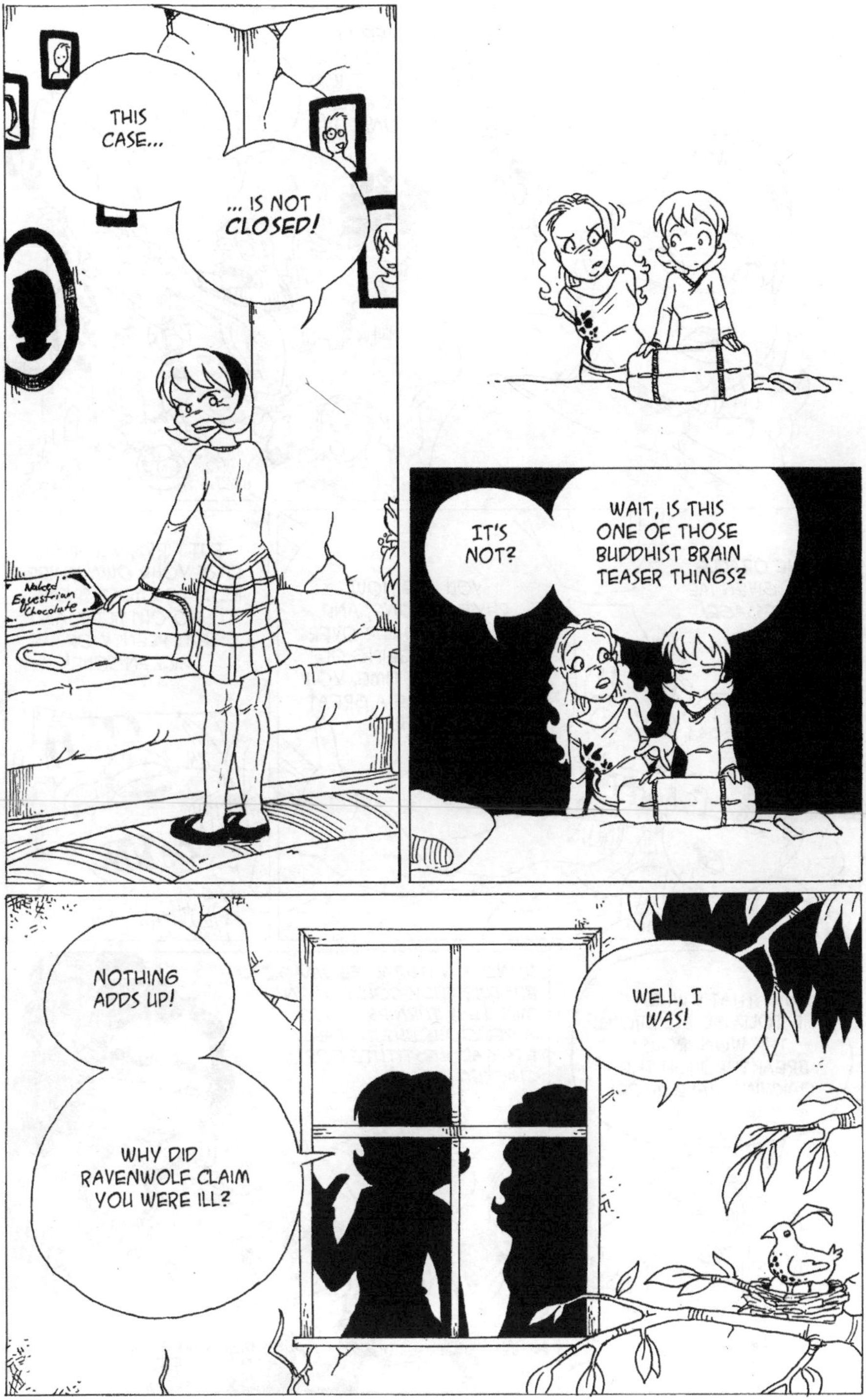
THIS CASE...
... IS NOT CLOSED!
Naked Equestrian Chocolate
IT'S NOT?
WAIT, IS THIS ONE OF THOSE BUDDHIST BRAIN TEASER THINGS?
NOTHING ADDS UP!
WHY DID RAVENWOLF CLAIM YOU WERE ILL?
WELL, I WAS!

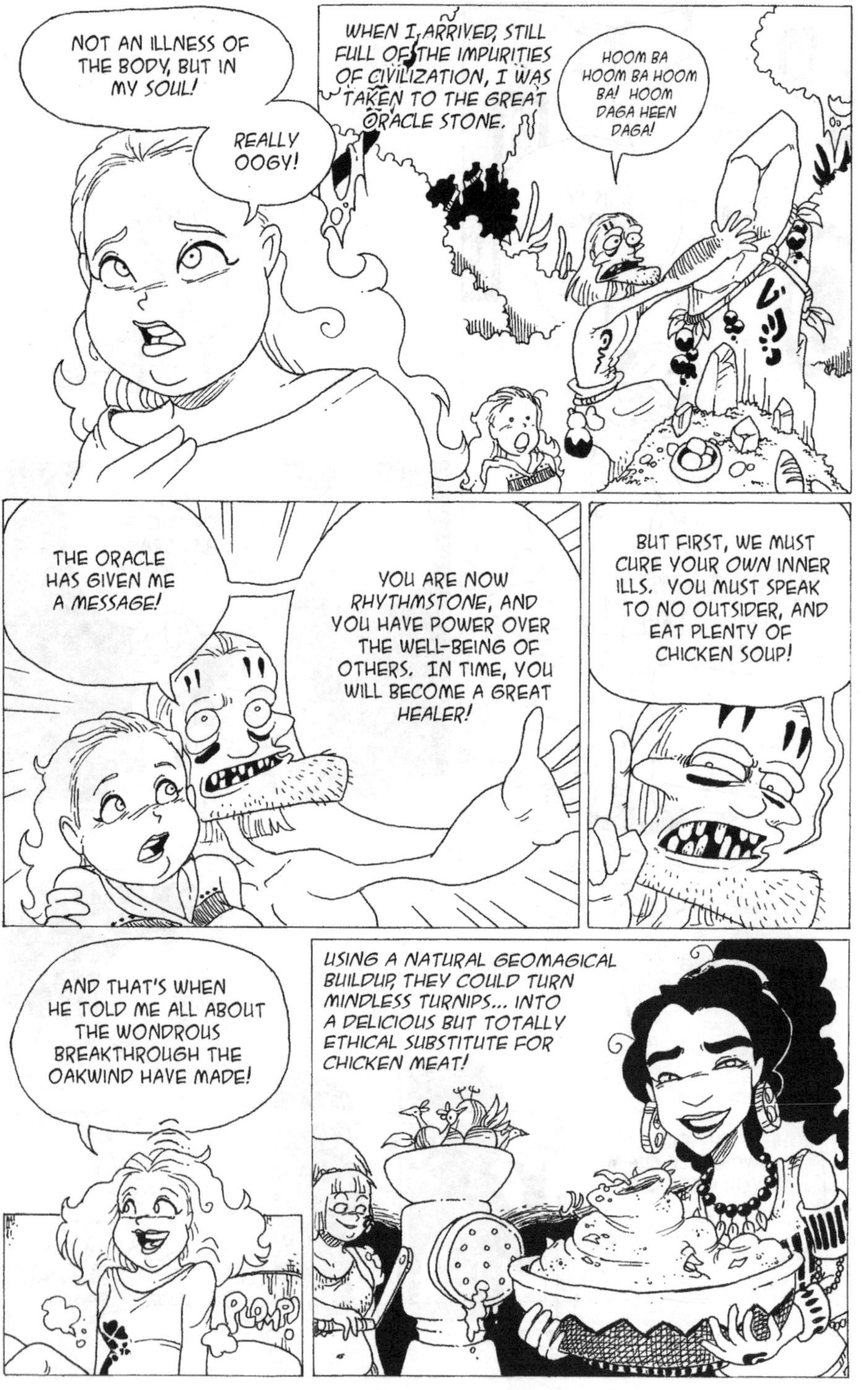
NOT AN ILLNESS OF THE BODY, BUT IN MY SOUL!
REALLY OOGY!
WHEN I ARRIVED, STILL FULL OF THE IMPURITIES OF CIVILIZATION, I WAS TAKEN TO THE GREAT ORACLE STONE.
HOOM BA HOOM BA HOOM BA! HOOM DAGA HEEN DAGA!
THE ORACLE HAS GIVEN ME A MESSAGE!
YOU ARE NOW RHYTHMSTONE, AND YOU HAVE POWER OVER THE WELL-BEING OF OTHERS. IN TIME, YOU WILL BECOME A GREAT HEALER!
BUT FIRST, WE MUST CURE YOUR OWN INNER ILLS. YOU MUST SPEAK TO NO OUTSIDER, AND EAT PLENTY OF CHICKEN SOUP!
AND THAT'S WHEN HE TOLD ME ALL ABOUT THE WONDROUS BREAKTHROUGH THE OAKWIND HAVE MADE!
PLOMP!
USING A NATURAL GEOMAGICAL BUILDUP, THEY COULD TURN MINDLESS TURNIPS... INTO A DELICIOUS BUT TOTALLY ETHICAL SUBSTITUTE FOR CHICKEN MEAT!

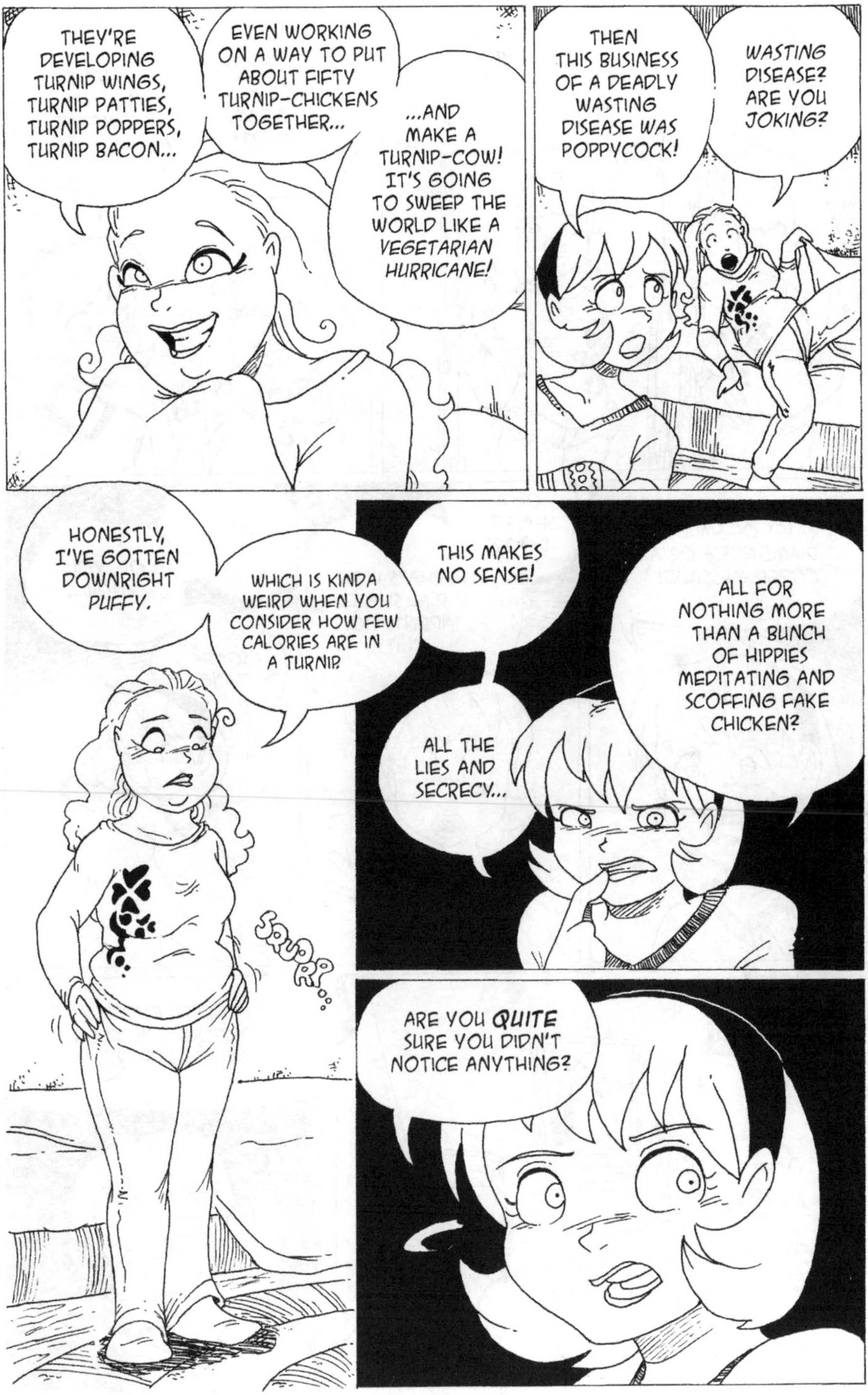
THEY'RE DEVELOPING TURNIP WINGS, TURNIP PATTIES, TURNIP POPPERS, TURNIP BACON...
EVEN WORKING ON A WAY TO PUT ABOUT FIFTY TURNIP-CHICKENS TOGETHER...
...AND MAKE A TURNIP-COW! IT'S GOING TO SWEEP THE WORLD LIKE A VEGETARIAN HURRICANE!
THEN THIS BUSINESS OF A DEADLY WASTING DISEASE WAS POPPYCOCK!
WASTING DISEASE? ARE YOU JOKING?
HONESTLY, I'VE GOTTEN DOWNRIGHT PUFFY.
WHICH IS KINDA WEIRD WHEN YOU CONSIDER HOW FEW CALORIES ARE IN A TURNIP.
SQUORP
THIS MAKES NO SENSE!
ALL THE LIES AND SECRECY...
ALL FOR NOTHING MORE THAN A BUNCH OF HIPPIES MEDITATING AND SCOFFING FAKE CHICKEN?
ARE YOU QUITE SURE YOU DIDN'T NOTICE ANYTHING?

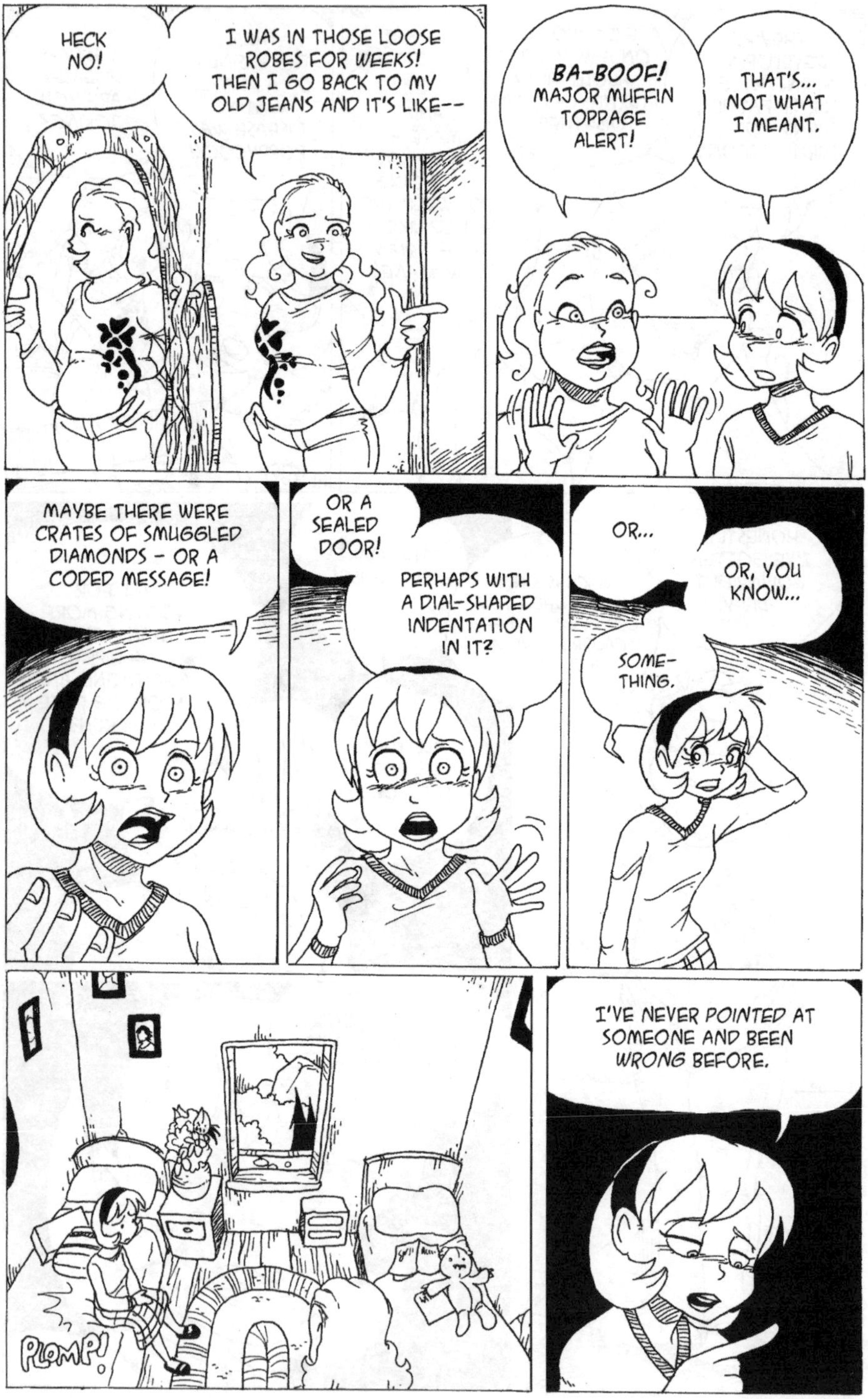
HECK NO!
I WAS IN THOSE LOOSE ROBES FOR WEEKS! THEN I GO BACK TO MY OLD JEANS AND IT'S LIKE--
BA-BOOF! MAJOR MUFFIN TOPPAGE ALERT!
THAT'S... NOT WHAT I MEANT.
MAYBE THERE WERE CRATES OF SMUGGLED DIAMONDS - OR A CODED MESSAGE!
OR A SEALED DOOR!
PERHAPS WITH A DIAL-SHAPED INDENTATION IN IT?
OR...
OR, YOU KNOW...
SOME-THING.
PLOMP!
I'VE NEVER POINTED AT SOMEONE AND BEEN WRONG BEFORE.

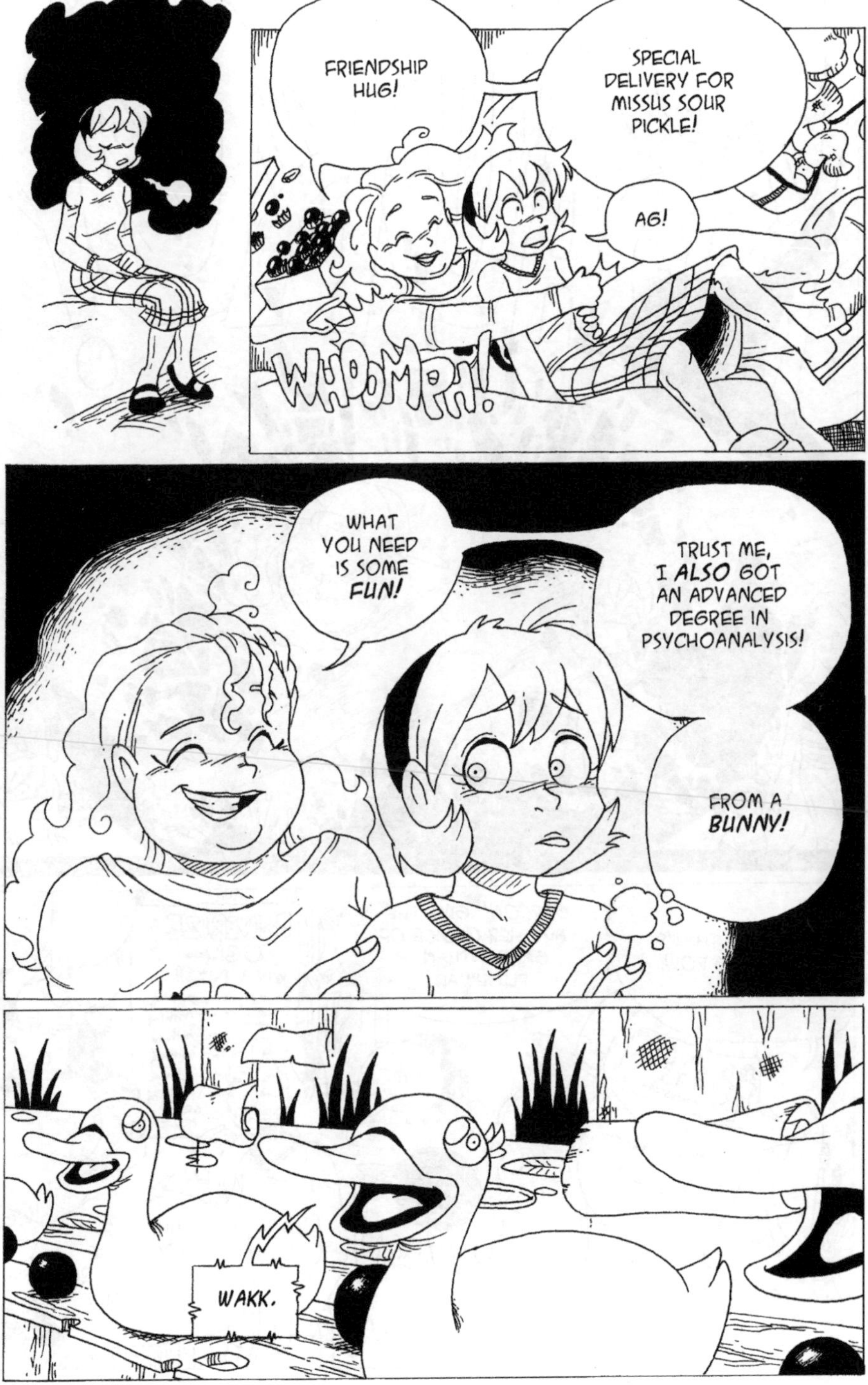
FRIENDSHIP HUG!
SPECIAL DELIVERY FOR MISSUS SOUR PICKLE!
AG!
WHOOMPH!
WHAT YOU NEED IS SOME FUN!
TRUST ME, I ALSO GOT AN ADVANCED DEGREE IN PSYCHOANALYSIS!
FROM A BUNNY!
WAKK.

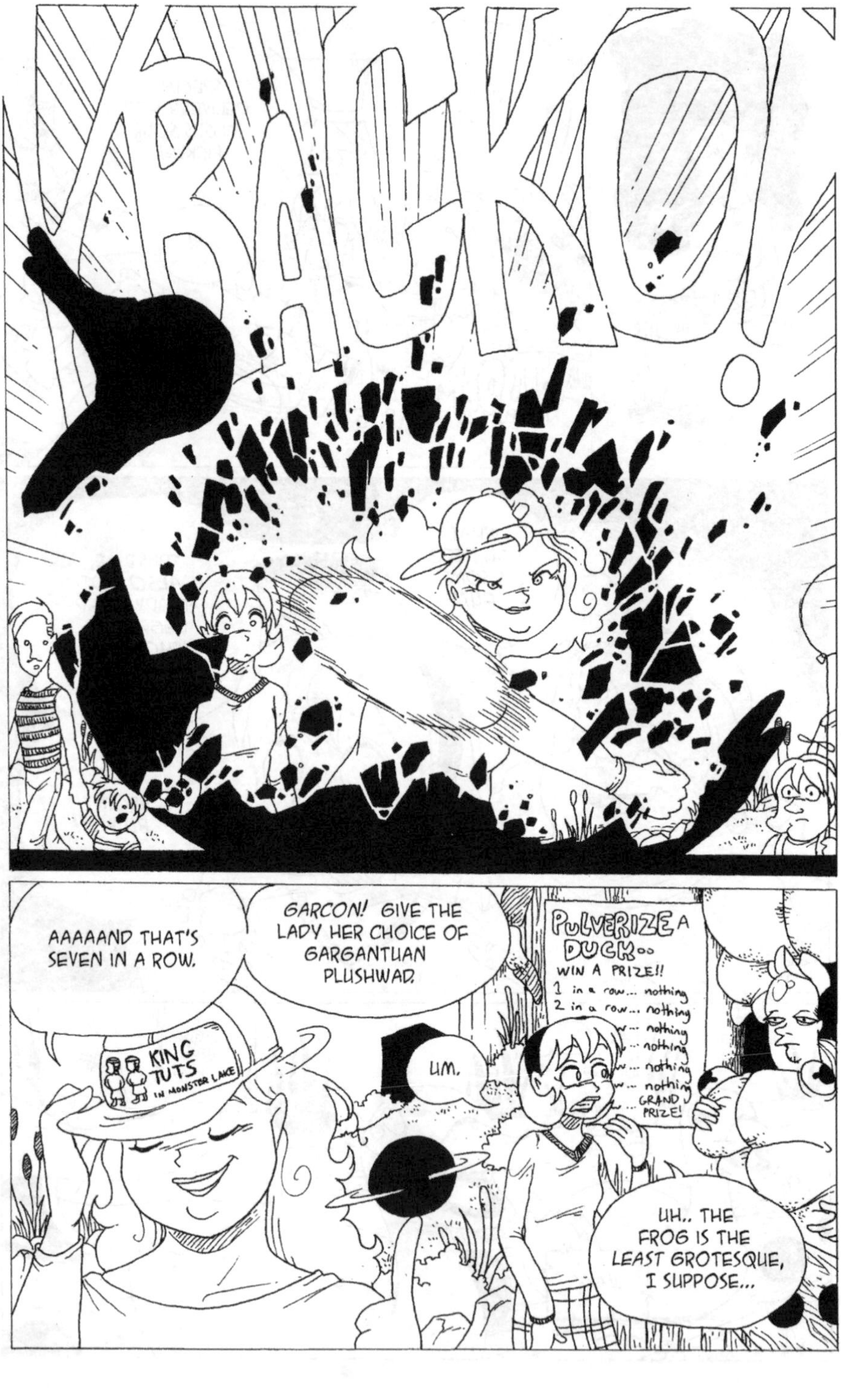
BACKO!
AAAAAND THAT'S SEVEN IN A ROW.
GARCON! GIVE THE LADY HER CHOICE OF GARGANTUAN PLUSHWAD.
PULVERIZE A DUCK.. WIN A PRIZE!!
1 in a row... nothing
2 in a row... nothing
nothing
nothing
nothing
nothing
GRAND PRIZE!
KING TUTS IN MONSTER LAKE
UM.
UH.. THE FROG IS THE LEAST GROTESQUE, I SUPPOSE...

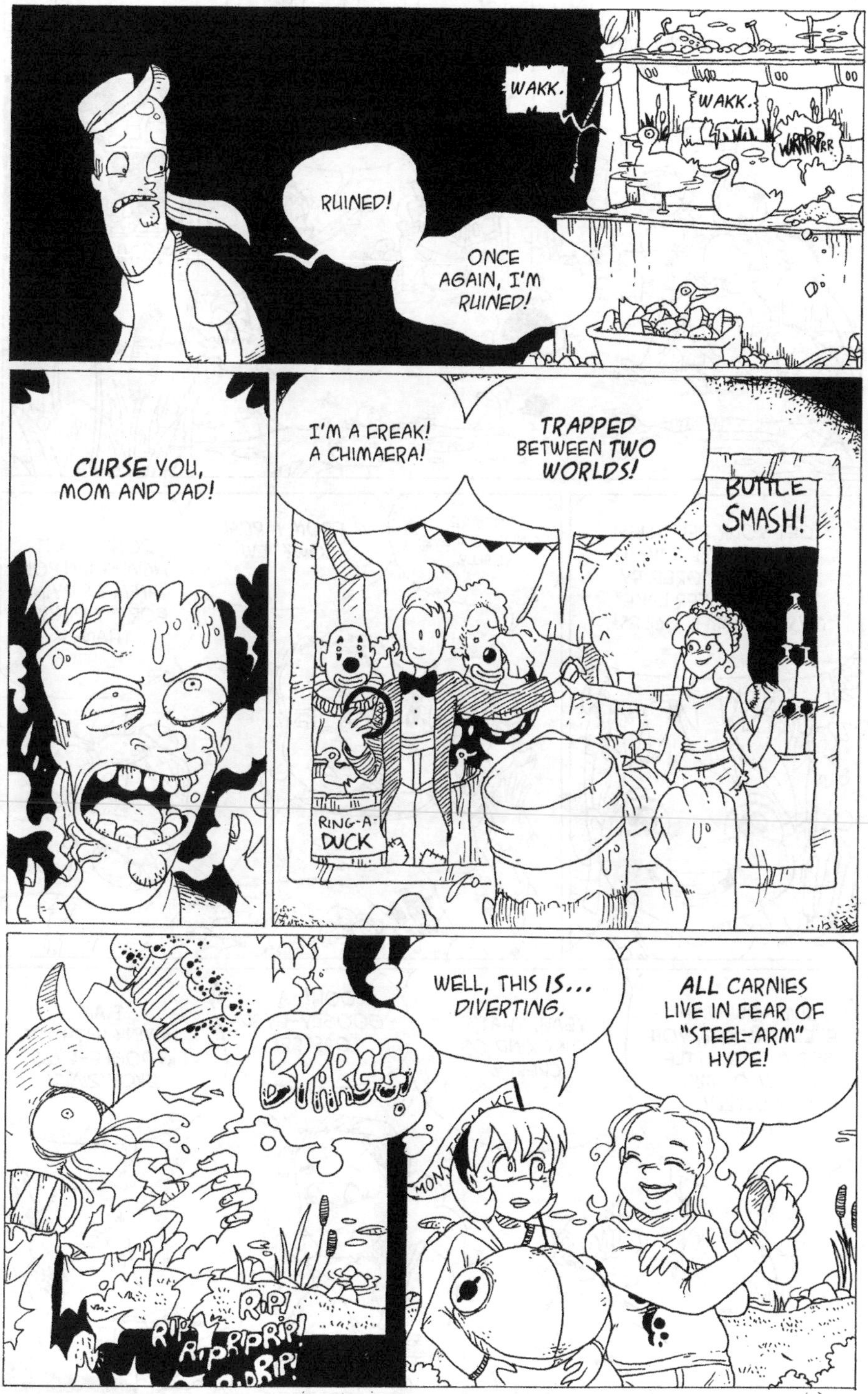
WAKK.
WAKK.
WRRRPRRR
RUINED!
ONCE AGAIN, I'M RUINED!
CURSE YOU, MOM AND DAD!
I'M A FREAK! A CHIMAERA!
TRAPPED BETWEEN TWO WORLDS!
BOTTLE SMASH!
RING-A-DUCK
BYARGS!
WELL, THIS IS... DIVERTING.
ALL CARNIES LIVE IN FEAR OF "STEEL-ARM" HYDE!
RIP!
RIP RIP RIP RIP!

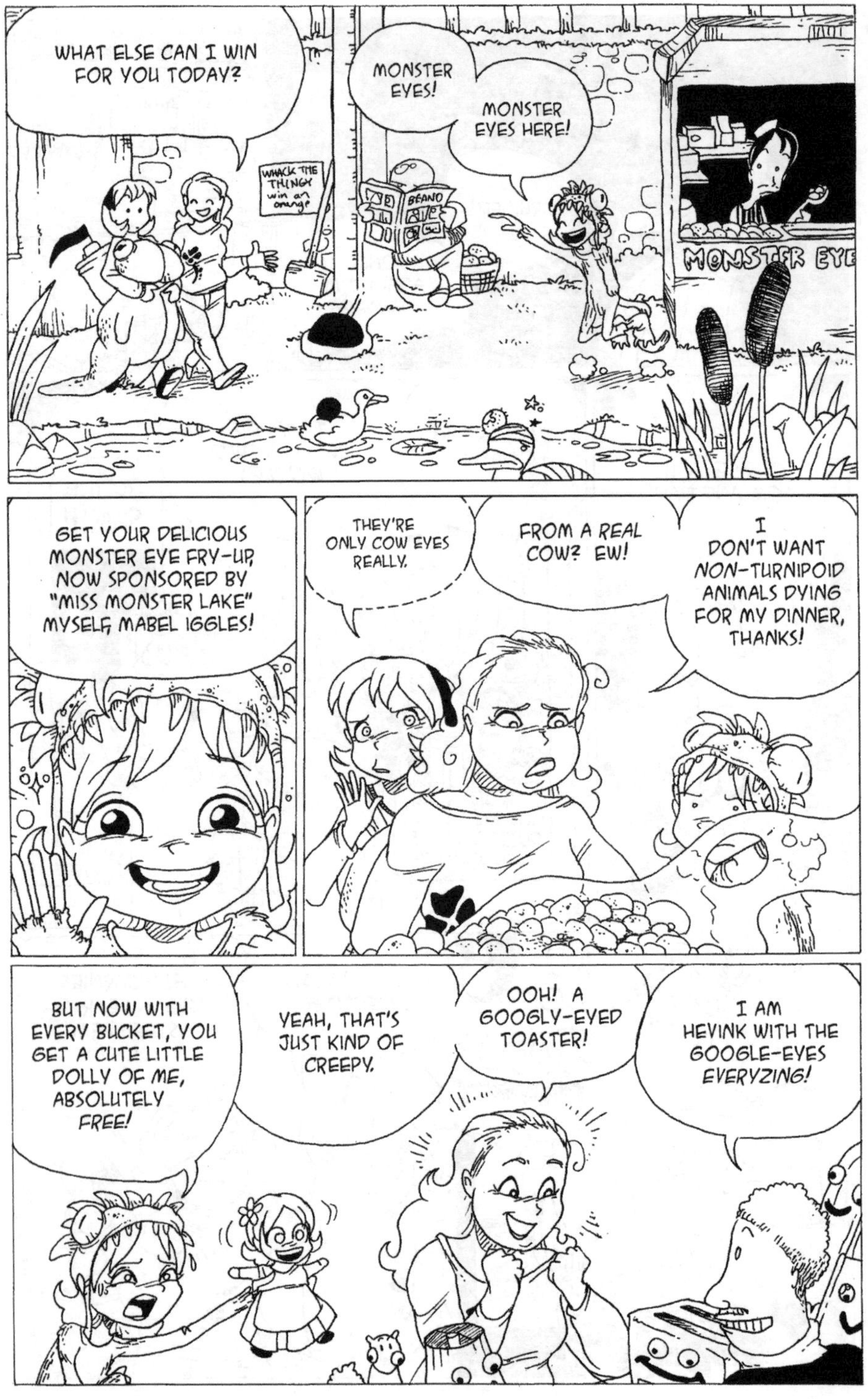
WHAT ELSE CAN I WIN FOR YOU TODAY?
WHACK THE THINGY win an orange
MONSTER EYES!
MONSTER EYES HERE!
BEANO
MONSTER EYE
GET YOUR DELICIOUS MONSTER EYE FRY-UP, NOW SPONSORED BY "MISS MONSTER LAKE" MYSELF, MABEL IGGLES!
THEY'RE ONLY COW EYES REALLY.
FROM A REAL COW? EW!
I DON'T WANT NON-TURNIPOID ANIMALS DYING FOR MY DINNER, THANKS!
BUT NOW WITH EVERY BUCKET, YOU GET A CUTE LITTLE DOLLY OF ME, ABSOLUTELY FREE!
YEAH, THAT'S JUST KIND OF CREEPY.
OOH! A GOOGLY-EYED TOASTER!
I AM HEVINK WITH THE GOOGLE-EYES EVERYZING!

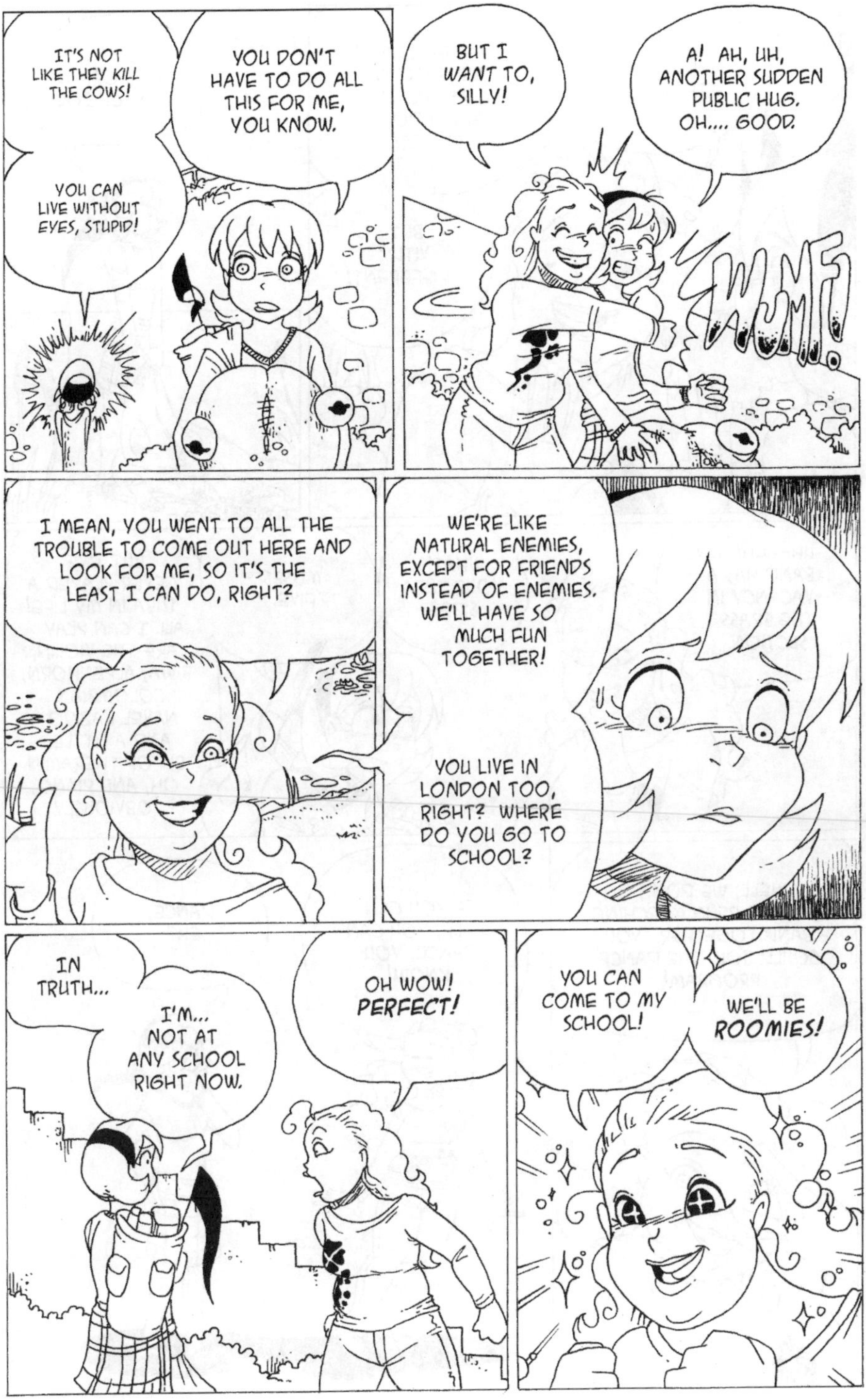

IT'S NOT LIKE THEY KILL THE COWS!
YOU CAN LIVE WITHOUT EYES, STUPID!
YOU DON'T HAVE TO DO ALL THIS FOR ME, YOU KNOW.
BUT I WANT TO, SILLY!
A! AH, UH, ANOTHER SUDDEN PUBLIC HUG. OH.... GOOD.
WUMF!
I MEAN, YOU WENT TO ALL THE TROUBLE TO COME OUT HERE AND LOOK FOR ME, SO IT'S THE LEAST I CAN DO, RIGHT?
WE'RE LIKE NATURAL ENEMIES, EXCEPT FOR FRIENDS INSTEAD OF ENEMIES. WE'LL HAVE SO MUCH FUN TOGETHER!
YOU LIVE IN LONDON TOO, RIGHT? WHERE DO YOU GO TO SCHOOL?
IN TRUTH...
I'M... NOT AT ANY SCHOOL RIGHT NOW.
OH WOW! PERFECT!
YOU CAN COME TO MY SCHOOL!
WE'LL BE ROOMIES!

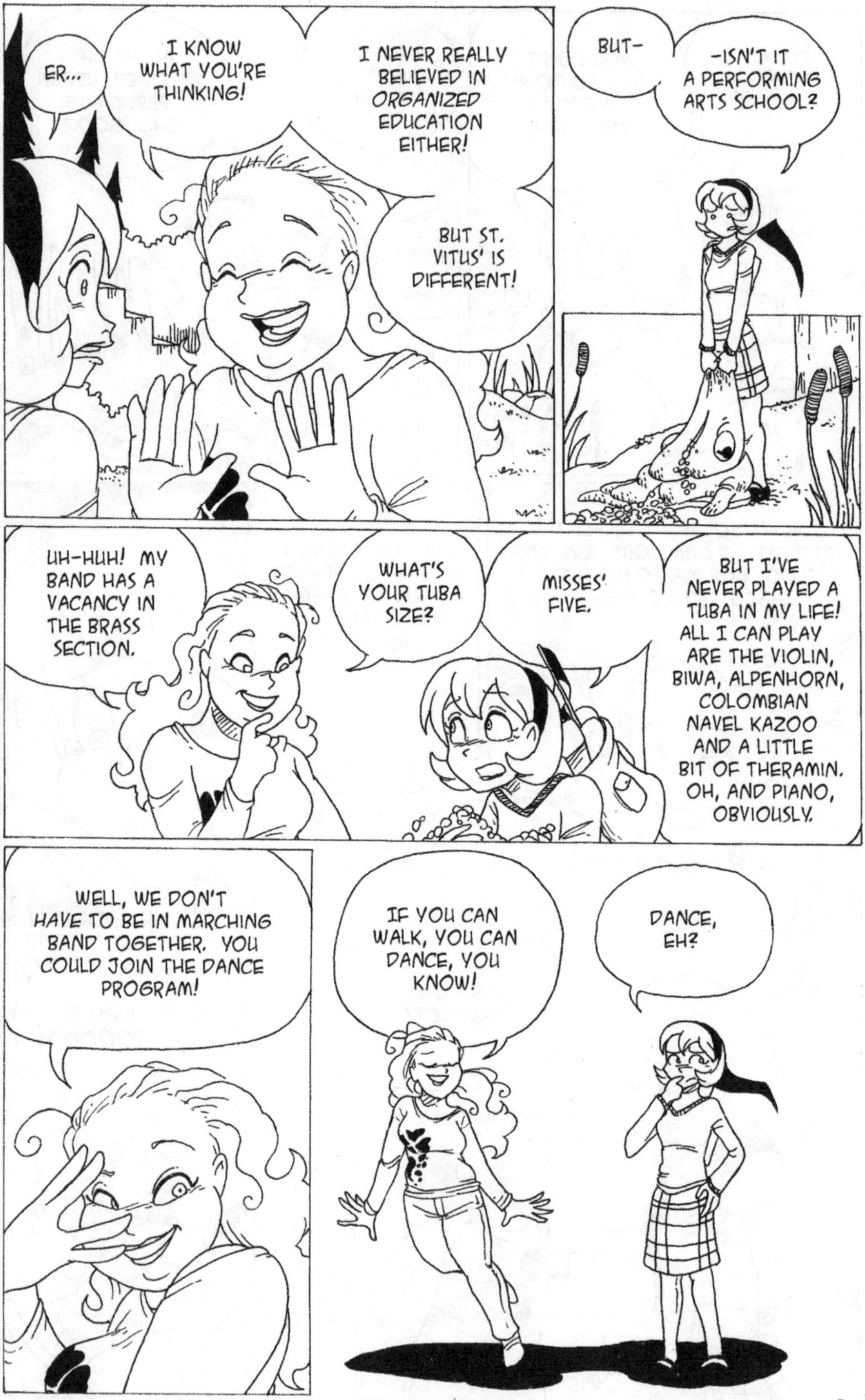
ER...
I KNOW WHAT YOU'RE THINKING!
I NEVER REALLY BELIEVED IN ORGANIZED EDUCATION EITHER!
BUT ST. VITUS' IS DIFFERENT!
BUT-
-ISN'T IT A PERFORMING ARTS SCHOOL?
UH-HUH! MY BAND HAS A VACANCY IN THE BRASS SECTION.
WHAT'S YOUR TUBA SIZE?
MISSES' FIVE.
BUT I'VE NEVER PLAYED A TUBA IN MY LIFE! ALL I CAN PLAY ARE THE VIOLIN, BIWA, ALPENHORN, COLOMBIAN NAVEL KAZOO AND A LITTLE BIT OF THERAMIN. OH, AND PIANO, OBVIOUSLY.
WELL, WE DON'T HAVE TO BE IN MARCHING BAND TOGETHER. YOU COULD JOIN THE DANCE PROGRAM!
IF YOU CAN WALK, YOU CAN DANCE, YOU KNOW!
DANCE, EH?

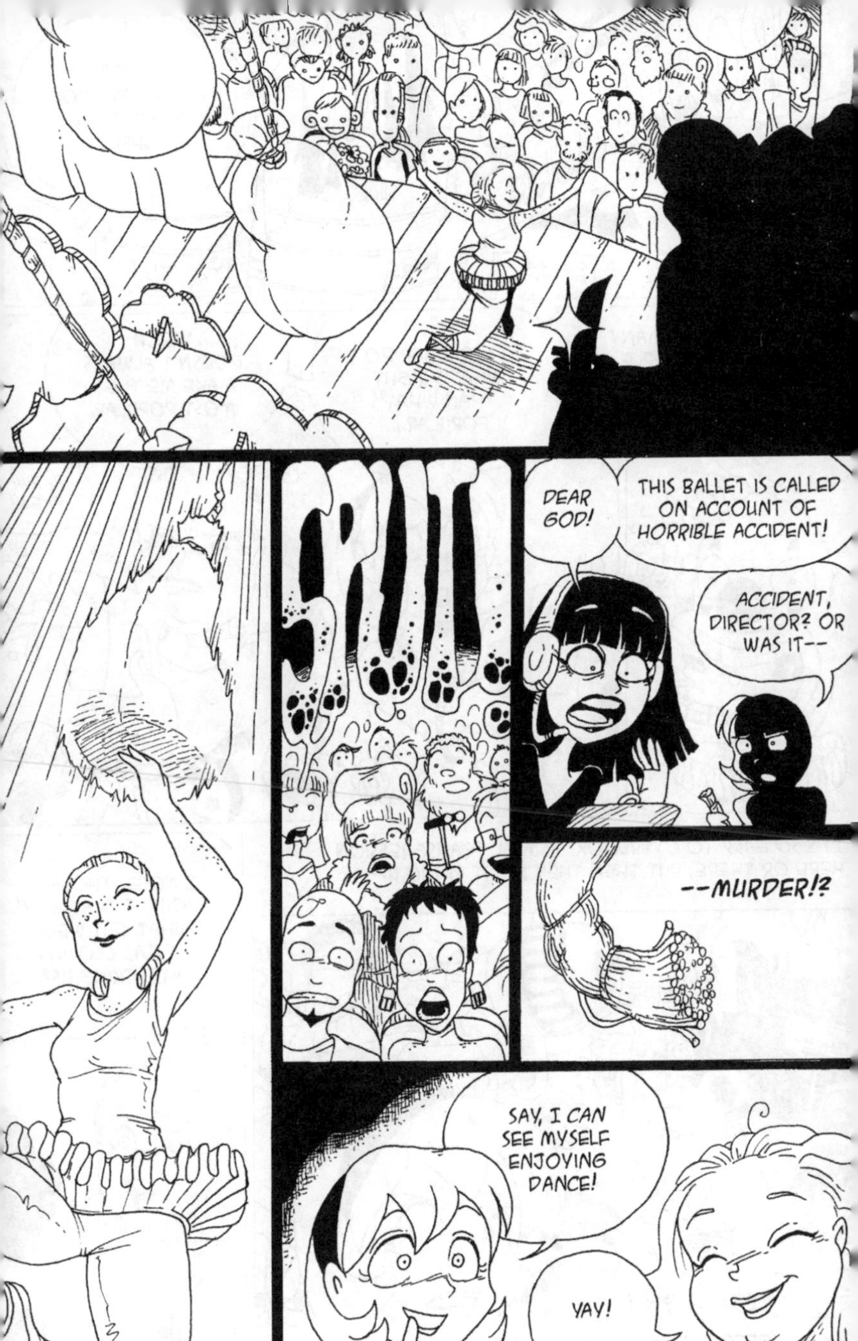
SPLUT
DEAR GOD!
THIS BALLET IS CALLED ON ACCOUNT OF HORRIBLE ACCIDENT!
ACCIDENT, DIRECTOR? OR WAS IT--
--MURDER!?
SAY, I CAN SEE MYSELF ENJOYING DANCE!
YAY!

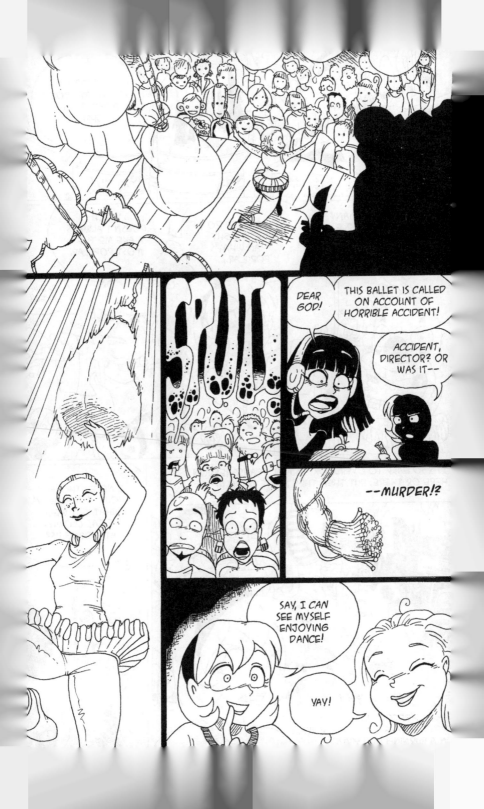

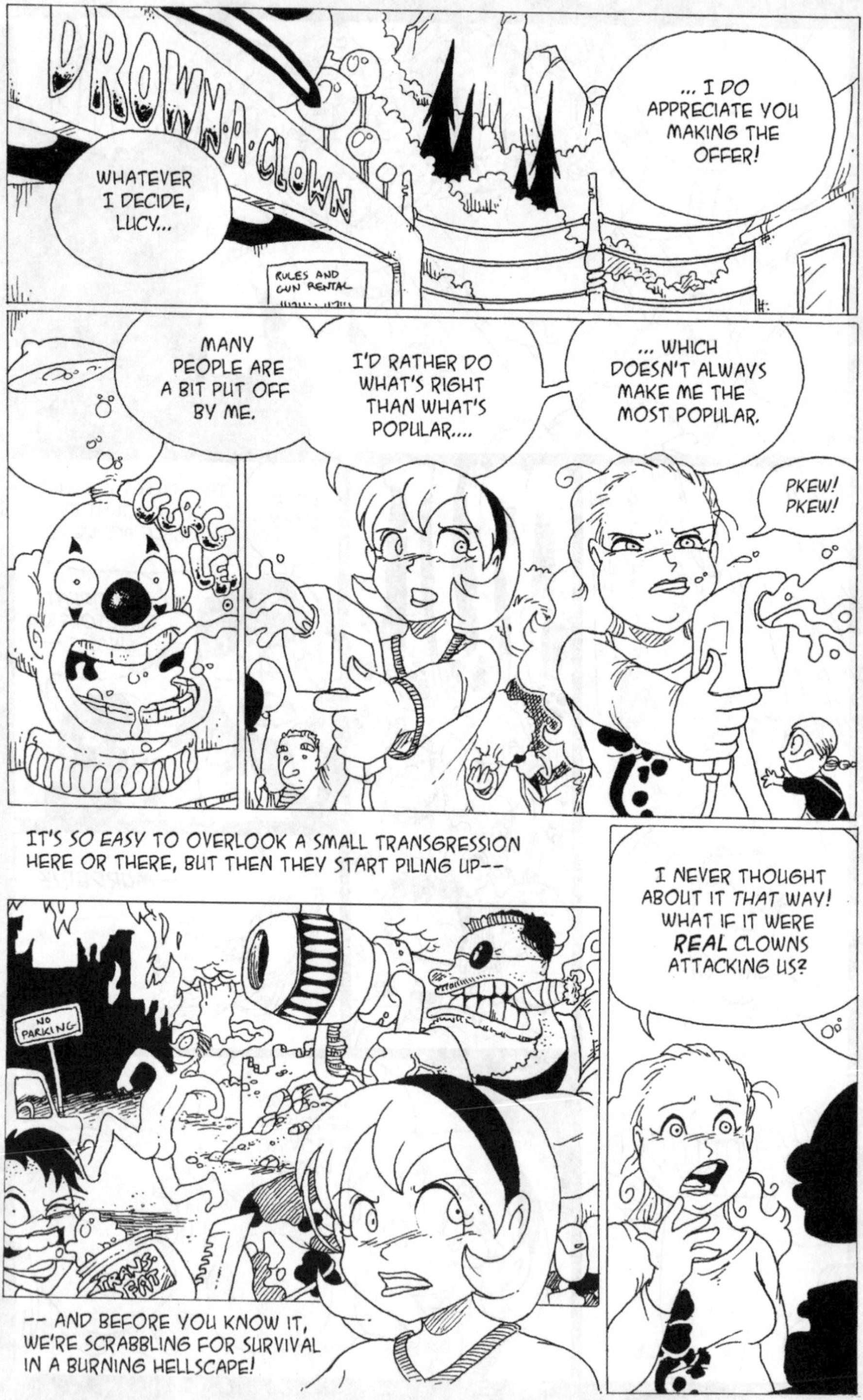
DROWN-A-CLOWN
WHATEVER I DECIDE, LUCY...
... I DO APPRECIATE YOU MAKING THE OFFER!
RULES AND GUN RENTAL
MANY PEOPLE ARE A BIT PUT OFF BY ME.
I'D RATHER DO WHAT'S RIGHT THAN WHAT'S POPULAR....
... WHICH DOESN'T ALWAYS MAKE ME THE MOST POPULAR.
GURGLE
PKEW! PKEW!
IT'S SO *EASY* TO OVERLOOK A SMALL TRANSGRESSION HERE OR THERE, BUT THEN THEY START PILING UP--
NO PARKING
TRANS FAT
-- AND BEFORE YOU KNOW IT, WE'RE SCRABBLING FOR SURVIVAL IN A BURNING HELLSCAPE!
I NEVER THOUGHT ABOUT IT *THAT* WAY! WHAT IF IT WERE **REAL** CLOWNS ATTACKING US?

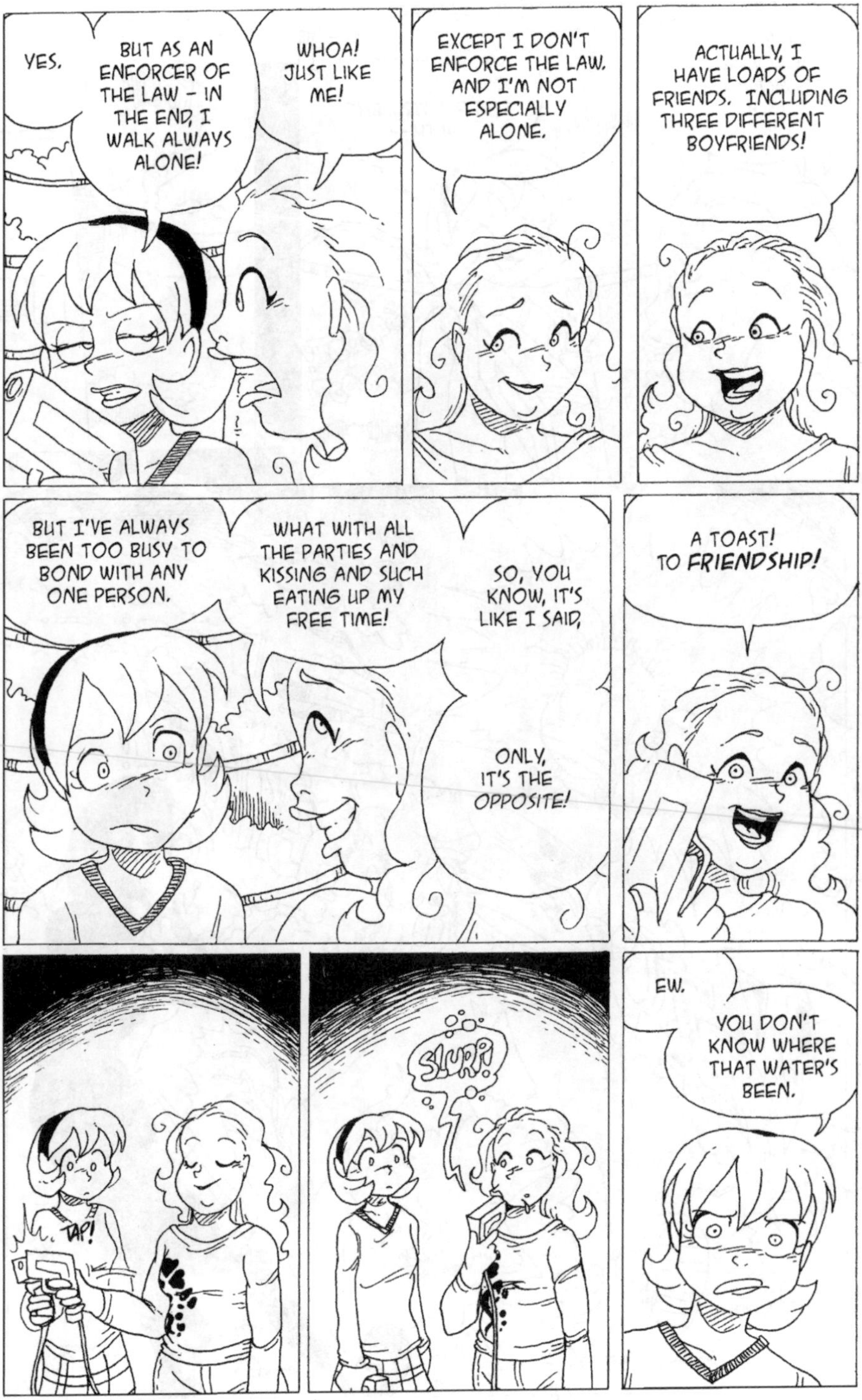
YES.
BUT AS AN ENFORCER OF THE LAW - IN THE END, I WALK ALWAYS ALONE!
WHOA! JUST LIKE ME!
EXCEPT I DON'T ENFORCE THE LAW. AND I'M NOT ESPECIALLY ALONE.
ACTUALLY, I HAVE LOADS OF FRIENDS. INCLUDING THREE DIFFERENT BOYFRIENDS!
BUT I'VE ALWAYS BEEN TOO BUSY TO BOND WITH ANY ONE PERSON.
WHAT WITH ALL THE PARTIES AND KISSING AND SUCH EATING UP MY FREE TIME!
SO, YOU KNOW, IT'S LIKE I SAID,
ONLY, IT'S THE OPPOSITE!
A TOAST! TO FRIENDSHIP!
TAP!
SLURP!
EW.
YOU DON'T KNOW WHERE THAT WATER'S BEEN.

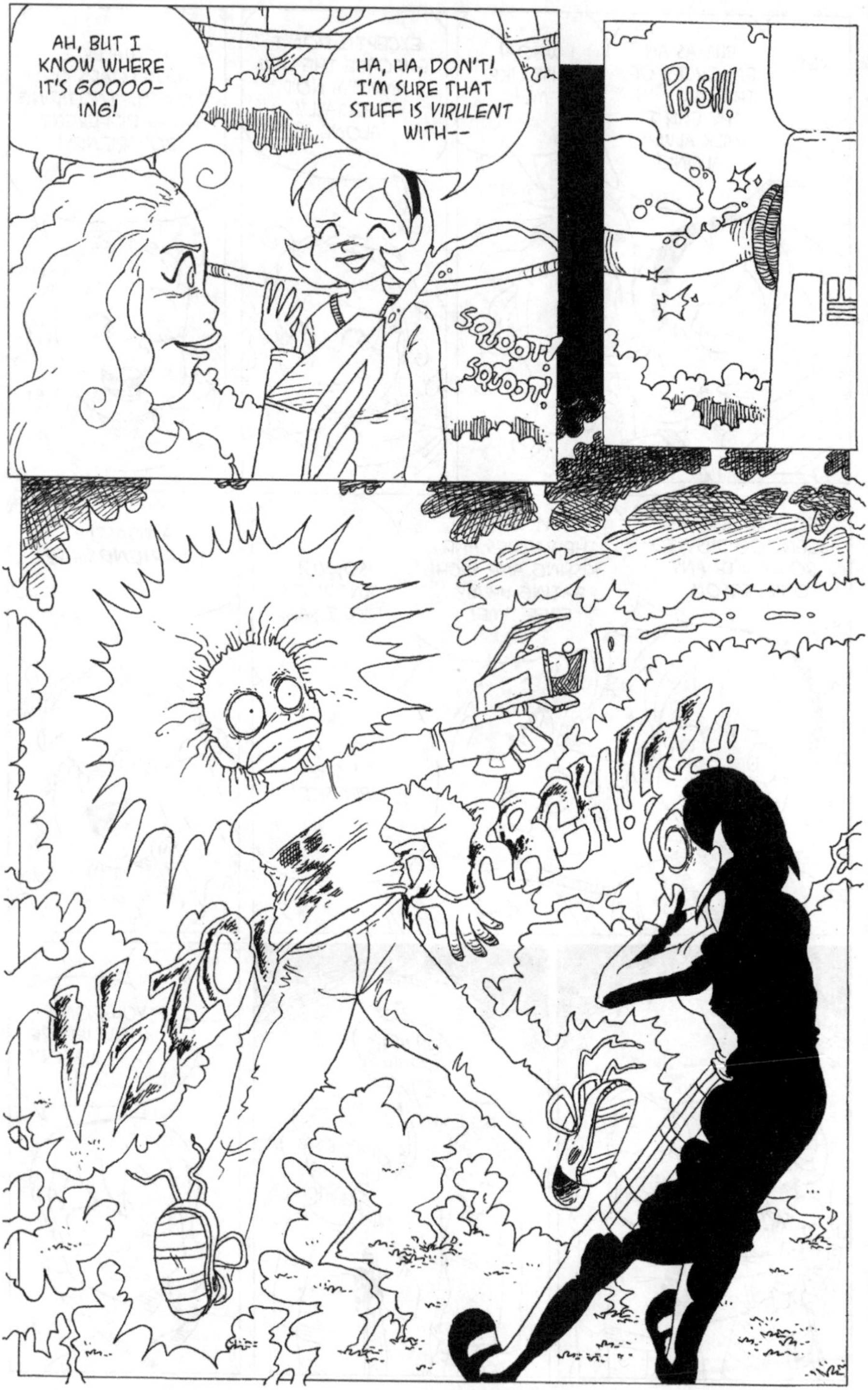

AH, BUT I KNOW WHERE IT'S GOOOO-ING!
HA, HA, DON'T! I'M SURE THAT STUFF IS VIRULENT WITH--
SQUOOT! SQUOOT!
PLUSH!
SPLOOSH!!
ZZOT

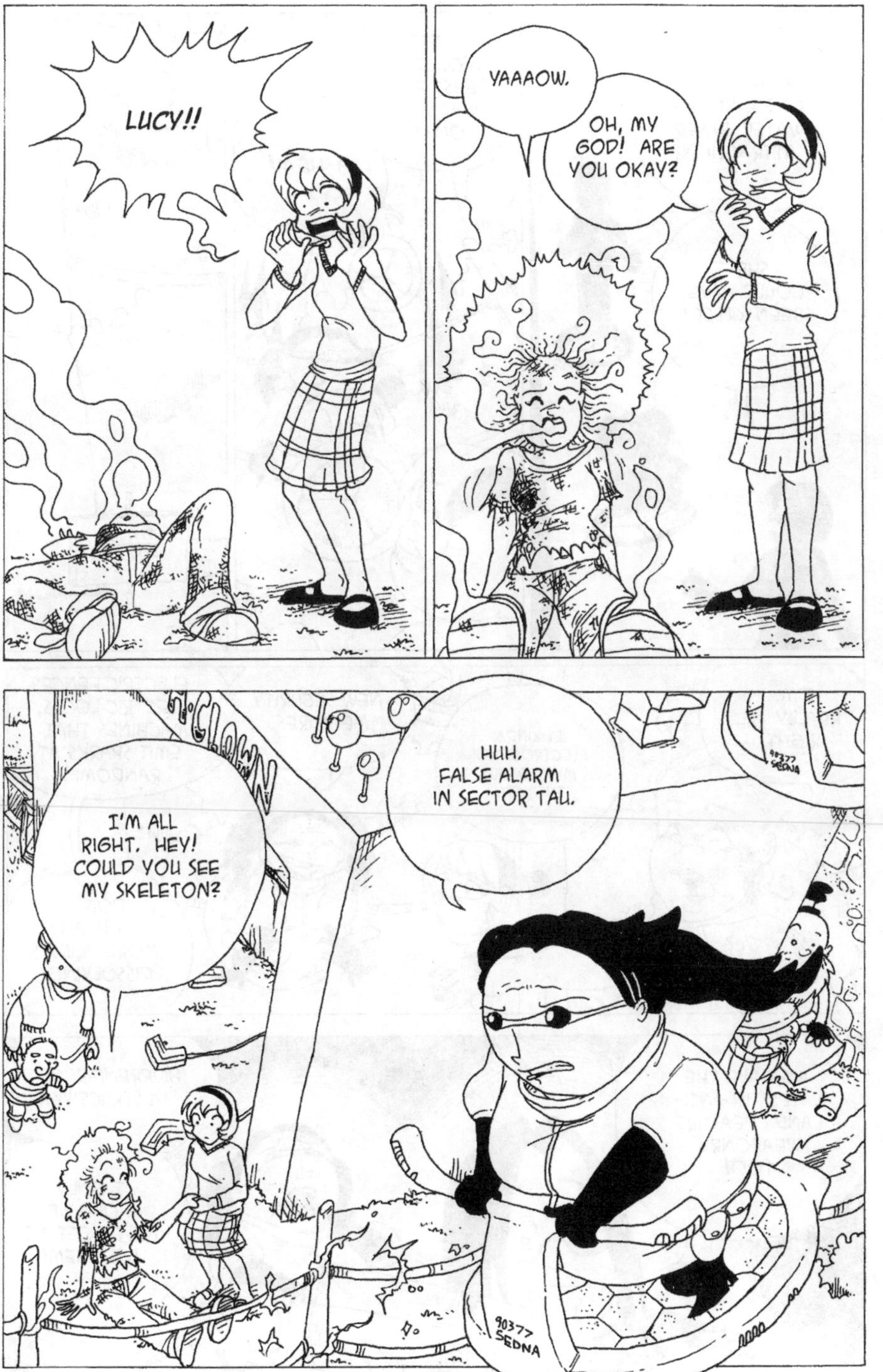
LUCY!!
YAAAOW.
OH, MY GOD! ARE YOU OKAY?
I'M ALL RIGHT. HEY! COULD YOU SEE MY SKELETON?
HUH. FALSE ALARM IN SECTOR TAU.
90377 SEDNA

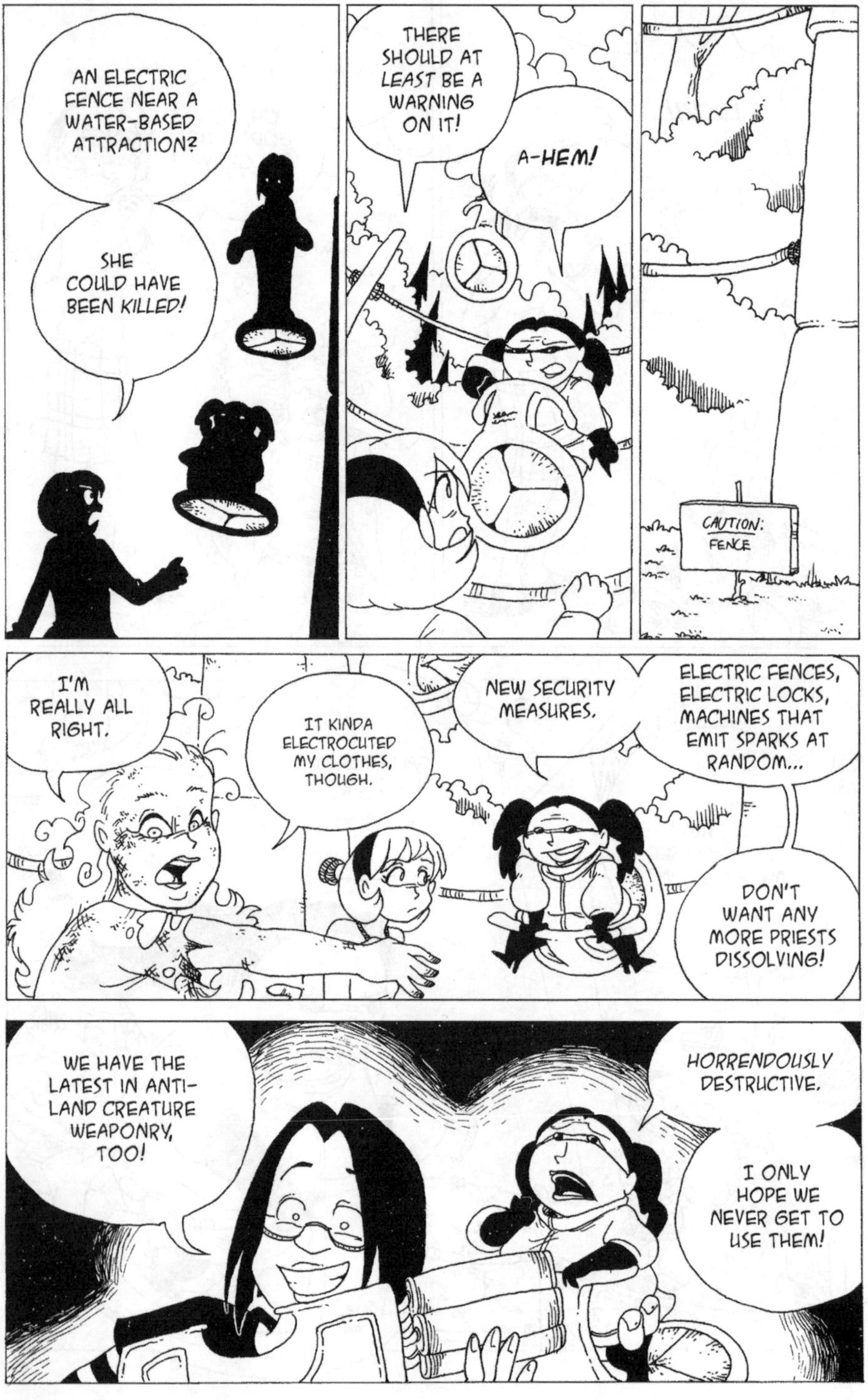
AN ELECTRIC FENCE NEAR A WATER-BASED ATTRACTION?
SHE COULD HAVE BEEN KILLED!
THERE SHOULD AT LEAST BE A WARNING ON IT!
A-HEM!
CAUTION: FENCE
I'M REALLY ALL RIGHT.
IT KINDA ELECTROCUTED MY CLOTHES, THOUGH.
NEW SECURITY MEASURES.
ELECTRIC FENCES, ELECTRIC LOCKS, MACHINES THAT EMIT SPARKS AT RANDOM...
DON'T WANT ANY MORE PRIESTS DISSOLVING!
WE HAVE THE LATEST IN ANTI-LAND CREATURE WEAPONRY, TOO!
HORRENDOUSLY DESTRUCTIVE.
I ONLY HOPE WE NEVER GET TO USE THEM!

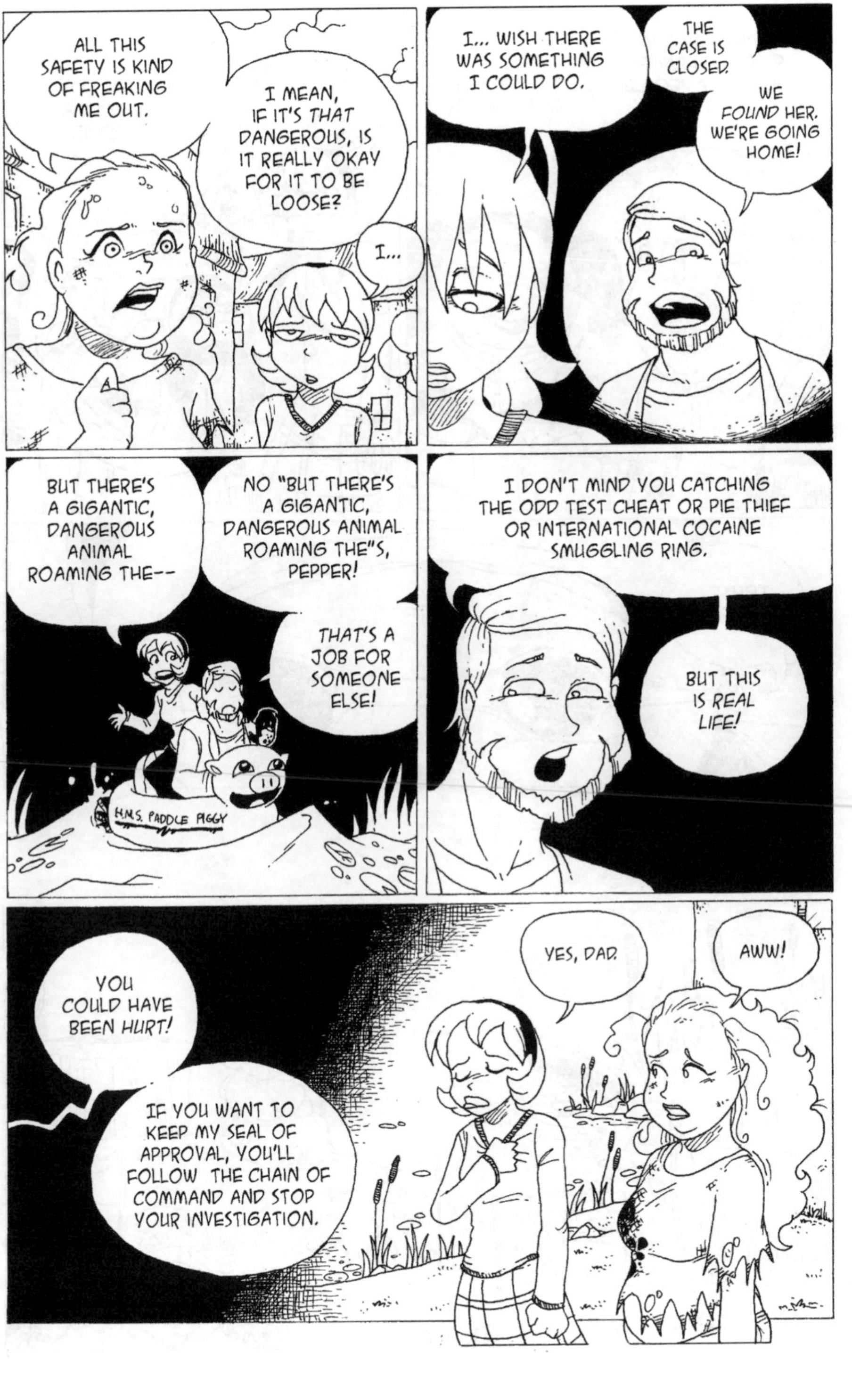
ALL THIS SAFETY IS KIND OF FREAKING ME OUT.
I MEAN, IF IT'S THAT DANGEROUS, IS IT REALLY OKAY FOR IT TO BE LOOSE?
I...
I... WISH THERE WAS SOMETHING I COULD DO.
THE CASE IS CLOSED.
WE FOUND HER. WE'RE GOING HOME!
BUT THERE'S A GIGANTIC, DANGEROUS ANIMAL ROAMING THE--
NO "BUT THERE'S A GIGANTIC, DANGEROUS ANIMAL ROAMING THE"S, PEPPER!
THAT'S A JOB FOR SOMEONE ELSE!
H.M.S. PADDLE PIGGY
I DON'T MIND YOU CATCHING THE ODD TEST CHEAT OR PIE THIEF OR INTERNATIONAL COCAINE SMUGGLING RING.
BUT THIS IS REAL LIFE!
YOU COULD HAVE BEEN HURT!
IF YOU WANT TO KEEP MY SEAL OF APPROVAL, YOU'LL FOLLOW THE CHAIN OF COMMAND AND STOP YOUR INVESTIGATION.
YES, DAD.
AWW!

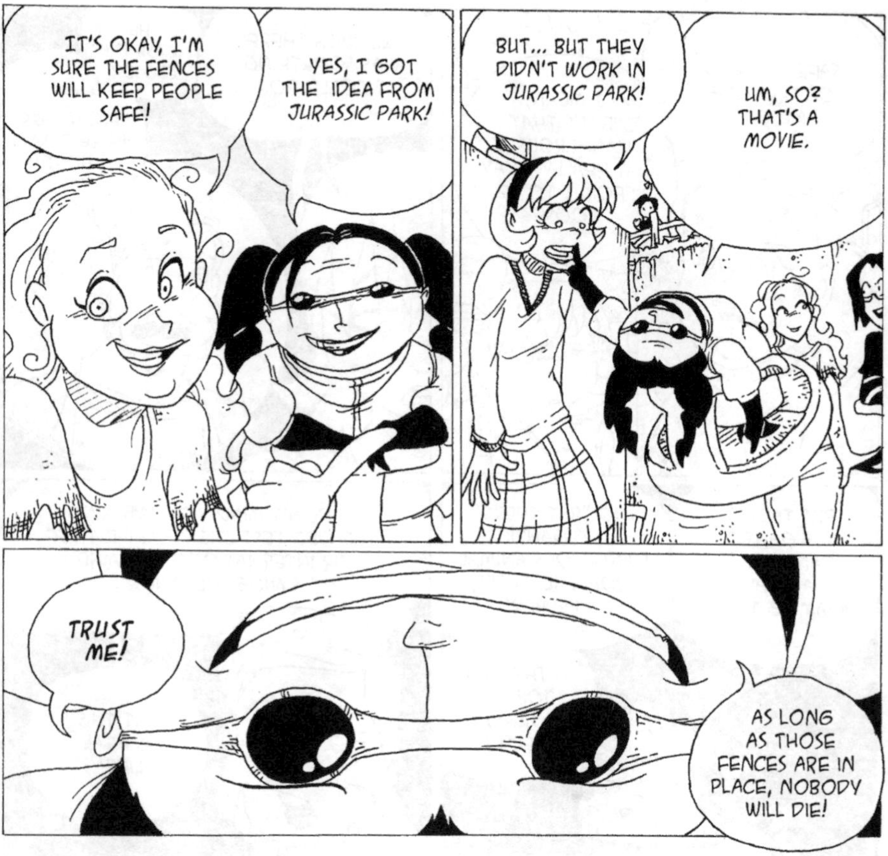
IT'S OKAY, I'M SURE THE FENCES WILL KEEP PEOPLE SAFE!
YES, I GOT THE IDEA FROM JURASSIC PARK!
BUT... BUT THEY DIDN'T WORK IN JURASSIC PARK!
UM, SO? THAT'S A MOVIE.
TRUST ME!
AS LONG AS THOSE FENCES ARE IN PLACE, NOBODY WILL DIE!

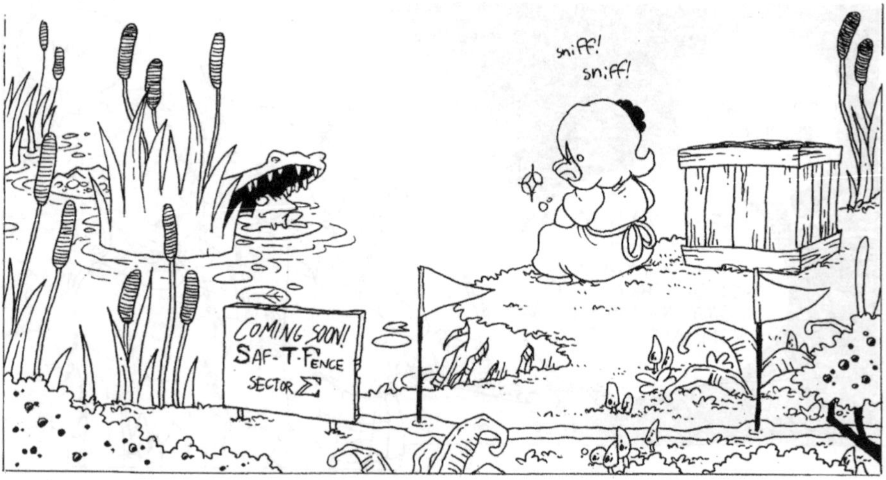
sniff!
sniff!
COMING SOON!
SAF-T-FENCE
SECTOR Σ

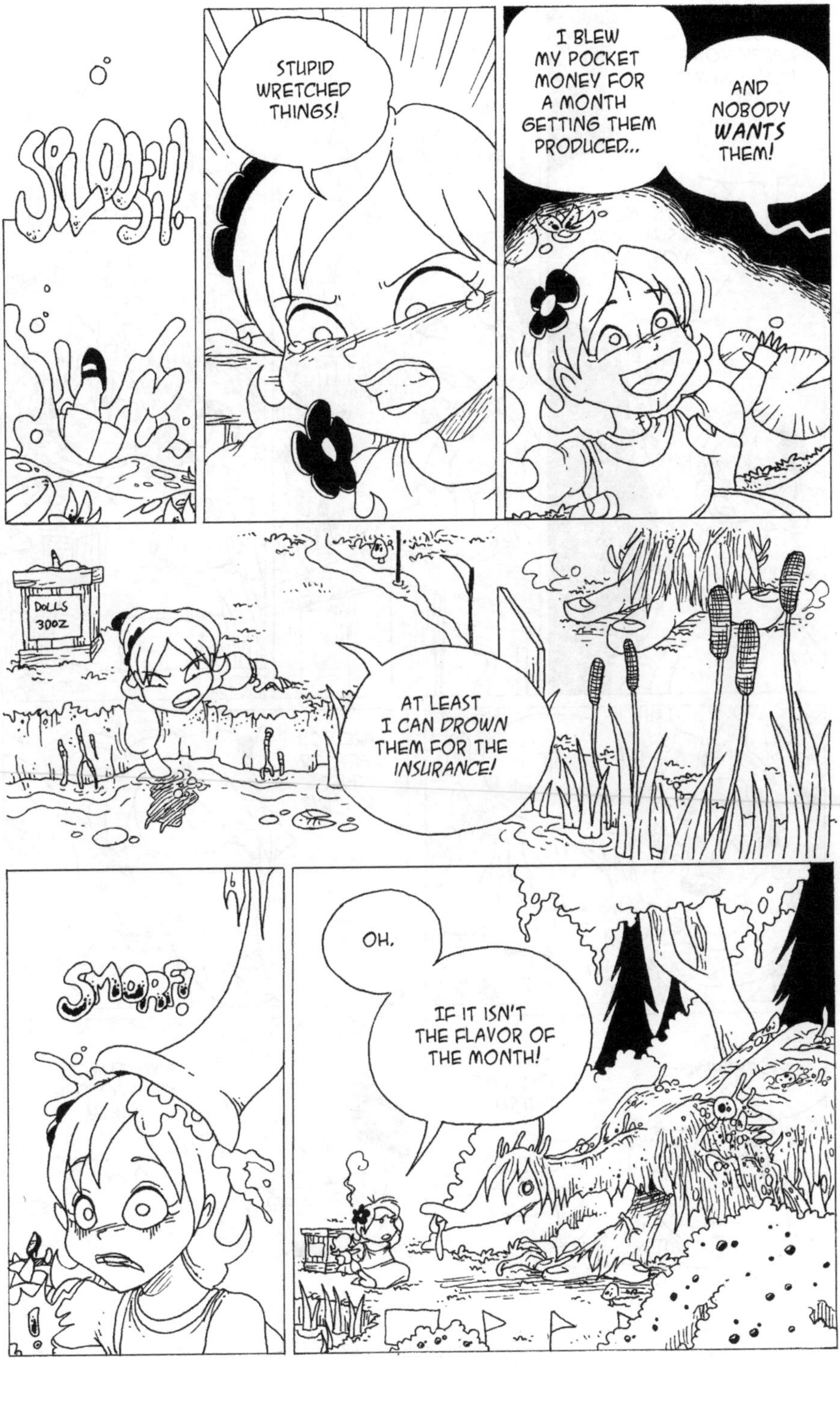
SPLOOSH!
STUPID WRETCHED THINGS!
I BLEW MY POCKET MONEY FOR A MONTH GETTING THEM PRODUCED...
AND NOBODY *WANTS* THEM!
DOLLS 3DOZ
AT LEAST I CAN *DROWN* THEM FOR THE *INSURANCE!*
SMORF!
OH.
IF IT ISN'T THE FLAVOR OF THE MONTH!

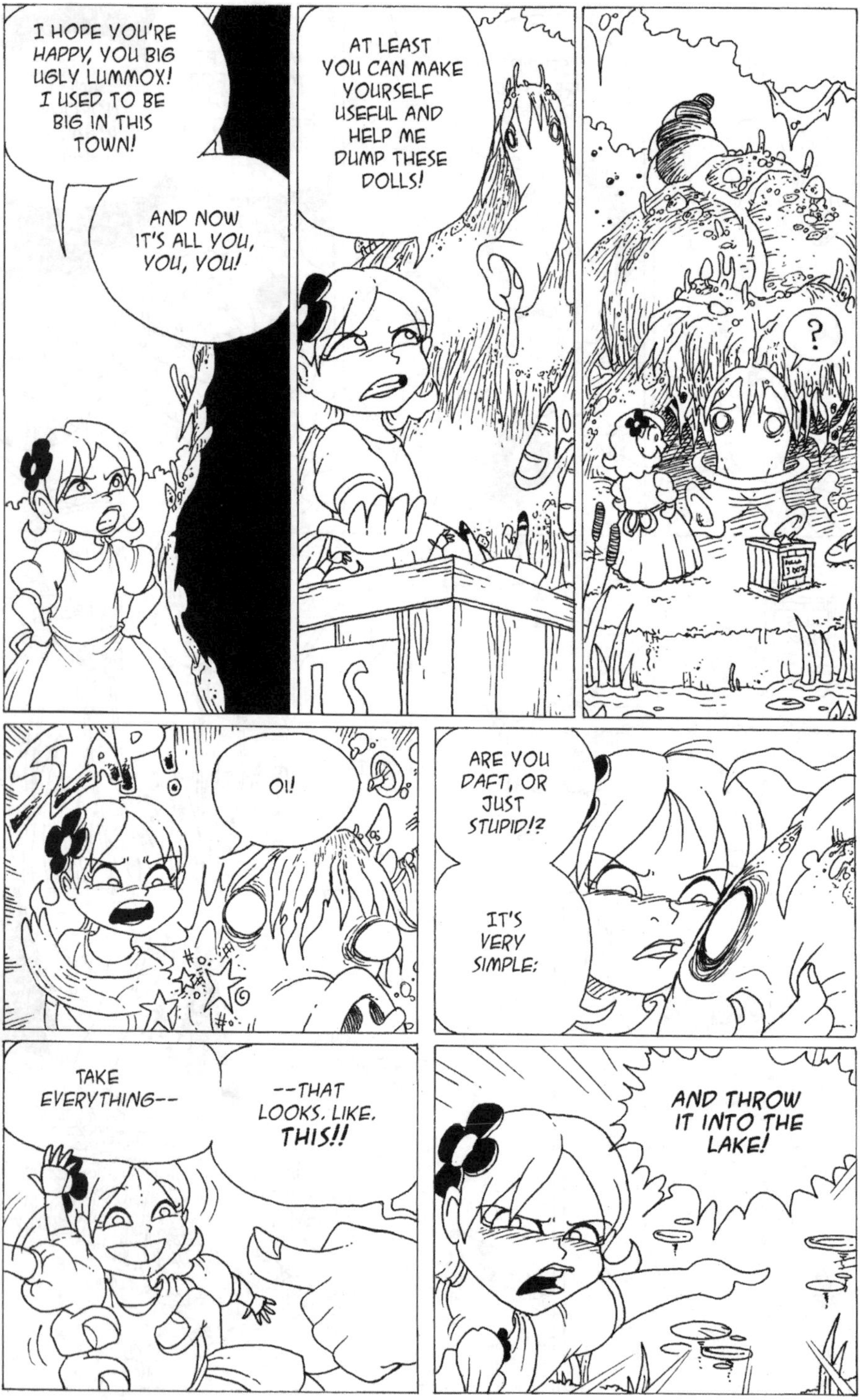
I HOPE YOU'RE HAPPY, YOU BIG UGLY LUMMOX! I USED TO BE BIG IN THIS TOWN!
AND NOW IT'S ALL YOU, YOU, YOU!
AT LEAST YOU CAN MAKE YOURSELF USEFUL AND HELP ME DUMP THESE DOLLS!
?
SLAP!
OI!
ARE YOU DAFT, OR JUST STUPID!?
IT'S VERY SIMPLE:
TAKE EVERYTHING--
--THAT LOOKS. LIKE. THIS!!
AND THROW IT INTO THE LAKE!

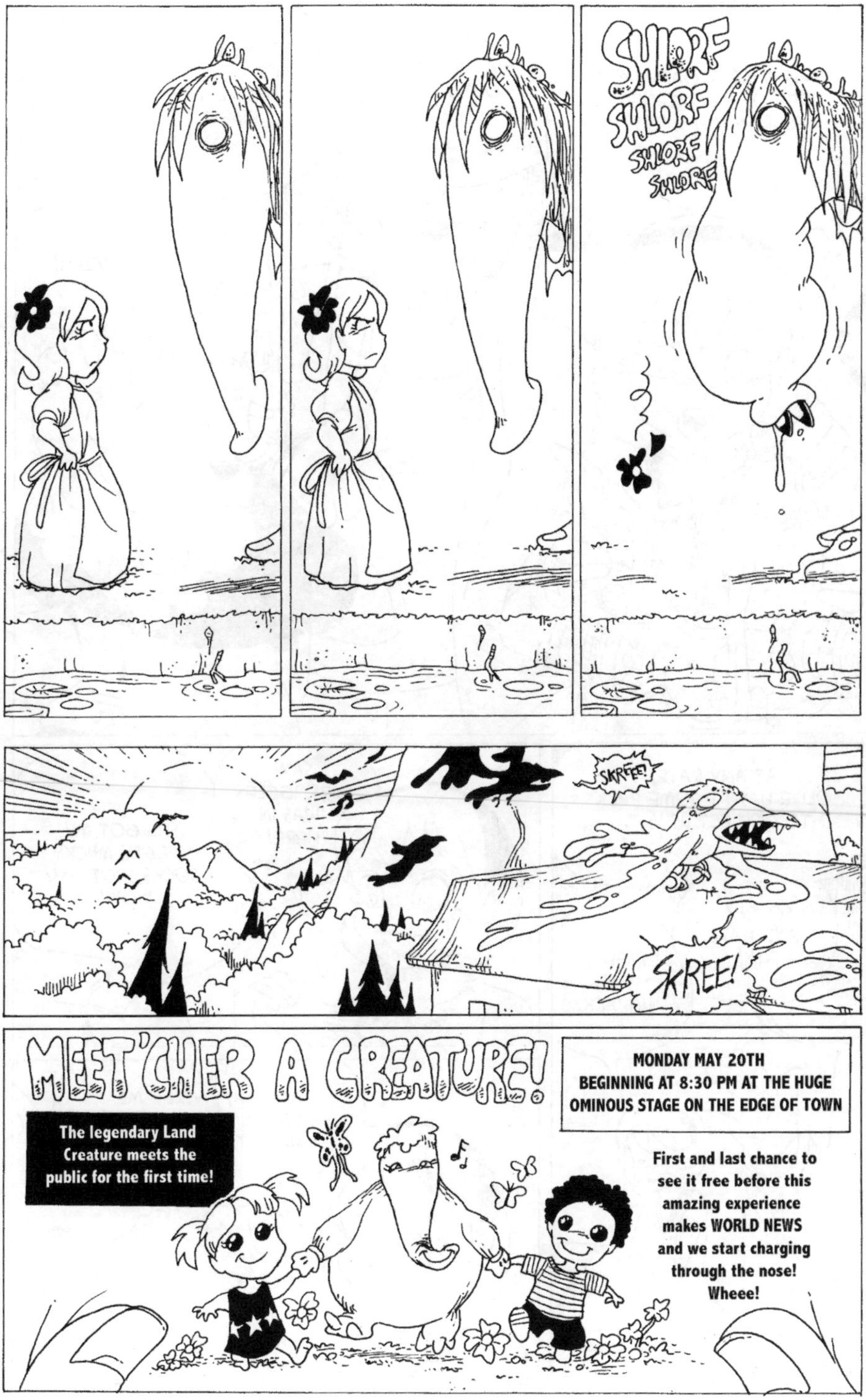
SHLORF
SHLORF
SHLORF
SHLORF
SKREEE!
SKREE!
MEET'CHER A CREATURE!
MONDAY MAY 20TH
BEGINNING AT 8:30 PM AT THE HUGE OMINOUS STAGE ON THE EDGE OF TOWN
The legendary Land Creature meets the public for the first time!
First and last chance to see it free before this amazing experience makes WORLD NEWS and we start charging through the nose! Wheee!

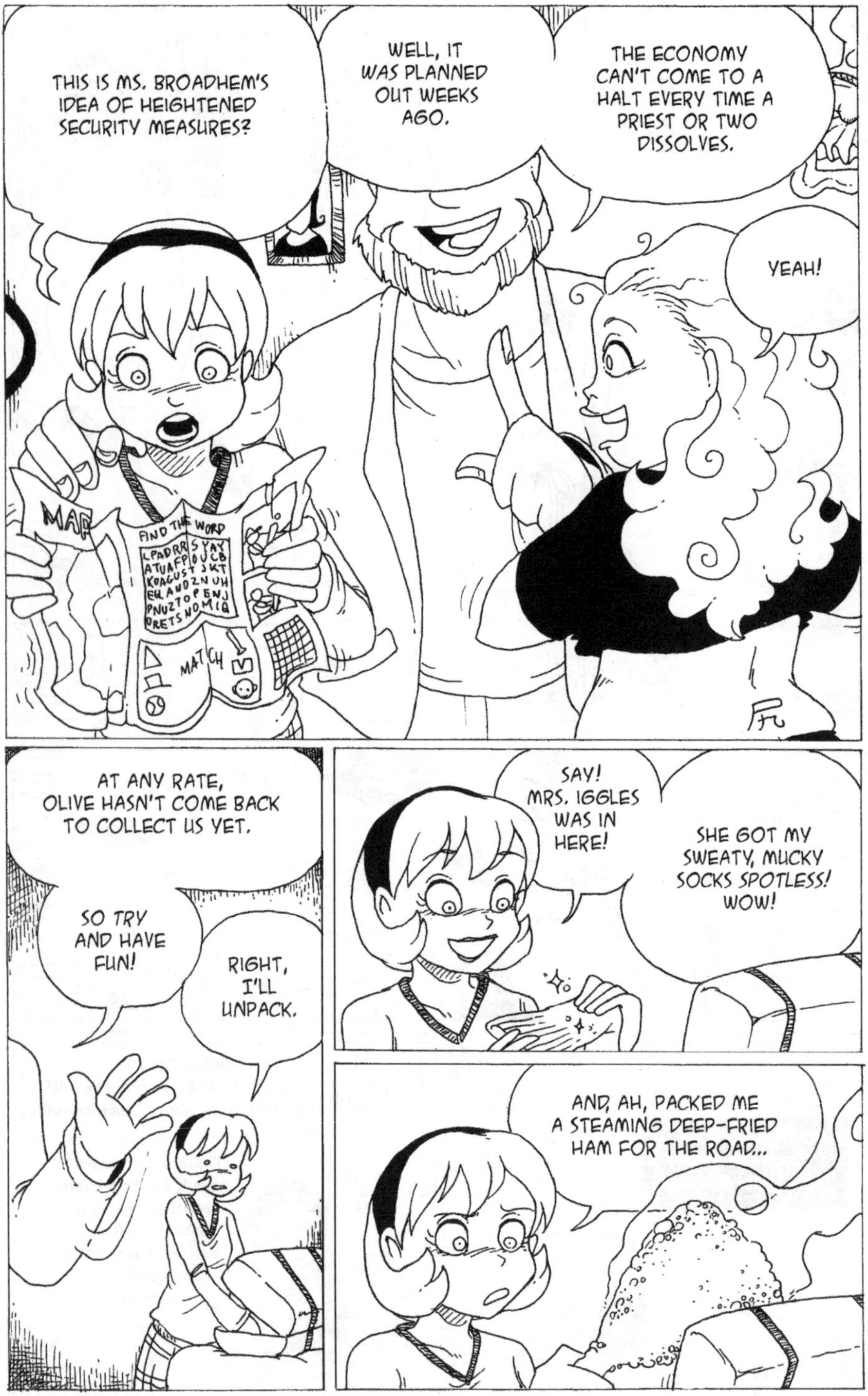
THIS IS MS. BROADHEM'S IDEA OF HEIGHTENED SECURITY MEASURES?
WELL, IT WAS PLANNED OUT WEEKS AGO.
THE ECONOMY CAN'T COME TO A HALT EVERY TIME A PRIEST OR TWO DISSOLVES.
YEAH!
FIND THE WORD
MATCH
AT ANY RATE, OLIVE HASN'T COME BACK TO COLLECT US YET.
SO TRY AND HAVE FUN!
RIGHT, I'LL UNPACK.
SAY! MRS. IGGLES WAS IN HERE!
SHE GOT MY SWEATY, MUCKY SOCKS SPOTLESS! WOW!
AND, AH, PACKED ME A STEAMING DEEP-FRIED HAM FOR THE ROAD...

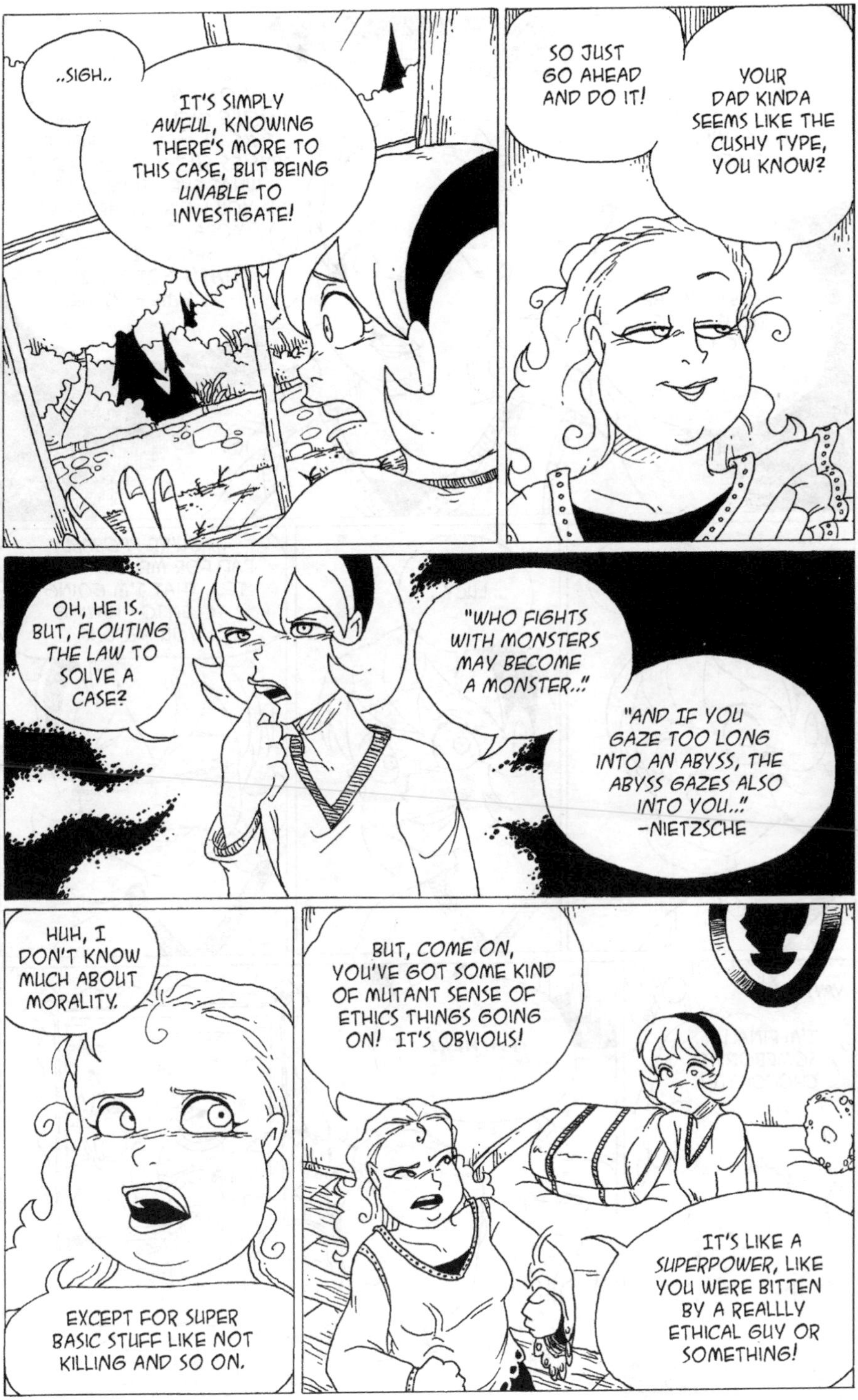
..SIGH..
IT'S SIMPLY AWFUL, KNOWING THERE'S MORE TO THIS CASE, BUT BEING UNABLE TO INVESTIGATE!
SO JUST GO AHEAD AND DO IT!
YOUR DAD KINDA SEEMS LIKE THE CUSHY TYPE, YOU KNOW?
OH, HE IS. BUT, FLOUTING THE LAW TO SOLVE A CASE?
"WHO FIGHTS WITH MONSTERS MAY BECOME A MONSTER..."
"AND IF YOU GAZE TOO LONG INTO AN ABYSS, THE ABYSS GAZES ALSO INTO YOU..." -NIETZSCHE
HUH, I DON'T KNOW MUCH ABOUT MORALITY.
EXCEPT FOR SUPER BASIC STUFF LIKE NOT KILLING AND SO ON.
BUT, COME ON, YOU'VE GOT SOME KIND OF MUTANT SENSE OF ETHICS THINGS GOING ON! IT'S OBVIOUS!
IT'S LIKE A SUPERPOWER, LIKE YOU WERE BITTEN BY A REALLLY ETHICAL GUY OR SOMETHING!

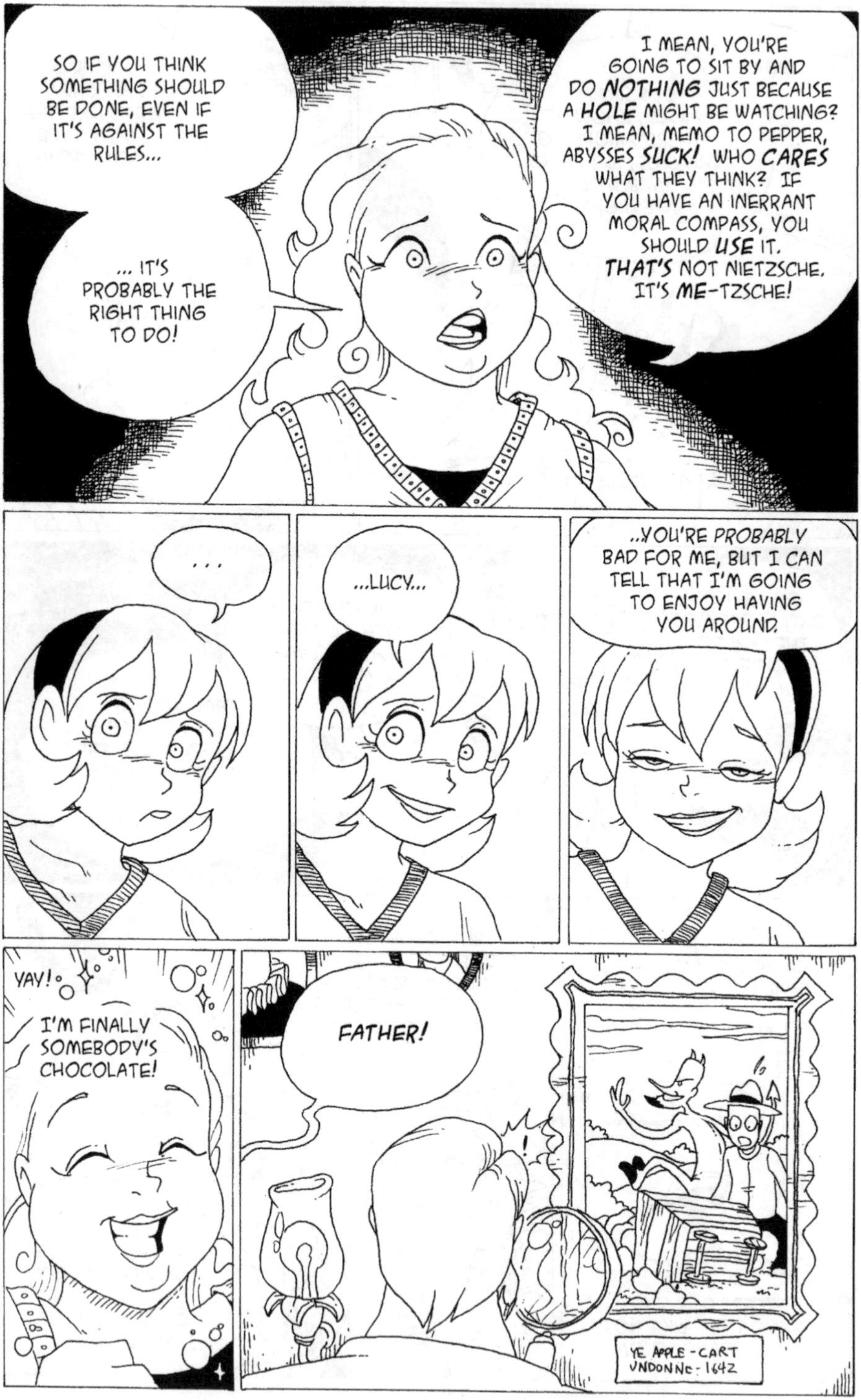
SO IF YOU THINK SOMETHING SHOULD BE DONE, EVEN IF IT'S AGAINST THE RULES...
... IT'S PROBABLY THE RIGHT THING TO DO!
I MEAN, YOU'RE GOING TO SIT BY AND DO NOTHING JUST BECAUSE A HOLE MIGHT BE WATCHING? I MEAN, MEMO TO PEPPER, ABYSSES SUCK! WHO CARES WHAT THEY THINK? IF YOU HAVE AN INERRANT MORAL COMPASS, YOU SHOULD USE IT. THAT'S NOT NIETZSCHE. IT'S ME-TZSCHE!
...
...LUCY...
..YOU'RE PROBABLY BAD FOR ME, BUT I CAN TELL THAT I'M GOING TO ENJOY HAVING YOU AROUND.
YAY!
I'M FINALLY SOMEBODY'S CHOCOLATE!
FATHER!
!
YE APPLE-CART UNDONNE - 1642

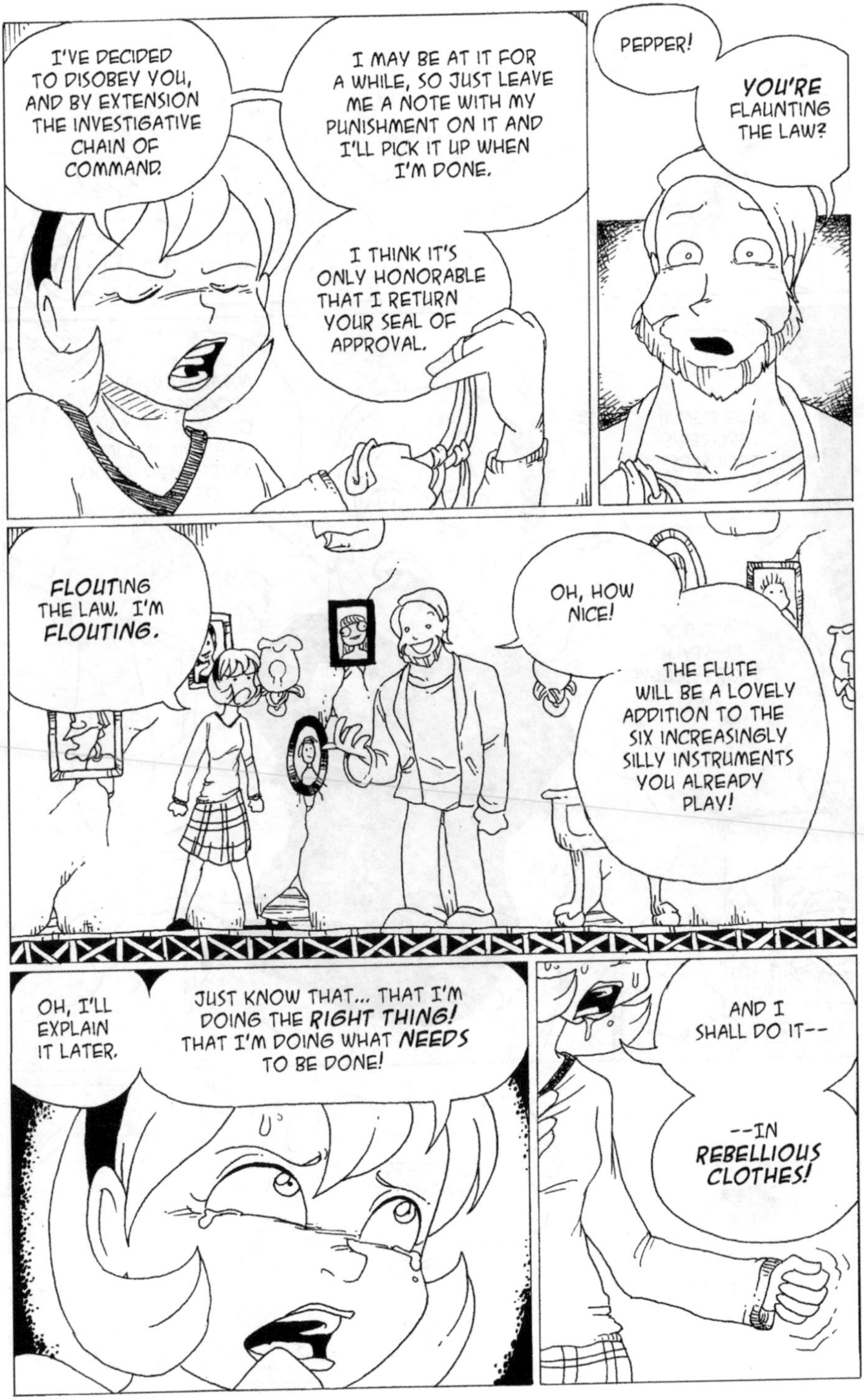
I'VE DECIDED TO DISOBEY YOU, AND BY EXTENSION THE INVESTIGATIVE CHAIN OF COMMAND.
I MAY BE AT IT FOR A WHILE, SO JUST LEAVE ME A NOTE WITH MY PUNISHMENT ON IT AND I'LL PICK IT UP WHEN I'M DONE.
I THINK IT'S ONLY HONORABLE THAT I RETURN YOUR SEAL OF APPROVAL.
PEPPER!
YOU'RE FLAUNTING THE LAW?
FLOUTING THE LAW. I'M FLOUTING.
OH, HOW NICE!
THE FLUTE WILL BE A LOVELY ADDITION TO THE SIX INCREASINGLY SILLY INSTRUMENTS YOU ALREADY PLAY!
OH, I'LL EXPLAIN IT LATER.
JUST KNOW THAT... THAT I'M DOING THE RIGHT THING! THAT I'M DOING WHAT NEEDS TO BE DONE!
AND I SHALL DO IT--
--IN REBELLIOUS CLOTHES!

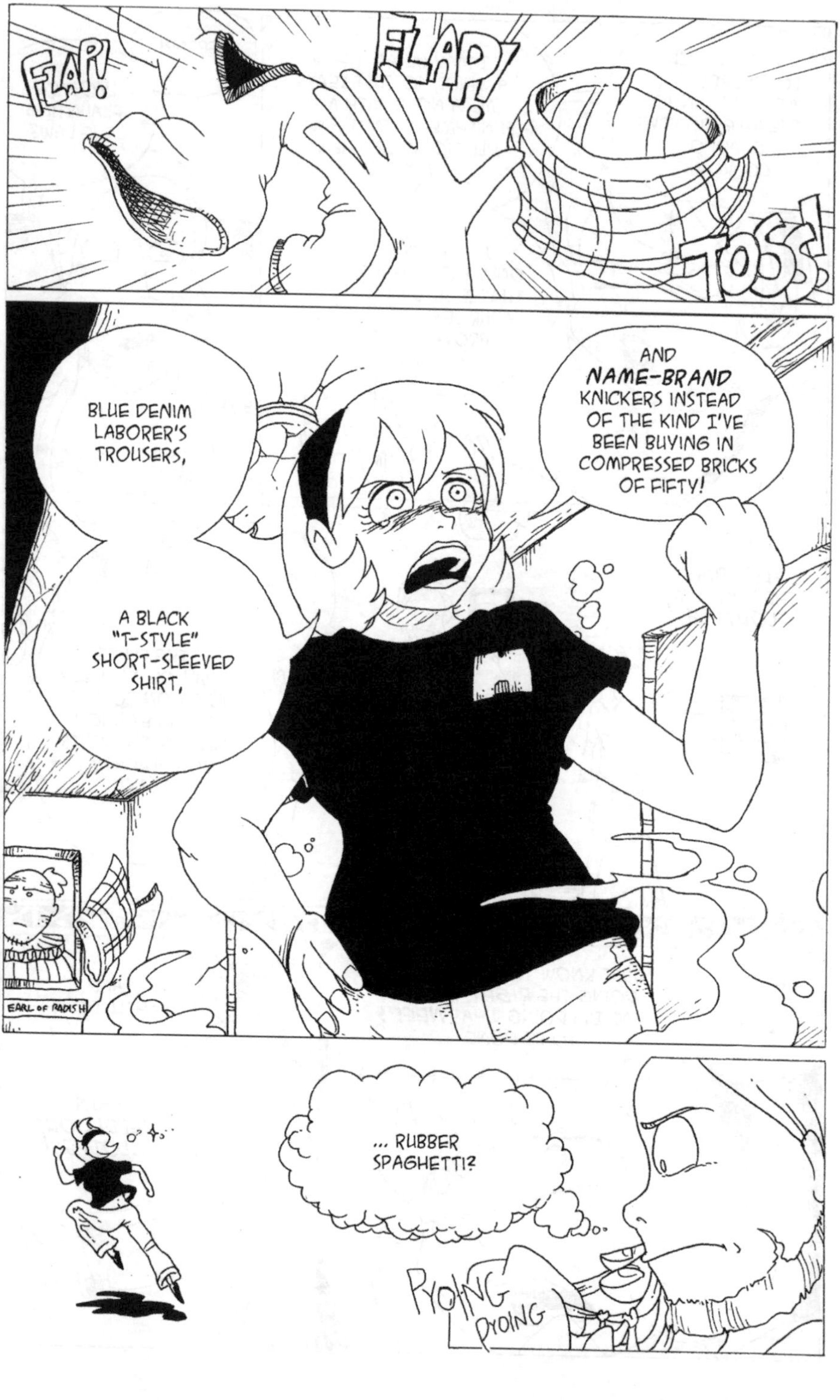
FLAP!
FLAP!
TOSS!
BLUE DENIM LABORER'S TROUSERS,
A BLACK "T-STYLE" SHORT-SLEEVED SHIRT,
AND NAME-BRAND KNICKERS INSTEAD OF THE KIND I'VE BEEN BUYING IN COMPRESSED BRICKS OF FIFTY!
EARL OF RADISH
... RUBBER SPAGHETTI?
PYOING
PYOING

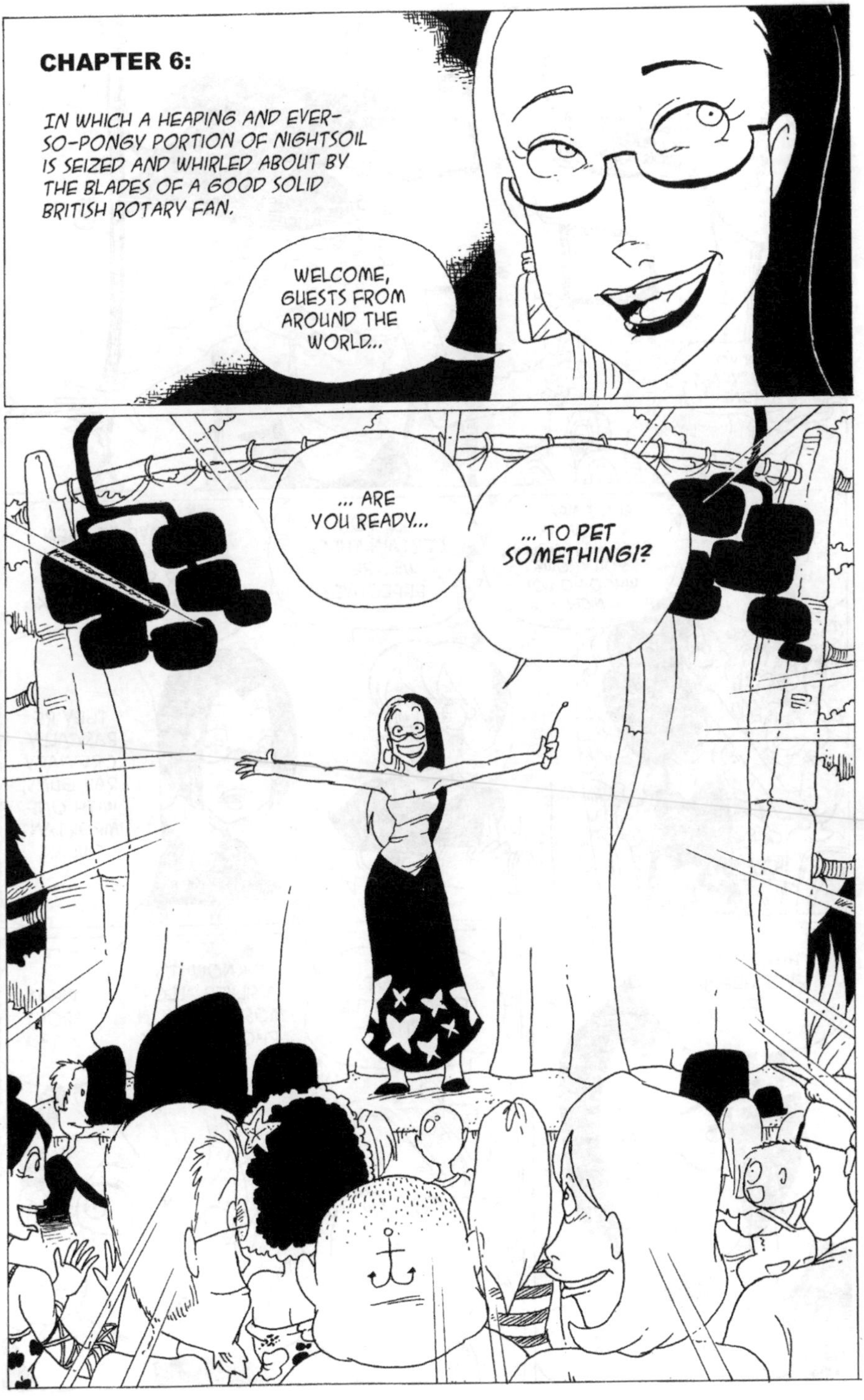
CHAPTER 6:
IN WHICH A HEAPING AND EVER-SO-PONGY PORTION OF NIGHTSOIL IS SEIZED AND WHIRLED ABOUT BY THE BLADES OF A GOOD SOLID BRITISH ROTARY FAN.
WELCOME, GUESTS FROM AROUND THE WORLD...
... ARE YOU READY...
... TO PET SOMETHING!?

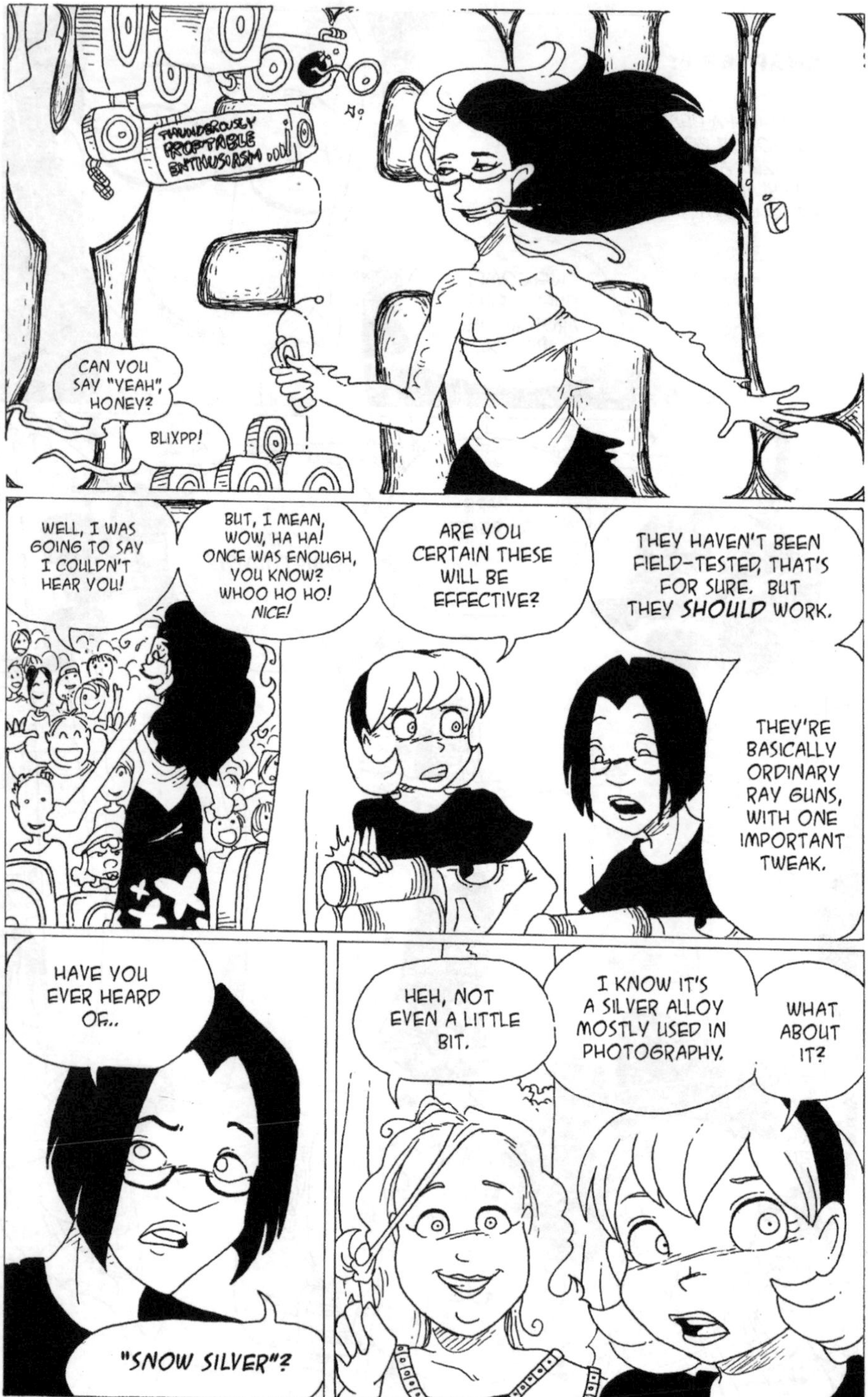
THUNDEROUSLY PROFITABLE ENTHUSIASM
CAN YOU SAY "YEAH", HONEY?
BLIXPP!
WELL, I WAS GOING TO SAY I COULDN'T HEAR YOU!
BUT, I MEAN, WOW, HA HA! ONCE WAS ENOUGH, YOU KNOW? WHOO HO HO! NICE!
ARE YOU CERTAIN THESE WILL BE EFFECTIVE?
THEY HAVEN'T BEEN FIELD-TESTED, THAT'S FOR SURE. BUT THEY *SHOULD* WORK.
THEY'RE BASICALLY ORDINARY RAY GUNS, WITH ONE IMPORTANT TWEAK.
HAVE YOU EVER HEARD OF..
"SNOW SILVER"?
HEH, NOT EVEN A LITTLE BIT.
I KNOW IT'S A SILVER ALLOY MOSTLY USED IN PHOTOGRAPHY.
WHAT ABOUT IT?

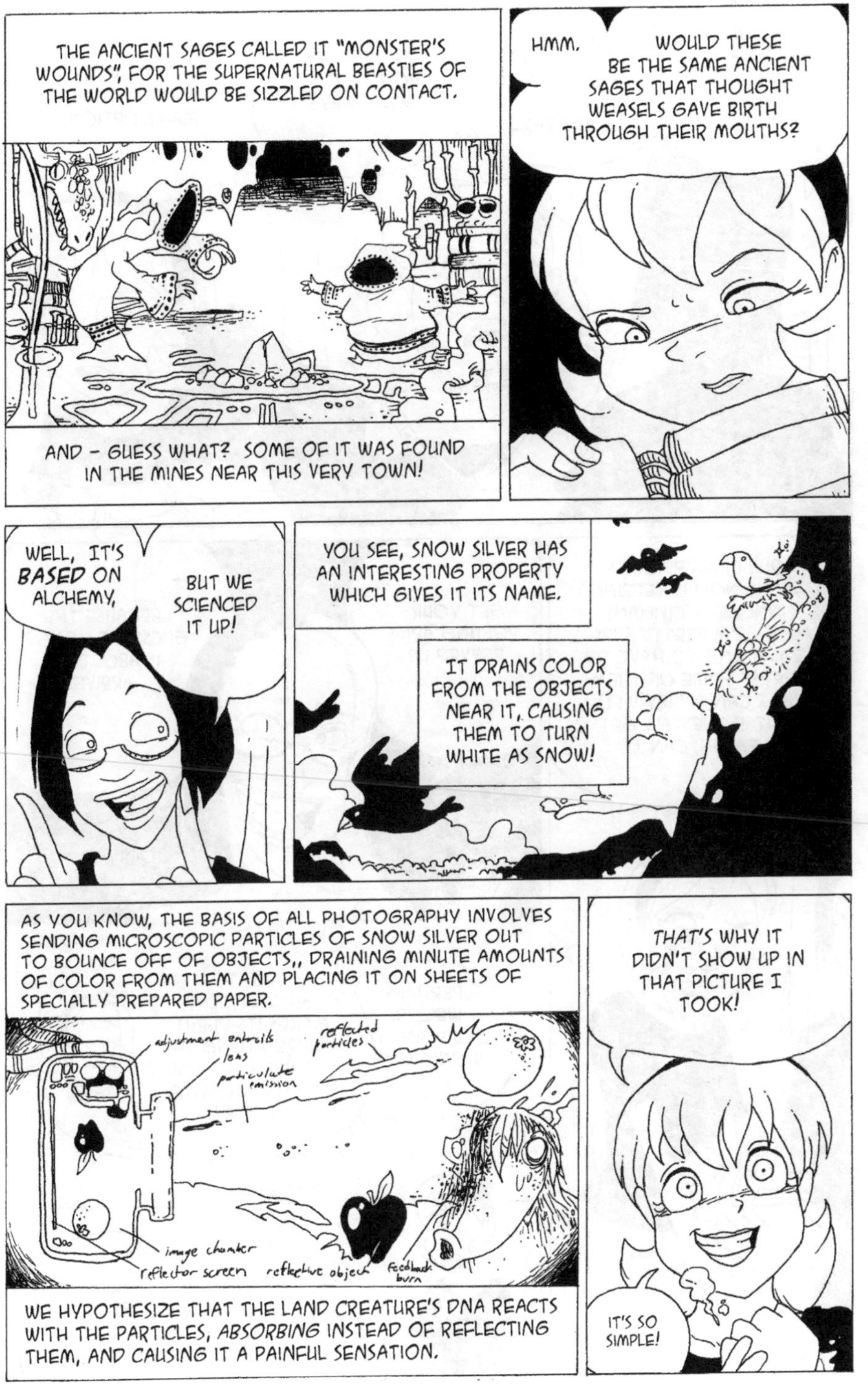
THE ANCIENT SAGES CALLED IT "MONSTER'S WOUNDS", FOR THE SUPERNATURAL BEASTIES OF THE WORLD WOULD BE SIZZLED ON CONTACT.
AND – GUESS WHAT? SOME OF IT WAS FOUND IN THE MINES NEAR THIS VERY TOWN!
HMM.
WOULD THESE BE THE SAME ANCIENT SAGES THAT THOUGHT WEASELS GAVE BIRTH THROUGH THEIR MOUTHS?
WELL, IT'S *BASED* ON ALCHEMY,
BUT WE SCIENCED IT UP!
YOU SEE, SNOW SILVER HAS AN INTERESTING PROPERTY WHICH GIVES IT ITS NAME.
IT DRAINS COLOR FROM THE OBJECTS NEAR IT, CAUSING THEM TO TURN WHITE AS SNOW!
AS YOU KNOW, THE BASIS OF ALL PHOTOGRAPHY INVOLVES SENDING MICROSCOPIC PARTICLES OF SNOW SILVER OUT TO BOUNCE OFF OF OBJECTS,, DRAINING MINUTE AMOUNTS OF COLOR FROM THEM AND PLACING IT ON SHEETS OF SPECIALLY PREPARED PAPER.
adjustment controls
lens
particulate emission
reflected particles
image chamber
reflector screen
reflective object
feedback burn
WE HYPOTHESIZE THAT THE LAND CREATURE'S DNA REACTS WITH THE PARTICLES, *ABSORBING* INSTEAD OF REFLECTING THEM, AND CAUSING IT A PAINFUL SENSATION.
THAT'S WHY IT DIDN'T SHOW UP IN THAT PICTURE I TOOK!
IT'S SO SIMPLE!

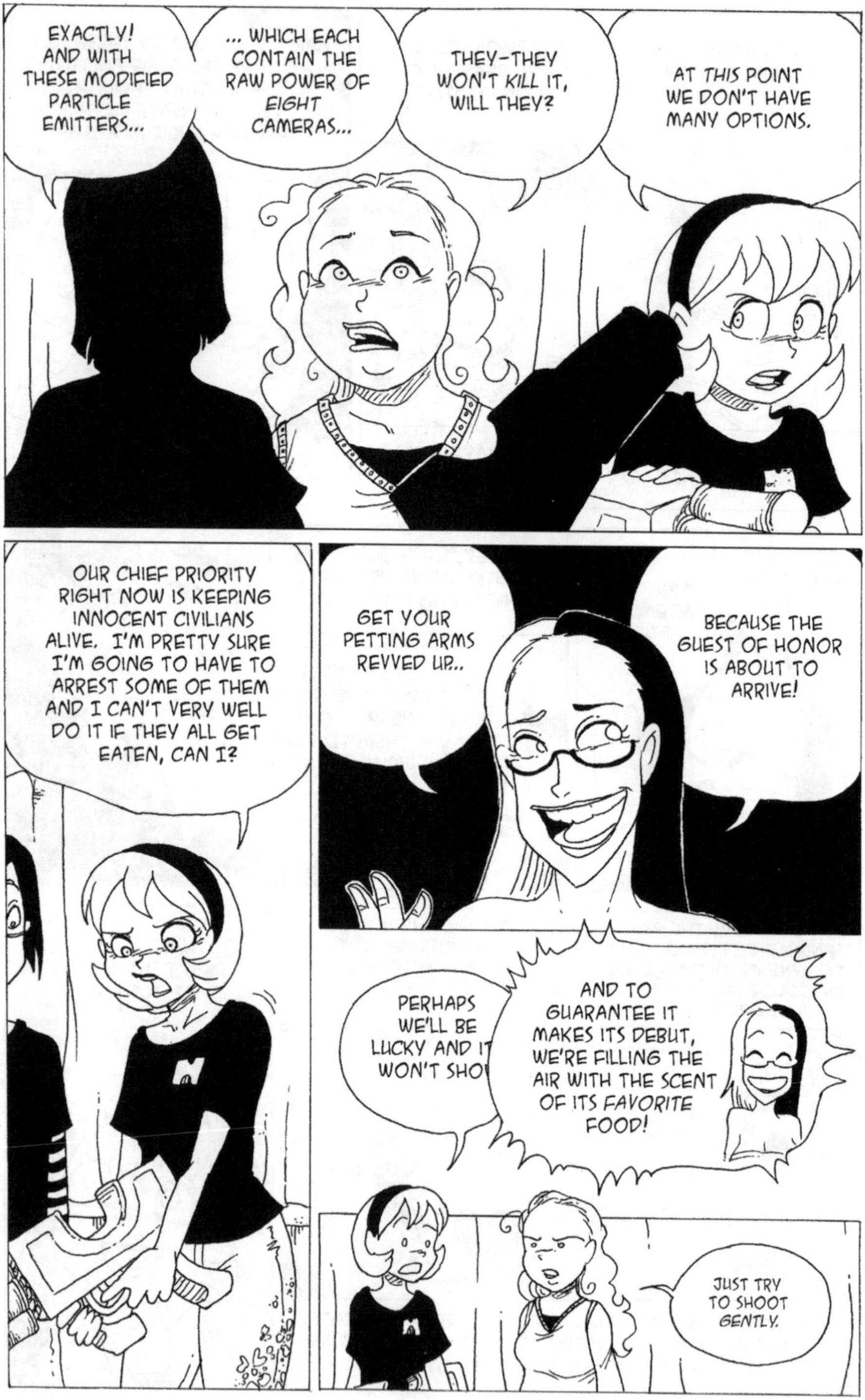
EXACTLY! AND WITH THESE MODIFIED PARTICLE EMITTERS...
... WHICH EACH CONTAIN THE RAW POWER OF *EIGHT* CAMERAS...
THEY-THEY WON'T *KILL* IT, WILL THEY?
AT *THIS* POINT WE DON'T HAVE MANY OPTIONS.
OUR CHIEF PRIORITY RIGHT NOW IS KEEPING INNOCENT CIVILIANS ALIVE. I'M PRETTY SURE I'M GOING TO HAVE TO ARREST SOME OF THEM AND I CAN'T VERY WELL DO IT IF THEY ALL GET EATEN, CAN I?
GET YOUR PETTING ARMS REVVED UP..
BECAUSE THE GUEST OF HONOR IS ABOUT TO ARRIVE!
PERHAPS WE'LL BE LUCKY AND IT WON'T SHO
AND TO GUARANTEE IT MAKES ITS DEBUT, WE'RE FILLING THE AIR WITH THE SCENT OF ITS *FAVORITE* FOOD!
JUST TRY TO SHOOT *GENTLY.*

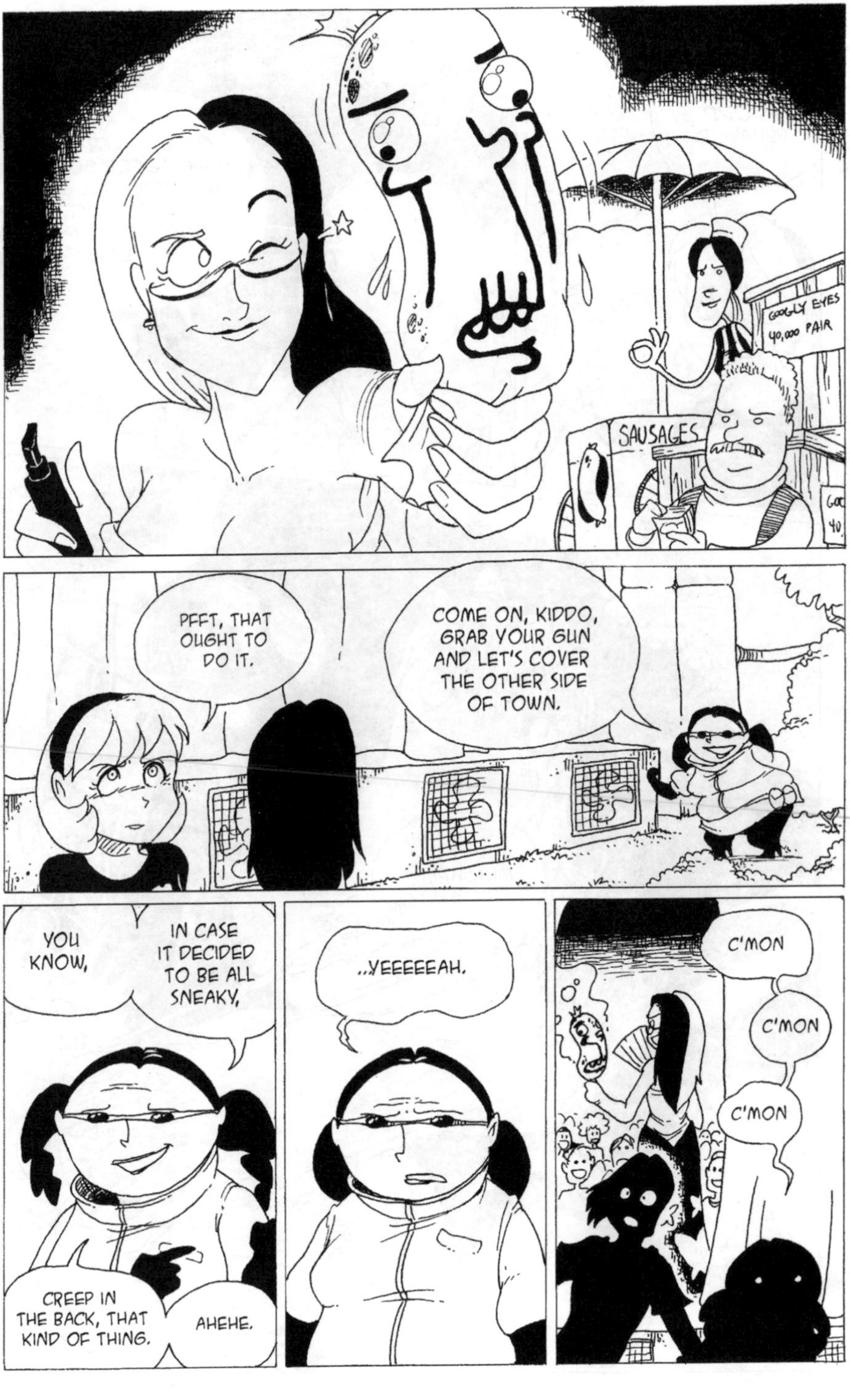
GOOGLY EYES
40,000 PAIR
SAUSAGES
PFFT, THAT OUGHT TO DO IT.
COME ON, KIDDO, GRAB YOUR GUN AND LET'S COVER THE OTHER SIDE OF TOWN.
YOU KNOW,
IN CASE IT DECIDED TO BE ALL SNEAKY,
CREEP IN THE BACK, THAT KIND OF THING.
AHEHE.
...YEEEEEAH.
C'MON
C'MON
C'MON

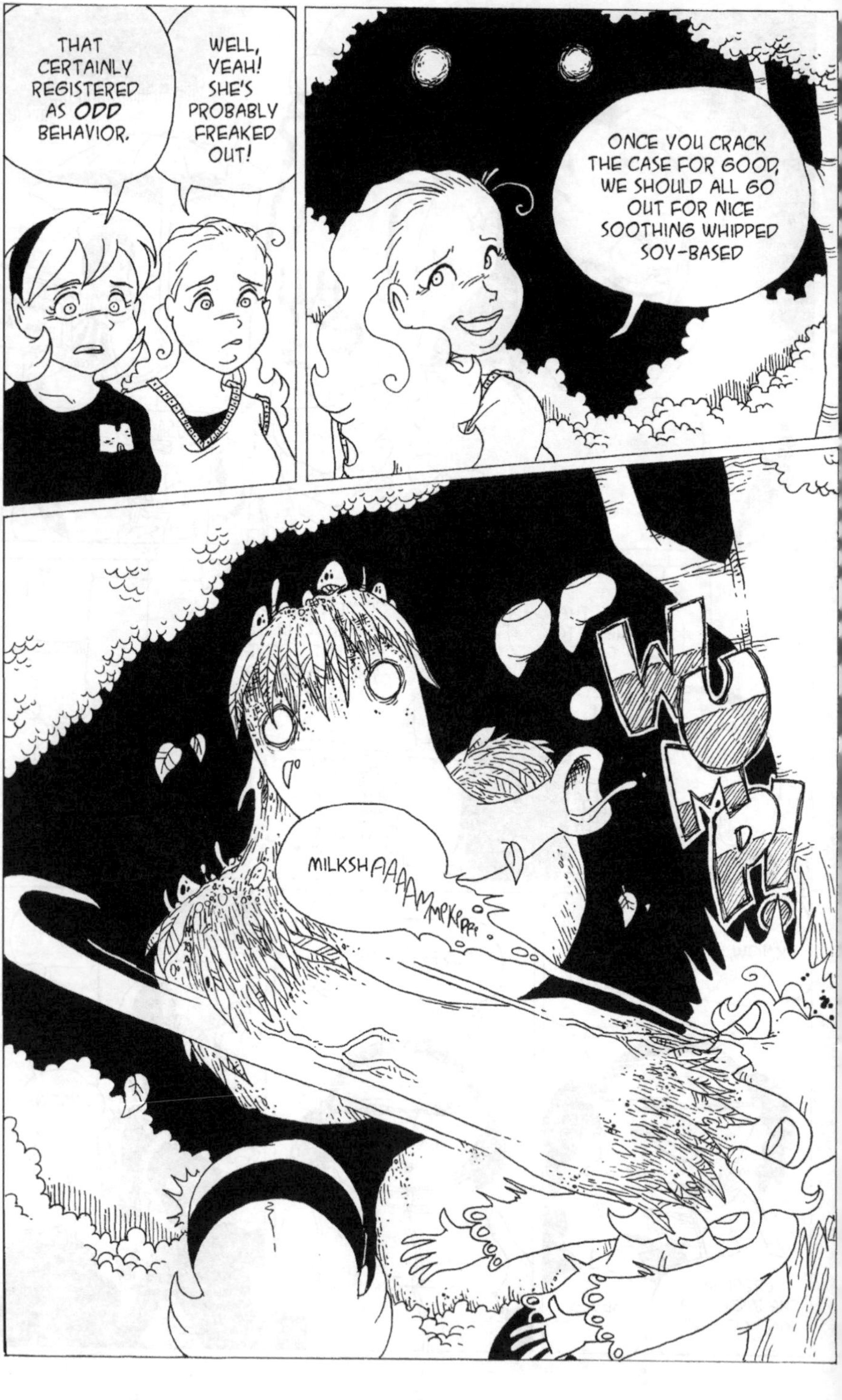
THAT CERTAINLY REGISTERED AS ODD BEHAVIOR.
WELL, YEAH! SHE'S PROBABLY FREAKED OUT!
ONCE YOU CRACK THE CASE FOR GOOD, WE SHOULD ALL GO OUT FOR NICE SOOTHING WHIPPED SOY-BASED
MILKSHAAAAAMMPKIPP!
WUMP!

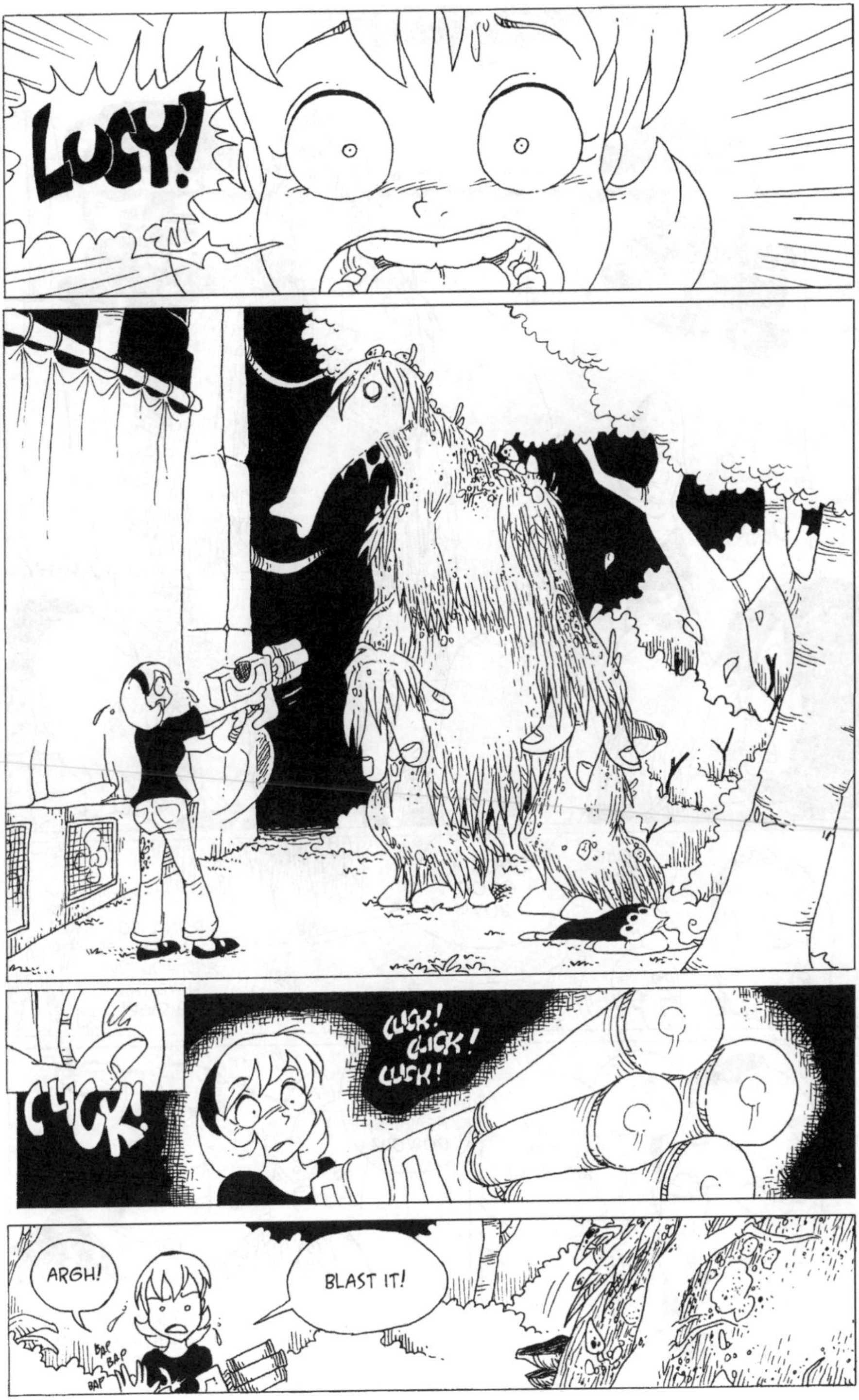
LUCY!
CLICK!
CLICK!
CLICK!
CLICK!
ARGH!
BAP
BAP
BAP
BLAST IT!

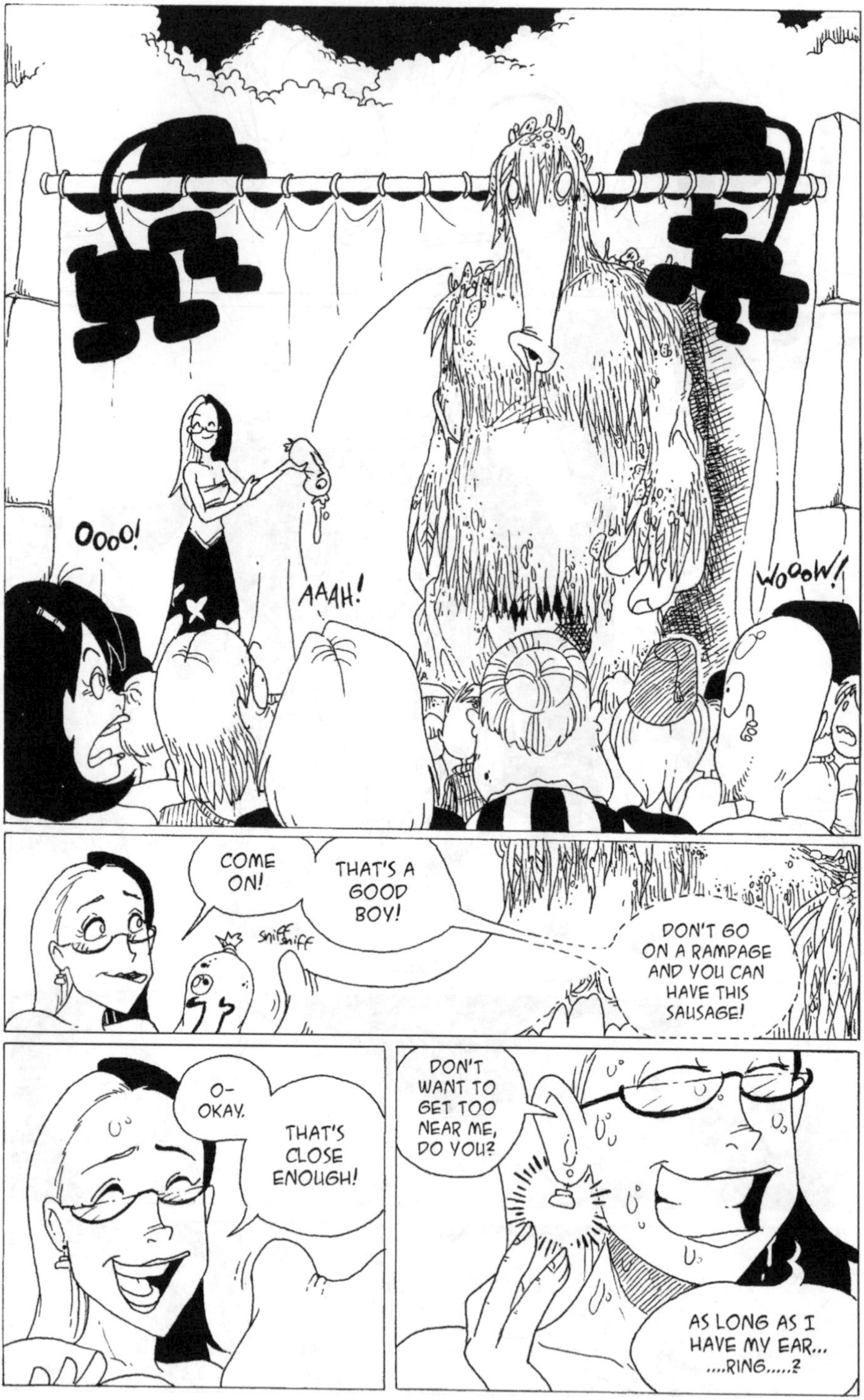
OOOO!
AAAH!
WOOOW!
COME ON!
THAT'S A GOOD BOY!
SNIFF SNIFF
DON'T GO ON A RAMPAGE AND YOU CAN HAVE THIS SAUSAGE!
O-OKAY.
THAT'S CLOSE ENOUGH!
DON'T WANT TO GET TOO NEAR ME, DO YOU?
AS LONG AS I HAVE MY EAR... ....RING.....?

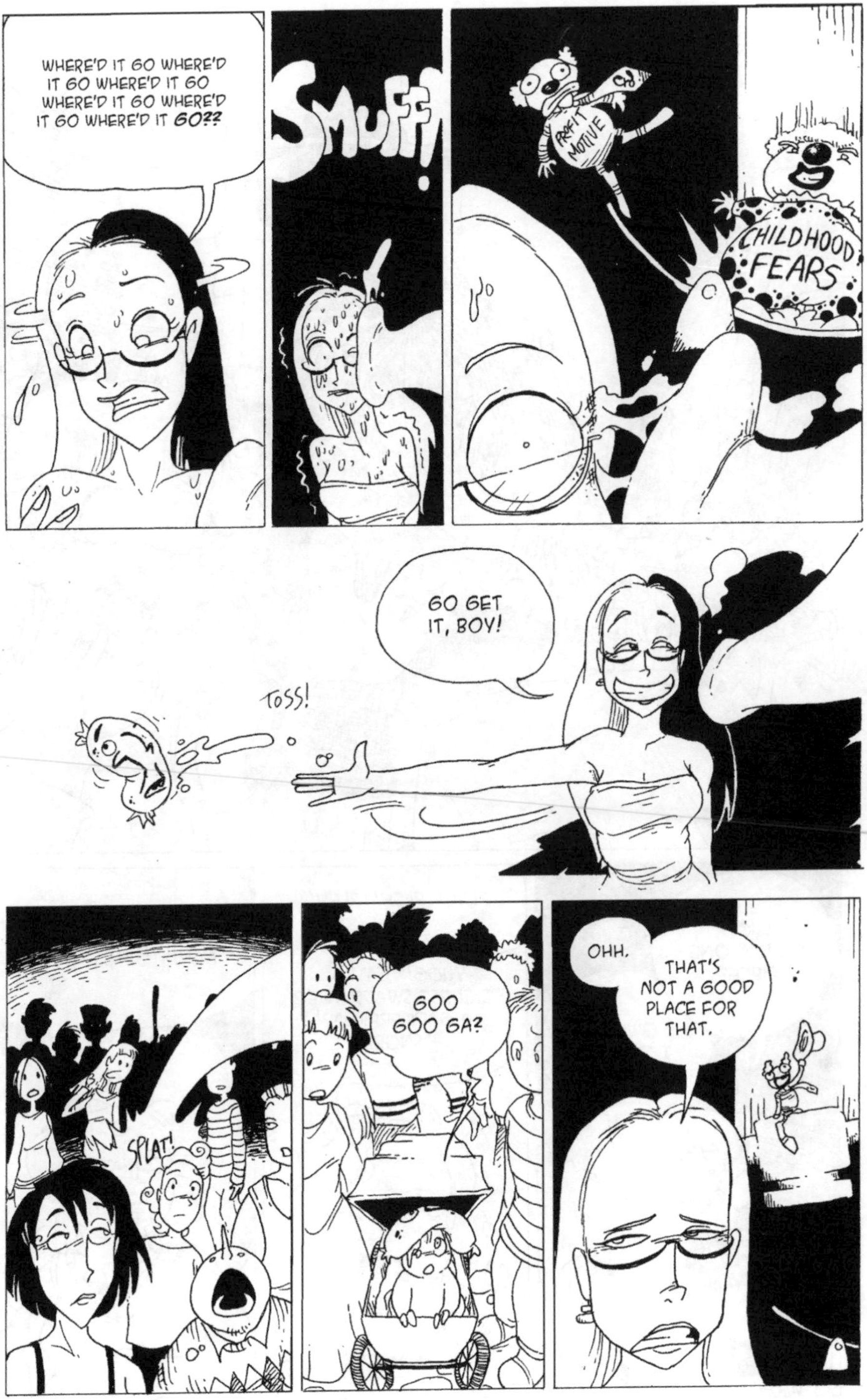
WHERE'D IT GO WHERE'D IT GO WHERE'D IT GO WHERE'D IT GO WHERE'D IT GO WHERE'D IT GO??
SMUFF!
PROFIT MOTIVE
CHILDHOOD FEARS
GO GET IT, BOY!
TOSS!
SPLAT!
GOO GOO GA?
OHH.
THAT'S NOT A GOOD PLACE FOR THAT.

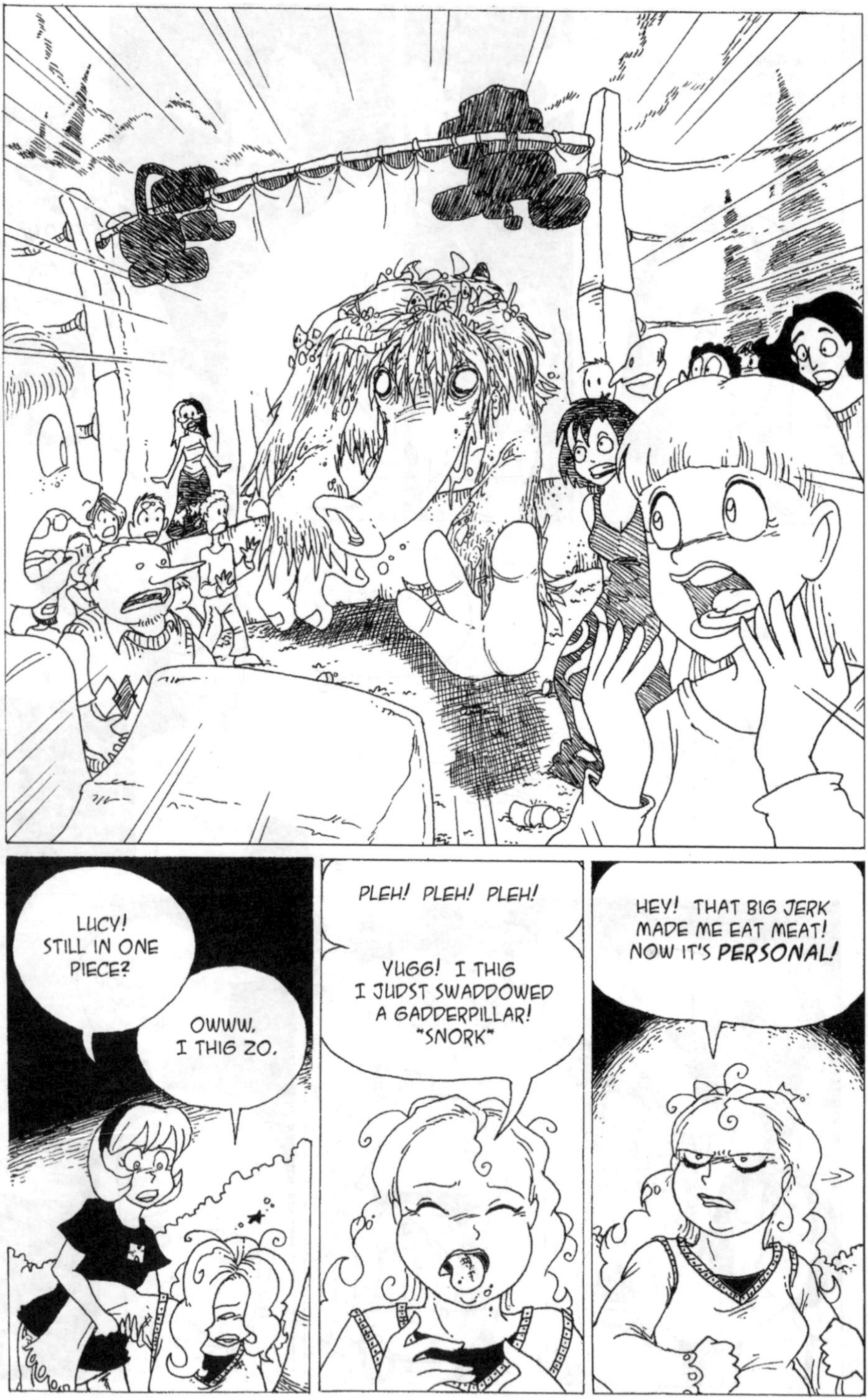
LUCY! STILL IN ONE PIECE?
OWWW. I THIG ZO.
PLEH! PLEH! PLEH!
YUGG! I THIG I JUDST SWADDOWED A GADDERPILLAR! *SNORK*
HEY! THAT BIG JERK MADE ME EAT MEAT! NOW IT'S PERSONAL!

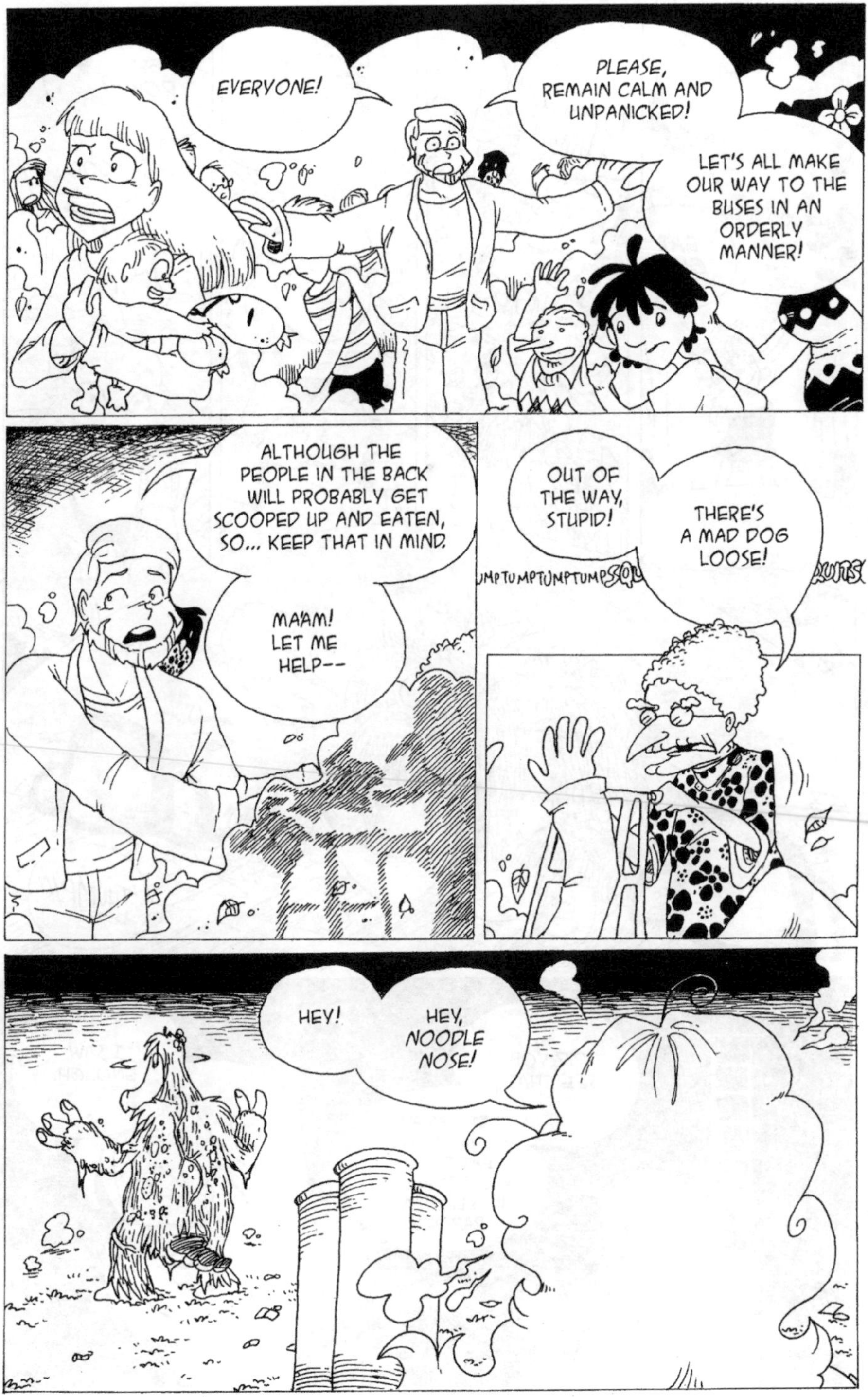
EVERYONE!
PLEASE, REMAIN CALM AND UNPANICKED!
LET'S ALL MAKE OUR WAY TO THE BUSES IN AN ORDERLY MANNER!
ALTHOUGH THE PEOPLE IN THE BACK WILL PROBABLY GET SCOOPED UP AND EATEN, SO... KEEP THAT IN MIND.
MA'AM! LET ME HELP--
OUT OF THE WAY, STUPID!
THERE'S A MAD DOG LOOSE!
HEY!
HEY, NOODLE NOSE!

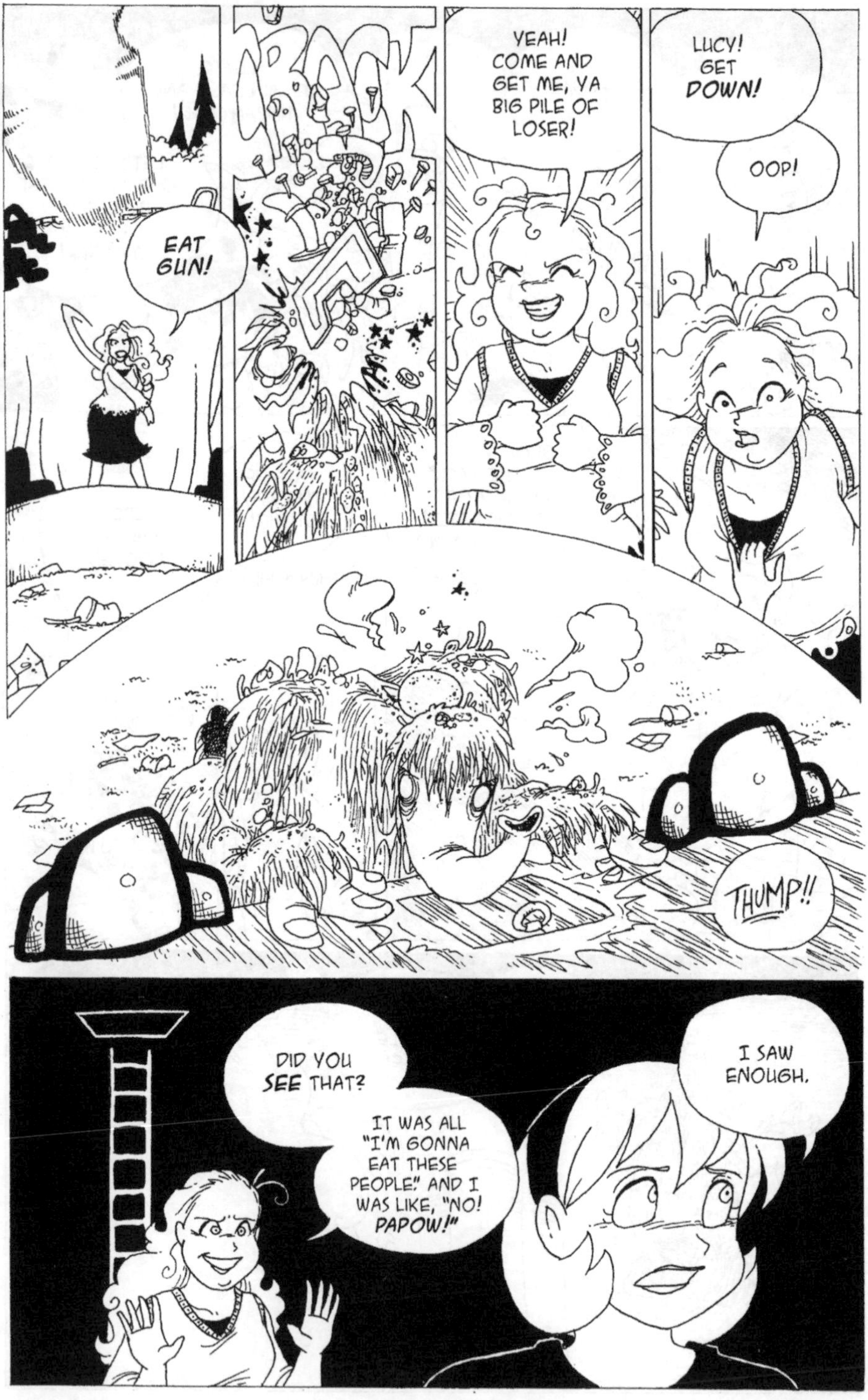
EAT GUN!
CRACK
YEAH! COME AND GET ME, YA BIG PILE OF LOSER!
LUCY! GET DOWN!
OOP!
THUMP!!
DID YOU SEE THAT?
IT WAS ALL "I'M GONNA EAT THESE PEOPLE!" AND I WAS LIKE, "NO! PAPOW!"
I SAW ENOUGH.

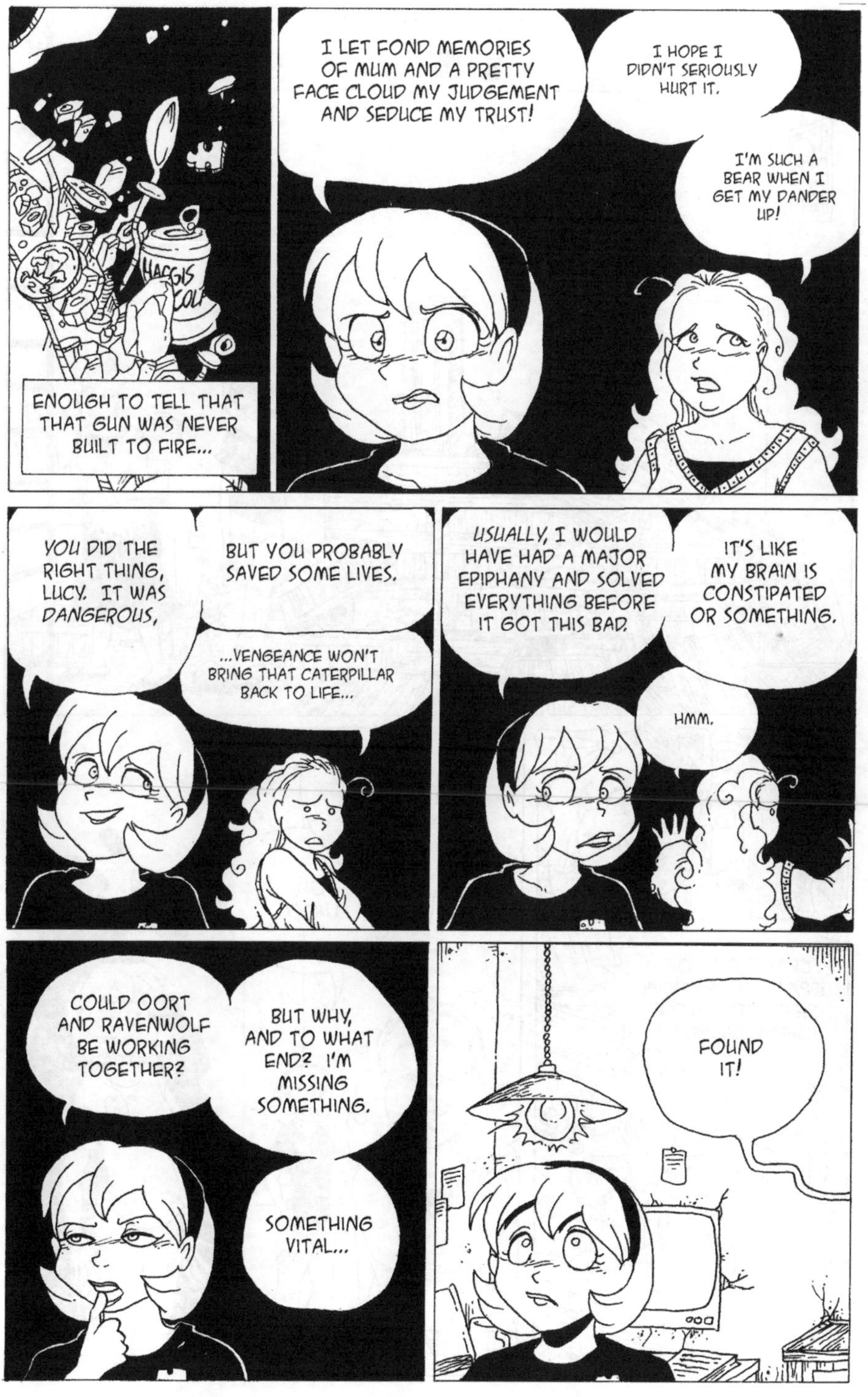

ENOUGH TO TELL THAT THAT GUN WAS NEVER BUILT TO FIRE...
HAGGIS COLA
I LET FOND MEMORIES OF MUM AND A PRETTY FACE CLOUD MY JUDGEMENT AND SEDUCE MY TRUST!
I HOPE I DIDN'T SERIOUSLY HURT IT.
I'M SUCH A BEAR WHEN I GET MY DANDER UP!
YOU DID THE RIGHT THING, LUCY. IT WAS DANGEROUS,
BUT YOU PROBABLY SAVED SOME LIVES.
...VENGEANCE WON'T BRING THAT CATERPILLAR BACK TO LIFE...
USUALLY, I WOULD HAVE HAD A MAJOR EPIPHANY AND SOLVED EVERYTHING BEFORE IT GOT THIS BAD.
IT'S LIKE MY BRAIN IS CONSTIPATED OR SOMETHING.
HMM.
COULD OORT AND RAVENWOLF BE WORKING TOGETHER?
BUT WHY, AND TO WHAT END? I'M MISSING SOMETHING.
SOMETHING VITAL...
FOUND IT!

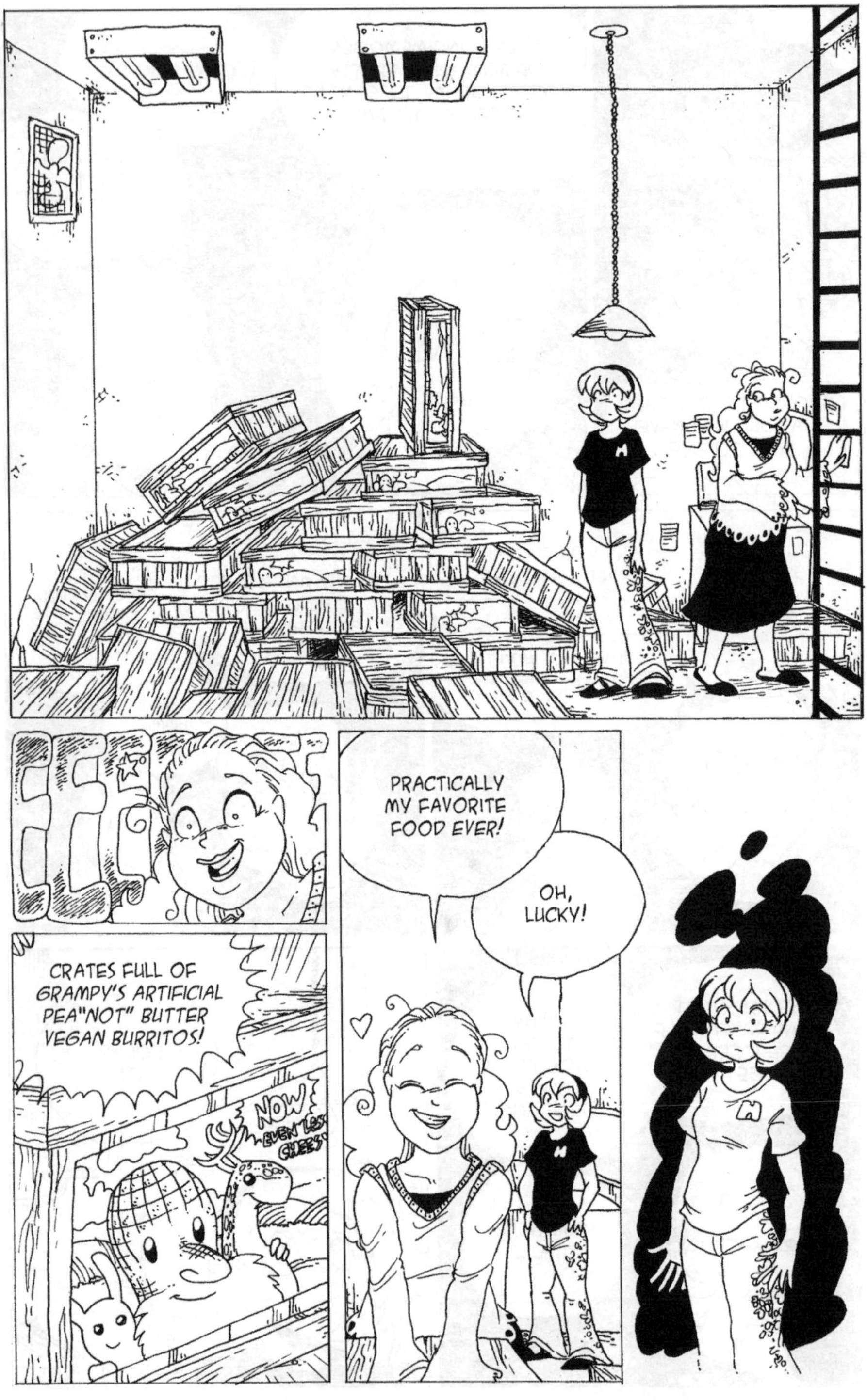
CRATES FULL OF GRAMPY'S ARTIFICIAL PEA"NOT" BUTTER VEGAN BURRITOS!
NOW
PRACTICALLY MY FAVORITE FOOD EVER!
OH, LUCKY!

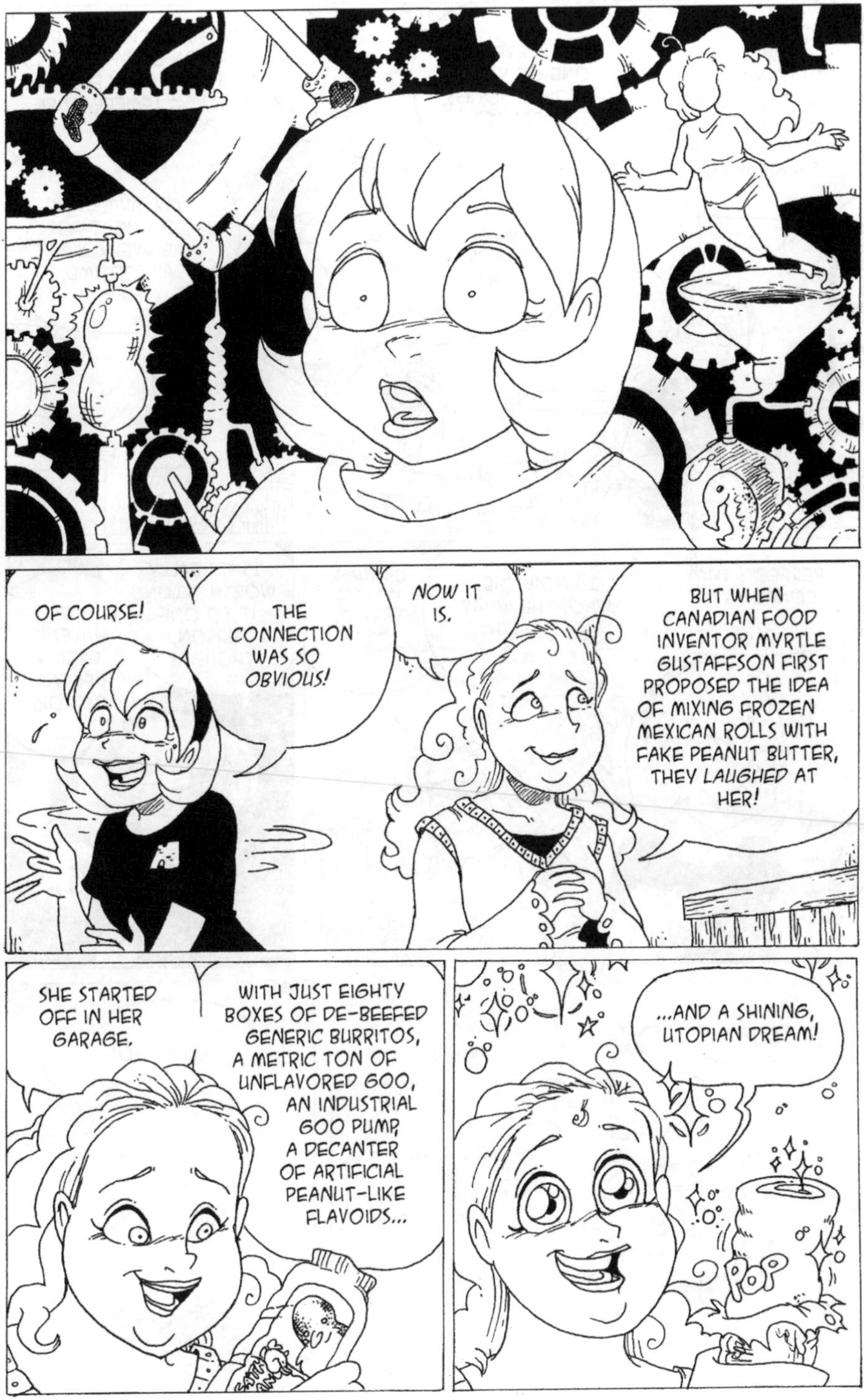
OF COURSE!
THE CONNECTION WAS SO OBVIOUS!
NOW IT IS.
BUT WHEN CANADIAN FOOD INVENTOR MYRTLE GUSTAFFSON FIRST PROPOSED THE IDEA OF MIXING FROZEN MEXICAN ROLLS WITH FAKE PEANUT BUTTER, THEY LAUGHED AT HER!
SHE STARTED OFF IN HER GARAGE,
WITH JUST EIGHTY BOXES OF DE-BEEFED GENERIC BURRITOS, A METRIC TON OF UNFLAVORED GOO, AN INDUSTRIAL GOO PUMP, A DECANTER OF ARTIFICIAL PEANUT-LIKE FLAVOIDS...
...AND A SHINING, UTOPIAN DREAM!
POP

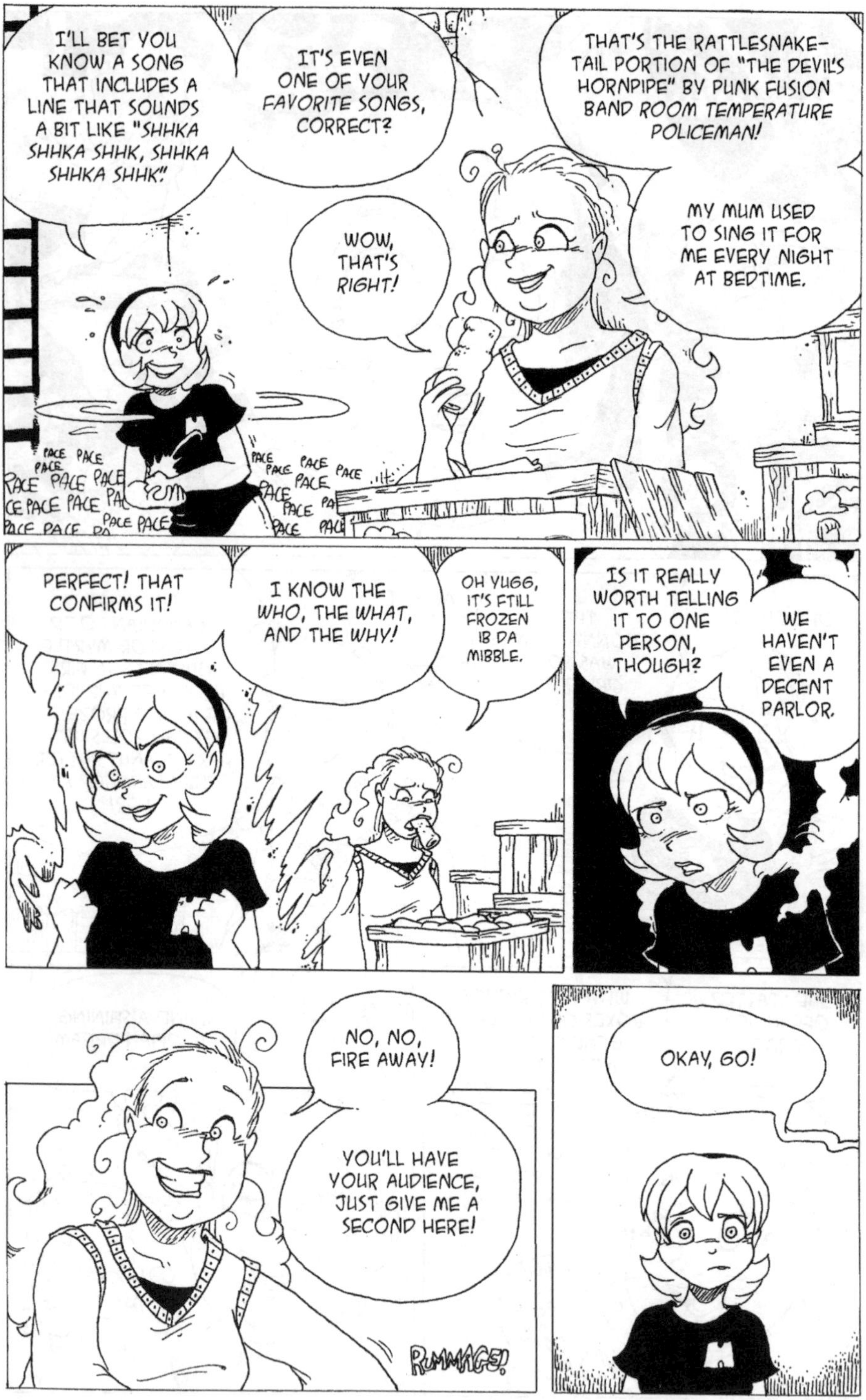
I'LL BET YOU KNOW A SONG THAT INCLUDES A LINE THAT SOUNDS A BIT LIKE "SHHKA SHHKA SHHK, SHHKA SHHKA SHHK."
IT'S EVEN ONE OF YOUR FAVORITE SONGS, CORRECT?
WOW, THAT'S RIGHT!
THAT'S THE RATTLESNAKE-TAIL PORTION OF "THE DEVIL'S HORNPIPE" BY PUNK FUSION BAND ROOM TEMPERATURE POLICEMAN!
MY MUM USED TO SING IT FOR ME EVERY NIGHT AT BEDTIME.
PACE PACE PACE PACE PACE PACE PACE PACE
PERFECT! THAT CONFIRMS IT!
I KNOW THE WHO, THE WHAT, AND THE WHY!
OH YUGG, IT'S FTILL FROZEN IB DA MIBBLE.
IS IT REALLY WORTH TELLING IT TO ONE PERSON, THOUGH?
WE HAVEN'T EVEN A DECENT PARLOR.
NO, NO, FIRE AWAY!
YOU'LL HAVE YOUR AUDIENCE, JUST GIVE ME A SECOND HERE!
RUMMAGE!
OKAY, GO!

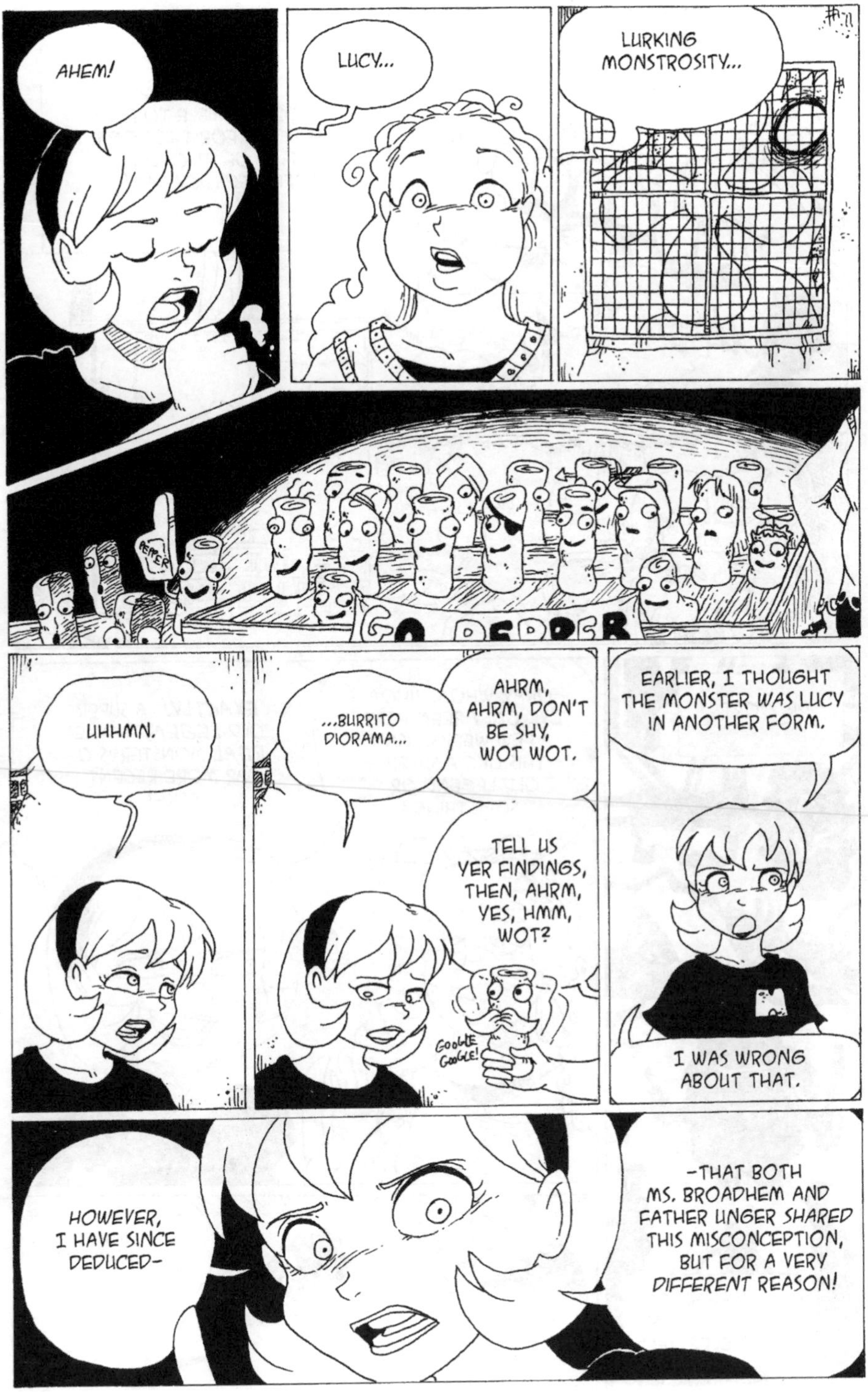
AHEM!
LUCY...
LURKING MONSTROSITY...
PEPPER
GO PEPPER
UHHMN.
...BURRITO DIORAMA...
AHRM, AHRM, DON'T BE SHY, WOT WOT.
TELL US YER FINDINGS, THEN, AHRM, YES, HMM, WOT?
GOOGLE GOOGLE!
EARLIER, I THOUGHT THE MONSTER WAS LUCY IN ANOTHER FORM.
I WAS WRONG ABOUT THAT.
HOWEVER, I HAVE SINCE DEDUCED-
-THAT BOTH MS. BROADHEM AND FATHER UNGER SHARED THIS MISCONCEPTION, BUT FOR A VERY DIFFERENT REASON!

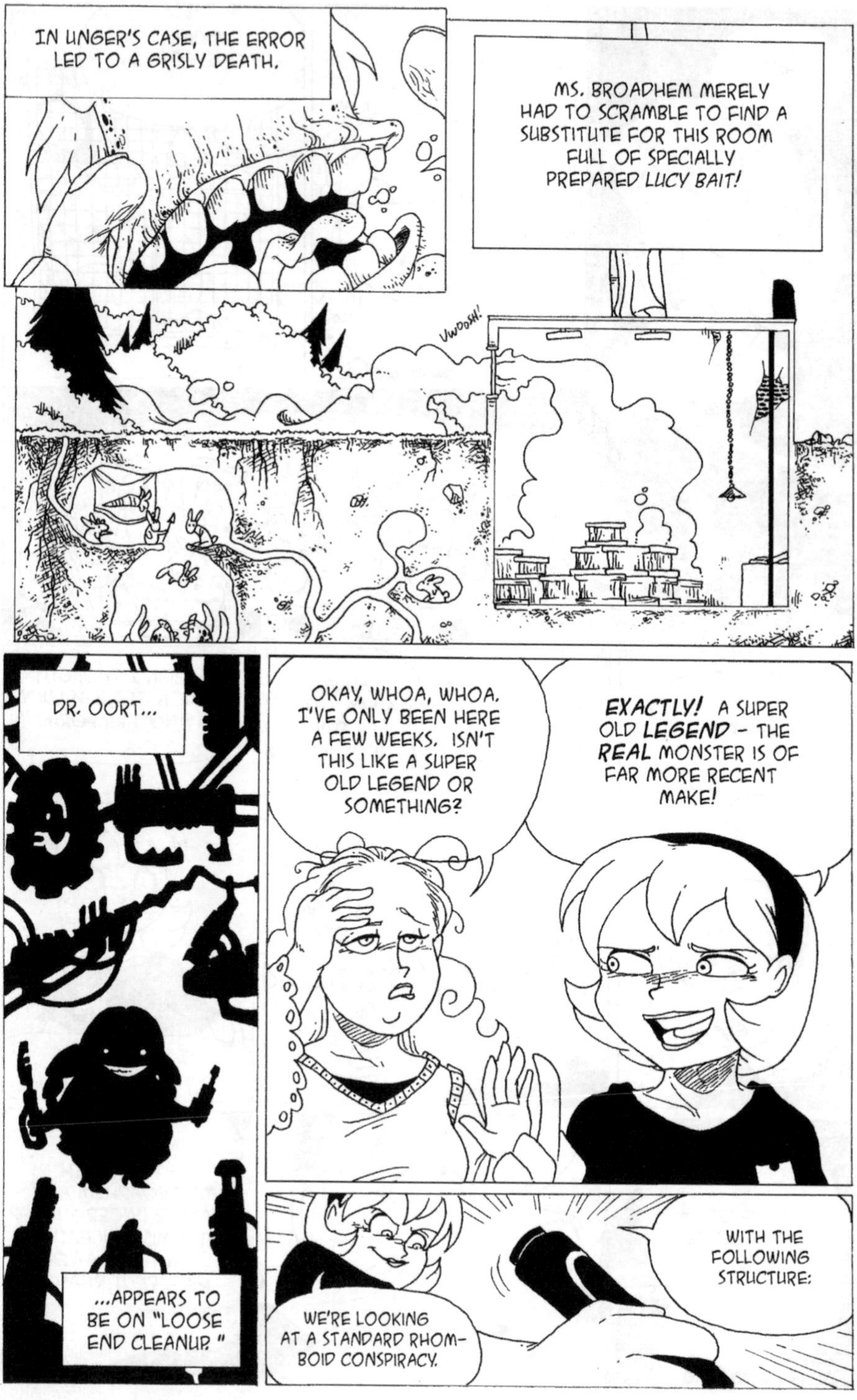
IN UNGER'S CASE, THE ERROR LED TO A GRISLY DEATH.
MS. BROADHEM MERELY HAD TO SCRAMBLE TO FIND A SUBSTITUTE FOR THIS ROOM FULL OF SPECIALLY PREPARED LUCY BAIT!
VWOOSH!
DR. OORT...
...APPEARS TO BE ON "LOOSE END CLEANUP."
OKAY, WHOA, WHOA. I'VE ONLY BEEN HERE A FEW WEEKS. ISN'T THIS LIKE A SUPER OLD LEGEND OR SOMETHING?
EXACTLY! A SUPER OLD LEGEND - THE REAL MONSTER IS OF FAR MORE RECENT MAKE!
WE'RE LOOKING AT A STANDARD RHOM-BOID CONSPIRACY.
WITH THE FOLLOWING STRUCTURE:

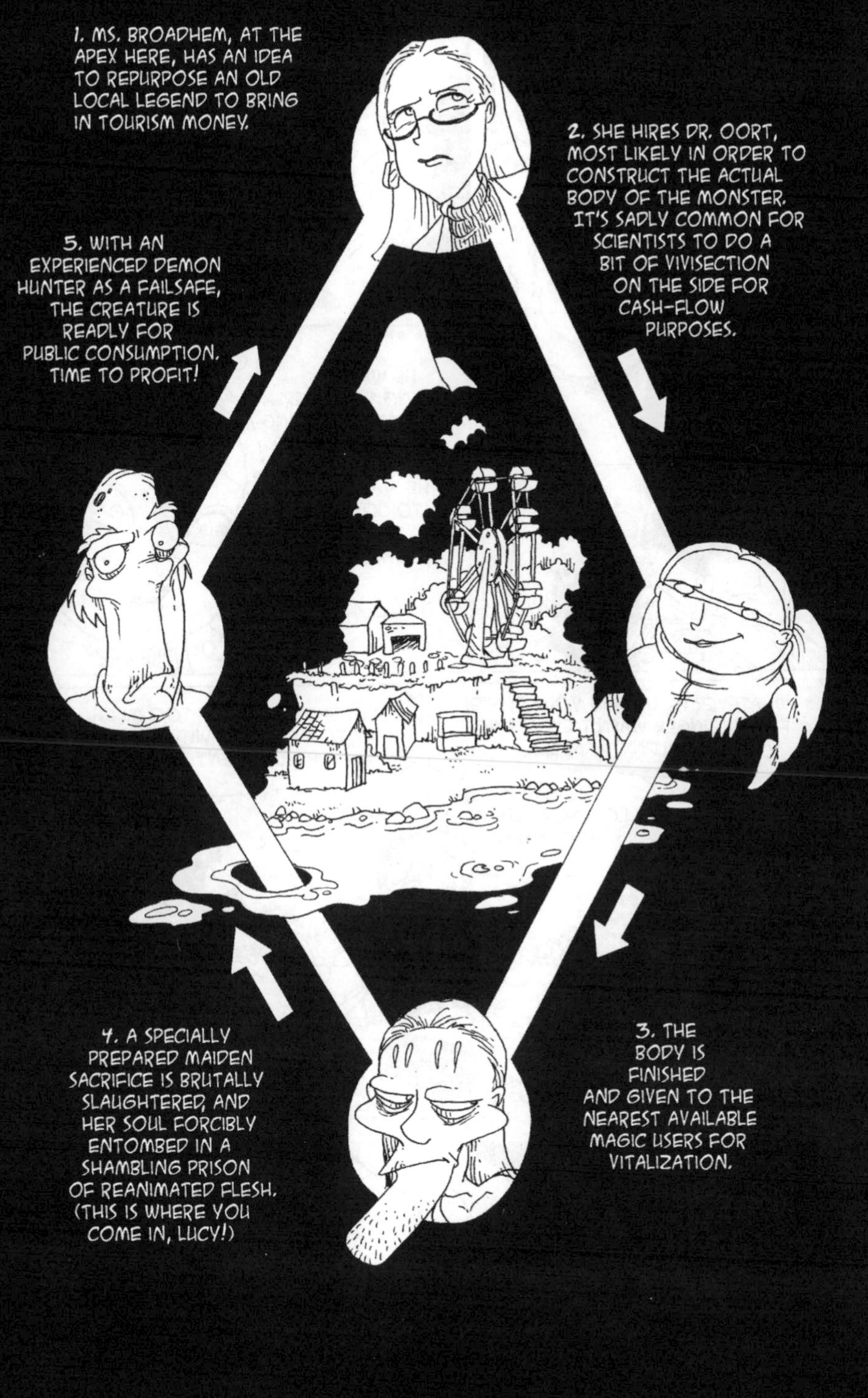
1. MS. BROADHEM, AT THE APEX HERE, HAS AN IDEA TO REPURPOSE AN OLD LOCAL LEGEND TO BRING IN TOURISM MONEY.
2. SHE HIRES DR. OORT, MOST LIKELY IN ORDER TO CONSTRUCT THE ACTUAL BODY OF THE MONSTER. IT'S SADLY COMMON FOR SCIENTISTS TO DO A BIT OF VIVISECTION ON THE SIDE FOR CASH-FLOW PURPOSES.
3. THE BODY IS FINISHED AND GIVEN TO THE NEAREST AVAILABLE MAGIC USERS FOR VITALIZATION.
4. A SPECIALLY PREPARED MAIDEN SACRIFICE IS BRUTALLY SLAUGHTERED, AND HER SOUL FORCIBLY ENTOMBED IN A SHAMBLING PRISON OF REANIMATED FLESH. (THIS IS WHERE YOU COME IN, LUCY!)
5. WITH AN EXPERIENCED DEMON HUNTER AS A FAILSAFE, THE CREATURE IS READLY FOR PUBLIC CONSUMPTION. TIME TO PROFIT!

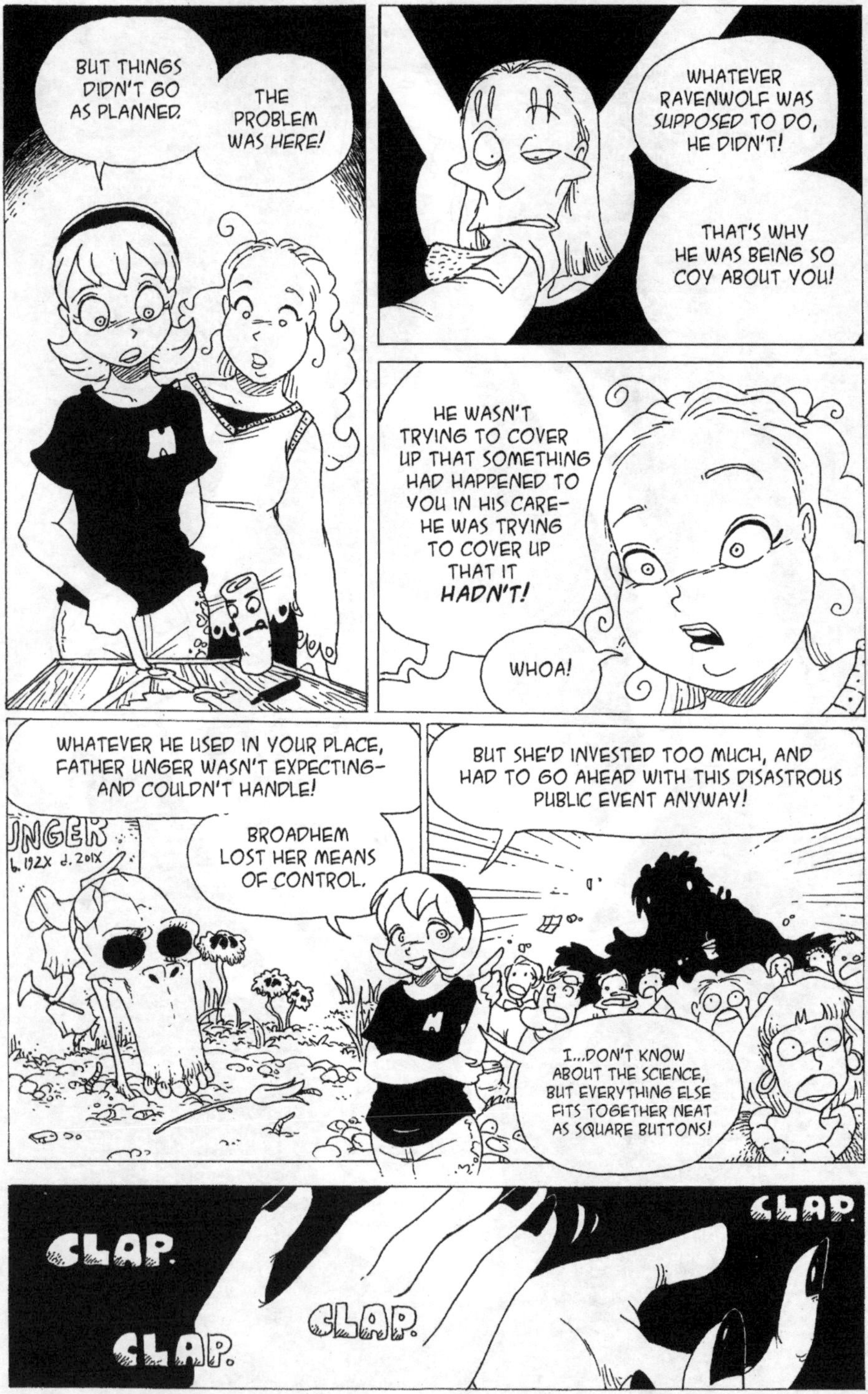
BUT THINGS DIDN'T GO AS PLANNED.
THE PROBLEM WAS HERE!
WHATEVER RAVENWOLF WAS SUPPOSED TO DO, HE DIDN'T!
THAT'S WHY HE WAS BEING SO COY ABOUT YOU!
HE WASN'T TRYING TO COVER UP THAT SOMETHING HAD HAPPENED TO YOU IN HIS CARE- HE WAS TRYING TO COVER UP THAT IT HADN'T!
WHOA!
WHATEVER HE USED IN YOUR PLACE, FATHER UNGER WASN'T EXPECTING- AND COULDN'T HANDLE!
UNGER
b. 192X d. 201X
BROADHEM LOST HER MEANS OF CONTROL.
BUT SHE'D INVESTED TOO MUCH, AND HAD TO GO AHEAD WITH THIS DISASTROUS PUBLIC EVENT ANYWAY!
I...DON'T KNOW ABOUT THE SCIENCE, BUT EVERYTHING ELSE FITS TOGETHER NEAT AS SQUARE BUTTONS!
CLAP.
CLAP.
CLAP.
CLAP.

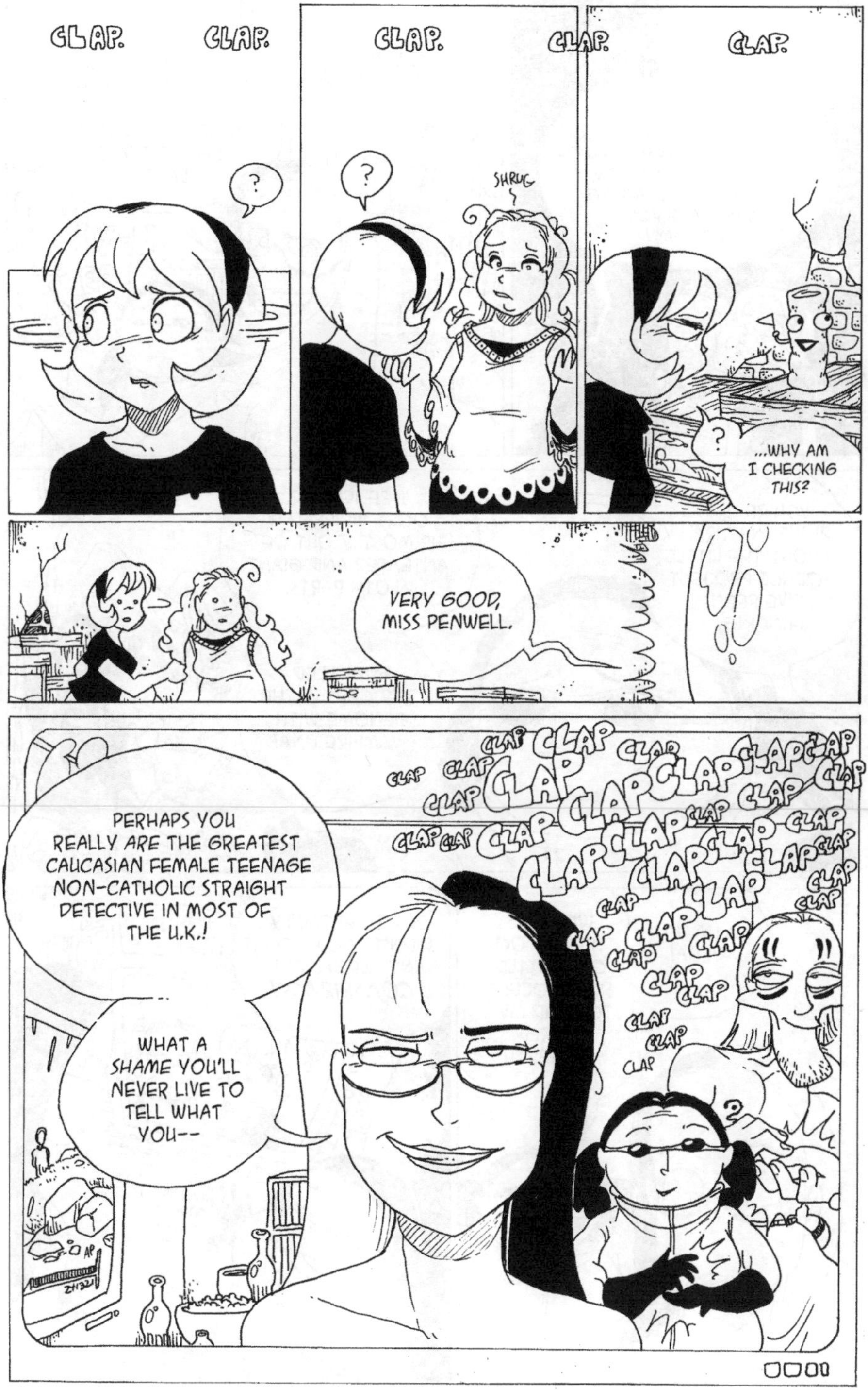
CLAP.
CLAP.
?
CLAP.
CLAP.
?
SHRUG
CLAP.
?
...WHY AM I CHECKING THIS?
VERY GOOD, MISS PENWELL.
CLAP CLAP CLAP CLAP CLAP CLAP
PERHAPS YOU REALLY ARE THE GREATEST CAUCASIAN FEMALE TEENAGE NON-CATHOLIC STRAIGHT DETECTIVE IN MOST OF THE U.K.!
WHAT A SHAME YOU'LL NEVER LIVE TO TELL WHAT YOU--
?
0001

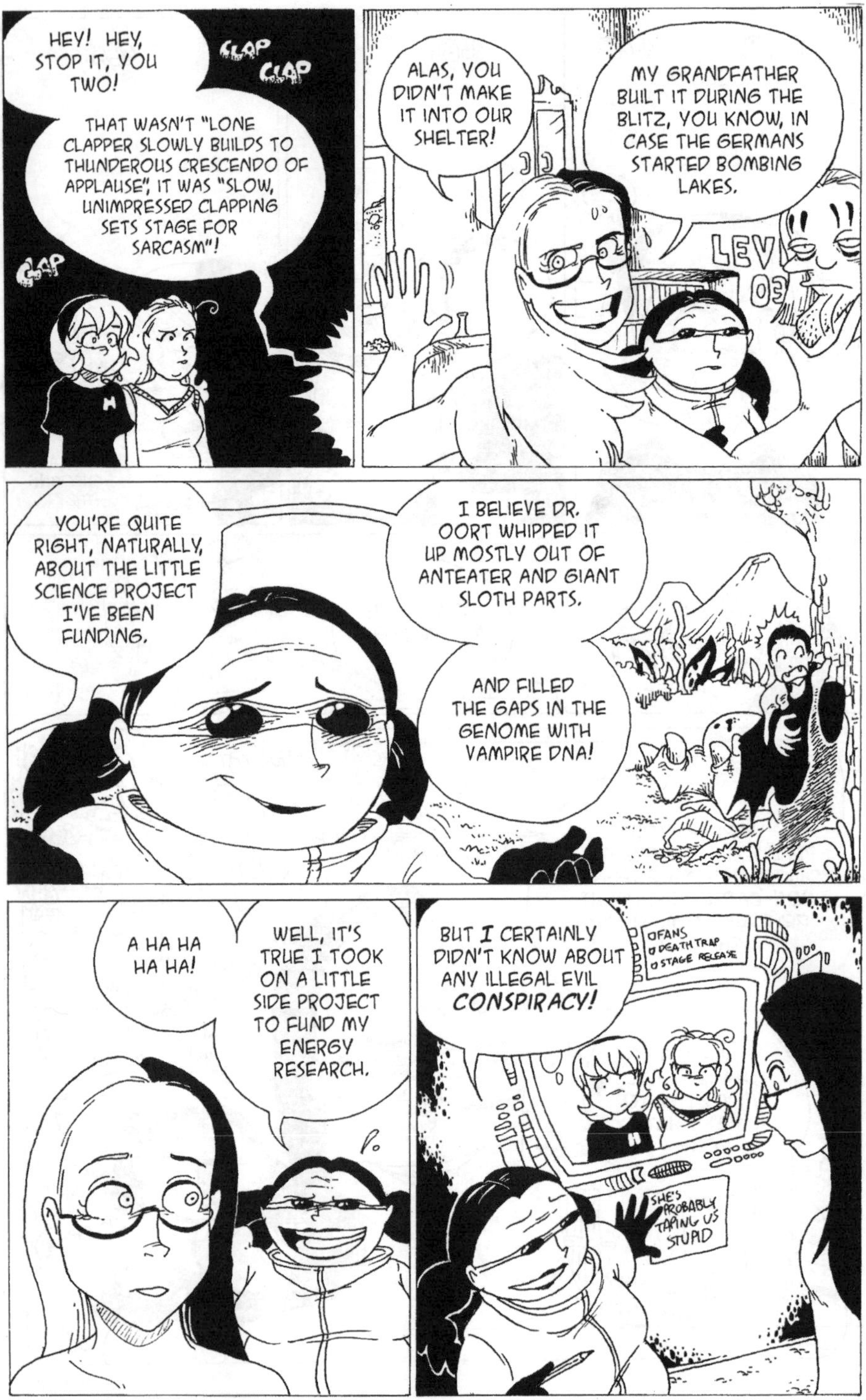
HEY! HEY, STOP IT, YOU TWO!
CLAP CLAP
THAT WASN'T "LONE CLAPPER SLOWLY BUILDS TO THUNDEROUS CRESCENDO OF APPLAUSE", IT WAS "SLOW, UNIMPRESSED CLAPPING SETS STAGE FOR SARCASM"!
CLAP
ALAS, YOU DIDN'T MAKE IT INTO OUR SHELTER!
MY GRANDFATHER BUILT IT DURING THE BLITZ, YOU KNOW, IN CASE THE GERMANS STARTED BOMBING LAKES.
LEV
03
YOU'RE QUITE RIGHT, NATURALLY, ABOUT THE LITTLE SCIENCE PROJECT I'VE BEEN FUNDING.
I BELIEVE DR. OORT WHIPPED IT UP MOSTLY OUT OF ANTEATER AND GIANT SLOTH PARTS.
AND FILLED THE GAPS IN THE GENOME WITH VAMPIRE DNA!
A HA HA HA HA!
WELL, IT'S TRUE I TOOK ON A LITTLE SIDE PROJECT TO FUND MY ENERGY RESEARCH.
BUT I CERTAINLY DIDN'T KNOW ABOUT ANY ILLEGAL EVIL CONSPIRACY!
FANS
DEATH TRAP
STAGE RELEASE
SHE'S PROBABLY TAPING US STUPID

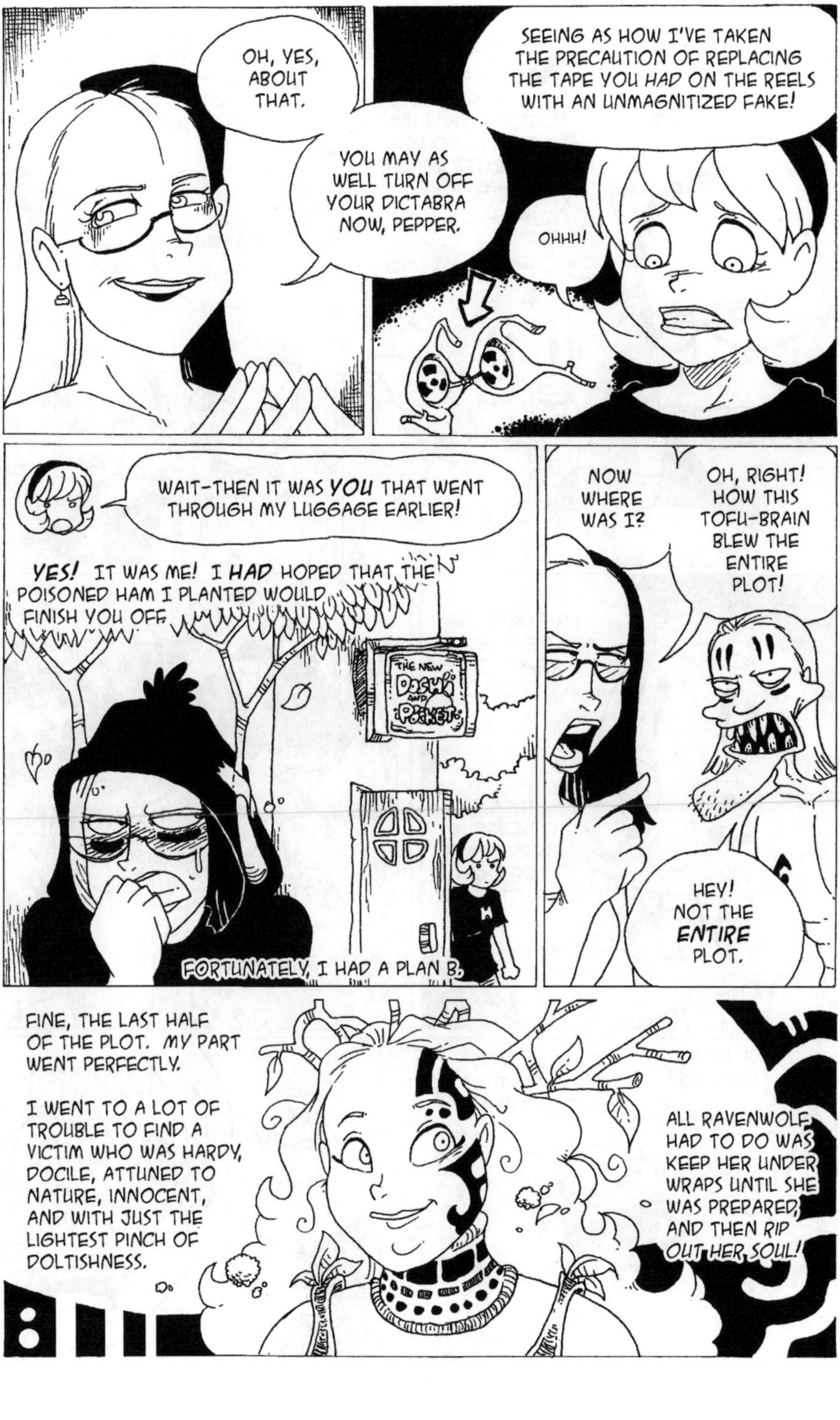

OH, YES, ABOUT THAT.
YOU MAY AS WELL TURN OFF YOUR DICTABRA NOW, PEPPER.
SEEING AS HOW I'VE TAKEN THE PRECAUTION OF REPLACING THE TAPE YOU *HAD* ON THE REELS WITH AN UNMAGNITIZED FAKE!
OHHH!
WAIT–THEN IT WAS ***YOU*** THAT WENT THROUGH MY LUGGAGE EARLIER!
YES! IT WAS ME! I ***HAD*** HOPED THAT THE POISONED HAM I PLANTED WOULD FINISH YOU OFF.
THE NEW DOSHUN AND POCKET
FORTUNATELY, I HAD A PLAN B.
NOW WHERE WAS I?
OH, RIGHT! HOW THIS TOFU-BRAIN BLEW THE ENTIRE PLOT!
HEY! NOT THE ***ENTIRE*** PLOT.
FINE, THE LAST HALF OF THE PLOT. MY PART WENT PERFECTLY.
I WENT TO A LOT OF TROUBLE TO FIND A VICTIM WHO WAS HARDY, DOCILE, ATTUNED TO NATURE, INNOCENT, AND WITH JUST THE LIGHTEST PINCH OF DOLTISHNESS.
ALL RAVENWOLF HAD TO DO WAS KEEP HER UNDER WRAPS UNTIL SHE WAS PREPARED, AND THEN *RIP* OUT HER SOUL!

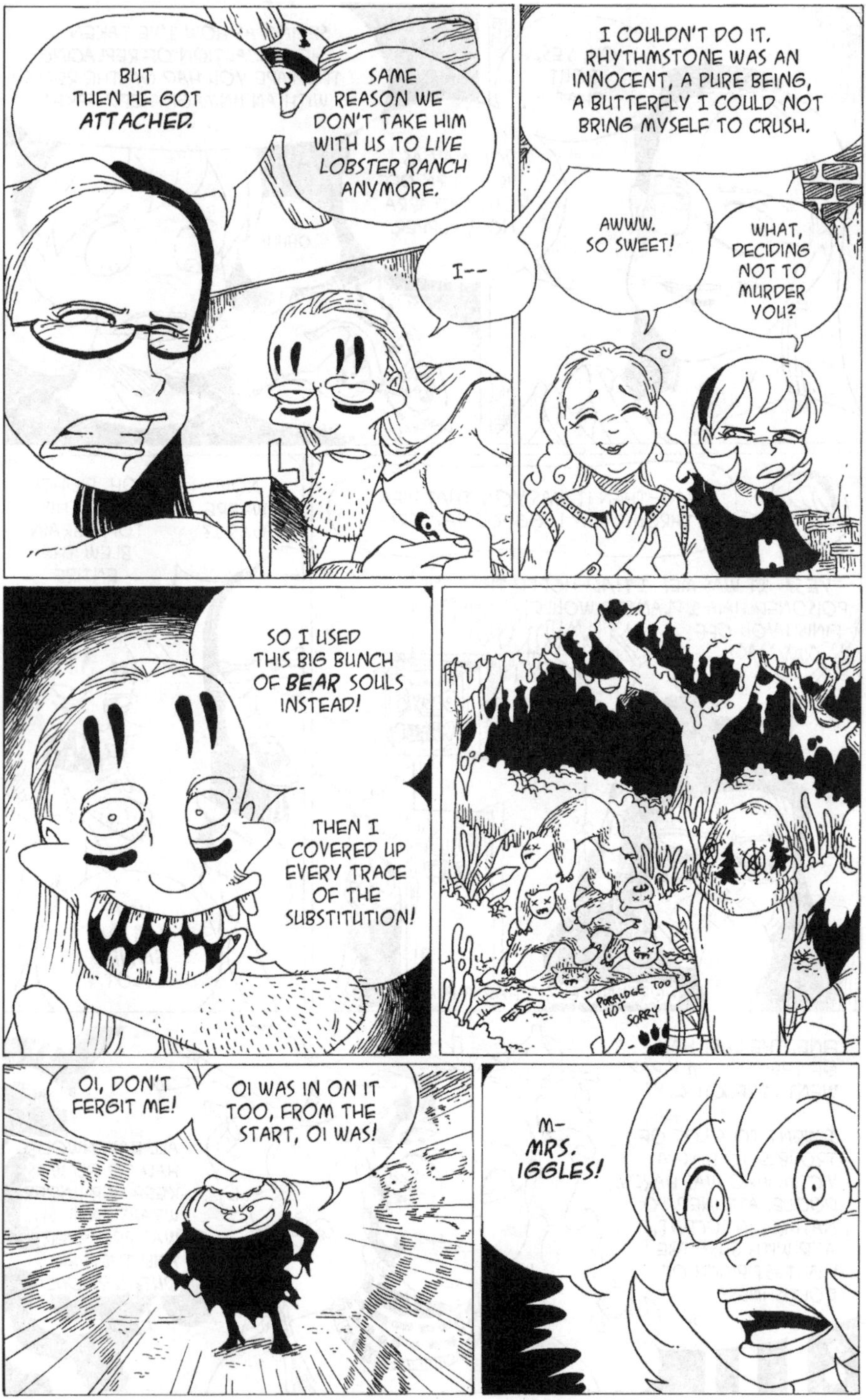
BUT THEN HE GOT ATTACHED.
SAME REASON WE DON'T TAKE HIM WITH US TO LIVE LOBSTER RANCH ANYMORE.
I--
I COULDN'T DO IT. RHYTHMSTONE WAS AN INNOCENT, A PURE BEING, A BUTTERFLY I COULD NOT BRING MYSELF TO CRUSH.
AWWW. SO SWEET!
WHAT, DECIDING NOT TO MURDER YOU?
SO I USED THIS BIG BUNCH OF BEAR SOULS INSTEAD!
THEN I COVERED UP EVERY TRACE OF THE SUBSTITUTION!
PORRIDGE TOO HOT SORRY
OI, DON'T FERGIT ME!
OI WAS IN ON IT TOO, FROM THE START, OI WAS!
M- MRS. IGGLES!

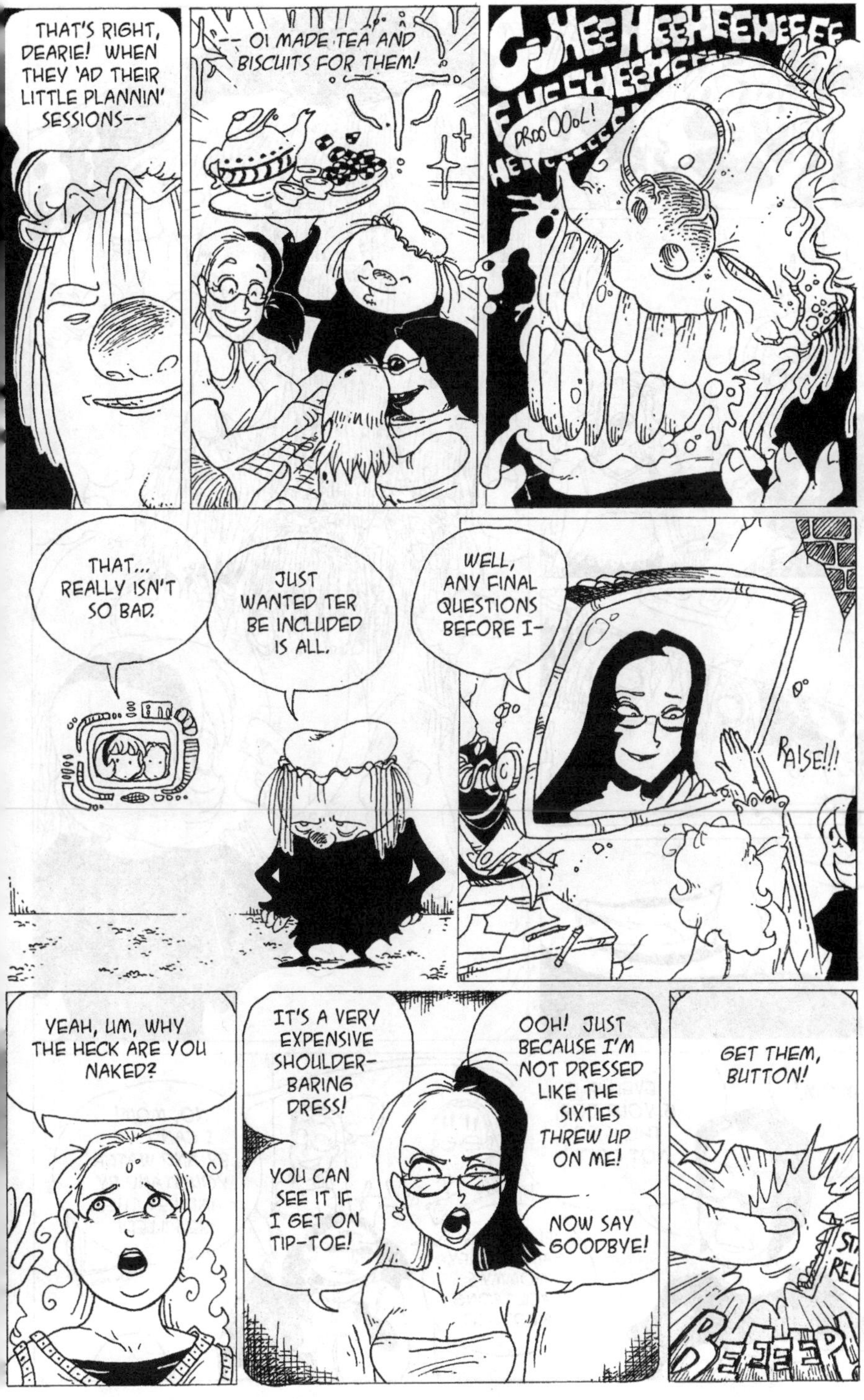

THAT'S RIGHT, DEARIE! WHEN THEY 'AD THEIR LITTLE PLANNIN' SESSIONS--
--OI MADE TEA AND BISCUITS FOR THEM!
DROOOOOL!
THAT... REALLY ISN'T SO BAD.
JUST WANTED TER BE INCLUDED IS ALL.
WELL, ANY FINAL QUESTIONS BEFORE I-
RAISE!!!
YEAH, UM, WHY THE HECK ARE YOU NAKED?
IT'S A VERY EXPENSIVE SHOULDER-BARING DRESS!
YOU CAN SEE IT IF I GET ON TIP-TOE!
OOH! JUST BECAUSE I'M NOT DRESSED LIKE THE SIXTIES THREW UP ON ME!
NOW SAY GOODBYE!
GET THEM, BUTTON!

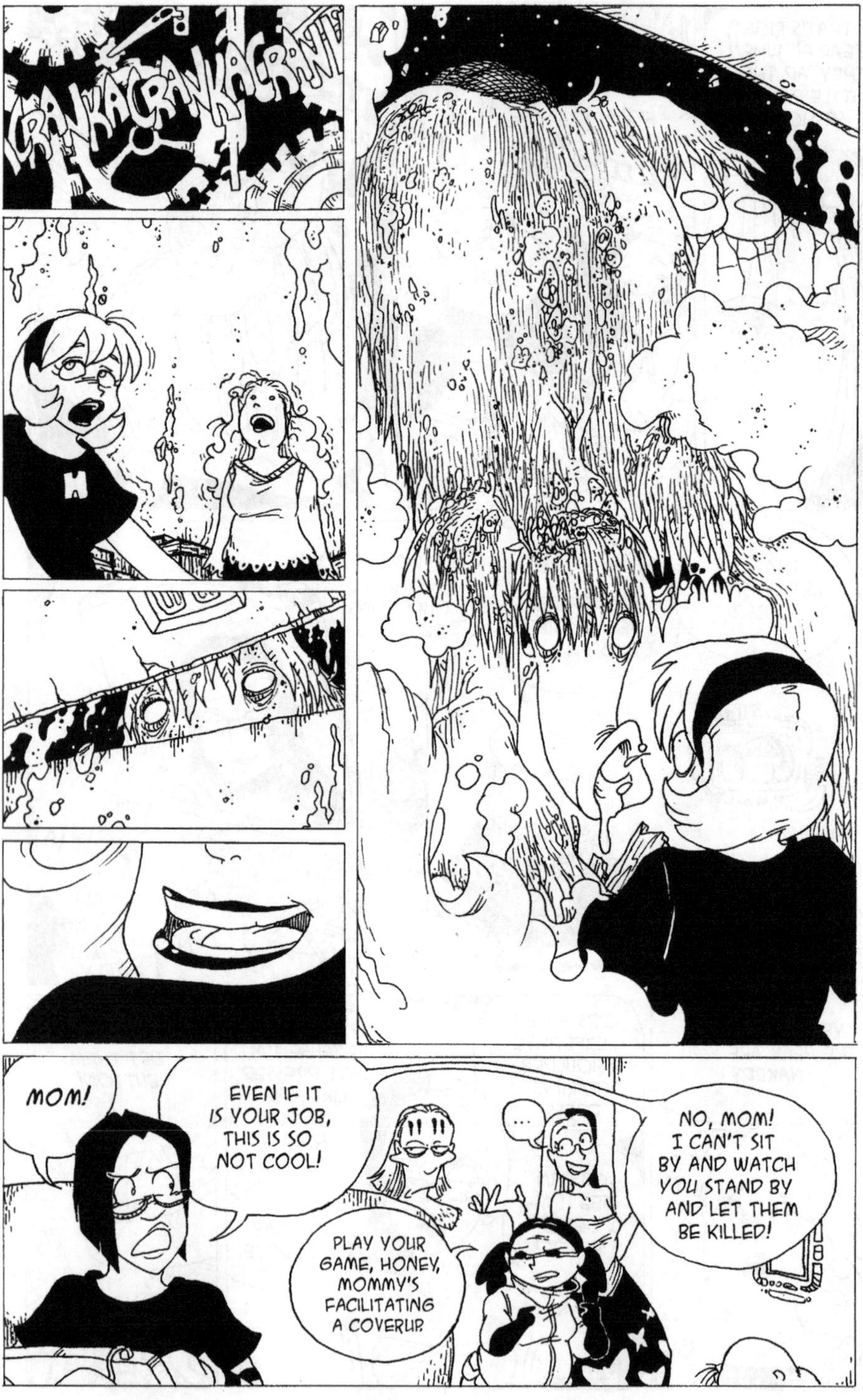
CRANKACRANKACRANK
MOM!
EVEN IF IT IS YOUR JOB, THIS IS SO NOT COOL!
!!!
...
NO, MOM! I CAN'T SIT BY AND WATCH YOU STAND BY AND LET THEM BE KILLED!
PLAY YOUR GAME, HONEY, MOMMY'S FACILITATING A COVERUP.

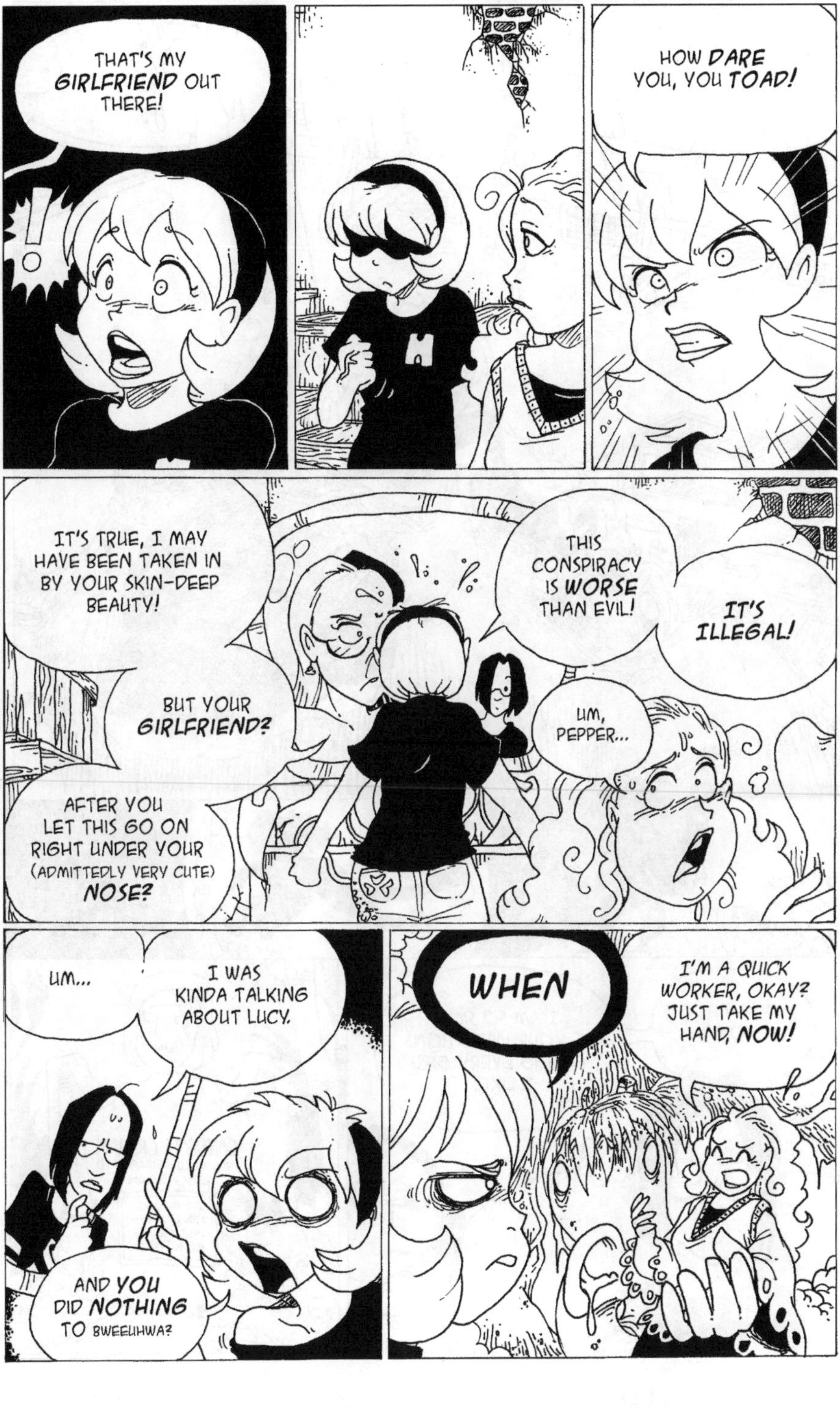

THAT'S MY GIRLFRIEND OUT THERE!
!
HOW DARE YOU, YOU TOAD!
IT'S TRUE, I MAY HAVE BEEN TAKEN IN BY YOUR SKIN-DEEP BEAUTY!
BUT YOUR GIRLFRIEND?
AFTER YOU LET THIS GO ON RIGHT UNDER YOUR (ADMITTEDLY VERY CUTE) NOSE?
THIS CONSPIRACY IS WORSE THAN EVIL!
IT'S ILLEGAL!
UM, PEPPER...
UM...
I WAS KINDA TALKING ABOUT LUCY.
AND YOU DID NOTHING TO BWEEUHWA?
WHEN
I'M A QUICK WORKER, OKAY? JUST TAKE MY HAND, NOW!

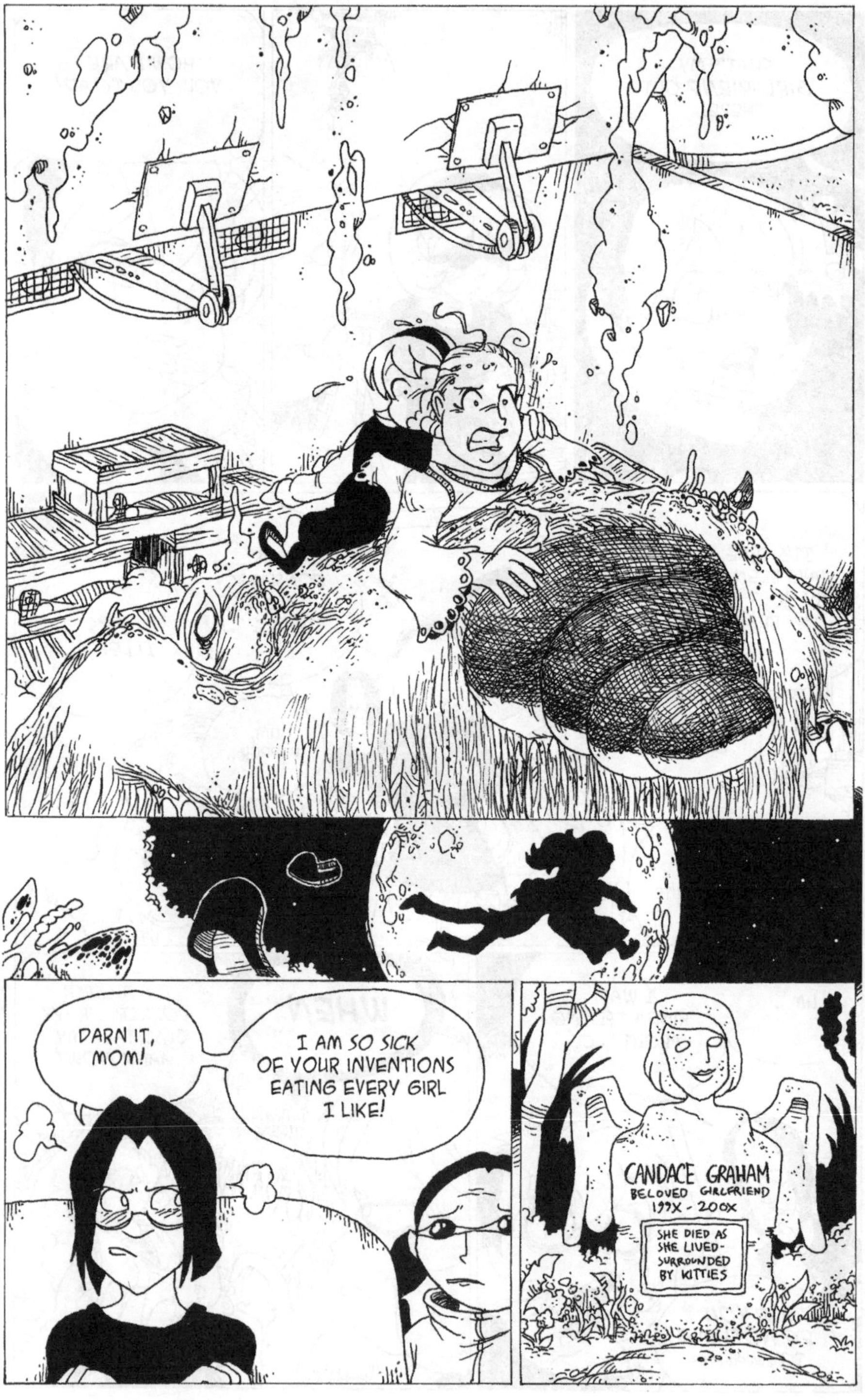
DARN IT, MOM!
I AM SO SICK OF YOUR INVENTIONS EATING EVERY GIRL I LIKE!
CANDACE GRAHAM
BELOVED GIRLFRIEND
199X - 200X
SHE DIED AS SHE LIVED- SURROUNDED BY KITTIES

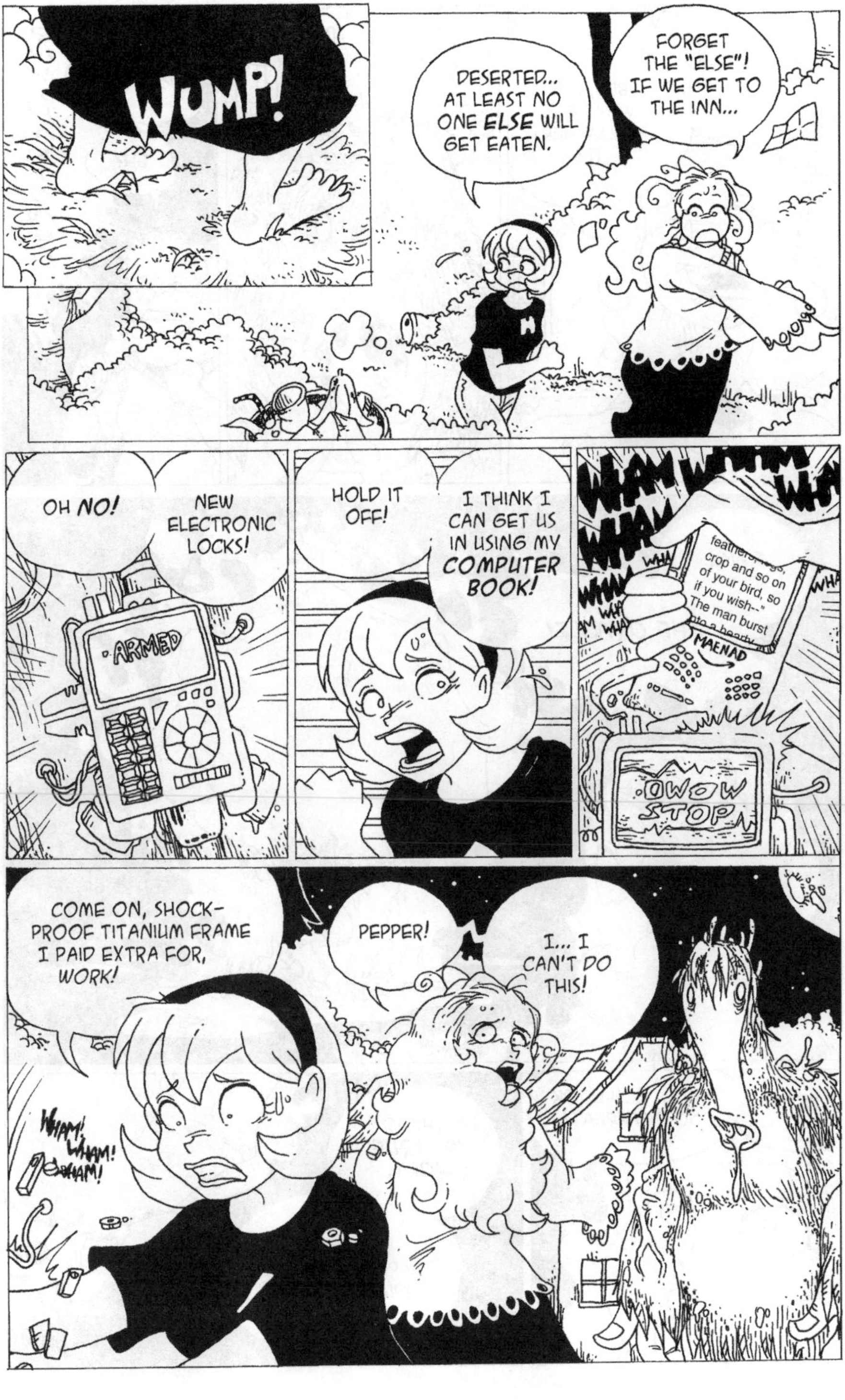
WUMP!
DESERTED... AT LEAST NO ONE ELSE WILL GET EATEN.
FORGET THE "ELSE"! IF WE GET TO THE INN...
OH NO!
NEW ELECTRONIC LOCKS!
ARMED
HOLD IT OFF!
I THINK I CAN GET US IN USING MY COMPUTER BOOK!
WHAM WHAM WHAM
feathers, legs, crop and so on of your bird, so if you wish--" The man burst
MAENAD
OWOW STOP
COME ON, SHOCK-PROOF TITANIUM FRAME I PAID EXTRA FOR, WORK!
PEPPER!
I... I CAN'T DO THIS!
WHAM! WHAM! WHAM!

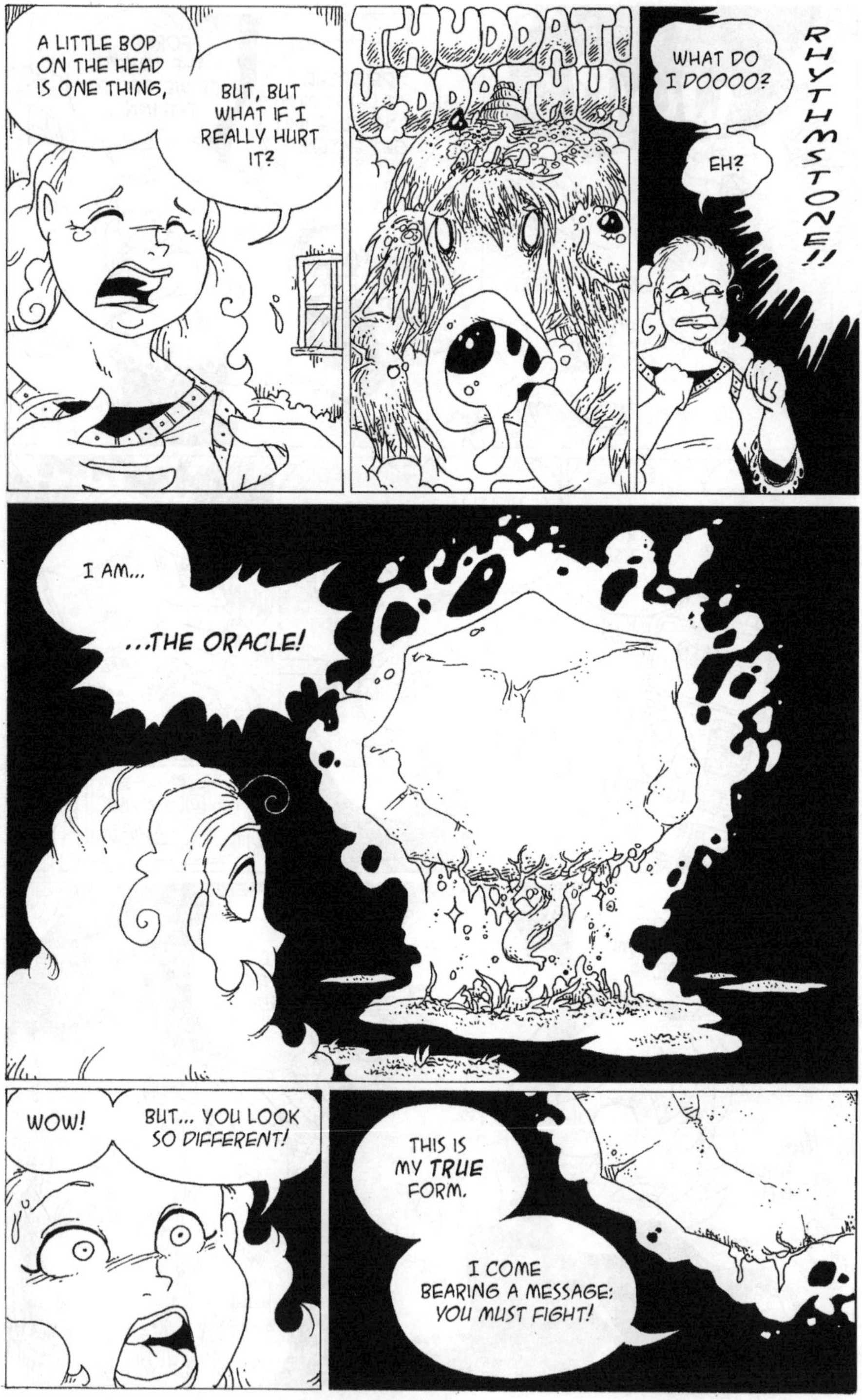
A LITTLE BOP ON THE HEAD IS ONE THING,
BUT, BUT WHAT IF I REALLY HURT IT?
THUDDAT!
WHAT DO I DOOOO?
EH?
RHYTHMSTONE!!
I AM...
...THE ORACLE!
WOW!
BUT... YOU LOOK SO DIFFERENT!
THIS IS MY TRUE FORM.
I COME BEARING A MESSAGE: YOU MUST FIGHT!

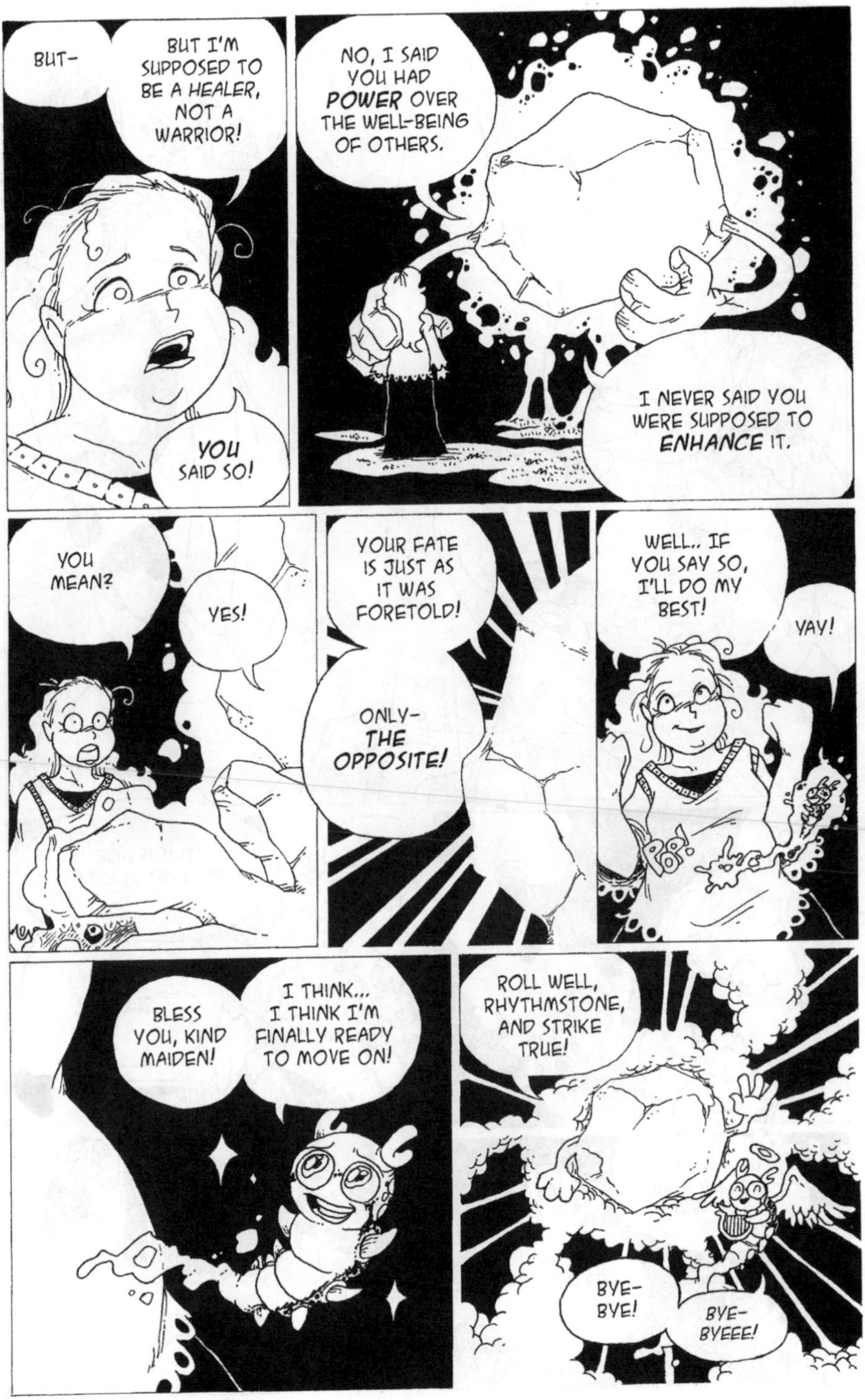
BUT-
BUT I'M SUPPOSED TO BE A HEALER, NOT A WARRIOR!
YOU SAID SO!
NO, I SAID YOU HAD POWER OVER THE WELL-BEING OF OTHERS.
I NEVER SAID YOU WERE SUPPOSED TO ENHANCE IT.
YOU MEAN?
YES!
YOUR FATE IS JUST AS IT WAS FORETOLD!
ONLY- THE OPPOSITE!
WELL.. IF YOU SAY SO, I'LL DO MY BEST!
YAY!
POP!
BLESS YOU, KIND MAIDEN!
I THINK... I THINK I'M FINALLY READY TO MOVE ON!
ROLL WELL, RHYTHMSTONE, AND STRIKE TRUE!
BYE-BYE!
BYE-BYEEE!

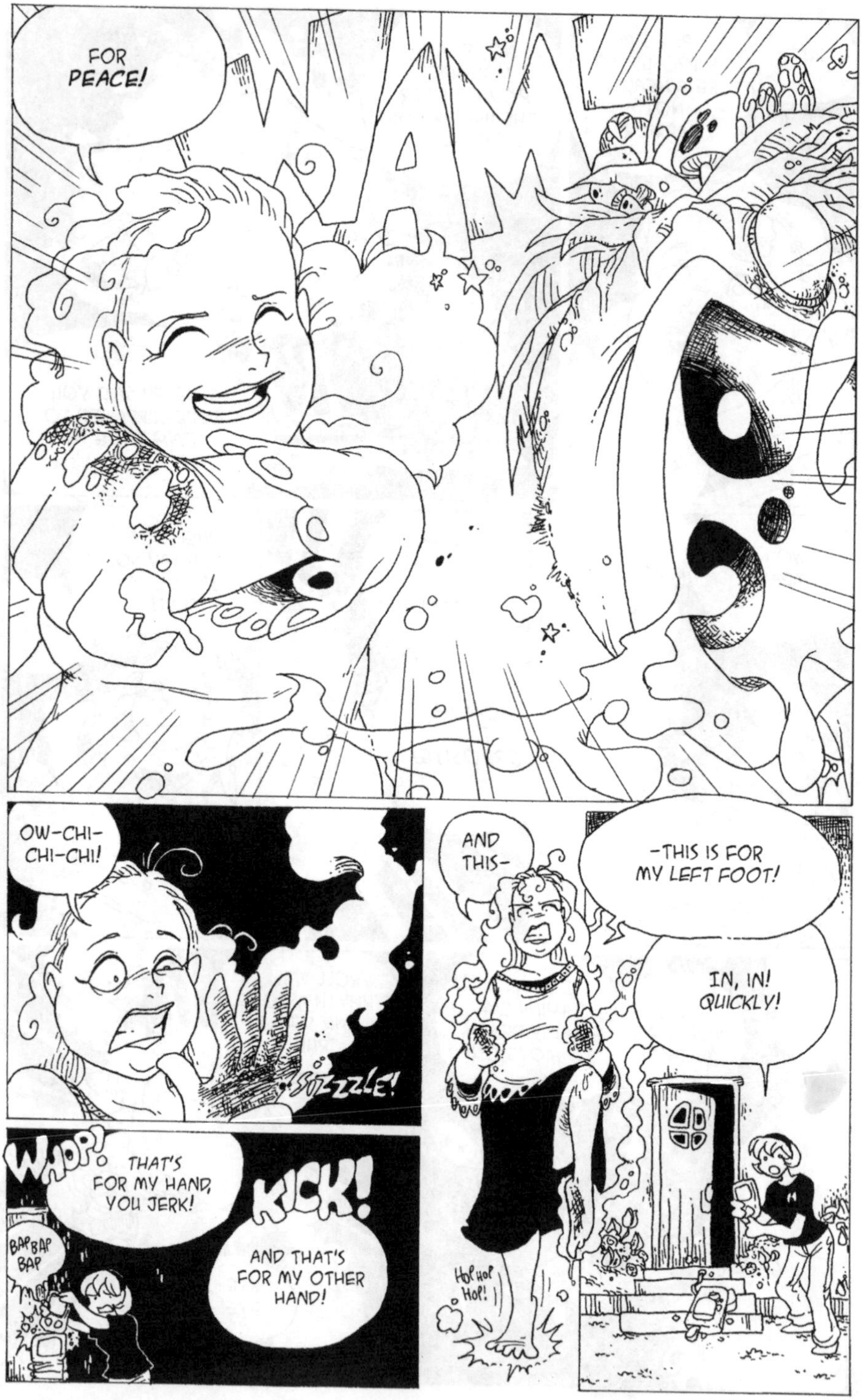
FOR PEACE!
WAM
OW-CHI-CHI-CHI!
SIZZZLE!
WHOP!
THAT'S FOR MY HAND, YOU JERK!
BAP BAP BAP
KICK!
AND THAT'S FOR MY OTHER HAND!
AND THIS-
-THIS IS FOR MY LEFT FOOT!
HOP HOP HOP!
IN, IN! QUICKLY!

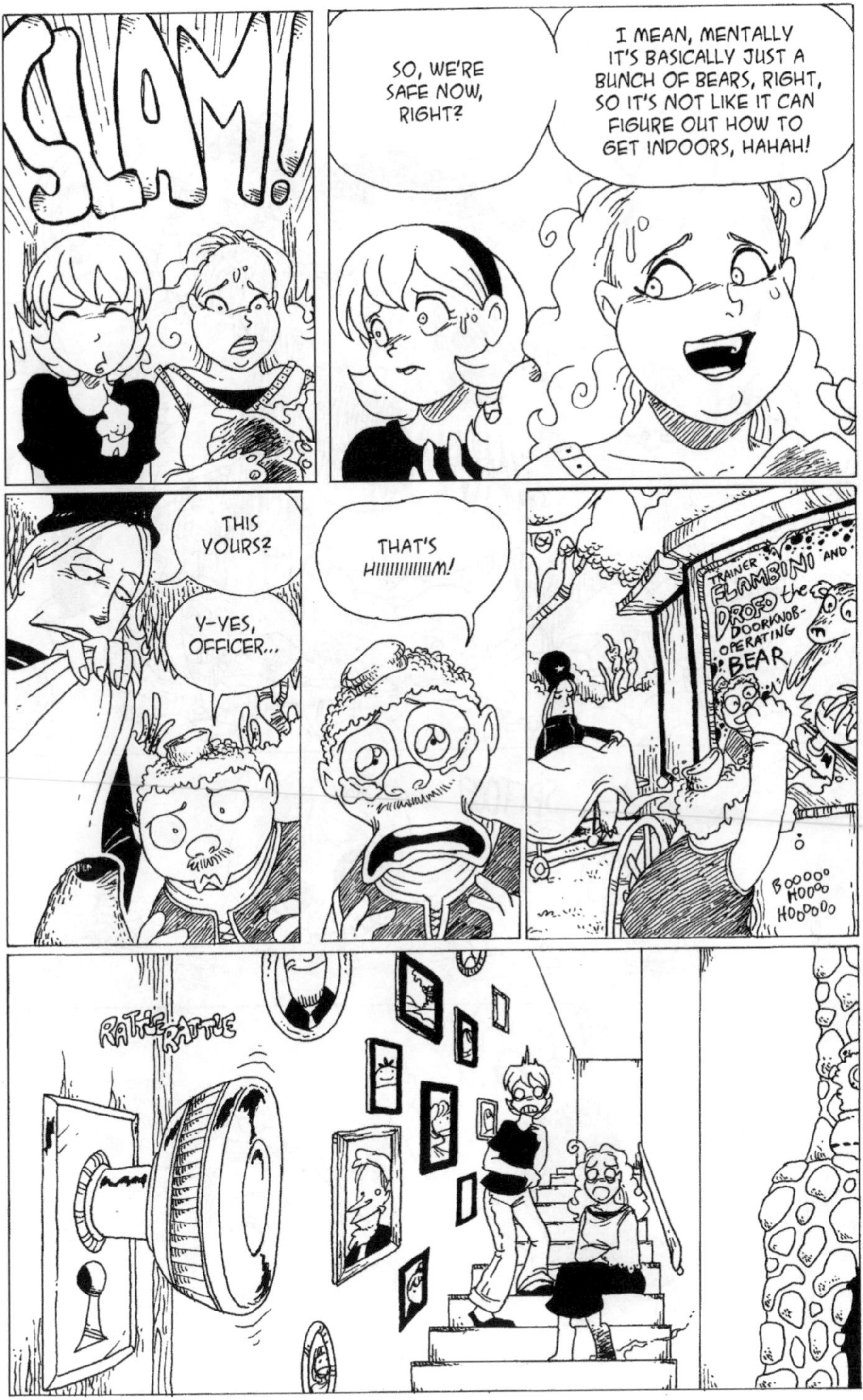
SLAM!
SO, WE'RE SAFE NOW, RIGHT?
I MEAN, MENTALLY IT'S BASICALLY JUST A BUNCH OF BEARS, RIGHT, SO IT'S NOT LIKE IT CAN FIGURE OUT HOW TO GET INDOORS, HAHAH!
THIS YOURS?
Y-YES, OFFICER...
THAT'S HIIIIIIIIIIIM!
TRAINER FLAMBINI AND DROFO the DOORKNOB-OPERATING BEAR
BOOOOO HOOO HOOOOO
RATTLE RATTLE

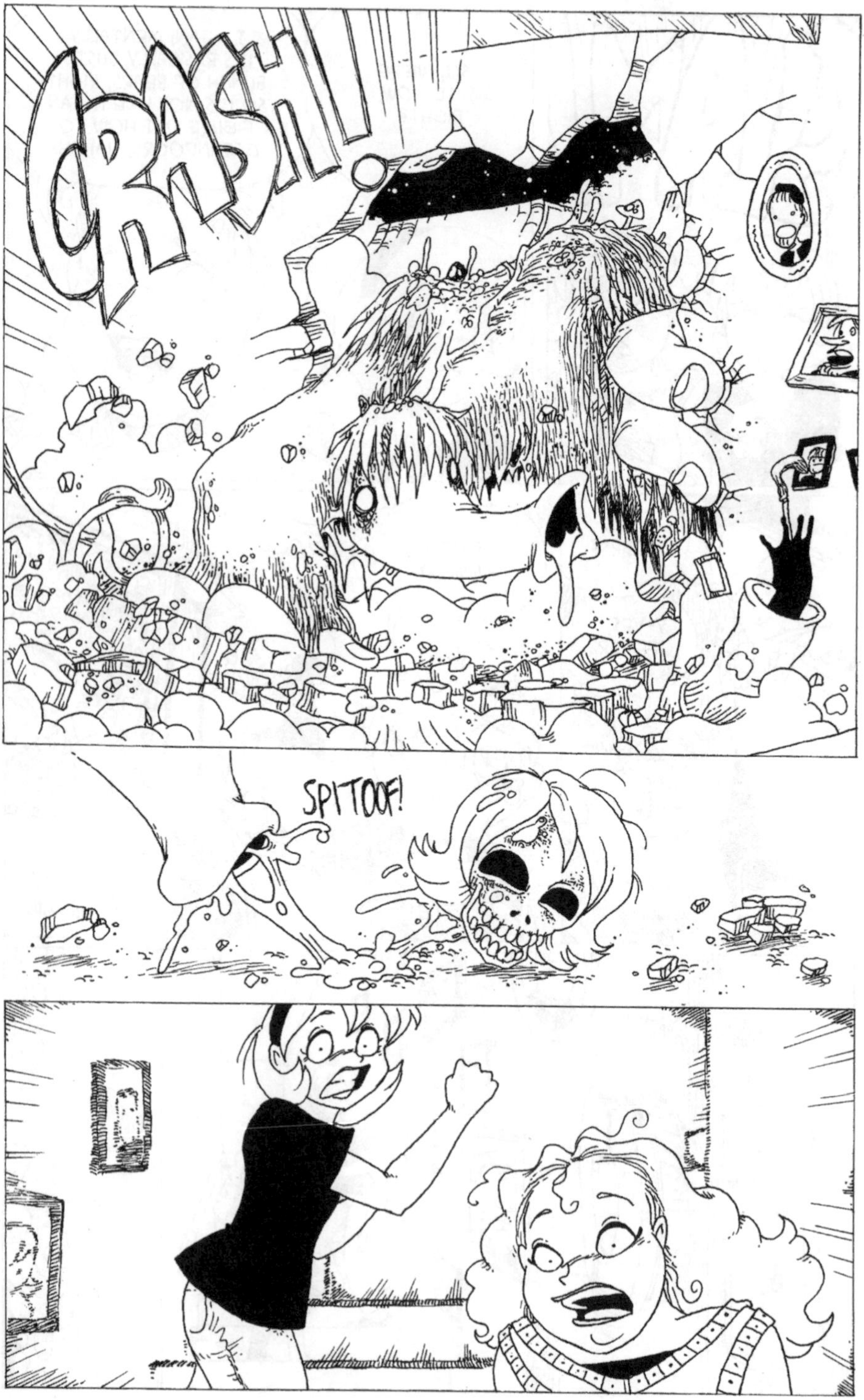
CRASH!!
SPITOOF!

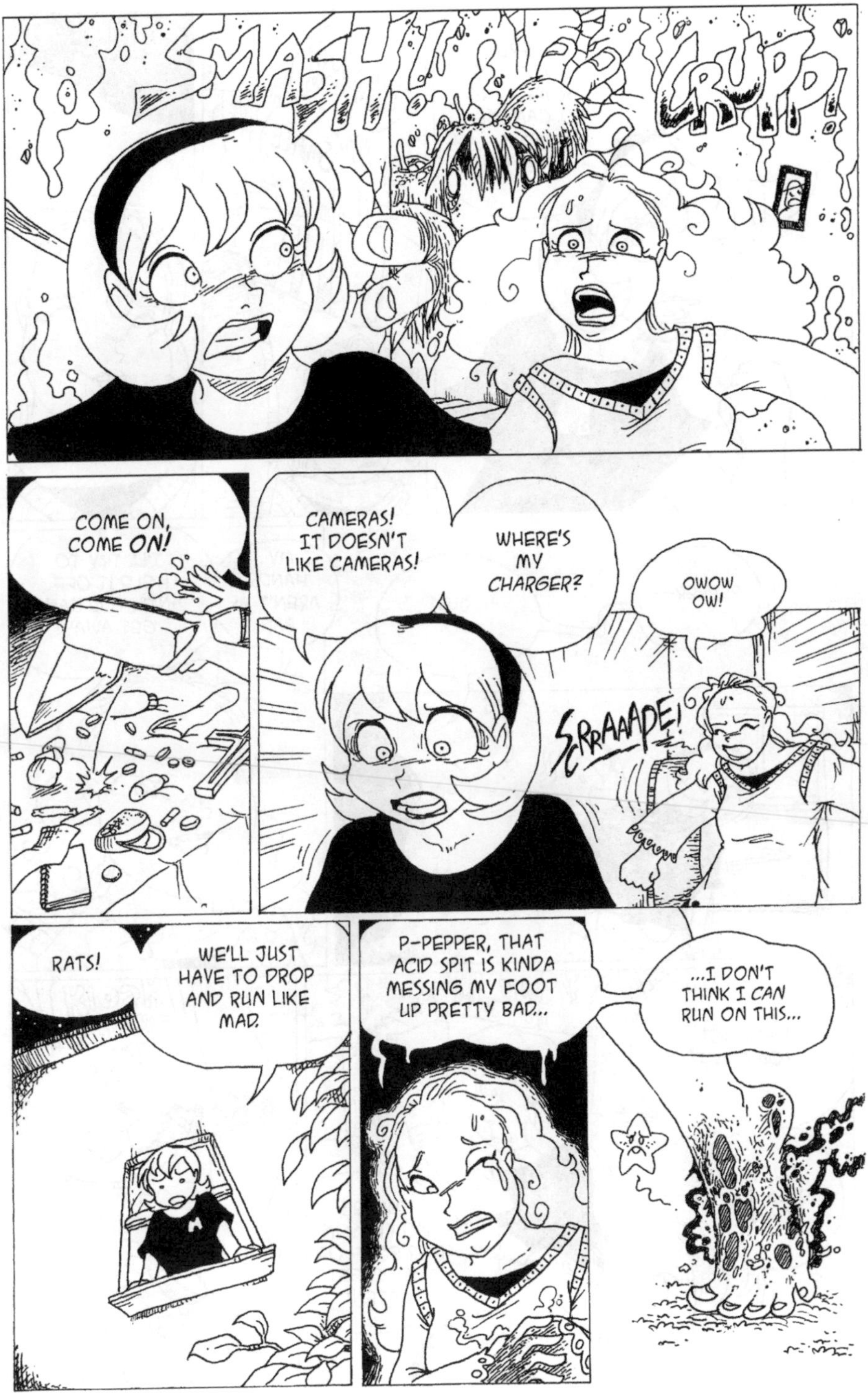
SMASH!
CRUDD!
COME ON, COME ON!
CAMERAS! IT DOESN'T LIKE CAMERAS!
WHERE'S MY CHARGER?
OWOW OW!
SCRRAAAPE!
RATS!
WE'LL JUST HAVE TO DROP AND RUN LIKE MAD.
P-PEPPER, THAT ACID SPIT IS KINDA MESSING MY FOOT UP PRETTY BAD...
...I DON'T THINK I CAN RUN ON THIS...

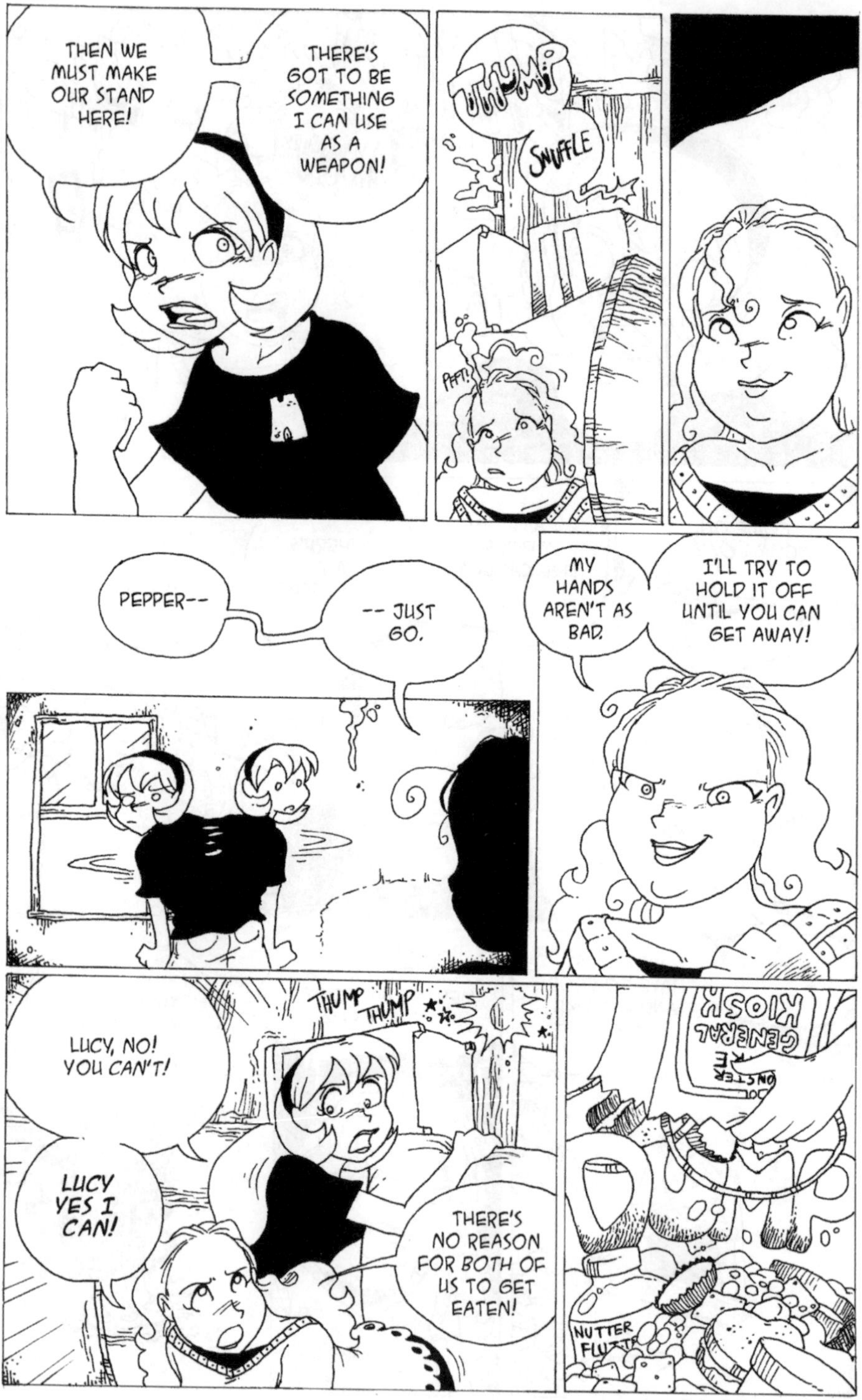

THEN WE MUST MAKE OUR STAND HERE!
THERE'S GOT TO BE SOMETHING I CAN USE AS A WEAPON!
THUMP
SNUFFLE
PFFT!
PEPPER--
-- JUST GO.
MY HANDS AREN'T AS BAD.
I'LL TRY TO HOLD IT OFF UNTIL YOU CAN GET AWAY!
THUMP
THUMP
LUCY, NO! YOU CAN'T!
LUCY YES I CAN!
THERE'S NO REASON FOR BOTH OF US TO GET EATEN!
GENERAL KIOSK
NUTTER

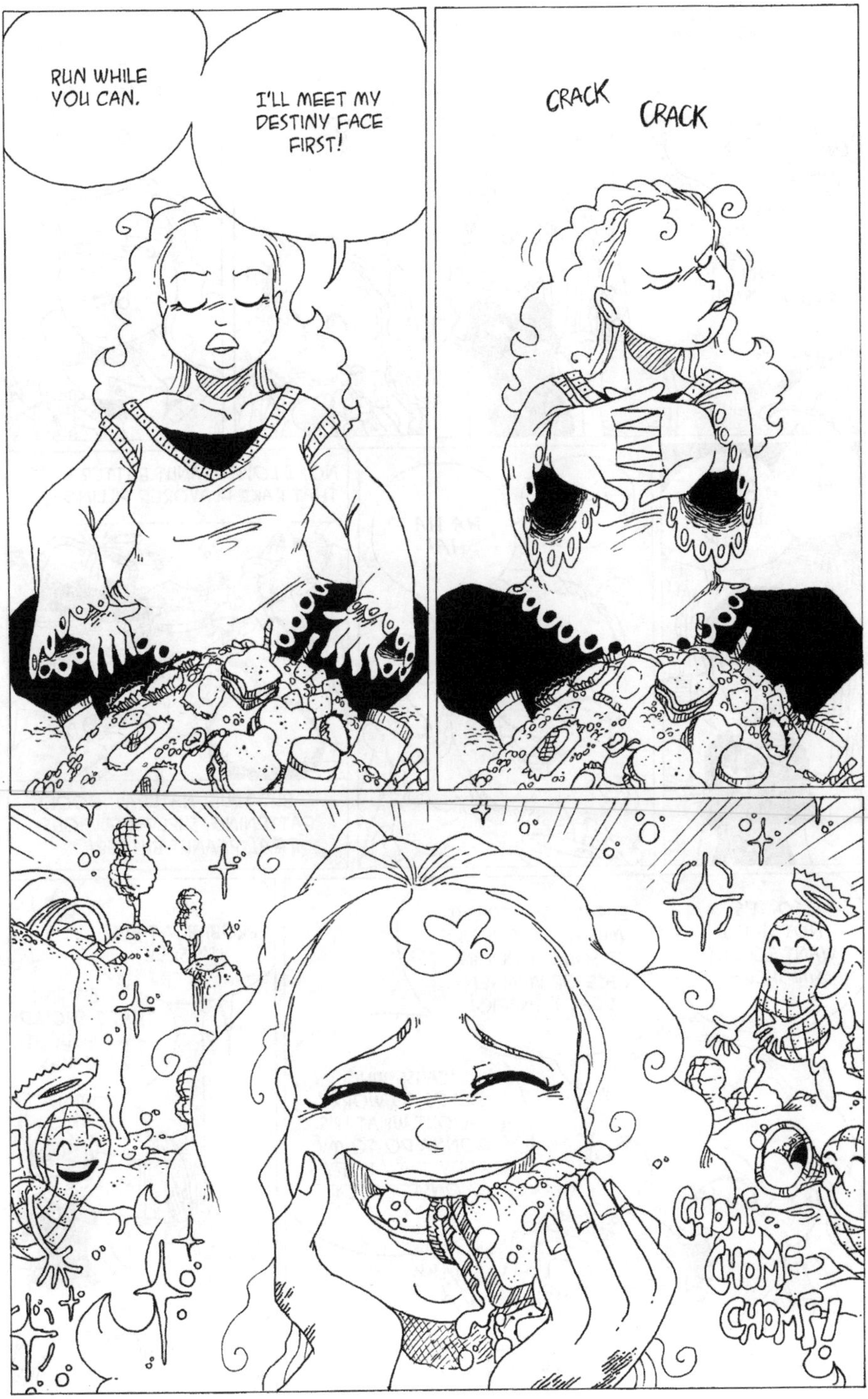
RUN WHILE YOU CAN.
I'LL MEET MY DESTINY FACE FIRST!
CRACK
CRACK
CHOMF
CHOMF
CHOMF!

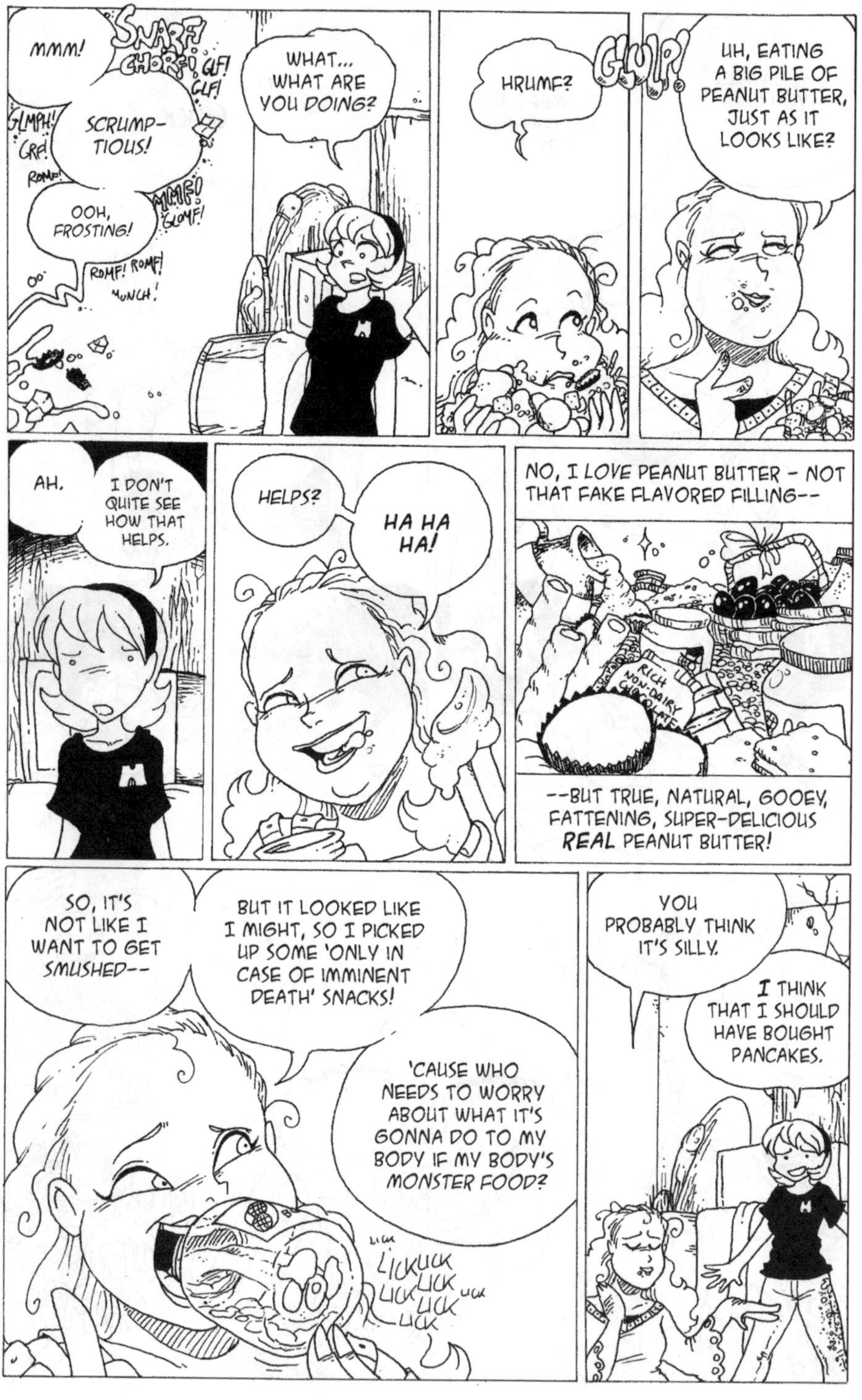
MMM!
SNARF! CHORF! GLF! GLF!
SCRUMP-TIOUS!
GLMPH! GRF! ROMF!
MMF! GLOMF!
OOH, FROSTING!
ROMF! ROMF! MUNCH!
WHAT... WHAT ARE YOU DOING?
HRUMF?
GLULP!
UH, EATING A BIG PILE OF PEANUT BUTTER, JUST AS IT LOOKS LIKE?
AH.
I DON'T QUITE SEE HOW THAT HELPS.
HELPS?
HA HA HA!
NO, I LOVE PEANUT BUTTER - NOT THAT FAKE FLAVORED FILLING--
RICH NON-DAIRY CHOCOLATE
--BUT TRUE, NATURAL, GOOEY, FATTENING, SUPER-DELICIOUS REAL PEANUT BUTTER!
SO, IT'S NOT LIKE I WANT TO GET SMUSHED--
BUT IT LOOKED LIKE I MIGHT, SO I PICKED UP SOME 'ONLY IN CASE OF IMMINENT DEATH' SNACKS!
'CAUSE WHO NEEDS TO WORRY ABOUT WHAT IT'S GONNA DO TO MY BODY IF MY BODY'S MONSTER FOOD?
LICK LICK LICK LICK LICK LICK LICK LICK
YOU PROBABLY THINK IT'S SILLY.
I THINK THAT I SHOULD HAVE BOUGHT PANCAKES.

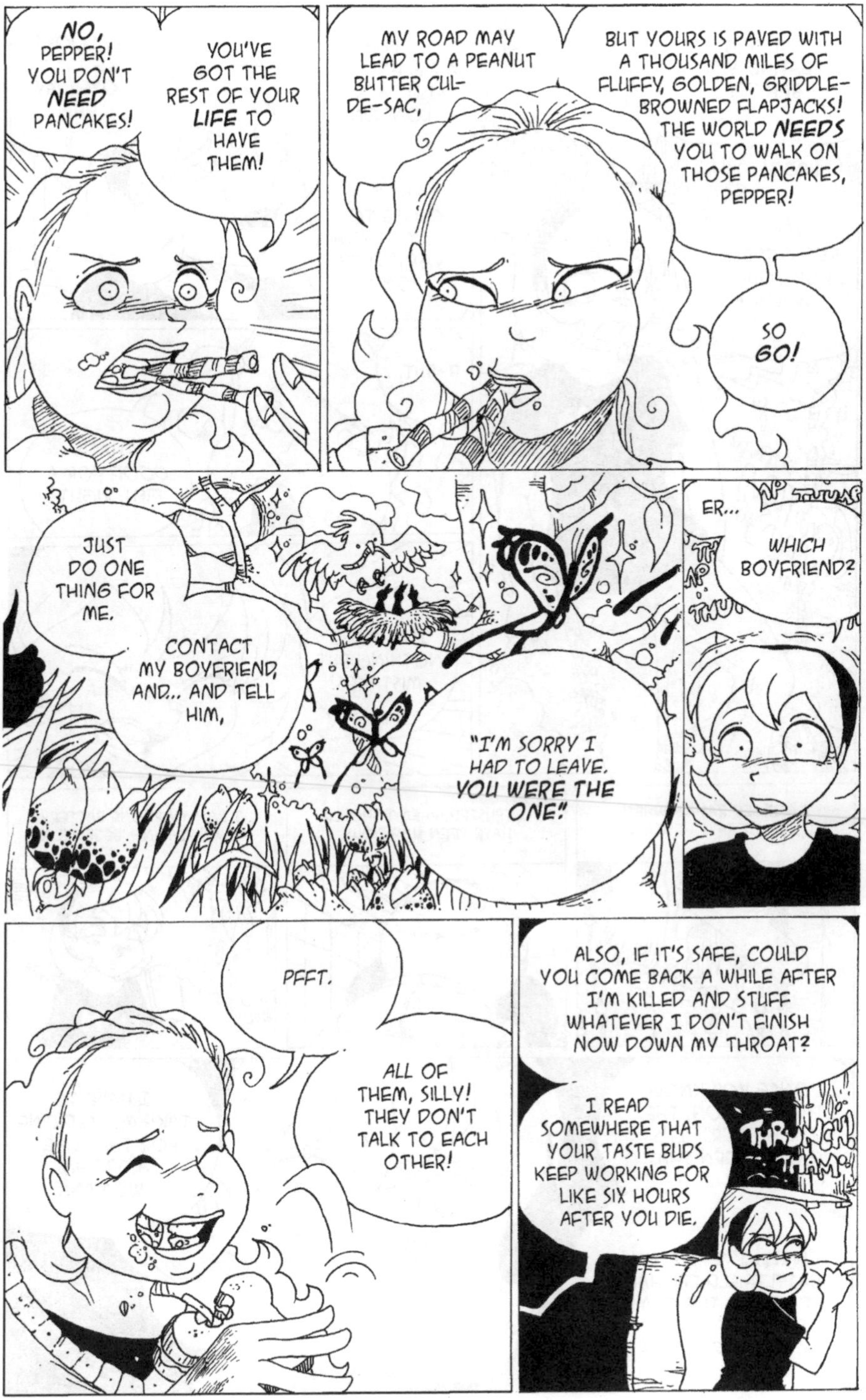
NO, PEPPER! YOU DON'T NEED PANCAKES!
YOU'VE GOT THE REST OF YOUR LIFE TO HAVE THEM!
MY ROAD MAY LEAD TO A PEANUT BUTTER CUL-DE-SAC,
BUT YOURS IS PAVED WITH A THOUSAND MILES OF FLUFFY, GOLDEN, GRIDDLE-BROWNED FLAPJACKS! THE WORLD NEEDS YOU TO WALK ON THOSE PANCAKES, PEPPER!
SO GO!
JUST DO ONE THING FOR ME.
CONTACT MY BOYFRIEND, AND... AND TELL HIM,
"I'M SORRY I HAD TO LEAVE. YOU WERE THE ONE!"
ER...
WHICH BOYFRIEND?
PFFT.
ALL OF THEM, SILLY! THEY DON'T TALK TO EACH OTHER!
ALSO, IF IT'S SAFE, COULD YOU COME BACK A WHILE AFTER I'M KILLED AND STUFF WHATEVER I DON'T FINISH NOW DOWN MY THROAT?
I READ SOMEWHERE THAT YOUR TASTE BUDS KEEP WORKING FOR LIKE SIX HOURS AFTER YOU DIE.
THRUNCH!
THAM

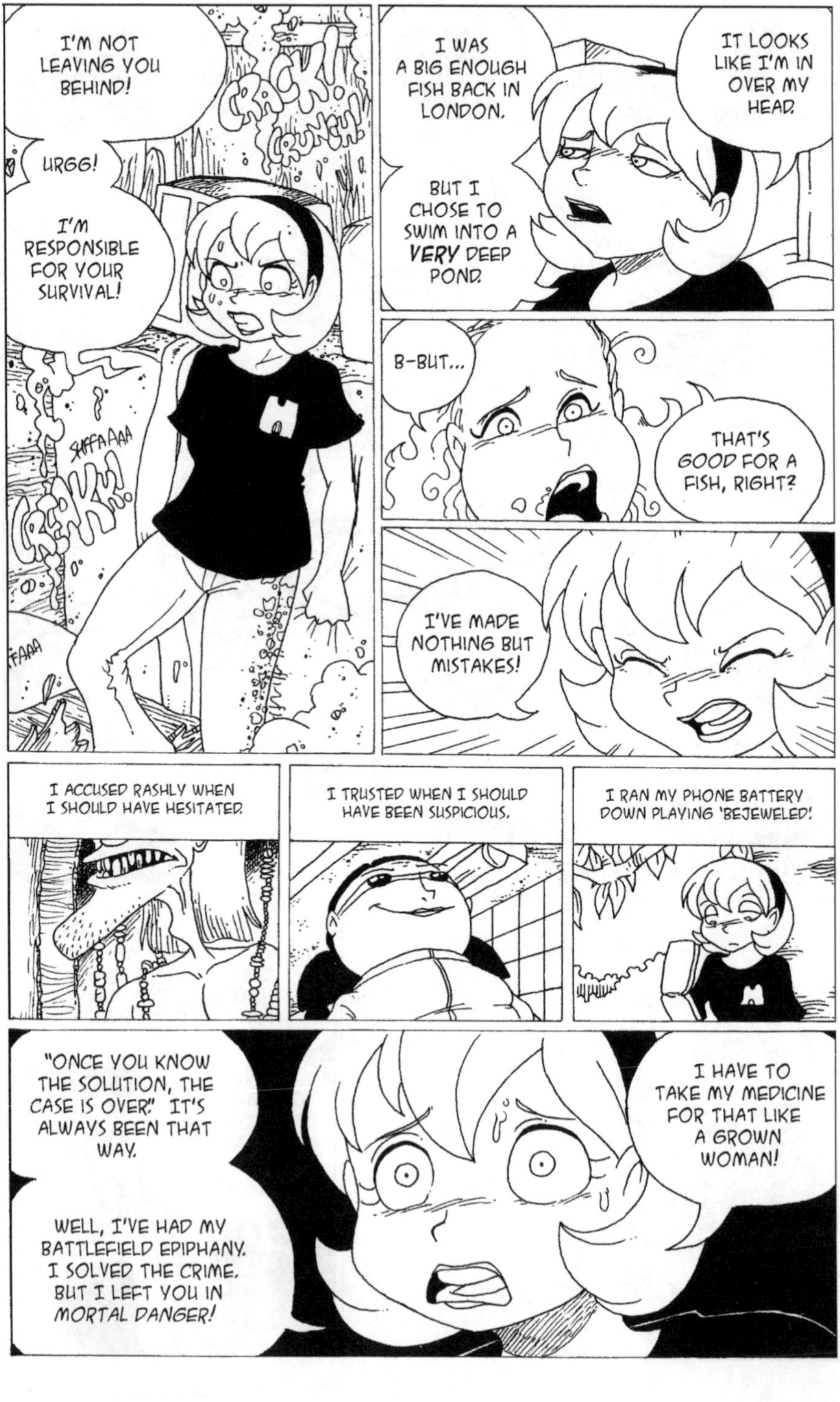
I'M NOT LEAVING YOU BEHIND!
CRACK!
CRUNCH!
URGG!
I'M RESPONSIBLE FOR YOUR SURVIVAL!
SHFFAAAA
CREAK!!
I WAS A BIG ENOUGH FISH BACK IN LONDON.
BUT I CHOSE TO SWIM INTO A *VERY* DEEP POND.
IT LOOKS LIKE I'M IN OVER MY HEAD.
B-BUT...
THAT'S *GOOD* FOR A FISH, RIGHT?
I'VE MADE NOTHING BUT MISTAKES!
I ACCUSED RASHLY WHEN I SHOULD HAVE HESITATED.
I TRUSTED WHEN I SHOULD HAVE BEEN SUSPICIOUS.
I RAN MY PHONE BATTERY DOWN PLAYING 'BEJEWELED.'
"ONCE YOU KNOW THE SOLUTION, THE CASE IS OVER." IT'S ALWAYS BEEN THAT WAY.
WELL, I'VE HAD MY BATTLEFIELD EPIPHANY. I SOLVED THE CRIME. BUT I LEFT YOU IN *MORTAL DANGER!*
I HAVE TO TAKE MY MEDICINE FOR THAT LIKE A GROWN WOMAN!

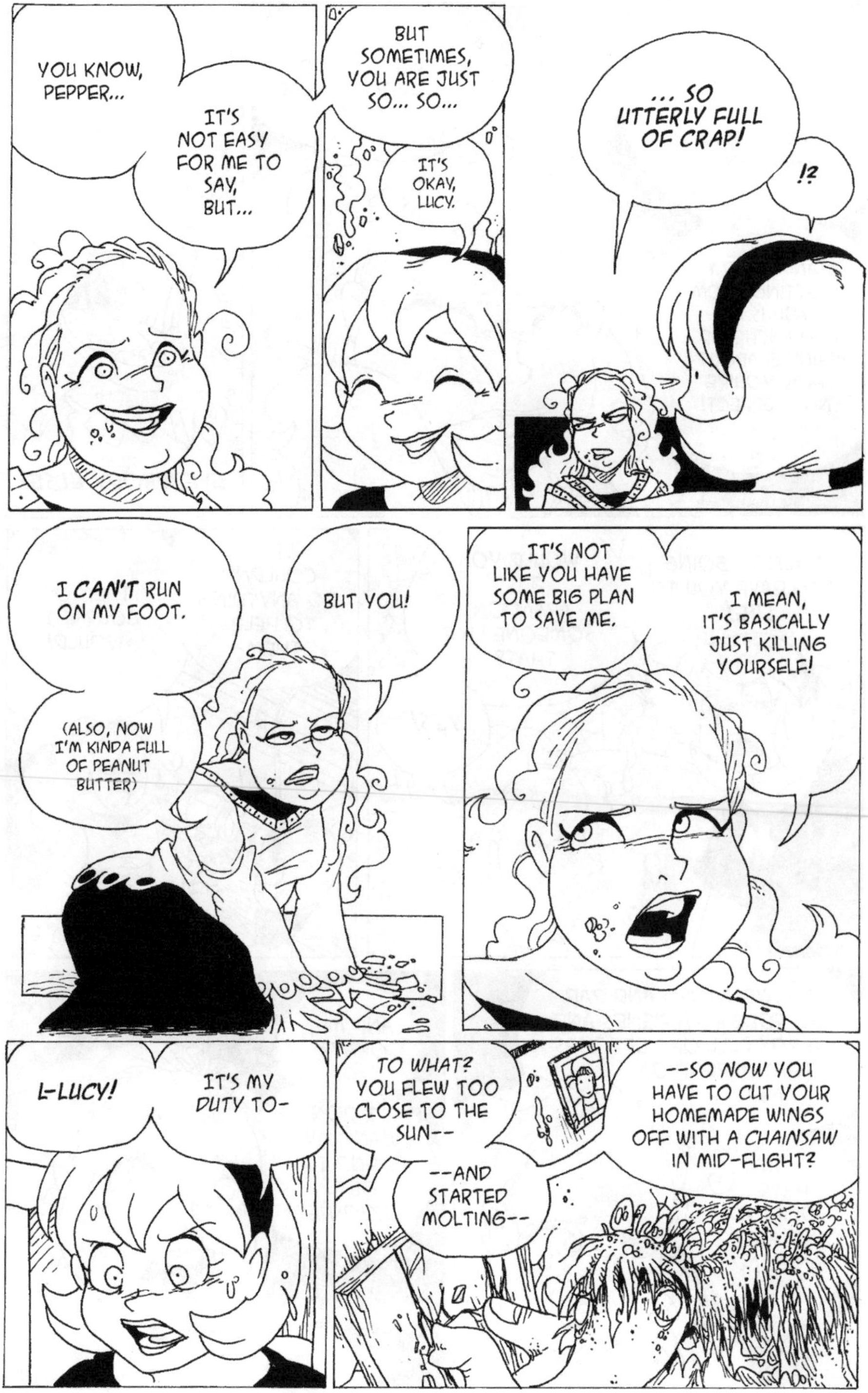
YOU KNOW, PEPPER...
IT'S NOT EASY FOR ME TO SAY, BUT...
BUT SOMETIMES, YOU ARE JUST SO... SO...
IT'S OKAY, LUCY.
... SO UTTERLY FULL OF CRAP!
!?
I CAN'T RUN ON MY FOOT.
(ALSO, NOW I'M KINDA FULL OF PEANUT BUTTER)
BUT YOU!
IT'S NOT LIKE YOU HAVE SOME BIG PLAN TO SAVE ME.
I MEAN, IT'S BASICALLY JUST KILLING YOURSELF!
L-LUCY!
IT'S MY DUTY TO-
TO WHAT? YOU FLEW TOO CLOSE TO THE SUN--
--AND STARTED MOLTING--
--SO NOW YOU HAVE TO CUT YOUR HOMEMADE WINGS OFF WITH A CHAINSAW IN MID-FLIGHT?

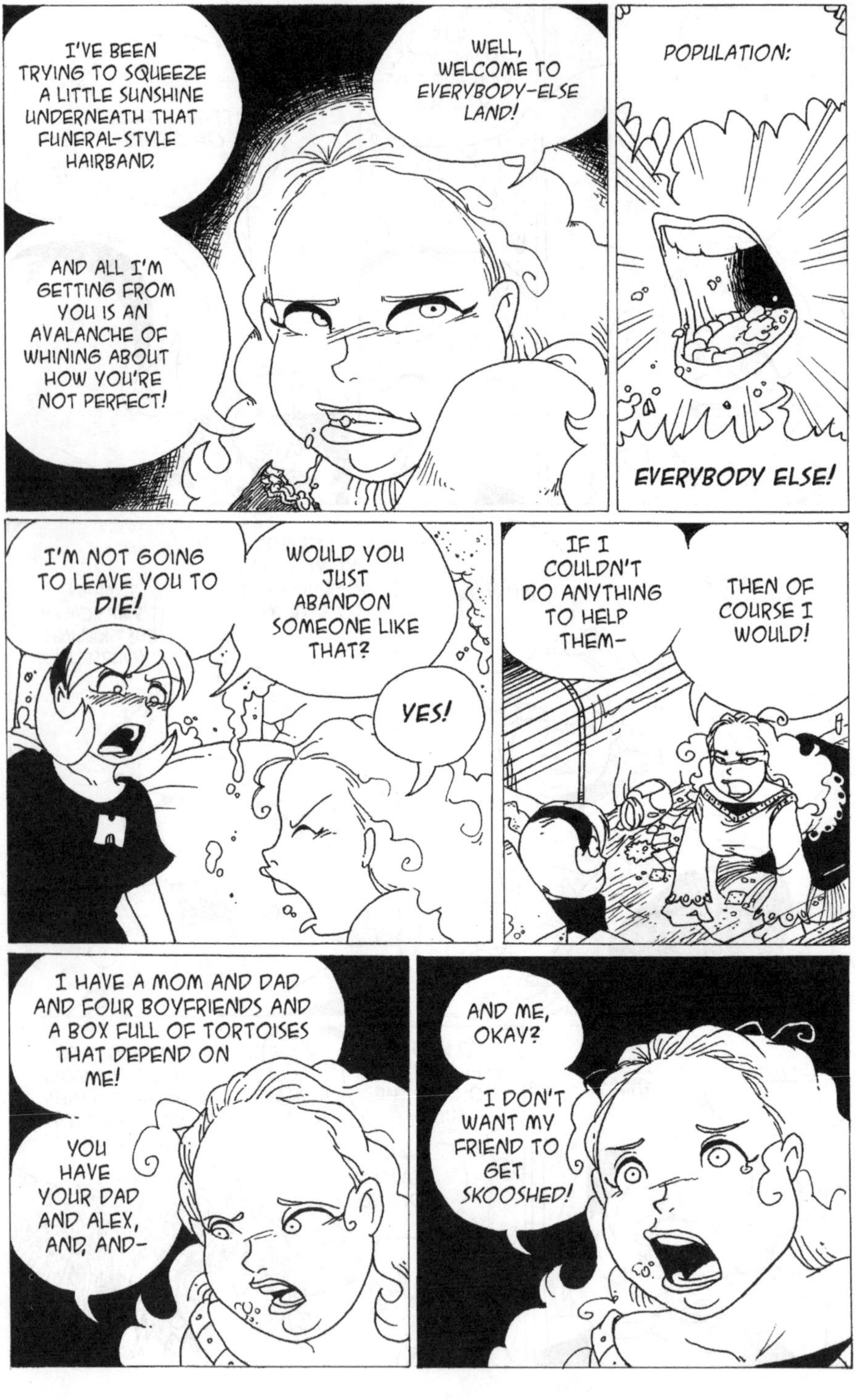
I'VE BEEN TRYING TO SQUEEZE A LITTLE SUNSHINE UNDERNEATH THAT FUNERAL-STYLE HAIRBAND.
AND ALL I'M GETTING FROM YOU IS AN AVALANCHE OF WHINING ABOUT HOW YOU'RE NOT PERFECT!
WELL, WELCOME TO EVERYBODY-ELSE LAND!
POPULATION:
EVERYBODY ELSE!
I'M NOT GOING TO LEAVE YOU TO DIE!
WOULD YOU JUST ABANDON SOMEONE LIKE THAT?
YES!
IF I COULDN'T DO ANYTHING TO HELP THEM-
THEN OF COURSE I WOULD!
I HAVE A MOM AND DAD AND FOUR BOYFRIENDS AND A BOX FULL OF TORTOISES THAT DEPEND ON ME!
YOU HAVE YOUR DAD AND ALEX, AND, AND-
AND ME, OKAY?
I DON'T WANT MY FRIEND TO GET SKOOSHED!

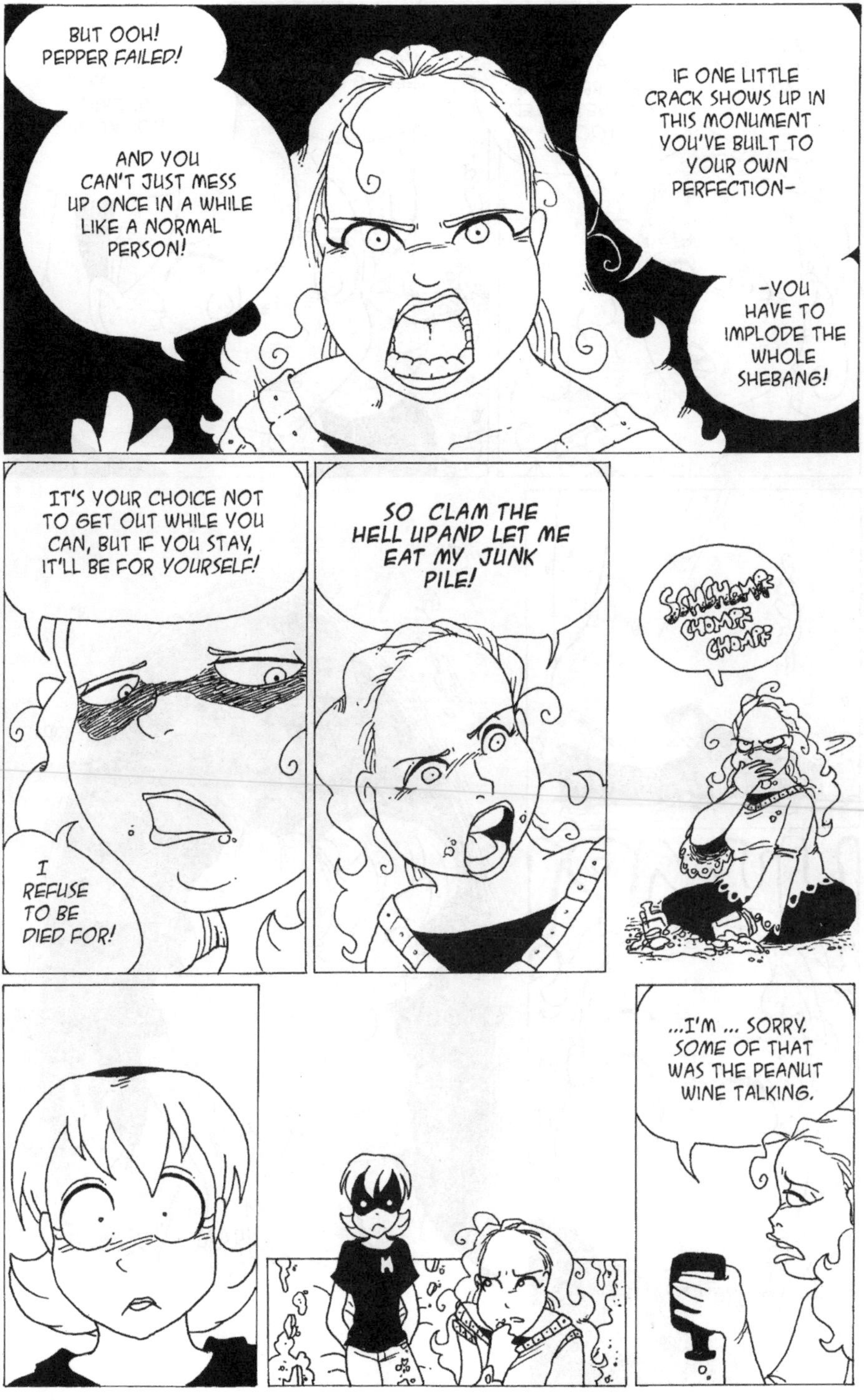
BUT OOH! PEPPER FAILED!
AND YOU CAN'T JUST MESS UP ONCE IN A WHILE LIKE A NORMAL PERSON!
IF ONE LITTLE CRACK SHOWS UP IN THIS MONUMENT YOU'VE BUILT TO YOUR OWN PERFECTION-
-YOU HAVE TO IMPLODE THE WHOLE SHEBANG!
IT'S YOUR CHOICE NOT TO GET OUT WHILE YOU CAN, BUT IF YOU STAY, IT'LL BE FOR *YOURSELF!*
I REFUSE TO BE DIED FOR!
SO CLAM THE HELL UPAND LET ME EAT MY JUNK PILE!
CHOMP! CHOMP!
...I'M ... SORRY. SOME OF THAT WAS THE PEANUT WINE TALKING.

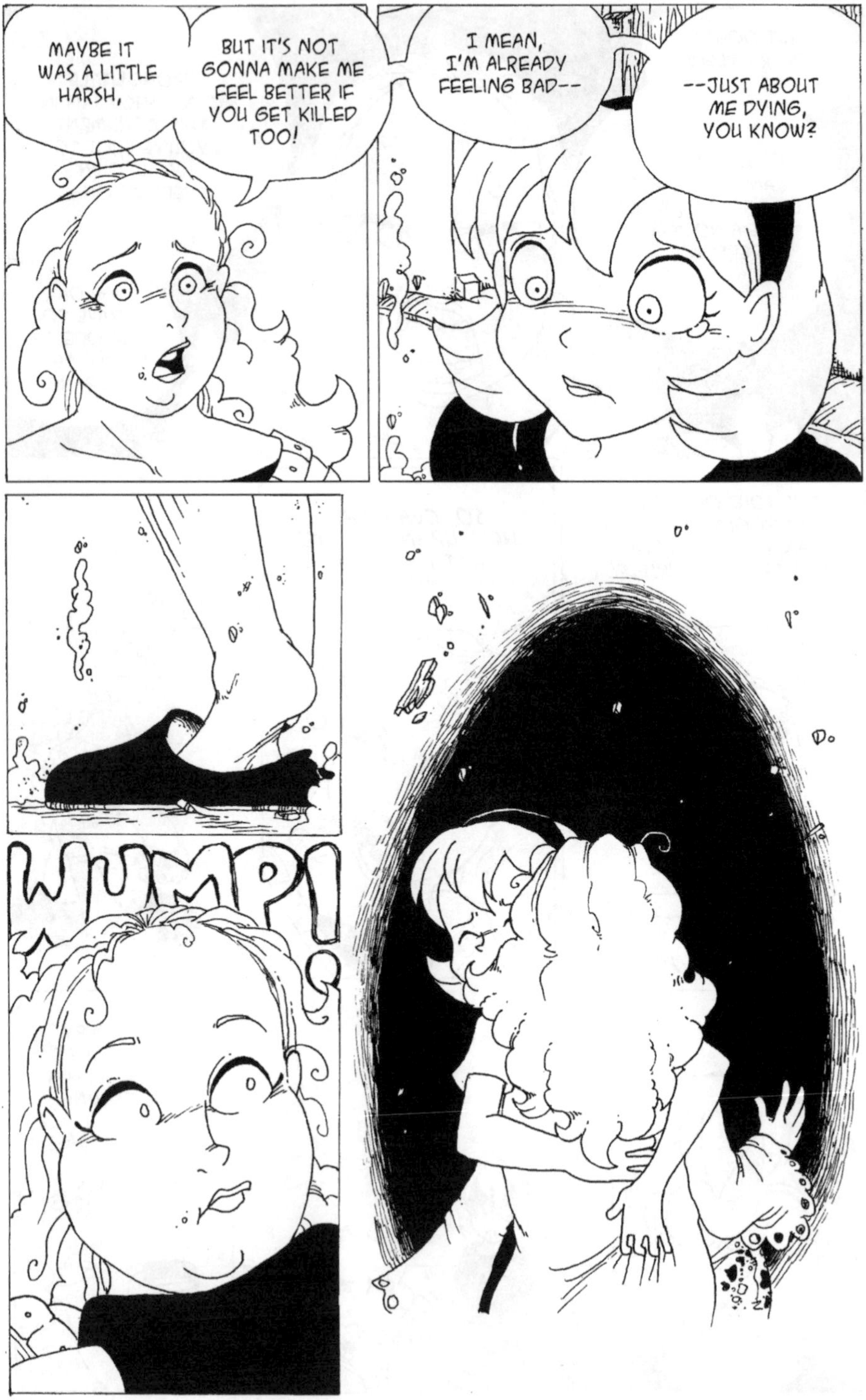
MAYBE IT WAS A LITTLE HARSH,
BUT IT'S NOT GONNA MAKE ME FEEL BETTER IF YOU GET KILLED TOO!
I MEAN, I'M ALREADY FEELING BAD--
--JUST ABOUT ME DYING, YOU KNOW?
WUMP!

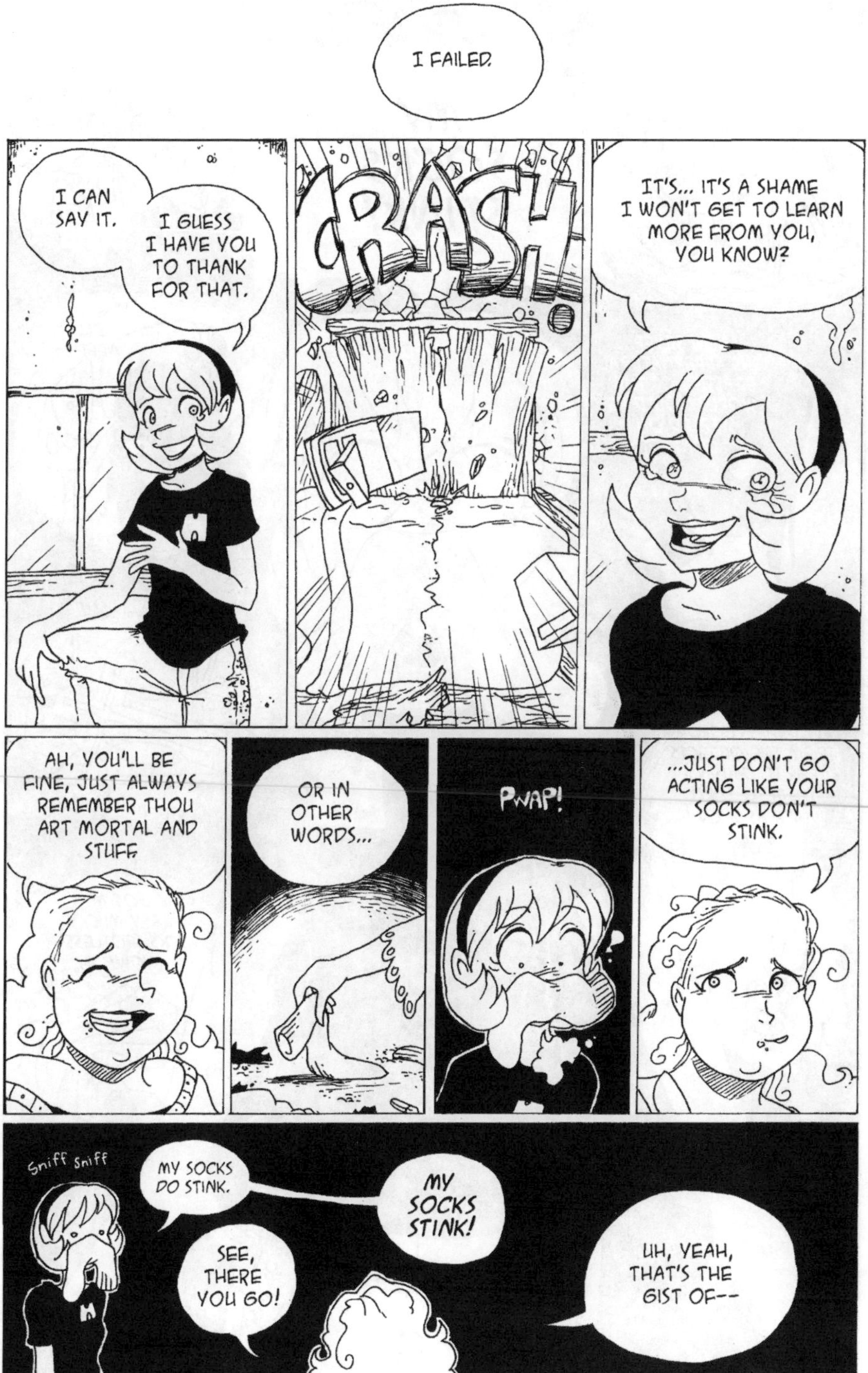
I FAILED.
I CAN SAY IT.
I GUESS I HAVE YOU TO THANK FOR THAT.
CRASH!
IT'S... IT'S A SHAME I WON'T GET TO LEARN MORE FROM YOU, YOU KNOW?
AH, YOU'LL BE FINE, JUST ALWAYS REMEMBER THOU ART MORTAL AND STUFF.
OR IN OTHER WORDS...
PWAP!
...JUST DON'T GO ACTING LIKE YOUR SOCKS DON'T STINK.
Sniff sniff
MY SOCKS DO STINK.
MY SOCKS STINK!
SEE, THERE YOU GO!
UH, YEAH, THAT'S THE GIST OF--

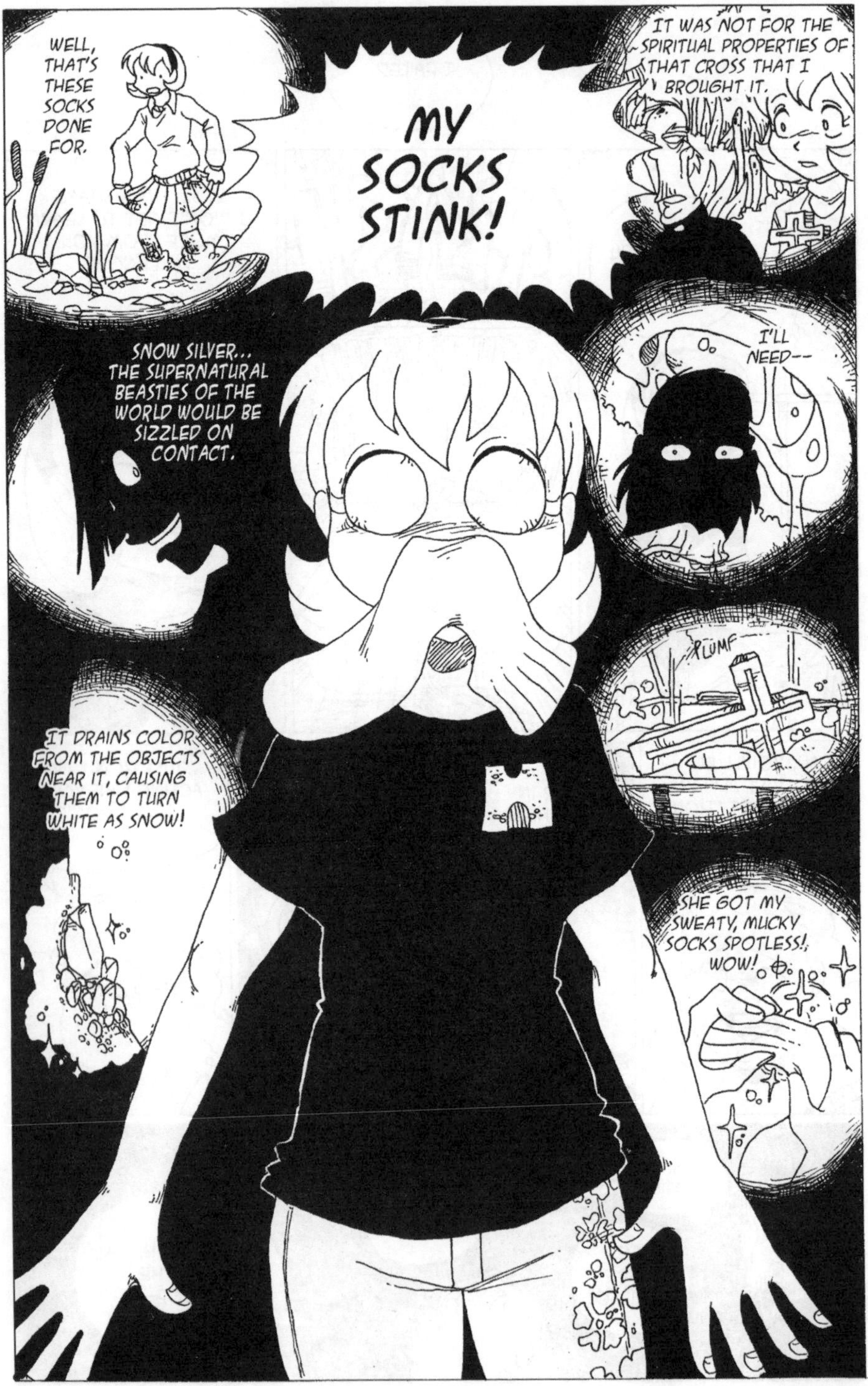
WELL, THAT'S THESE SOCKS DONE FOR.
MY SOCKS STINK!
IT WAS NOT FOR THE SPIRITUAL PROPERTIES OF THAT CROSS THAT I BROUGHT IT.
SNOW SILVER... THE SUPERNATURAL BEASTIES OF THE WORLD WOULD BE SIZZLED ON CONTACT.
I'LL NEED--
PLUMF
IT DRAINS COLOR FROM THE OBJECTS NEAR IT, CAUSING THEM TO TURN WHITE AS SNOW!
SHE GOT MY SWEATY, MUCKY SOCKS SPOTLESS! WOW!

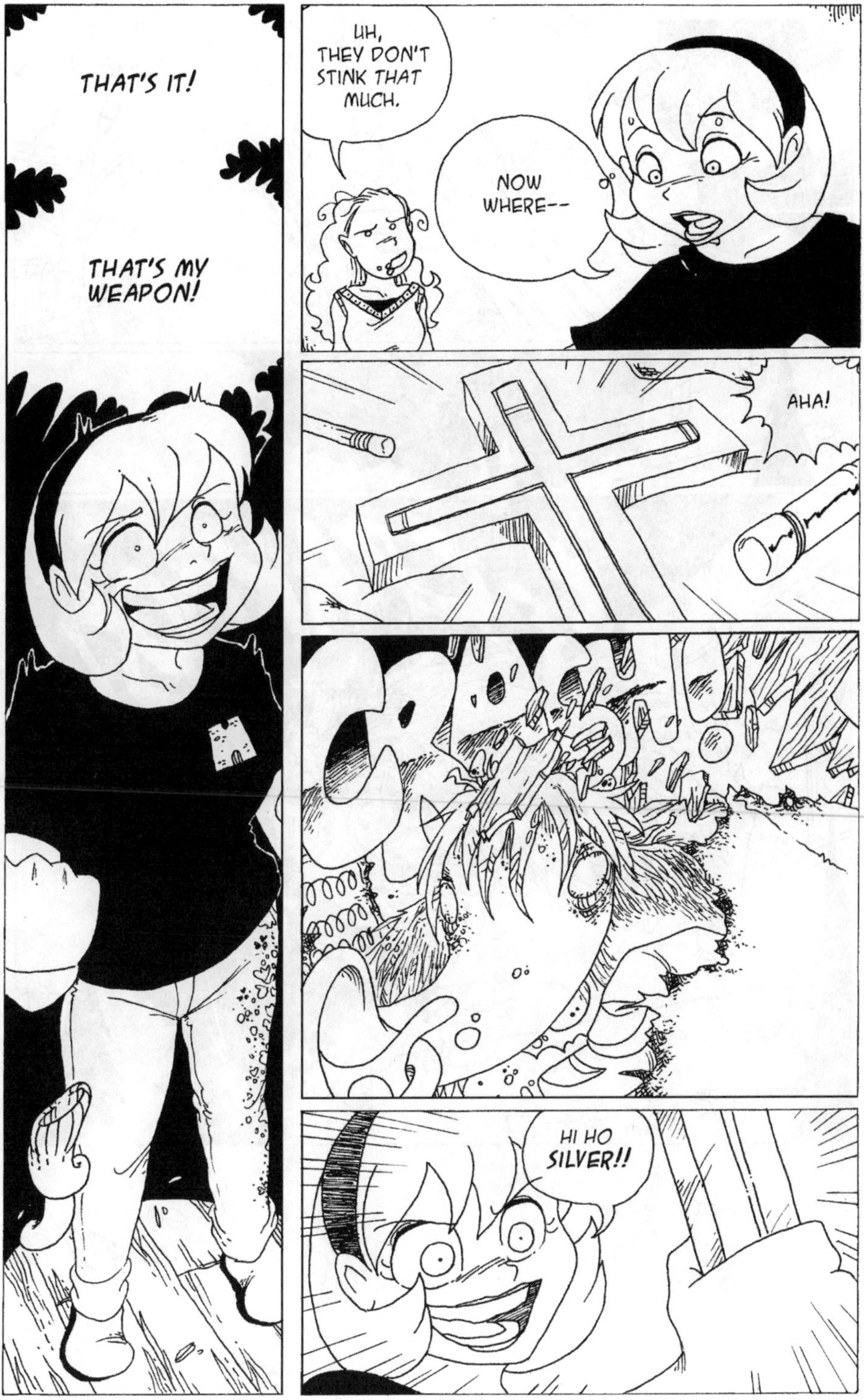
THAT'S IT!
THAT'S MY WEAPON!
UH, THEY DON'T STINK THAT MUCH.
NOW WHERE--
AHA!
HI HO SILVER!!

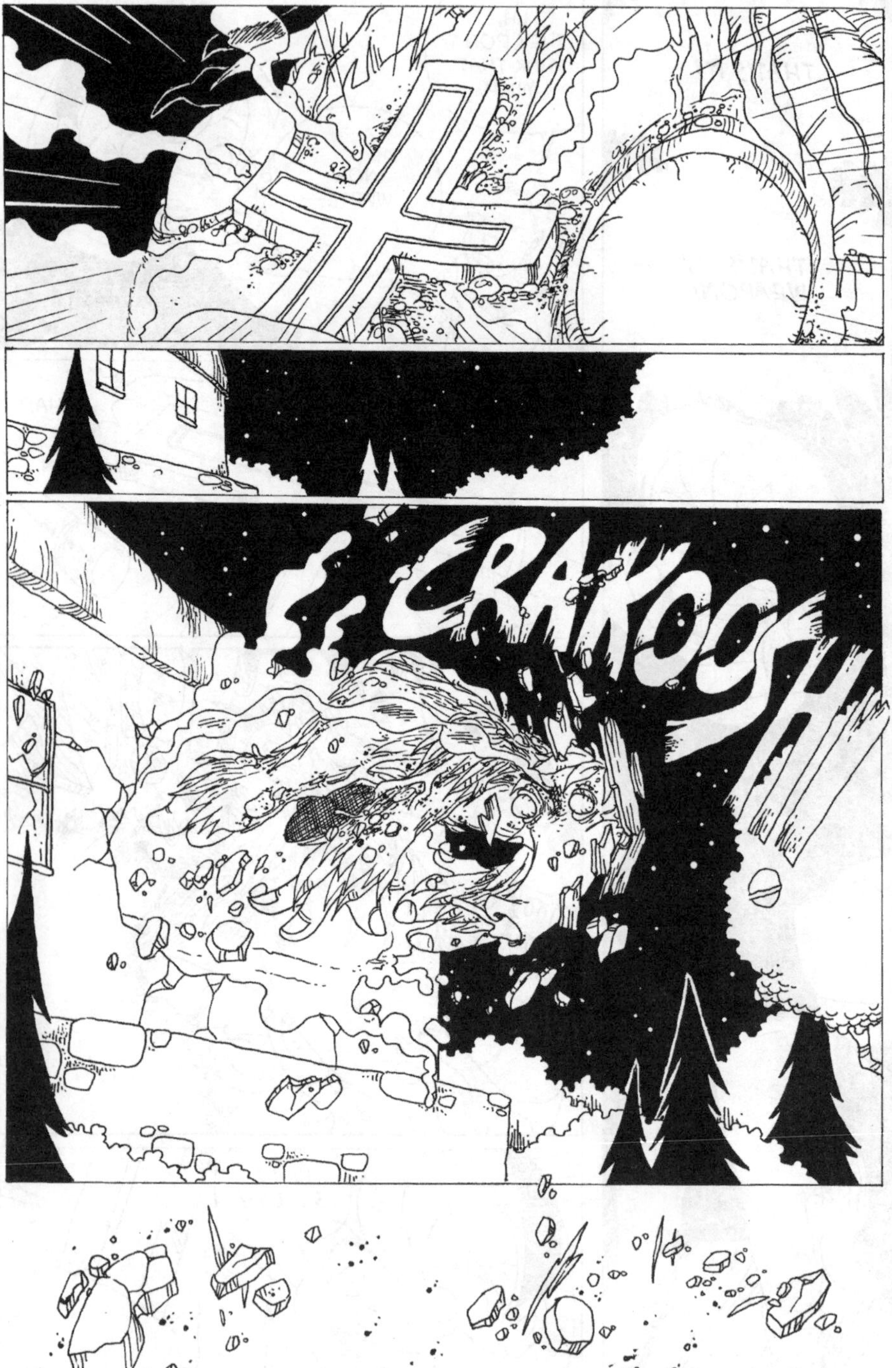
CRAKOOSH

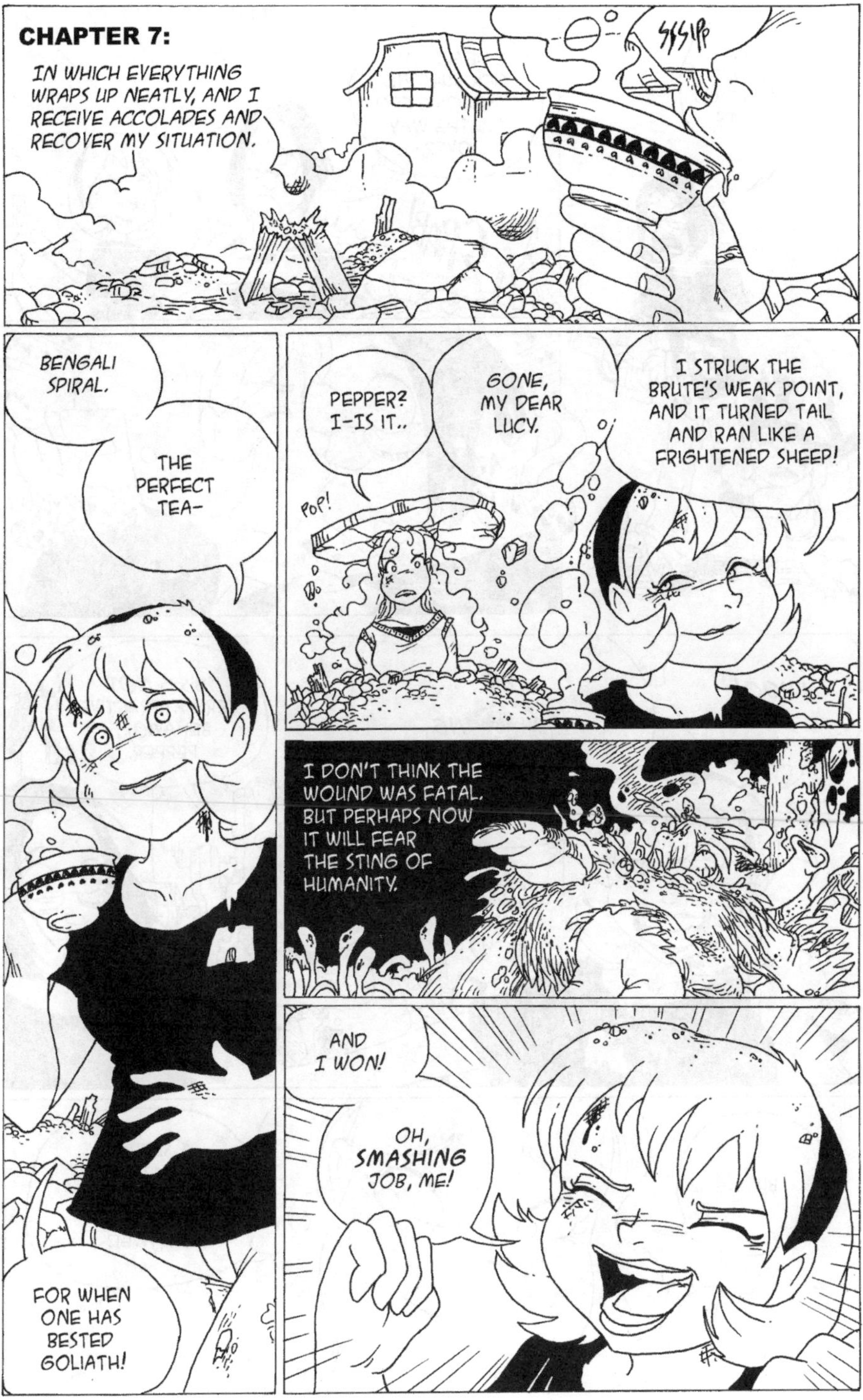
CHAPTER 7:
IN WHICH EVERYTHING WRAPS UP NEATLY, AND I RECEIVE ACCOLADES AND RECOVER MY SITUATION.
SSSIPP
BENGALI SPIRAL.
THE PERFECT TEA-
FOR WHEN ONE HAS BESTED GOLIATH!
PEPPER? I-IS IT..
POP!
GONE, MY DEAR LUCY.
I STRUCK THE BRUTE'S WEAK POINT, AND IT TURNED TAIL AND RAN LIKE A FRIGHTENED SHEEP!
I DON'T THINK THE WOUND WAS FATAL. BUT PERHAPS NOW IT WILL FEAR THE STING OF HUMANITY.
AND I WON!
OH, SMASHING JOB, ME!

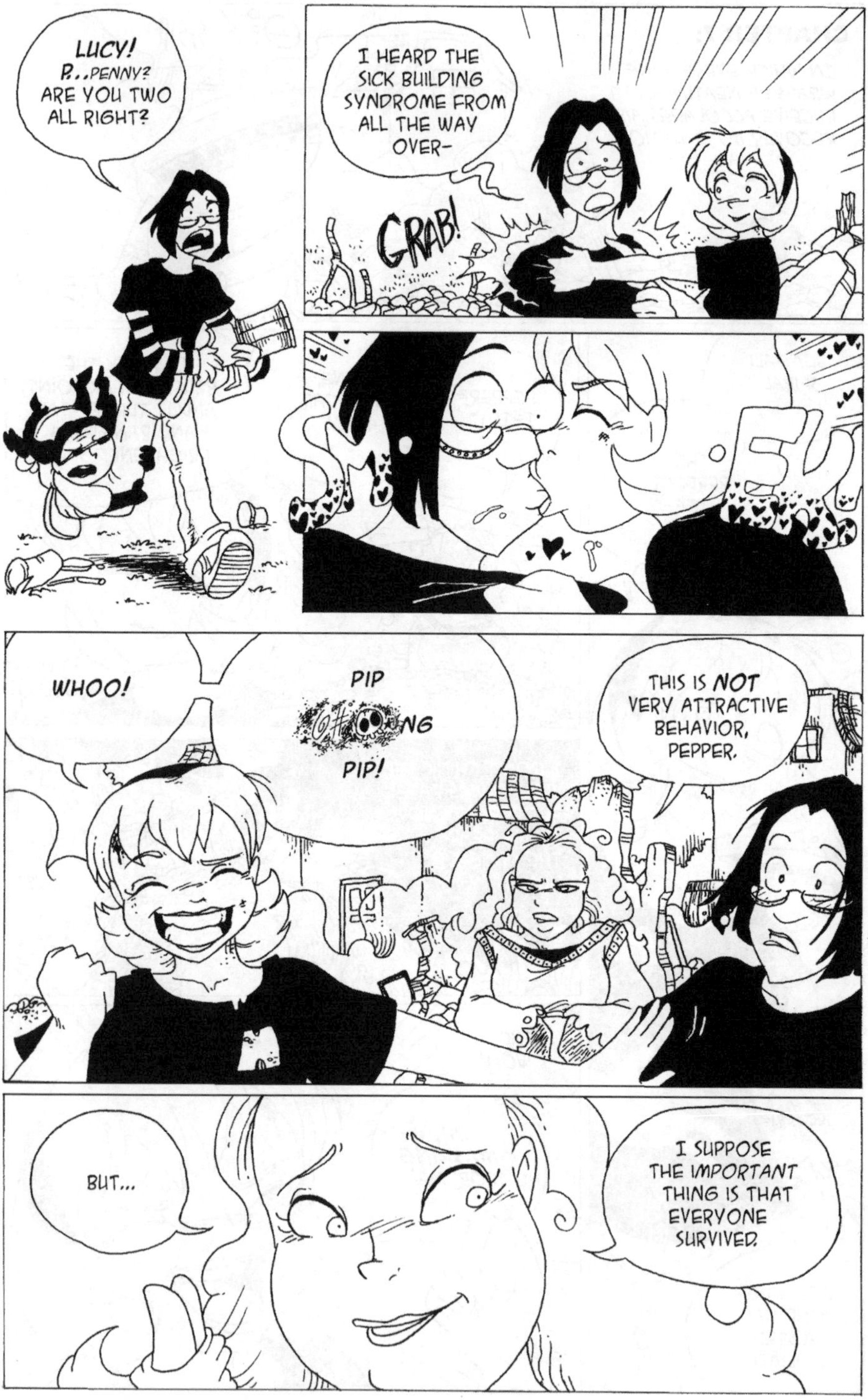
LUCY! P...PENNY? ARE YOU TWO ALL RIGHT?
I HEARD THE SICK BUILDING SYNDROME FROM ALL THE WAY OVER-
GRAB!
WHOO!
PIP
NG
PIP!
THIS IS NOT VERY ATTRACTIVE BEHAVIOR, PEPPER.
BUT...
I SUPPOSE THE IMPORTANT THING IS THAT EVERYONE SURVIVED.

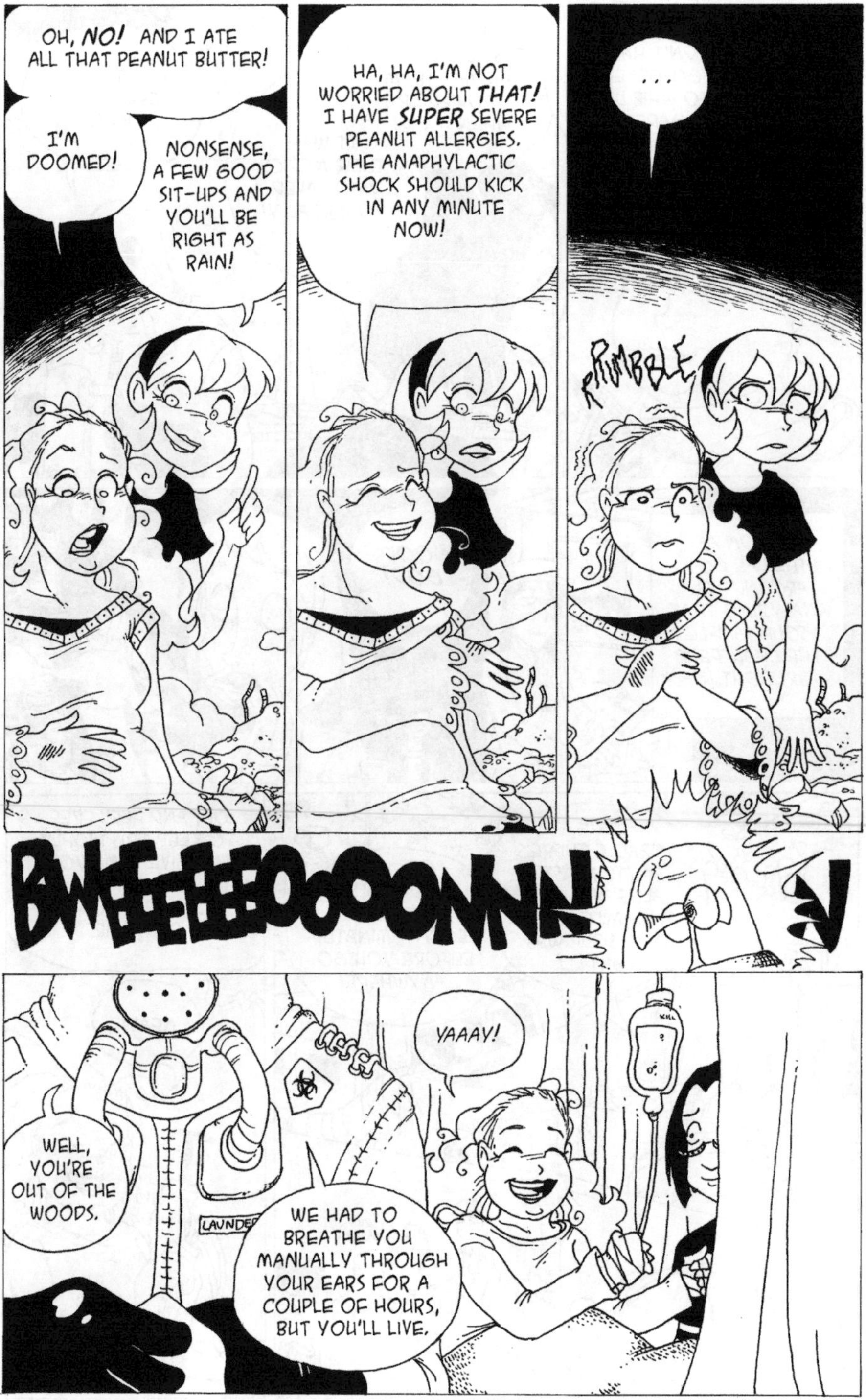
OH, NO! AND I ATE ALL THAT PEANUT BUTTER!
I'M DOOMED!
NONSENSE, A FEW GOOD SIT-UPS AND YOU'LL BE RIGHT AS RAIN!
HA, HA, I'M NOT WORRIED ABOUT THAT! I HAVE SUPER SEVERE PEANUT ALLERGIES. THE ANAPHYLACTIC SHOCK SHOULD KICK IN ANY MINUTE NOW!
...
RUMBLE
BWEEEEOOOONNN
YAAAY!
WELL, YOU'RE OUT OF THE WOODS.
WE HAD TO BREATHE YOU MANUALLY THROUGH YOUR EARS FOR A COUPLE OF HOURS, BUT YOU'LL LIVE.

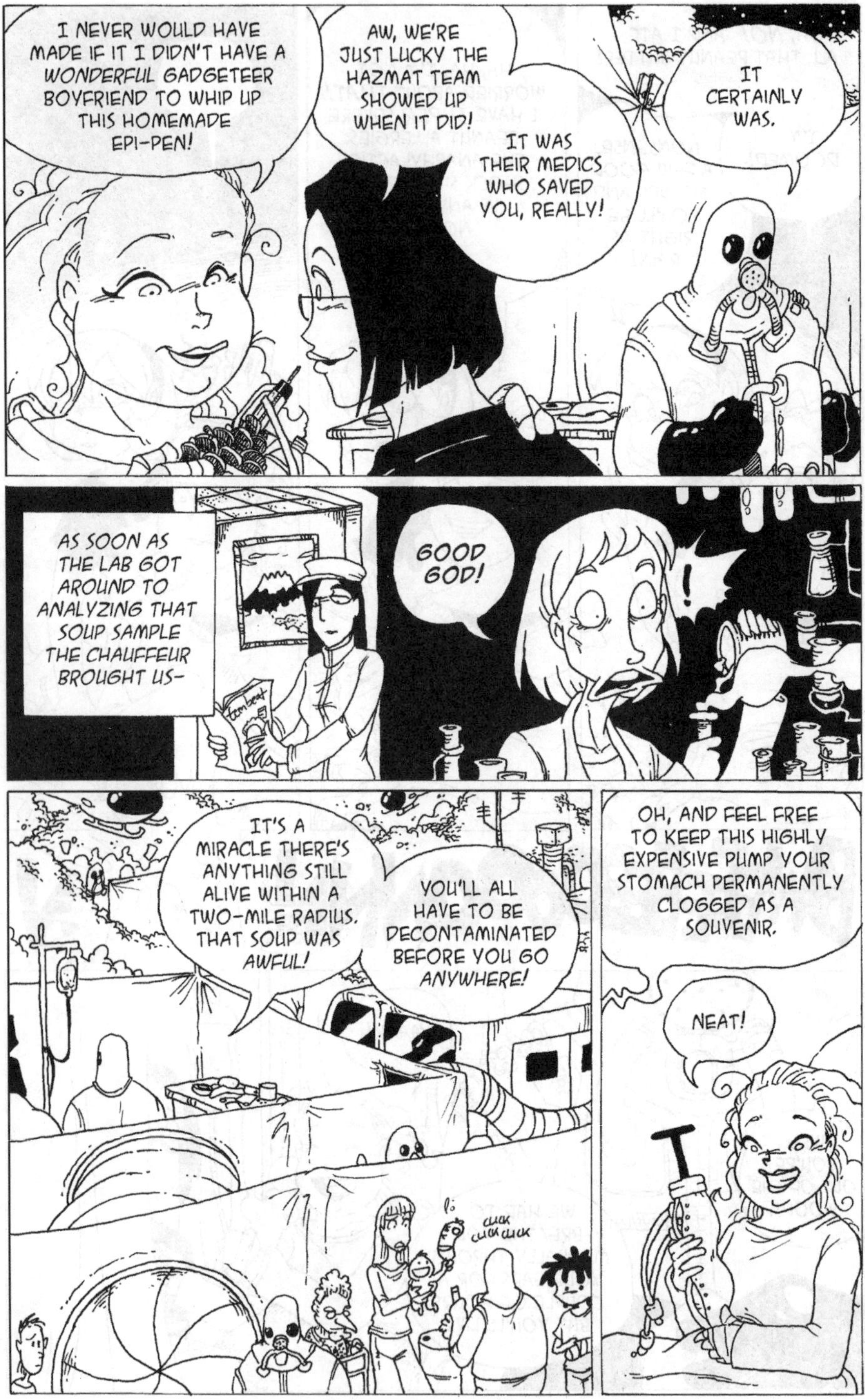
I NEVER WOULD HAVE MADE IF IT I DIDN'T HAVE A WONDERFUL GADGETEER BOYFRIEND TO WHIP UP THIS HOMEMADE EPI-PEN!
AW, WE'RE JUST LUCKY THE HAZMAT TEAM SHOWED UP WHEN IT DID!
IT WAS THEIR MEDICS WHO SAVED YOU, REALLY!
IT CERTAINLY WAS.
AS SOON AS THE LAB GOT AROUND TO ANALYZING THAT SOUP SAMPLE THE CHAUFFEUR BROUGHT US-
GOOD GOD!
!
IT'S A MIRACLE THERE'S ANYTHING STILL ALIVE WITHIN A TWO-MILE RADIUS. THAT SOUP WAS AWFUL!
YOU'LL ALL HAVE TO BE DECONTAMINATED BEFORE YOU GO ANYWHERE!
CLICK CLICK CLICK
OH, AND FEEL FREE TO KEEP THIS HIGHLY EXPENSIVE PUMP YOUR STOMACH PERMANENTLY CLOGGED AS A SOUVENIR.
NEAT!

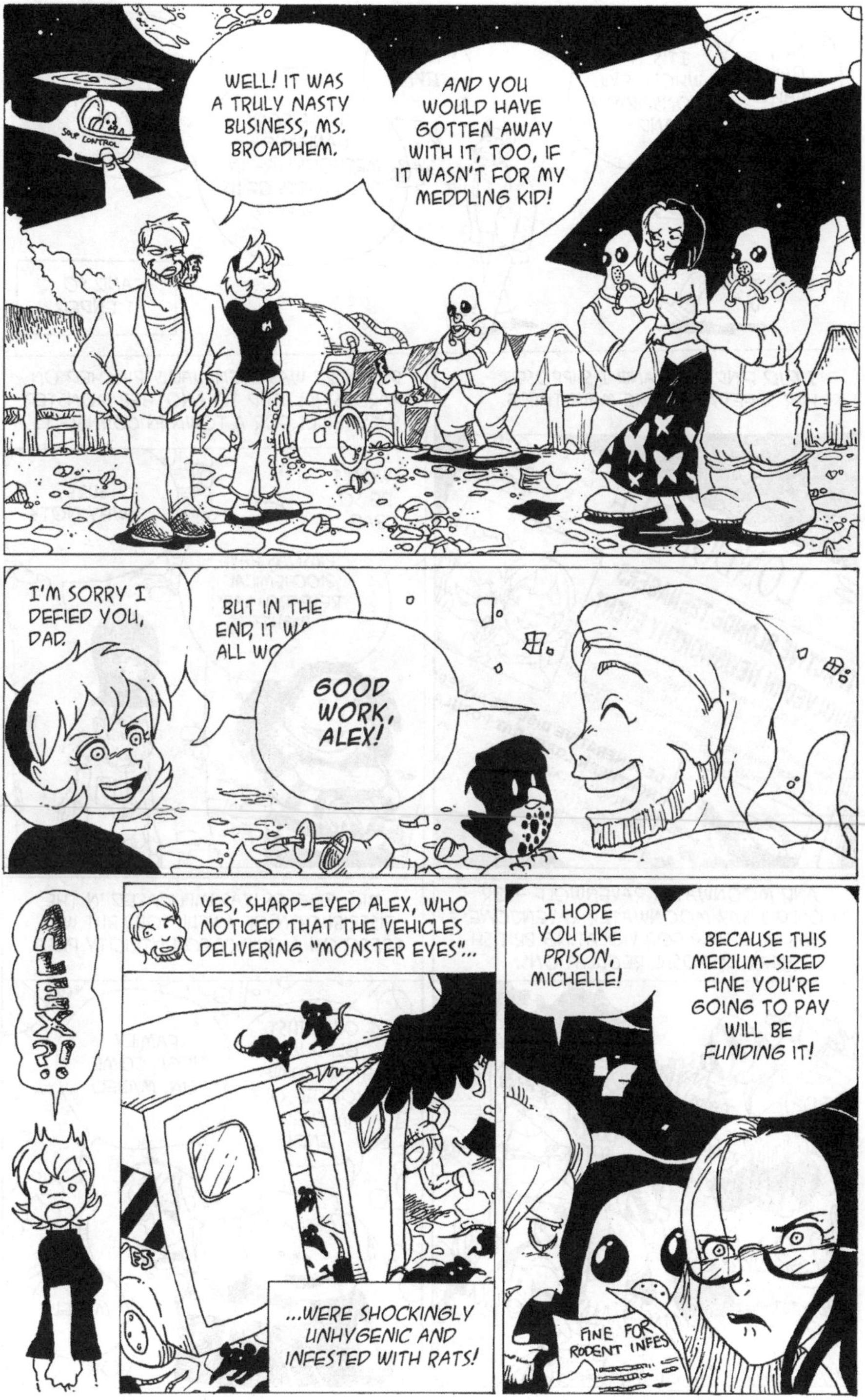
WELL! IT WAS A TRULY NASTY BUSINESS, MS. BROADHEM.
AND YOU WOULD HAVE GOTTEN AWAY WITH IT, TOO, IF IT WASN'T FOR MY MEDDLING KID!
I'M SORRY I DEFIED YOU, DAD.
BUT IN THE END, IT WA ALL WO
GOOD WORK, ALEX!
ALEX?!
YES, SHARP-EYED ALEX, WHO NOTICED THAT THE VEHICLES DELIVERING "MONSTER EYES"...
...WERE SHOCKINGLY UNHYGENIC AND INFESTED WITH RATS!
I HOPE YOU LIKE PRISON, MICHELLE!
BECAUSE THIS MEDIUM-SIZED FINE YOU'RE GOING TO PAY WILL BE FUNDING IT!
FINE FOR RODENT INFES

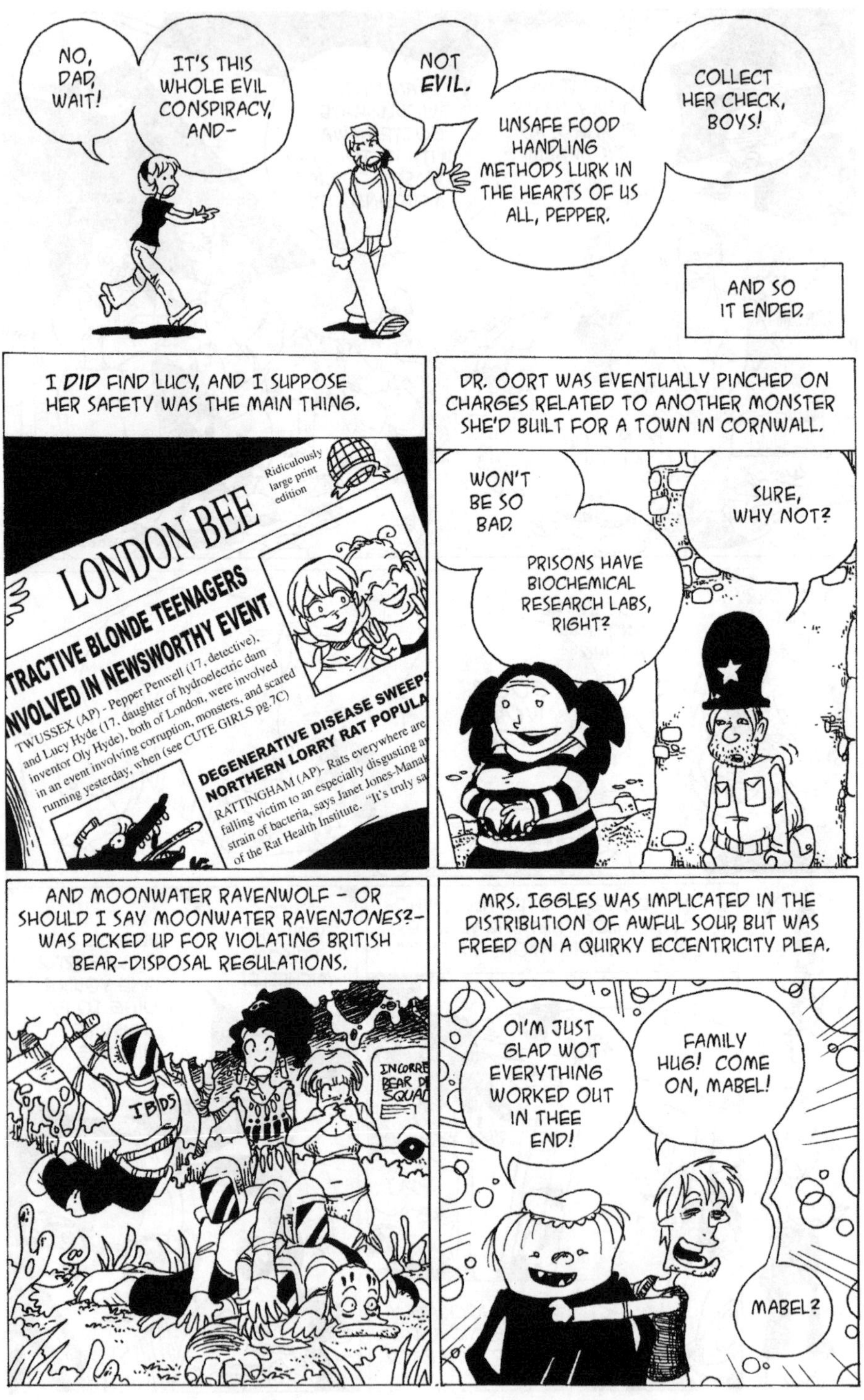

NO, DAD, WAIT!
IT'S THIS WHOLE EVIL CONSPIRACY, AND-
NOT *EVIL.*
UNSAFE FOOD HANDLING METHODS LURK IN THE HEARTS OF US ALL, PEPPER.
COLLECT HER CHECK, BOYS!
AND SO IT ENDED.
I *DID* FIND LUCY, AND I SUPPOSE HER SAFETY WAS THE MAIN THING.
Ridiculously large print edition
LONDON BEE
TRACTIVE BLONDE TEENAGERS
NVOLVED IN NEWSWORTHY EVENT
TWUSSEX (AP) - Pepper Penwell (17, detective), and Lucy Hyde (17, daughter of hydroelectric dam inventor Oly Hyde), both of London, were involved in an event involving corruption, monsters, and scared running yesterday, when (see CUTE GIRLS pg.7C)
DEGENERATIVE DISEASE SWEEPS NORTHERN LORRY RAT POPULA
RATTINGHAM (AP)- Rats everywhere are falling victim to an especially disgusting strain of bacteria, says Janet Jones-Manak of the Rat Health Institute. "It's truly sa
DR. OORT WAS EVENTUALLY PINCHED ON CHARGES RELATED TO ANOTHER MONSTER SHE'D BUILT FOR A TOWN IN CORNWALL.
WON'T BE SO BAD.
PRISONS HAVE BIOCHEMICAL RESEARCH LABS, RIGHT?
SURE, WHY NOT?
AND MOONWATER RAVENWOLF - OR SHOULD I SAY MOONWATER RAVENJONES?- WAS PICKED UP FOR VIOLATING BRITISH BEAR-DISPOSAL REGULATIONS.
IBDS
INCORRE BEAR D SQUAD
MRS. IGGLES WAS IMPLICATED IN THE DISTRIBUTION OF AWFUL SOUP, BUT WAS FREED ON A QUIRKY ECCENTRICITY PLEA.
OI'M JUST GLAD WOT EVERYTHING WORKED OUT IN THEE END!
FAMILY HUG! COME ON, MABEL!
MABEL?

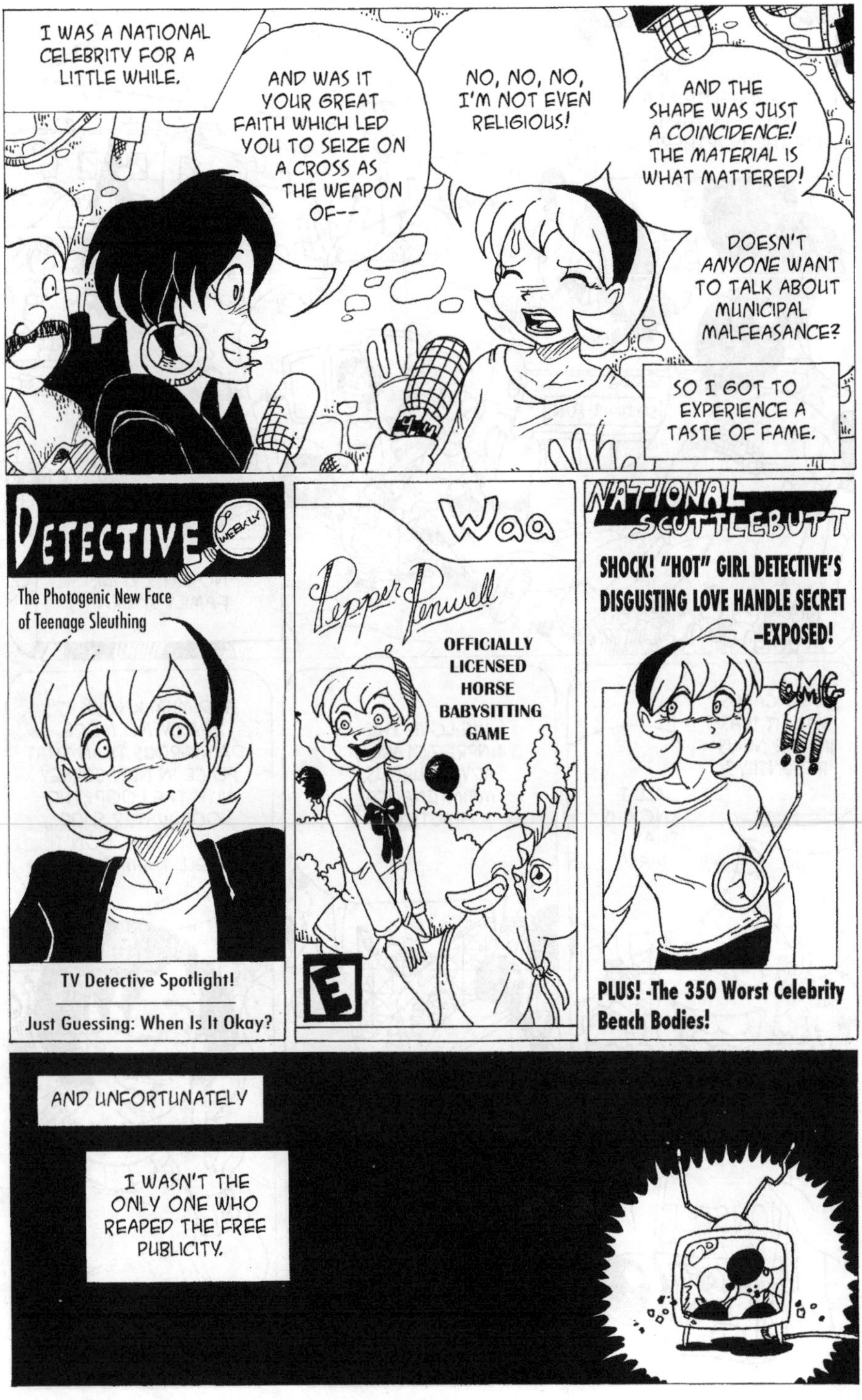
I WAS A NATIONAL CELEBRITY FOR A LITTLE WHILE.
AND WAS IT YOUR GREAT FAITH WHICH LED YOU TO SEIZE ON A CROSS AS THE WEAPON OF--
NO, NO, NO, I'M NOT EVEN RELIGIOUS!
AND THE SHAPE WAS JUST A COINCIDENCE! THE MATERIAL IS WHAT MATTERED!
DOESN'T ANYONE WANT TO TALK ABOUT MUNICIPAL MALFEASANCE?
SO I GOT TO EXPERIENCE A TASTE OF FAME.
DETECTIVE WEEKLY
The Photogenic New Face of Teenage Sleuthing
TV Detective Spotlight!
Just Guessing: When Is It Okay?
Waa
Pepper Penwell
OFFICIALLY LICENSED HORSE BABYSITTING GAME
E
NATIONAL SCUTTLEBUTT
SHOCK! "HOT" GIRL DETECTIVE'S DISGUSTING LOVE HANDLE SECRET —EXPOSED!
OMG!!!
PLUS! -The 350 Worst Celebrity Beach Bodies!
AND UNFORTUNATELY
I WASN'T THE ONLY ONE WHO REAPED THE FREE PUBLICITY.

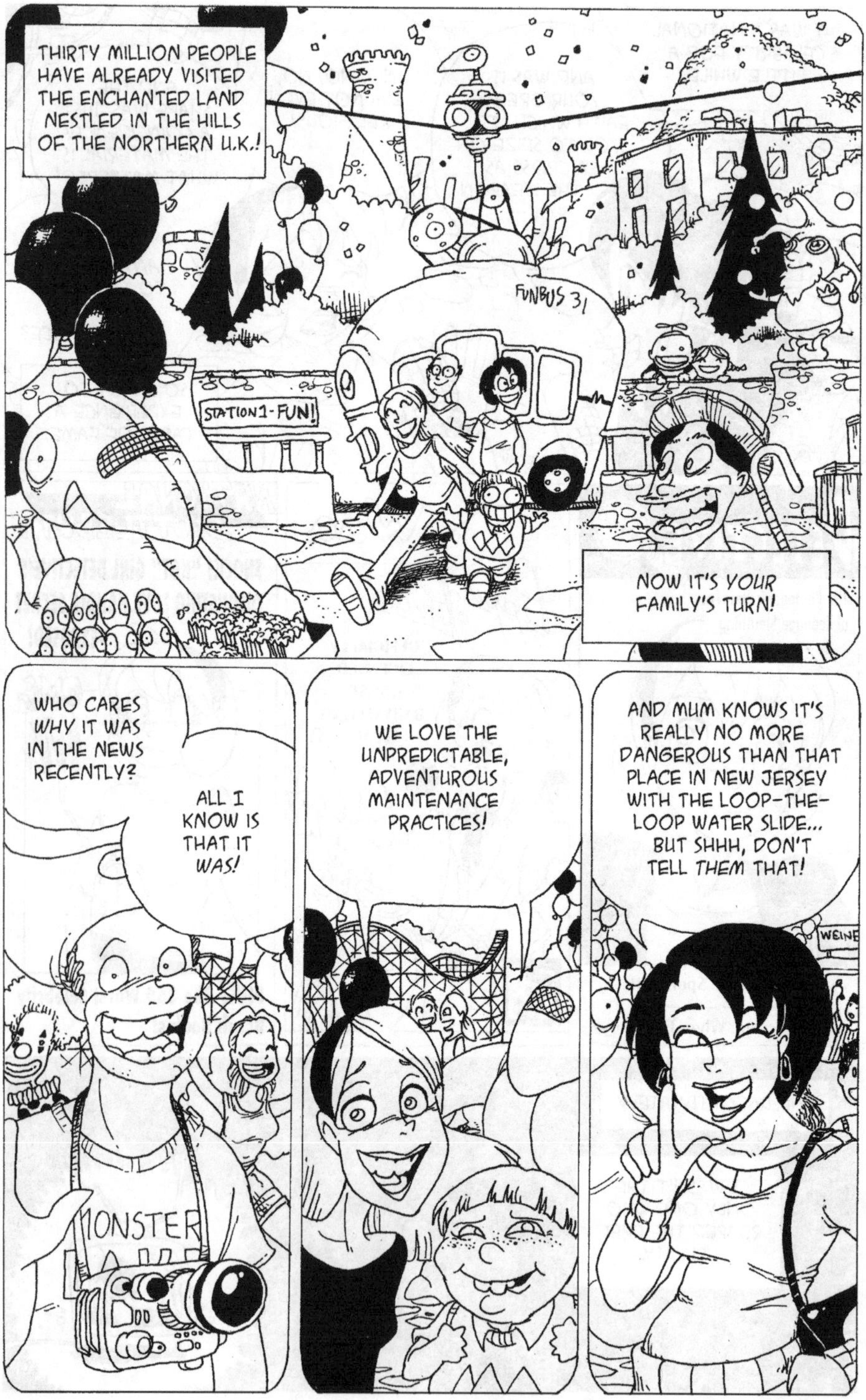
THIRTY MILLION PEOPLE HAVE ALREADY VISITED THE ENCHANTED LAND NESTLED IN THE HILLS OF THE NORTHERN U.K.!
FUNBUS 31
STATION 1-FUN!
NOW IT'S YOUR FAMILY'S TURN!
WHO CARES WHY IT WAS IN THE NEWS RECENTLY?
ALL I KNOW IS THAT IT WAS!
MONSTER
WE LOVE THE UNPREDICTABLE, ADVENTUROUS MAINTENANCE PRACTICES!
AND MUM KNOWS IT'S REALLY NO MORE DANGEROUS THAN THAT PLACE IN NEW JERSEY WITH THE LOOP-THE-LOOP WATER SLIDE... BUT SHHH, DON'T TELL THEM THAT!
WEINE

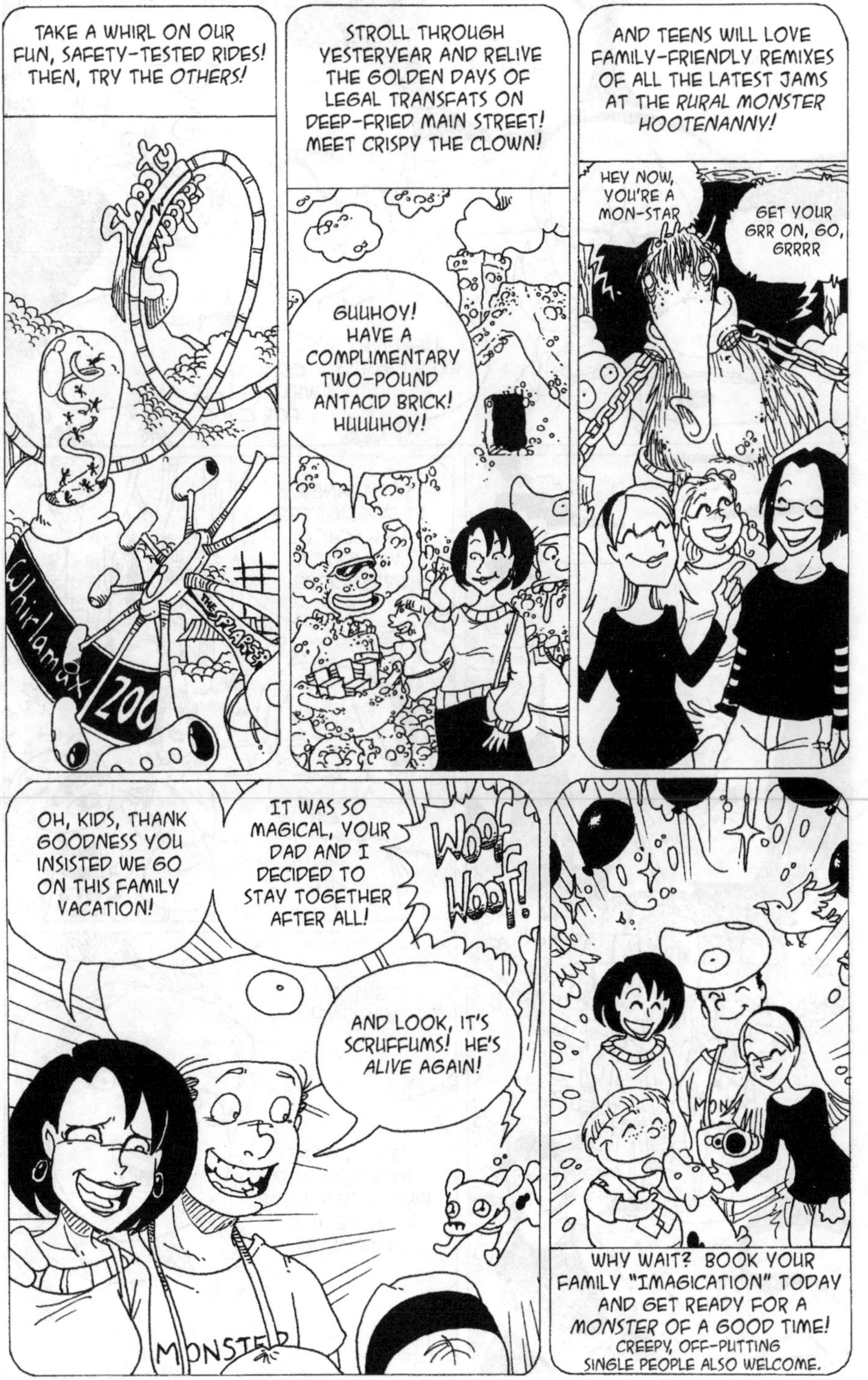
TAKE A WHIRL ON OUR FUN, SAFETY-TESTED RIDES! THEN, TRY THE OTHERS!
Whirlamux
ZOC
THE SPLARSH
STROLL THROUGH YESTERYEAR AND RELIVE THE GOLDEN DAYS OF LEGAL TRANSFATS ON DEEP-FRIED MAIN STREET! MEET CRISPY THE CLOWN!
GUUHOY! HAVE A COMPLIMENTARY TWO-POUND ANTACID BRICK! HUUUHOY!
AND TEENS WILL LOVE FAMILY-FRIENDLY REMIXES OF ALL THE LATEST JAMS AT THE RURAL MONSTER HOOTENANNY!
HEY NOW, YOU'RE A MON-STAR
GET YOUR GRR ON, GO, GRRRR
OH, KIDS, THANK GOODNESS YOU INSISTED WE GO ON THIS FAMILY VACATION!
IT WAS SO MAGICAL, YOUR DAD AND I DECIDED TO STAY TOGETHER AFTER ALL!
WOOF WOOF!
AND LOOK, IT'S SCRUFFUMS! HE'S ALIVE AGAIN!
MONSTER
WHY WAIT? BOOK YOUR FAMILY "IMAGICATION" TODAY AND GET READY FOR A MONSTER OF A GOOD TIME!
CREEPY, OFF-PUTTING SINGLE PEOPLE ALSO WELCOME.

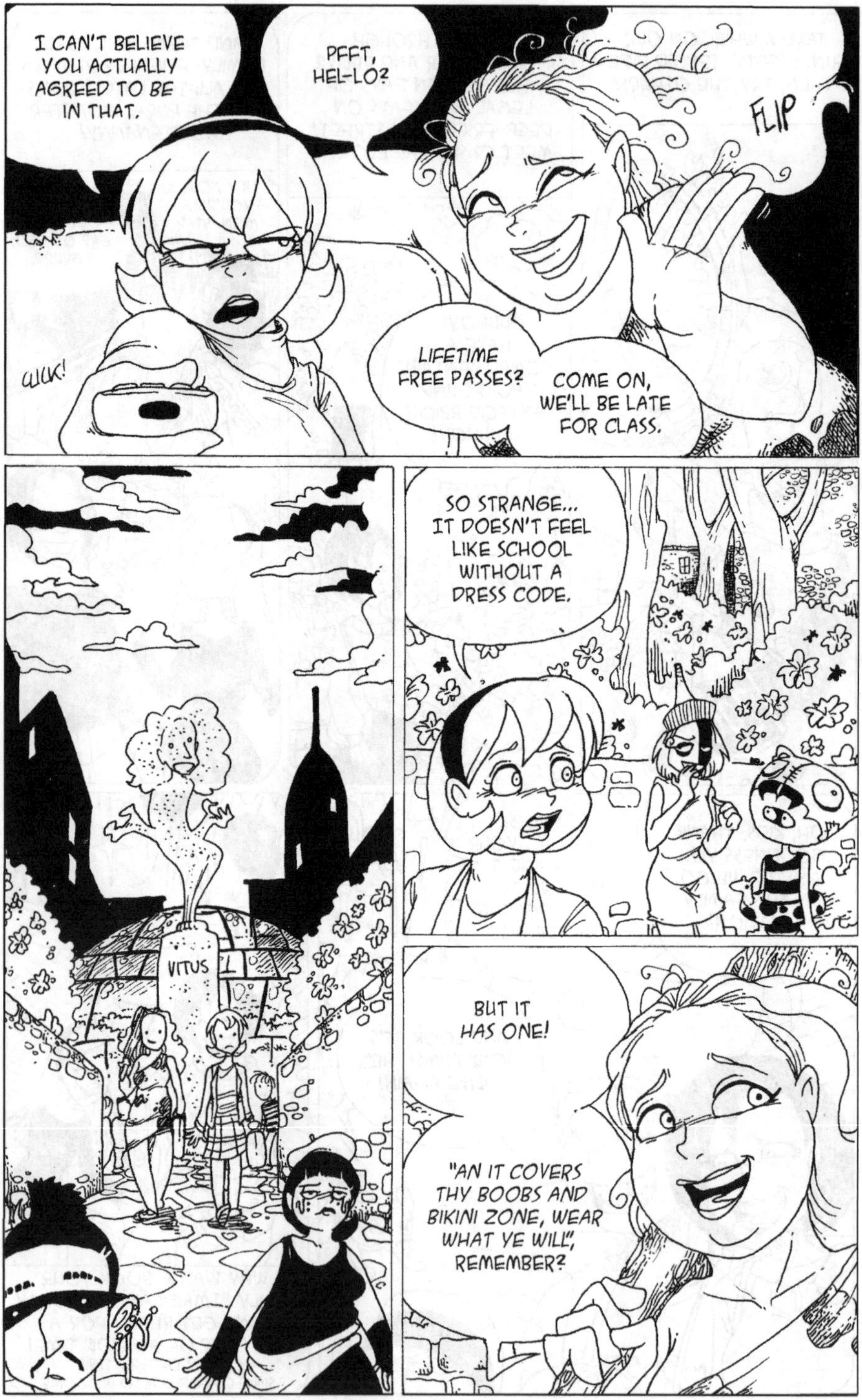
I CAN'T BELIEVE YOU ACTUALLY AGREED TO BE IN THAT.
CLICK!
PFFT, HEL-LO?
FLIP
LIFETIME FREE PASSES?
COME ON, WE'LL BE LATE FOR CLASS.
VITUS
SO STRANGE... IT DOESN'T FEEL LIKE SCHOOL WITHOUT A DRESS CODE.
BUT IT HAS ONE!
"AN IT COVERS THY BOOBS AND BIKINI ZONE, WEAR WHAT YE WILL", REMEMBER?

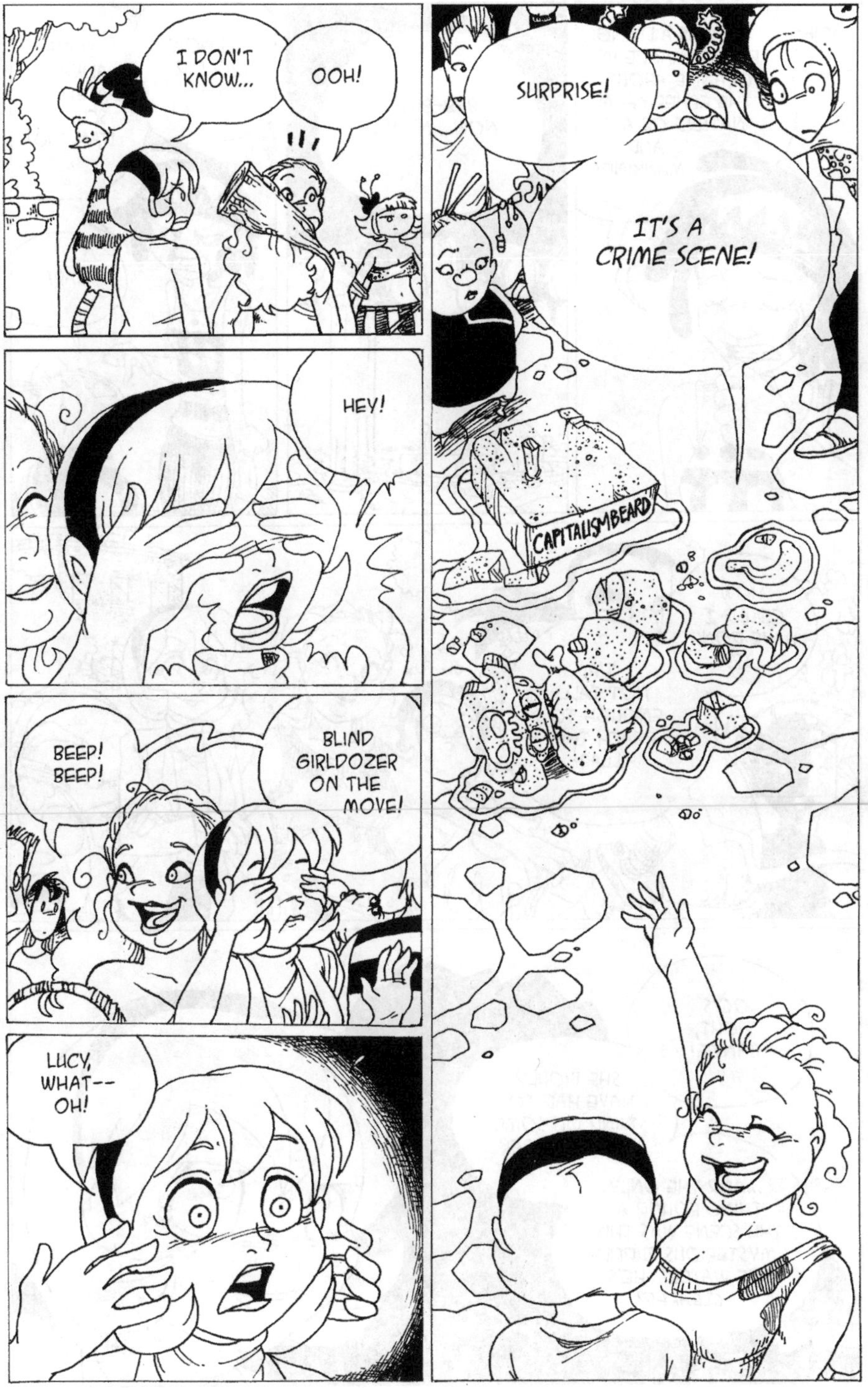
I DON'T KNOW...
OOH!
HEY!
BEEP! BEEP!
BLIND GIRLDOZER ON THE MOVE!
LUCY, WHAT-- OH!
SURPRISE!
IT'S A CRIME SCENE!
CAPITALISMBEARD

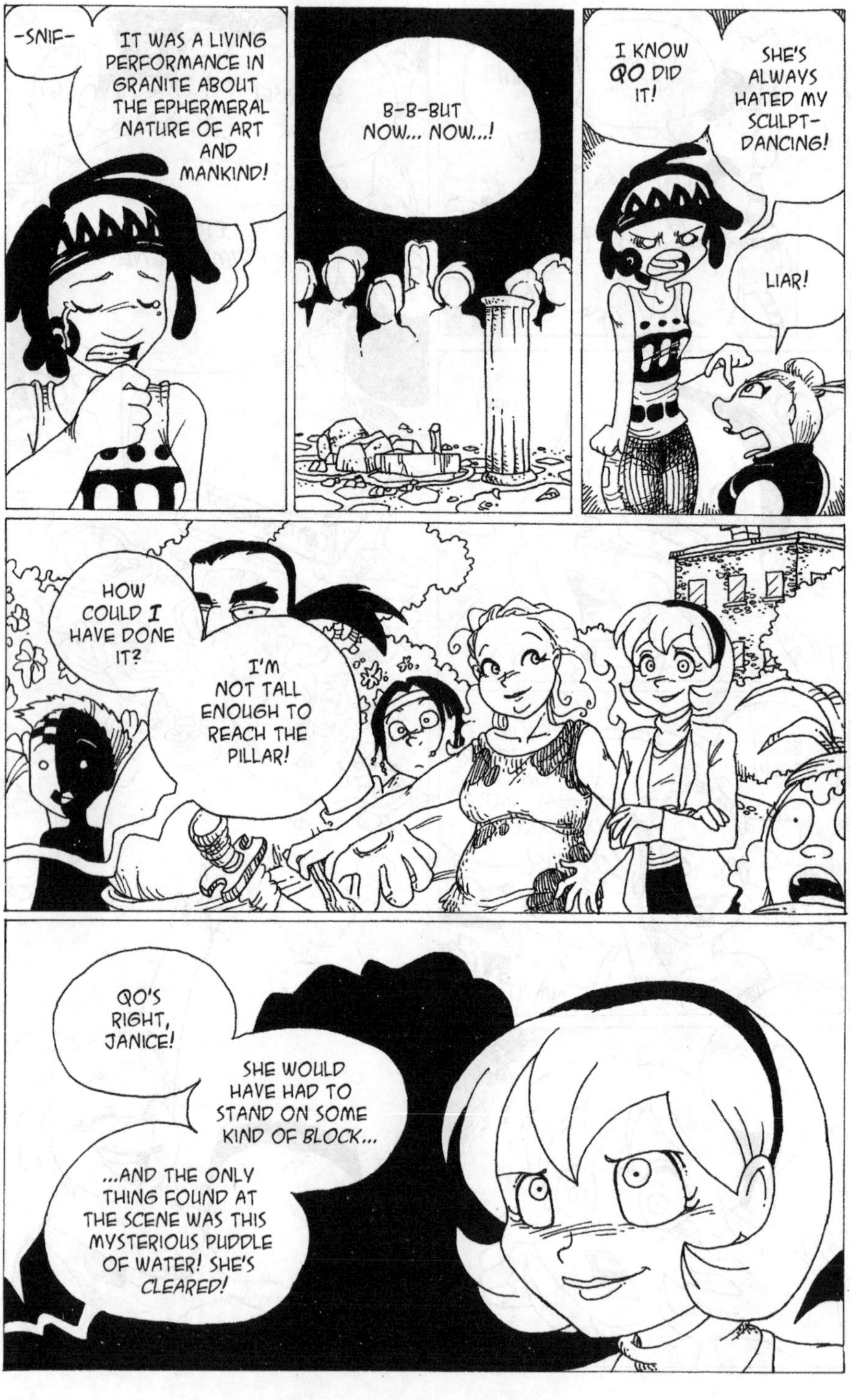
-SNIF-
IT WAS A LIVING PERFORMANCE IN GRANITE ABOUT THE EPHERMERAL NATURE OF ART AND MANKIND!
B-B-BUT NOW... NOW...!
I KNOW QO DID IT!
SHE'S ALWAYS HATED MY SCULPT-DANCING!
LIAR!
HOW COULD I HAVE DONE IT?
I'M NOT TALL ENOUGH TO REACH THE PILLAR!
QO'S RIGHT, JANICE!
SHE WOULD HAVE HAD TO STAND ON SOME KIND OF BLOCK...
...AND THE ONLY THING FOUND AT THE SCENE WAS THIS MYSTERIOUS PUDDLE OF WATER! SHE'S CLEARED!

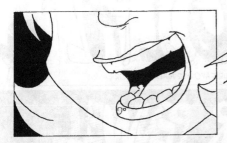

NOT SO FAST!

A LOT OF CRIMES INVOLVE ICE, AND MAYBE THAT'S BECAUSE THE FUNDAMENTAL NATURES OF ICE AND CRIME ARE SO SIMILAR.

TO THE AVERAGE PERSON, AN ICE CUBE SEEMS TRANSITORY, BECAUSE CONDITIONS THAT ARE LIVABLE FOR US ARE FATAL FOR THEM.

BUT THIS DIDN'T JUST *HAPPEN.* IN THE VOID, WITHOUT ENERGY, THAT CUBE WOULD PERSIST FOREVER. WE'VE GOT TO KEEP THE HEAT ON IN ORDER TO BREAK THROUGH THE FREEZE, MELT THE FORCES OF LAWLESSNESS, AND BRING THE SUNLIGHT OF ORDER INTO THE COLD CORNERS OF THIS UNIVERSE, MAKING THEM WARM AND HABITABLE.

I ENJOY THE AMENITIES HERE, FROM THE BIG SEALED ARBORETUM THAT'S PERFECT FOR ALEX, TO THE POINTY BUT EFFECTIVELY FITNESS-INDUCING ABSTRACT ART GYMNASIUM. LUCY PERFORMS AN EFFICIENT DUAL ROLE AS ROOMMATE AND BODYGUARD, AND I MUST ADMIT, IT CAN BE PLEASANT TO HAVE SOMEONE AROUND WHOSE COMPANY ONE ENJOYS.

OF COURSE THE PLACE IS PURE ANARCHY JUST NOW, BUT EVERYWHERE IS LIKE THAT UNTIL I GET IT STRAIGHTENED OUT. AT LEAST IT KEEPS ME BUSY! -P.

CECIL'S NOVELTY SHOPPE

EXHIBIT A

ONE (1) LADDER-SHAPED ICE MOLD... 99p
SOLD TO: QO ION
SEP 14, 1

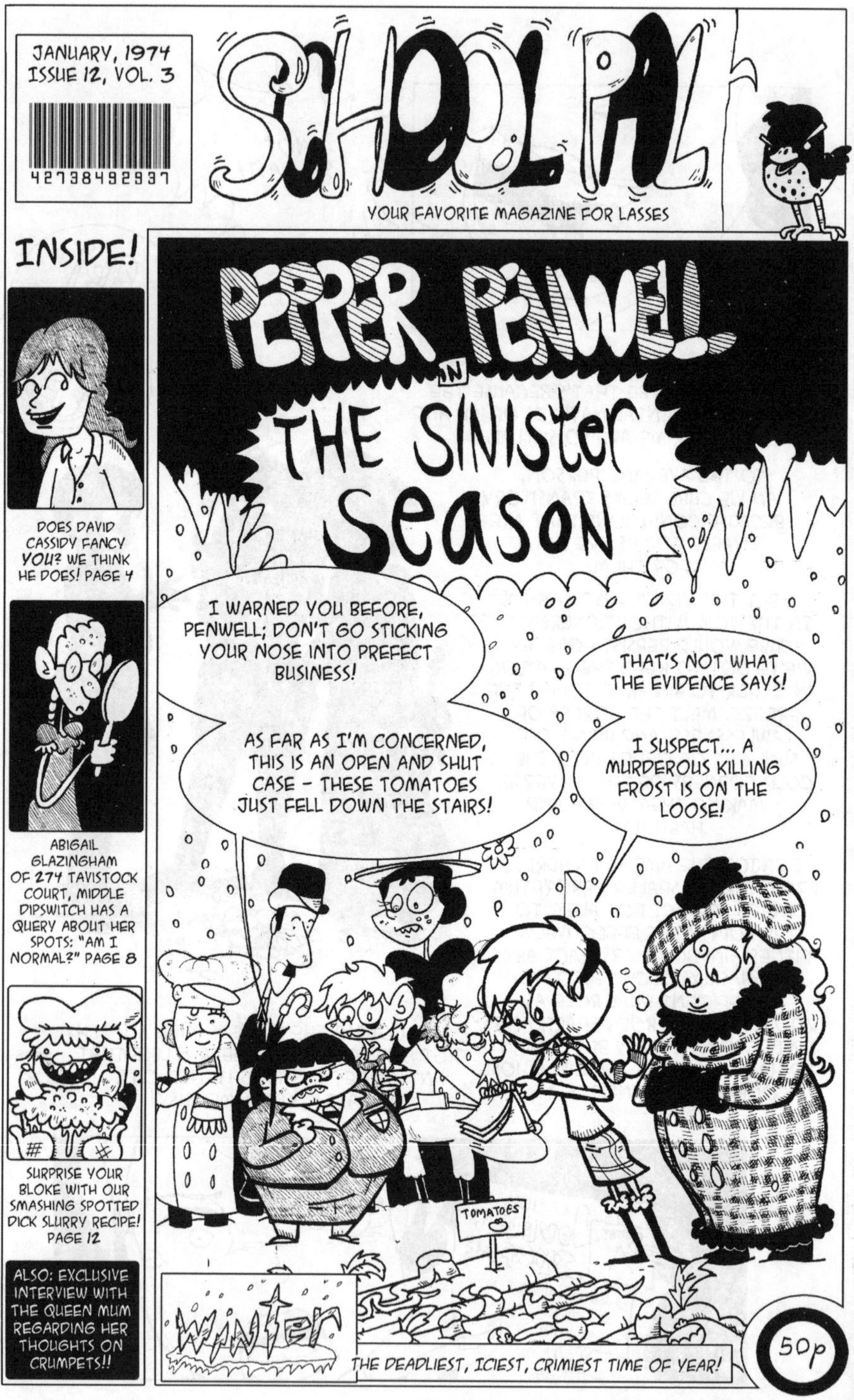

JANUARY, 1974
ISSUE 12, VOL. 3
42738492937
SCHOOL PAL
YOUR FAVORITE MAGAZINE FOR LASSES
INSIDE!
DOES DAVID CASSIDY FANCY YOU? WE THINK HE DOES! PAGE 4
ABIGAIL GLAZINGHAM OF 274 TAVISTOCK COURT, MIDDLE DIPSWITCH HAS A QUERY ABOUT HER SPOTS: "AM I NORMAL?" PAGE 8
SURPRISE YOUR BLOKE WITH OUR SMASHING SPOTTED DICK SLURRY RECIPE! PAGE 12
ALSO: EXCLUSIVE INTERVIEW WITH THE QUEEN MUM REGARDING HER THOUGHTS ON CRUMPETS!!
PEPPER PENWELL IN THE SINISTER SEASON
I WARNED YOU BEFORE, PENWELL; DON'T GO STICKING YOUR NOSE INTO PREFECT BUSINESS!
AS FAR AS I'M CONCERNED, THIS IS AN OPEN AND SHUT CASE - THESE TOMATOES JUST FELL DOWN THE STAIRS!
THAT'S NOT WHAT THE EVIDENCE SAYS!
I SUSPECT... A MURDEROUS KILLING FROST IS ON THE LOOSE!
TOMATOES
WINTER
THE DEADLIEST, ICIEST, CRIMIEST TIME OF YEAR!
50p

ILLUSTRATION BY MIKE ROSEN (WWW.GUTTERSNIPECOMIC.COM)

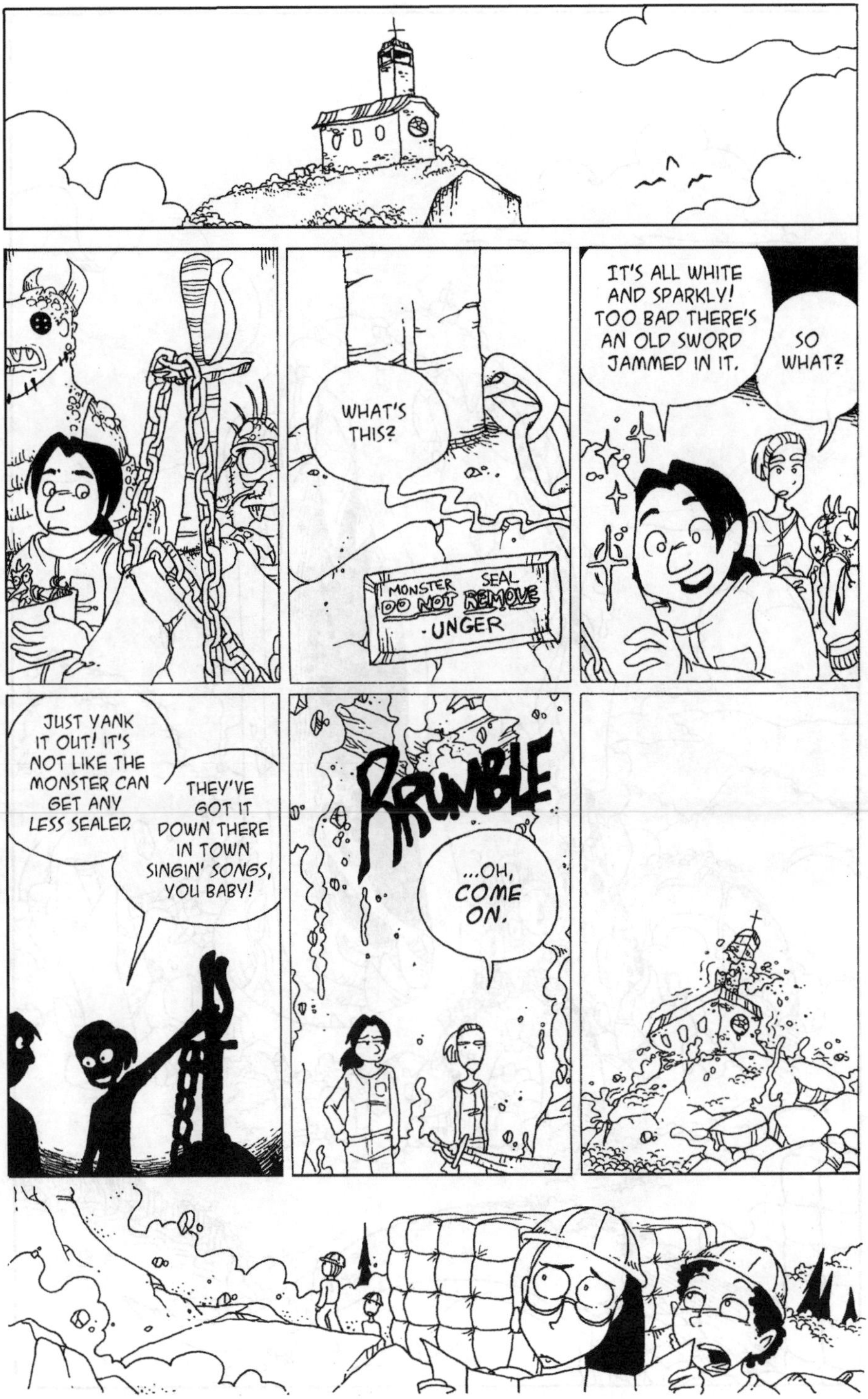
WHAT'S THIS?
MONSTER SEAL
DO NOT REMOVE
-UNGER
IT'S ALL WHITE AND SPARKLY! TOO BAD THERE'S AN OLD SWORD JAMMED IN IT.
SO WHAT?
JUST YANK IT OUT! IT'S NOT LIKE THE MONSTER CAN GET ANY LESS SEALED.
THEY'VE GOT IT DOWN THERE IN TOWN SINGIN' SONGS, YOU BABY!
RRUMBLE
...OH, COME ON.

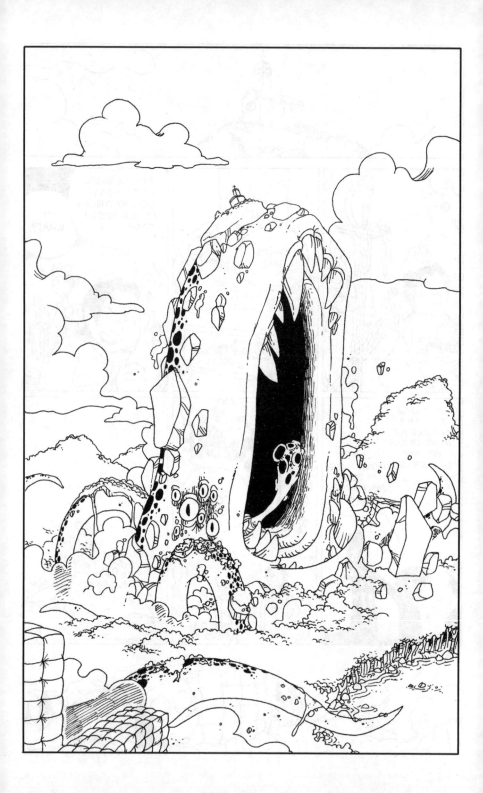